The
Shadow Network

Also by Edward Van Der Rhoer

Deadly Magic
Master Spy

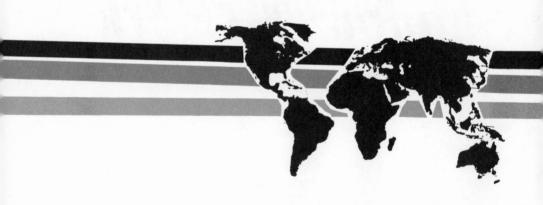

Edward Van Der Rhoer

The Shadow Network

Charles Scribner's Sons   New York

Copyright © 1983 Edward Van Der Rhoer

Library of Congress Cataloging in Publication Data
Van Der Rhoer, Edward.
  The shadow network.

  Bibliography: p.
  Includes index.
  1. Soviet Union. Komitet gosudarstvennoí bezopasnosti.
2. Intelligence service—Soviet Union. I. Title.
HV8224.V26   1983   363.2′83′0947   83–11524
ISBN 0–684–17960–1

This book published simultaneously in the
United States of America and in Canada—
Copyright under the Berne Convention.

1 3 5 7 9 11 13 15 17 19   F/C   20 18 16 14 12 10 8 6 4 2

Printed in the United States of America.

Contents

It is much easier to make a good man wise,
than to make a bad man good.
HENRY FIELDING

1

State Security, Soviet Style

IN THE CONCLUDING WORDS OF *Nineteen Eighty-Four*, George Orwell describes the state of the novel's hero:

> Two gin-scented tears trickled down the sides of his nose. But it was all right, everything was all right, the struggle was finished. . . . He loved Big Brother.[1]

The "Big Brother" of whom Orwell wrote could have been Stalin himself or, in the final analysis, the Soviet system. More important, however, those ominous words "He loved Big Brother" set forth succinctly yet significantly the real goal of Soviet State Security, the secret police. For this goal is far less concerned with the physical security of the regime than with the imposition of Soviet ideology wherever the State Security organization can extend its reach.

When Felix Edmundovich Dzerzhinsky, the founder and first head of Soviet State Security, established the organization in December 1917, a month after the Bolsheviks seized power, it was called the Extraordinary Commission for Combating Counterrevolution and Sabotage (*Chrezvychainaya komissiya po borbe s*

1

kontrrevolyutsiei i sabotazhem), or Cheka for short. Many Bolsheviks who had suffered at the hands of the Czarist Okhrana feared the reestablishment of a secret police but were comforted by the designation "extraordinary." The word suggested that as soon as the temporary danger of counterrevolution and sabotage was past, the Cheka would be abolished. But leaders of the Soviet regime like Lenin and Trotsky had a different view: the Cheka was "extraordinary" because it set aside all moral and ethical standards. Whatever benefited the dictatorship of the proletariat represented true morality and justice.

The theory upon which these leaders based their actions was both revolutionary and destructive, although they themselves lacked a profound understanding of its implications. Lenin grandly regarded his party of Bolsheviks as the vanguard of the proletariat. Dzerzhinsky characteristically expressed the idea in simple language: "A small but spiritually strong handful of people will rally the masses round them, give them what they lack and put new life and hope into them."[2] Both Lenin and Dzerzhinsky ignored the fact that the workers or proletariat represented only about 2 percent of the adult working population on the eve of World War I and probably even less in 1917, after the ravages of war.[3] As a self-styled elite of the proletariat, the Bolsheviks were only a tiny minority of a minority and ultimately could retain power only by force. The Cheka—or a similar institution of repression—was absolutely indispensable.

The Soviet leaders, however, did not come to this realization at once, and several years elapsed before they recognized that a tiny minority of a minority could not wait for opposition to develop but had to eradicate all potential opposition as well. Lenin, dissatisfied with the first Criminal Code in 1922, proposed amendments that developed into the notorious Article 58 of the RSFSR Criminal Code in 1926.[4] This article was directed against "counterrevolutionary crime," a convenient catchall for virtually anything of which the regime disapproved.

The eradication of potential opposition through the "organs" of State Security marked a new and higher phase in the development of Soviet democracy. This, in fact, introduced the "love Big Brother" syndrome that distinguishes Communist security organizations from all other types. In today's world this syndrome can be detected wherever State Security extends its reach into "enemy" territory, exploiting international movements and friendship societies and seeking to make people in general "love" the Soviet Union as the bulwark of peace and the quintessence of a system that has eliminated injustice and poverty.

In the USSR the principal props of the regime are, beyond doubt, the Communist Party of the Soviet Union (CPSU) and State Security. Since all State Security officers are party members, they constitute in a sense an elite of an elite and regard themselves as special guardians of the regime.

In speaking of State Security, reference will be made here as a general rule to the KGB (*Komitet gosudarstvennoi bezopasnosti*, or Committee for State Security), although the KGB did not officially come into existence until 1954. Before then State Security was known by a bewildering succession of initials: GPU, OGPU, NKVD, NKGB, MVD, and MGB.

Nevertheless, throughout its existence State Security has only nominally been a government body, although it has frequently masqueraded as a "people's commissariat" or ministry and is today a "committee" attached to the USSR Council of Ministers. In reality, State Security has never been subordinated to the government. Its chain of command runs up to the chairman of the KGB who, like Dzerzhinsky, is usually a member of the CPSU Politburo, where all the real political power of the Soviet Union is concentrated. On the lower echelons, there is a certain coordination of the work of State Security branches with local and regional party organizations. In a general sense, this takes place through the party cells within State Security, but in practical terms coordination is effected between the local party first secretary and the State Security chief or their immediate assistants. Effective control of State Security, however, is exercised only at the top level of the CPSU. At times the General Secretary, as head of the Politburo, has managed to concentrate this control in his hands. Nevertheless, with the horrible example of Stalin before them, the other Politburo members have remained on guard against the unrestricted exercise of such power by the General Secretary, whoever he might be.

It is axiomatic that the Soviet system cannot survive without its twin pillars of the Communist Party and State Security. And a corollary is that the Communist Party must retain a monopoly of political power, while State Security remains unhampered in its wielding of police power other than by the top political authority.

Past experience—Moscow in October 1941,[5] Hungary's withdrawal from the Warsaw Pact in 1956, "socialism with a human face" in Czechoslovakia in 1968, and the formation of the Solidarity trade union in Poland in 1980—suggests that, in a period of profound crisis, the Communist Party and State Security may literally melt away or at least become so altered that the Soviet system ceases to exist. Outside the USSR, Soviet intervention alone has succeeded thus far in restoring the situation. Thus the Soviet leadership has good reason to fear any threat to the Communist Party's monopoly of political power or legal restraint on State Security's exercise of police power.

It is a peculiarity of the KGB that the organization developed, so to speak, "from the inside out," becoming first the Soviet secret police and only later extending its scope to foreign espionage. The KGB's original functions, combating counterrevolution and sabotage inside the country, inevitably encompassed work against Allied Intelligence services, whose governments wished, not unreasonably, to overthrow the Bolshevik regime. The Bolsheviks, by making a separate peace with Germany, in violation of Russia's commitments to her allies in World War I, had made it possible for the Germans to transfer hundreds of thousands of troops from the eastern to the western front, thereby bringing them within a hairbreadth of victory. The resultant breach, manifesting itself in Allied support for the Russian opposition, challenged all the ingenuity and ruthlessness of Soviet State Security.

The experience would prove to be very useful when the KGB expanded into the field of foreign espionage.

Superficially, it could be said that the KGB combines the internal security functions of the FBI with the foreign Intelligence responsibilities of the CIA. But to put it in these terms alone would be misleading, since a simple comparison of this kind ignores the KGB's extralegal status, which sets it apart from Western security and Intelligence agencies.

The KGB is not subject to any Soviet laws. Any attempt by private citizens to invoke Soviet law against KGB abuses has no chance whatever and, moreover, will bring about prompt retaliation. Yet the KGB is prepared to invoke Soviet laws, such as the notorious Article 58, in legal proceedings, and in such cases the accused is presumed guilty before a trial takes place. The KGB often avoids court trials, which attract foreign publicity, preferring extralegal action or administrative measures, such as incarcerating dissidents in psychiatric hospitals.

The strength of Soviet State Security is based on long experience, proven methods, and notable efficiency. At the same time its success depends in no small degree on other favorable factors. A network of informers extends into every facet of Soviet life—into houses, schools, institutes, offices, factories, collective farms, railroads, ships, and the armed forces. Requirements are repeatedly imposed on all citizens to fill out questionnaires and applications, and KGB case officers pore over them in search of omissions and contradictions. The vaunted "patience" of the KGB enables it to postpone action against suspects for years until the right moment arrives to arrest or blackmail them. And possibly most important of all, ordinary Soviet people (as well as those who are not so ordinary) are aware of their complete powerlessness in the face of State Security.

As Genrikh Grigorievich Yagoda, a head of State Security during the 1930's, said: "We can turn anyone into a *seksot* [informer]. . . . Who is eager to die of hunger? When the GPU works over somebody in order to make him an informant, we already have him under our thumb, no matter how much he struggles against it. We take away his job, he won't find another one without the secret agreement of our organs. And, above all, if a man has a family, wife and children, he is forced to capitulate quickly."[6]

Nor are party members safe from punishment by the KGB. In the 1930's the party apparatus was ravaged from top to bottom, as Stalin ruthlessly exterminated all real or potential opposition. Although the situation then was extraordinary, State Security takes firm action (usually with the approval of the party apparatus) against individual members who get out of line. This does not point in any way to a conflict between State Security and the party but is simply evidence of the meshing of these organizations, which are dependent on one another for mutual survival.

Most of the internal security functions described above are handled organizationally by State Security's Second and Fifth Main Administrations. Foreign espionage is conducted by the First Main Administration (*Pervoye glavnoye upravleniye*, or PGU), and surveillance of Soviet officials stationed abroad is maintained by the PGU's Soviet colony (*Sovetskaya kolonia*, or SK) sections, which are alert for any sign of errant behavior or dangerous associations. (Delegations or touring groups are watched by so-called *nyanki* or "nursemaids," detailed by the Second Main Administration to accompany them.) In such cases, individuals are recalled home without delay and face administrative or legal punishment. This can take the form of dismissal from a privileged job permitting foreign travel (and permanent banishment from the elite) or, in more serious cases, involve a sentence in a labor camp or even execution for treason.

Thus, it is clear that the Soviet state regards its citizens as little more than pawns to be moved about in accordance with the strategy of the regime or, at times, the inscrutable whims of its bureaucracy. Personal considerations, such as the desires of the citizens themselves, play no part in these decisions. The behavior of the Soviet state is an exaggerated form of the behavior of other states in wartime; this, as Stalin might have said, is not accidental, since the Soviet state is permanently at war with the rest of the world. It is equally clear that a pivotal role falls to State Security, for nothing can be done at home or abroad without its review and approval.

State Security's all-pervasive position developed slowly, but as it extended its activities into foreign espionage, it soon began to treat foreign Communists much like its own citizens, demanding total submission to the Soviet state. In doing so, State Security pointed out that the possibility of creating other socialist states depended on the survival of the "first socialist state" and on Soviet aid to other Communist parties in their struggle for power. Most foreign Communists accepted these arguments, although they had little choice in the matter. A party member who refused to cooperate was promptly expelled. His own party could not back him up without losing the support of the Comintern, the international Communist organization located in Moscow and controlled by the Bolsheviks. Without that support any party would soon be supplanted by a rival party that enjoyed Moscow's favor.

In this way, State Security's PGU (or Foreign Administration as it was called in early years) used foreign Communists as auxiliaries, recruiting them to carry out covert missions of all kinds. The apparatus of a foreign Communist party often became little more than a spotting and recruiting mechanism for the PGU. Its functionaries were instructed to study party members with a view to their usefulness as Soviet Intelligence agents. Personal aptitudes and abilities entered into such an assessment, but another important element was the degree of access to secret information by virtue of one's position or profession. When a suitable candidate was found, he was approached by a functionary and told that the party had chosen him for an important assignment in its "underground apparatus." If the new recruit proved amenable, he was instructed to sever all overt connections with the party and publicize it to his friends, to discontinue subscriptions to Communist publications, and to take on the coloration of an anti-Communist in discussions with outsiders. The recruit might later be made aware that he was actually working for Soviet Intelligence, depending on his usefulness and the need to give him a more truthful picture of his own activities.

The PGU found it convenient to recruit foreign Communists because it was so easy. The foreign party did most of the work in finding and evaluating potential agents and generally possessed better sources of information inside the particular country. In these circumstances, the PGU had at its disposal an almost ready-made Intelligence apparatus, which soon began to rival, and in some cases outdo, opposing Intelligence services. Such agents penetrated the West's key governmental institutions or worked themselves into confidential positions as aides and secretaries of leading statesmen, feeding Moscow a steady diet of the West's most closely guarded secrets.

Yet the use of foreign Communists as spies had its reverse side. Even when agents dropped their contact with Communist parties, they could not completely cover their tracks. Their party membership had usually been recorded somewhere, witnesses had known them as Communists, and their sudden abandonment of communism was in itself a telltale sign. Had the Western security and Intelligence services been more alert, many PGU operations would have been aborted long before they began to pay off.

This, however, was not the case. While considerable public furor against the "Red menace" developed in the 1920's, the situation had changed within a decade. As fascism's shadow grew longer and more menacing, the Western public became indifferent to a Communist threat that seemed relatively harmless. Preoccupied by the saber rattling of Hitler's Germany, Mussolini's Italy, and a militaristic Japan, Western officialdom increasingly saw the Soviet Union and Communists everywhere as allies in the struggle against fascism. In such an atmosphere, Soviet Intelligence could work successfully with deep-cover agents recruited through the Communist parties.

Nevertheless, many of these agents ultimately turned out to be albatrosses rather than eagles, and the PGU had to explore new regions in search of its spies.

While the Bolsheviks under Lenin's leadership were engaged in a revolutionary struggle against the Czarist regime, Lenin consistently opposed the use of terrorism. His attitude was not based on moral or ethical inhibitions but was purely pragmatic, reflecting his conviction that terrorism was not effective in seeking to overthrow Czarism. On the contrary, he thought it might be harmful to that purpose.

But Lenin had no objection to violence. In those early years, he was a strong advocate of violence, not only planning the stockpiling of arms for an eventual uprising and studying tactics for fighting at the barricades, but also supporting holdups in which funds were raised for the Bolsheviks' activities by robbing banks or post offices.

Lenin's attitude toward terrorism changed after the Bolsheviks seized power. Again, the change was purely pragmatic. Earlier, terrorism had been "bad" because it would not directly aid in bringing about a revolution and could foment opposition among the people, disgusted with such violent deeds, against the revolutionaries. Now, it became "good" because "red terror" was the only effective response to what Lenin called "white terror," reflecting his conviction that the Bolsheviks had no chance to remain in power unless they were prepared to be ruthless in crushing all enemies of the new regime.

After the visit of a labor delegation in 1920, Lenin wrote to English workers:

> Several members of your delegation have asked me with surprise about red terror, about the absence of freedom of the press in Russia, freedom of assembly, and the persecution by us of Mensheviks and Menshevik workers, etc. I replied that those really guilty of terror were the imperialists of England and their "allies," who conducted and are conducting white terror in Finland and Hungary, in India and Ireland, who supported and are supporting Yudenich, Kolchak, Denikin, Pilsudski, and Wrangel. Our red terror is the defense of the working class against exploiters, who are supported by SRs, Mensheviks, and an insignificant number of Menshevik workers. . . .[7]

The first victims of "red terror" were Lenin's fellow countrymen, and the process has continued down to the present. Even emigration has not always protected Russians and other former Soviet subjects against the reprisals of State Security.

Although the KGB has reserved its hardest blows for real or suspected enemies of the regime who had fled the country, it has not hesitated to employ terror against former agents, whatever their nationality. And, finally, the KGB has eliminated other non-Soviet enemies of the regime abroad whenever it could do so with impunity.

The list of murders and kidnappings carried out by the KGB on foreign soil is a very, very long one. Unlike the Western intelligence services, *the KGB alone includes in its permanent organizational structure a unit whose sole function is to perform "special tasks,"* such as murder, kidnapping, and sabotage. When this unit was established by Nikolai Ivanovich Yezhov in December 1936, it included "mobile groups" to carry out assassinations abroad.[8]

While the KGB's capability in this regard remains intact, and the unit continues to refine its methods through research into poisons and the development of specially designed weapons, the direct use of terrorism has been drastically reduced in the past two decades. Now that the USSR has become one of the two superpowers in the world, the KGB probably finds fewer enemies outside the country to bother about. It is obvious, however, that the desire of the Soviet leadership since Khrushchev to establish a new international image in order to promote its twin policies of "peaceful coexistence" and "relaxation of tension" had more than a little to do with "reining in" the KGB.

Nevertheless, it is no coincidence that during this same period the KGB has found it profitable to sponsor terrorism by all sorts of foreign groups, leaving the USSR free, as one observer noted, "to practice the diplomacy of détente with its right hand, professing ignorance of what its left hand was doing."[9] In most instances, the KGB cannot be charged with directing international terrorism simply because it has no need to do so. If you furnish a hunting rifle to someone bent on murdering all people with red hair, you do not have to give an order to kill any particular redhead.

None of this excludes the possibility that, for reasons of state, the KGB might take a hand in assassinations, just as the CIA is alleged to have been involved in a plot to kill Castro. The possible involvement of the KGB and Cuban Intelligence in the 1963 assassination of President Kennedy can only be surmised on the basis of certain suspicious circumstances. In contrast, all available evidence points to the conclusion that the KGB gave the order for the nearly successful assassination of Pope John Paul II in St. Peter's Square on May 13, 1981. Most knowledgeable observers agree that the Bulgarian security service, which evidently recruited the Turkish terrorist Mehmet Ali Agca to carry out the shooting and furnished logistical support to him, would not have acted without instructions from the KGB.

The KGB's shift from direct to indirect terrorism was marked by the establishment of Patrice Lumumba University in Moscow in 1960 for students from Third World nations. The university operates under KGB direction and most of its staff are KGB officers. The nature of the instruction has been described by an African student:

> Originally I went to Soviet Russia to Lumumba University to become a physician. But instead of medical studies I was surprised to find myself being trained in making explosives and how to plant them at various strategic points of my homeland. That was why I, together with others in similar situations, mounted those strikes in Moscow and Baku to be returned home at once as peaceful citizens, not terrorists. We won. But some others did remain, to continue and complete such training.[10]

The KGB's top-level support for its new line is clear from the Politburo's decision as early as 1964 to increase Soviet expenditures on international terrorism by one thousand percent.[11] This was reported by General Jan Sejna, former secretary-general of the Czech Defense Ministry and a principal military adviser to the Czechoslovak Communist Party's Central Committee. Sejna, who defected in 1968, also reported that, beginning in 1964, the KGB had operated a school for terrorists at Karlovy Vary, while its sister intelligence service, the GRU (Soviet Military Intelligence), provided paramilitary training in another school at the Doupov parachutist camp near Prague. The students came, he said, from "all over Europe and the Third World."[12]

Viktor Sakharov, a KGB defector, described his work in the Kuwait *rezidentura* (residency), where the reports of agents from all over the Middle East crossed his desk. The KGB, he discovered, was engaged in creating terrorist cells in the Arab oil sheikhdoms around the Persian Gulf, offering training in the Soviet Union to prospective terrorists. The KGB also was making every effort to promote urban terrorism in Turkey; after the first Turkish cadre had been trained in the USSR, subsequent recruits were sent to Syria for training in Palestinian camps, although KGB officers in the Damascus embassy made the actual arrangements.[13]

Seeking to disengage itself from the training of terrorists, at least geographically, the KGB had initially arranged for this training in such countries as North Korea, North Vietnam, and Cuba, the latter taking on a special responsibility for Latin America.

During the 1968 student riots in Mexico City, it was established that the Cubans had helped to create a favorable psychological climate for the riots, but that several KGB officers in the Soviet Embassy provided tactical guidance to the hard core of the rioters,[14] which comprised three groups trained at Patrice Lumumba University in Moscow, North Korea, or North Vietnam.

Additional evidence of KGB support for terrorists resulted in the expulsion of five members of the Soviet Embassy from Mexico in March 1971. The next year KGB representatives enjoying diplomatic status were expelled from Bolivia and Colombia, after links with local terrorist groups had been uncovered.[15]

In 1968, by a secret agreement with Fidel Castro, the KGB took direct control over the Cuban Intelligence service, the Dirección

General de Inteligencia (DGI). A few years earlier the KGB had established training camps for terrorists from all over the world in Cuba, under the supervision of KGB Colonel Kochegin.[16] Also in 1968, responding to KGB urging, the Soviet leadership decided to reverse its position of avoiding involvement with the Palestinians. While Arab Communists were instructed to infiltrate the Palestinian organizations and seek to gain control of them, the Soviet Union began to train and arm the Palestinians.[17]

According to Claire Sterling:

> The Russians donated weapons, know-how, diplomatic cover, and strategic real estate to the Palestinians; the Palestinians passed all the benefits on to an international terrorist underground busily dismantling Western society at dozens of pressure points around the globe.[18]

Such facts far from exhaust the KGB's terrorist operations. A long-term KGB agent named Henri Curiel ran a cleverly camouflaged front organization called *Aide et Amitié* (Aid and Friendship); under a charitable guise, it acted as a support mechanism for all comers among the terrorists except those identified with Peking. The organization provided money, arms, documents, shelter, and other services to terrorists who made Paris a way station. Its sole purpose was to facilitate the development and expansion of terrorism in the West.[19]

In Paris (and possibly elsewhere) the KGB maintained contacts with the Croatian nationalists or *Ustasha*, whose past history is tarnished through connections with fascism. The Croatians are not only responsible for a number of bombings inside Yugoslavia and abroad, including the bloody one at New York's La Guardia Airport in 1975, but have also carried out the murder of Yugoslav diplomats abroad. What does the KGB have in mind when it associates itself with the Croatians? Anything that contributes to tension in Croatia and weakens the Yugoslav regime in Belgrade is obviously grist for the mill of the USSR, which has never forgiven Yugoslavia's withdrawal from the "Socialist bloc."

The KGB's activities on behalf of "national liberation movements" pose certain dangers for the USSR: such movements can also be directed against the Soviet Union. Despite a change in facade under the Soviet regime, the Russian empire still exists.

Certain Armenians abroad are already engaged in terrorism. The Armenians direct their attacks solely at Turkish representatives in revenge for atrocities committed in World War I and Turkey's occupation of some Armenian territory. Still, their attention may eventually turn to their compatriots inside the Soviet Union, where one-third of Armenia's territory and its ancient capital are located.

Nevertheless, sponsoring terrorism clearly contributes to the KGB's goal of destabilizing and demoralizing the countries of the free world. Whenever widespread discontent creates the right climate for terrorist activities, the KGB is bound to make a contribution of its own. An example is the demonstrations in 1980 and 1981 in West Berlin, which escalated after illegal occupation of abandoned houses by homeless young people and their forcible eviction by the police. While proof is lacking, it appears that both the KGB and East German Intelligence sent over agents from East Berlin to agitate and incite and, wherever possible, to take part in planning the violent actions developing out of otherwise peaceful demonstrations.

Summing up, the KGB supports international terrorism on an impressive scale for one reason only: the destruction of societies and institutions in the West fits in neatly with the Soviet Union's ultimate goal of overthrowing governments of the free world.

The primary mission of most Intelligence services is to collect secret information through espionage, usually against nations of special interest from the standpoint of the security of their own countries.

Some of the larger Intelligence services undertake subsidiary or secondary operations in terms of propaganda or so-called psychological warfare. They occasionally engage in "covert action," as the CIA did in overthrowing Mossadegh in Iran and Arbenz in Guatemala or in its abortive attack in the Bay of Pigs against the Castro regime. Both the British and French Intelligence services have engaged in less widely publicized "covert action" of their own.

But it is safe to say that Soviet State Security is unique among Intelligence services in making the overthrow of governments the primary goal of its foreign operations. The KGB also collects secret information on a vast scale, with outstanding success, and its propaganda operations are equally significant. Entire newspapers and magazines, as well as individual journalists, are in its employ, and its practice of "disinformation"—the dissemination of forged documents ostensibly originating from adversaries and aimed at discrediting them—has developed into a fine art. But the real goal of its espionage is to probe for soft spots and find fatal weaknesses, thereby paving the way for the ultimate destruction of "enemy" governments, while the real goal of its propaganda is to weaken these governments and undermine public support. The KGB can take its time. It is patient in pursuing its objectives and prepared to wait a hundred years to bring about the downfall of anyone offering resistance to Soviet objectives.

The KGB has discovered a valuable by-product of its espionage that contributes to the same goal. When an operation has outlived its usefulness or has finally been exposed, the KGB seeks to terminate it in such a way that maximum demoralization occurs on the other side, with accompanying loss of confidence of people in their government. If citizens at large believe that their government is infiltrated at many levels, if they find their leaders incompetent or venal, national stability is bound to be adversely affected. Something along these lines followed the revelation that West Germany's Willy Brandt's personal assistant was an agent of East German intelligence, the KGB's apt pupils. The disclosure aroused such a loss of confidence by the public that Brandt was forced to resign as chancellor in 1974.

Does the KGB have any reason for optimism about the outcome of its struggle?

Since World War II more than a dozen Communist states have come into existence. Despite national and ideological quarrels, or what some observers view as the "growing pains" of world Communism, there can be no question about the Communist gains. Furthermore, the "Brezhnev doctrine" declares in effect that Moscow will not permit any Communist state to cease being Communist. Even though some Communist states have broken with Moscow, one can only conjecture what might happen if, for example, the Cuban government decided to drop its adherence to Communism when Castro dies.

What does the expanded Communist world mean to the KGB? Undoubtedly this improvement in what Communists call the "bal-

STATE SECURITY, SOVIET STYLE 15

ance of forces" has given a new stimulus to its operations. As the USSR has emerged as a superpower, the KGB has also begun to operate in virtually every country of the world. Therefore, it is entirely accurate to say that Soviet spy rings are ubiquitous. The KGB is hydra-headed; for every spy ring that is lopped off, two others spring up in its place. Only the priorities change.

Unpalatable as it may be to many Americans who oppose the Central Intelligence Agency as a matter of principle, the KGB would be a far greater menace were it not for its existence. The KGB is a formidable organization, with an unrivaled continuity and depth of experience, and only the CIA possesses the resources to resist its encroachment on a worldwide scale. The importance of this can be best appreciated if one considers the position of those countries whose security services have little or no capability of collecting Intelligence in the same geographical area, let alone on a global scale. Confronted with the KGB's operations in its own country, unaware of the KGB's activities in other areas, the local security service is at a tremendous disadvantage, lacking the depth in personnel and the coverage required to cope with this threat. Nowadays the CIA is the only free-world Intelligence service equipped to grapple with the KGB on a nearly equal basis. Together with friendly local Intelligence and security agencies, the CIA can often (if not always) help to frustrate the KGB's efforts.

2

Grand Inquisitors

DISCUSSING THE ROLE of individuals in the structure of the Soviet ruling apparatus, the writer-artist Ernst Neizvestny, who emigrated from the USSR, said:

> These personalities are more likely to change in the direction required by the apparatus than the reverse. Moreover, it would be strange to think that the operation of a machine could be changed by being inside it and performing a separate function similar to that of a tiny, automatically replaceable component of a cybernetic machine.[1]

In any discussion of the KGB, it is necessary to consider the interrelationship of men and the institutions they create. In the beginning they apparently enjoy complete freedom of choice, but appearances are deceiving. Even then, men are limited in their choices by such factors as cultural tradition, history, geopolitics, and even language.

The Bolsheviks who created the Cheka were also limited by the system to which they had committed themselves, not only Marxism but also Leninism, which aimed at keeping power in the hands of an elite group. If the KGB as an institution reflects the vital needs of the Soviet regime, which has been built on a pseudodemocratic

16

base, the reason is that this regime cannot survive without an instrument of repression capable of maintaining strict control over the country at all levels.

Once an institution exists, it is easier to abolish it than to change it. Its very existence creates an ethos and traditions that bind those who work for it, whatever their original beliefs, background, and training. This is particularly manifested in military, police, and security organizations, which demand a special élan. To paraphrase de Maistre's observation, the KGB tends to get the kind of leaders it deserves. It is no accident that the men needed for its optimal functioning at any given period, in response to historical imperatives, have invariably risen to the top.

Every violent revolution needs its executioner, who must be completely ruthless, absolutely convinced of the rightness of his cause, and prepared to exterminate all enemies without hesitation. Robespierre filled this need for the French Revolution. Felix Edmundovich Dzerzhinsky took on this odious task for the Bolsheviks.

Dzerzhinsky was born near Vilnius, Lithuania (then part of the Russian empire), on September 11, 1877, on the estate of his parents, who were well born but not wealthy members of the Polish aristocracy. In his youth he planned to enter the Roman Catholic priesthood,[2] but he soon found a new and more enduring faith. Because of his "hasty and impulsive nature,"[3] as he himself said, he came into constant conflict with high-school authorities and, after joining a Social Democratic group, dropped out of school to become a professional revolutionary.

When the Czar was overthrown in 1917, Dzerzhinsky was released from prison after receiving a six-year sentence in 1916 for revolutionary work. He then joined the Bolshevik Party, which thereby acquired a seasoned revolutionary with twenty years of underground experience behind him, including thirteen years spent in jail and Siberian exile. Dzerzhinsky became a member of the Bolshevik Central Committee and was among those who supported Lenin in calling for an armed insurrection. In October 1917 he was appointed to the Military Revolutionary Committee set up by the Petrograd Soviet of Workers' and Soldiers' Deputies to carry out the insurrection. His specific task was to direct the seizure of the post and telegraph offices.

Following the successful uprising, the committee's mission was to maintain the new rulers in power, and to this task Dzerzhinsky unsparingly devoted all his strength and ardor. When the Military Revolutionary Committee was replaced by the Cheka in December 1917, Dzerzhinsky became chairman. Ever ready to take on the party's most thankless jobs, he had offered his services, and given his past experience in prison and exile and first-hand knowledge of the Czarist secret and regular police, he appeared to be well qualified for the post.

Dzerzhinsky, who lamented the hunger and suffering of the masses under the czars, believed that an elite group had to bring about the changes that the people could not or would not bring about themselves. This implied coercion, and it was only a short step to the use of force against all those who impeded such changes. Self-righteous as ever, Dzerzhinsky did not shrink from destroying the revolution's real or presumed enemies by the tens of thousands if necessary.

Dzerzhinsky was among those old revolutionaries who had endured great hardships, who were self-sacrificing, unprepossessing, and uninterested in personal comfort. Like most fanatics, he utterly lacked humor. In later years he would make passionate speeches at meetings of the Politburo, where his colleagues endured his harangues in painful silence. Once when Lev Borisovich Kamenev was acting as chairman, he said to Dzerzhinsky: "Felix, you're not at a public meeting, but at a meeting of the Politburo."[4]

Nevertheless, Dzerzhinsky's energy and enthusiasm obtained results, and he was frequently called upon in emergencies to assume the most onerous tasks, fulfilling them to the letter and exhausting his strength in the process.

Dzerzhinsky's dream of assuming a leading role in the direction of the Soviet economy came true when he was appointed president of the Supreme Council of the Soviet Economy (Sovnarkhoz) in February 1924. In this capacity he had something to do with the New Economic Policy, which represented a tactical retreat of the Bolsheviks in the direction of capitalism. He continued as head of the Cheka, however, and finally wore himself out with the burden of his duties.

On July 20, 1926, he suffered a fatal heart attack after making an impassioned speech at a stormy meeting of the Central Committee. He was mourned by many who had been his friends, people who knew him as considerate, humane, and by no means without culture. But he was—and exhorted the Cheka to be—merciless toward enemies, even if they had once been friends. Karl Radek said of him, "Felix died just in time. He was a dogmatist. He would not have shrunk from reddening his hands in our blood."[5] Radek was wrong in one respect; it was already too late. Frankenstein had created his monster, the KGB, which outlived him by many years.

Dzerzhinsky's successor, Vyacheslav Rudolfovich Menzhinsky, is more to be remembered for what he did not do than for anything he did.

Leon Trotsky, who knew him well, wrote: "The impression he made on me can be best described when I say: he made no impression on me at all. He seemed to me more like the shadow of another, unrealized human being or an unsatisfactory sketch for a portrait that was never painted."[6]

Dzerzhinsky and Menzhinsky had family origins in the lesser Polish aristocracy, but there all resemblance ceased between the passionate and morally dynamic Dzerzhinsky and the neutral, unresponsive, half-apologetic Menzhinsky.

Three years Dzerzhinsky's senior, Menzhinsky was born on August 31, 1874, in St. Petersburg. His father was a teacher, and he himself studied law at St. Petersburg University, graduating in 1898. As a student, he had already become involved in the revolutionary movement. He joined the Russian Social Democratic Party in 1902 and, after the split at the party's Second Congress, became a member of the Bolshevik faction. He was arrested because of his revolutionary activities in 1906 and fled the following year to Paris, where he worked as an emigré journalist and continued his political activities. He did not return to Russia until July 1917, after the fall of the Czar, during the period of Kerensky's provisional government.[7]

At first he worked for a Petrograd military organization, editing a newspaper, *Soldier*. Athough his part in the Bolshevik coup appears to have been relatively minor, he was installed immediately afterward by the Military Revolutionary Committee as People's Commissar for Finance. He did not exactly distinguish himself in the post. As Trotsky said, Menzhinsky was either inactive or only active enough to reveal his own inadequacy. In 1918 he was sent to Berlin as RSFSR Consul General, but a year later he went to the Ukraine as People's Commissar for Commerce and Industry.

Menzhinsky failed to win the respect of any of his fellow leaders, becoming an object of condescension to the top Soviet brass, who were put off by the nervousness reflected in his physical awkwardness.

Nevertheless, Dzerzhinsky decided in 1923 to appoint Menzhinsky his first deputy in the Cheka—to much muttering and doubt from Politburo members. Dzerzhinsky attempted to defend his decision: "Who else? There isn't anybody!" Only Stalin, preferring nonentities and weaklings in key jobs who would be at the mercy of the party apparatus, supported the appointment. He already had his own man, Genrikh Grigorievich Yagoda, as second deputy and correctly calculated that Menzhinsky would offer no real resistance.

The situation was resolved in the way foreseen by Stalin during the last years of Dzerzhinsky's leadership of the Cheka. Dzerzhinsky was usually busy with his duties as chairman of the Sovnarkhoz. Menzhinsky, who suffered from a rare disease of the spinal cord, spent most of his time lying on a sofa, although nominally he was in charge of the Special Section, which maintained secret surveillance and control of the armed forces. Thus, as a result of Dzerzhinsky's prolonged absences and Menzhinsky's inactivity, Yagoda, for all practical purposes, ran the secret police during those years.[8]

When Dzerzhinsky died, Stalin still did not have the power to place his own man at the head of State Security, so he was content to perpetuate the existing situation. His opponents in the Politburo also lacked the power to appoint one of their own trusted supporters to this key position. A compromise was reached, whereby Menzhinsky became the head of State Security and Yagoda was his first deputy. Inevitably, Yagoda continued to run the whole organization.

Menzhinsky was not averse to using his ill health as an excuse for avoiding unpleasant duties. He was an aesthete, an admirer of Oscar Wilde, and an accomplished pianist who kept a grand piano behind a screen in his office. Condemned men being escorted across the courtyard of the Lubyanka inner prison would sometimes hear piano selections from Chopin or Grieg.

Menzhinsky was not at all close to Stalin and had been friendly with some of his rivals. Once he even went so far as to warn Trotsky against Stalin, but he was unwilling to oppose Stalin in the latter's capacity of General Secretary of the party. When he received orders to deliver a warning to all those who had been expelled from the Central Committee, he complied without hesitation by inviting Trotsky, Lev Kamenev, Grigori Zinoviev, and Radek to his office. He informed them that he would be obliged to have them arrested if they continued their clandestine antiparty activities.

The four men complained that their comrades were being forced by Yagoda to sign false declarations against them. Menzhinsky promised to investigate this charge, but at their next meeting, when challenged to explain his attitude toward Stalin, he demanded: "Why did you ever allow him to obtain the immense power which he is wielding already?"[9]

Menzhinsky died, apparently of natural causes, on May 10, 1934, and was buried in Red Square. When his successor Yagoda was arrested and placed on trial, Yagoda was accused of poisoning a number of people, among them Menzhinsky.

The reign of Genrikh Grigorievich Yagoda lasted only slightly more than two years (1934–1936), but in reality, Yagoda had already been running Soviet State Security for at least ten years. Because his formal reign coincided with the first phase of the Great Purge, it left a much greater impression.

Born in 1891, Yagoda, a Jew, came from Nizhny Novgorod (now Gorky). His beginnings were obscure. According to Boris Bazhanov, a member of Stalin's secretariat who was well acquainted with him, Yagoda was by no means the pharmacist he claimed to be. Yagoda owed his early advancement to the Sverdlov family. The elder Sverdlov was an engraver, in whose establishment Yagoda came to work as an apprentice. Sverdlov had long taken part in revolutionary activities and involved his children in them as well. He helped the revolutionaries in various ways, making seals useful to them in forging documents and printing leaflets on a small printing press. Yagoda at first had little interest in the underground and aspired to set himself up in business as an engraver. He stole Sverdlov's equipment and made himself independent. Failing to get a foothold in the business, however, he returned to Sverdlov, full of contrition and asking for forgiveness. The old man took him back. After the Bolsheviks came to power, one of the Sverdlov sons, Yakov, became chairman of the All-Union Central Executive Committee, the nominal head of the Soviet government. By this time Yagoda had married Ida Averbakh, Yakov Sverdlov's niece, and thereby secured an entrée to the Kremlin,[10] presumably at some point prior to Sverdlov's death in 1919.

In any case, Yagoda soon attracted Dzerzhinsky's notice and obtained a job in the Cheka in 1919. As early as December 1920, Yagoda signed a Cheka order as "business manager" (*upravlyayushchi del*) together with Dzerzhinsky.[11] As a result of Dzerzhinsky's appointment as chairman of the Sovnarkhoz and Menzhinsky's abdication of his responsibilities, Yagoda took over virtual direction of State Security.

As a self-styled pharmacist, with a presumed knowledge of poisons, Yagoda must have also seemed useful to Stalin. According to one account, on January 20, 1924, the eve of Lenin's death, Stalin sent Yagoda with a Kremlin doctor to the estate at Gorky where Lenin had been under treatment during his lengthy illness. "There will soon be another attack," Stalin allegedly told Yagoda. "He has written a few lines to thank you for sending him a means of deliverance. He is terribly distressed by the thought of a fresh attack." Several empty bottles were reportedly found on Lenin's bedside table when Yagoda telephoned Stalin's office the following evening with the news that Lenin had died.[12]

Boris Souvarine, a founder of the French Communist Party and member of the Comintern Executive Committee, believed that if Stalin gave Lenin poison, he did so at Lenin's own wish. Souvarine recalled meeting Bukharin, who was very upset after a visit to Gorky. Bukharin told him that Lenin could not bear his condition any longer and was begging to be killed.[13]

Whatever his role in Lenin's death, Yagoda unquestionably established close ties with Stalin's personal secretariat at that time and did his best to please him. Nevertheless, he was careful not to place all his eggs in one basket, since he also established a cozy relationship with the so-called Right Opposition, especially with

Aleksei Ivanovich Rykov, then chairman of the Council of People's Commissars (Sovnarkom). Yagoda's relationship with the Right Opposition, which grew much closer at the time of all-out collectivization in the late 1920's, soon became known to Stalin. It would cost Yagoda dearly in the long run.

But although he had lost Stalin's confidence by the late 1920's because of these connections, Yagoda kept his post because Stalin still found him useful. Placed in charge of Gulag (the Main Administration of Corrective Labor Camps), established in 1930, he displayed exceptional energy and ruthlessness in carrying out grandiose construction projects with the prisoners, most of them peasants rounded up in the collectivization drive, about which he himself had expressed strong doubt.[14] Yagoda, together with other State Security leaders such as Menzhinsky and Mikhail Trilisser, the chief of foreign espionage, thought that the collectivization drive had created a dangerous situation. The three attempted to warn Stalin, but he apparently "threw them down the stairs." After that Yagoda and Trilisser supposedly joined the Right Opposition.[15]

Yagoda responded to the exigencies of the times, as seen by the Soviet leadership, in his direction of State Security for more than a decade. He was the prime mover in the organization of the infamous "show trials"—if Stalin's role can be overlooked. He also carried the purpose of the secret police one logical step further by focusing their efforts on potential enemies of the regime after most of its real enemies had been eliminated.

It was Yagoda, too, who made State Security a party within the party. All of its officers were party members, but they formed a separate caste, functioning independently outside the regular party organization. Yagoda had also become a member of the Supreme Council of Physical Culture in the 1920s,[16] and State Security's involvement in Soviet sports, which has lasted to the present day, dates from this time. Yagoda carried his interest so far that he organized the famous Dynamo sports club,[17] which includes members of the security forces among its players and is widely recognized as the KGB's very own.

Yagoda's ego if not his achievements ultimately brought about his own downfall. In the summer of 1936, after Kamenev and Zinoviev had agreed to "confess" at a show trial, he was riding high. He had already acquired the title of General Commissar of

State Security and had had a uniform especially designed for himself. Stalin invited him to take up residence in an apartment in the Kremlin, an honor reserved for only the highest personages of the Soviet regime. According to other high-ranking State Security officers, Stalin said to Yagoda, after Kamenev and Zinoviev surrendered, "Today you have earned for yourself a seat in the Politburo."[18]

All these signal honors should have warned Yagoda that he was treading on thin ice. Nevertheless, he was apparently stunned when he was suddenly ousted. A decree dated September 26, 1936, appointed Nikolai Ivanovich Yezhov to the post of People's Commissar for Internal Affairs, replacing Yagoda, while Yagoda was appointed by a decree of the same date as People's Commissar of Communications.

Ironically, Yagoda took the place of Rykov, his old associate from the Right Opposition. Perhaps this was just a wry touch on Stalin's part, but the post of People's Commissar of Communications was already known as a way station to extinction. Seven months later Yagoda was arrested, and on March 2, 1938, he went on trial with Rykov, Bukharin, Krestinsky, Rosengoltz, and seventeen others, accused of belonging to an anti-Soviet bloc of Rightists and Trotskyites. In a certain sense, Yagoda had prepared his own "show trial."

Yagoda was sentenced to death and subsequently executed.

Like Yagoda, Nikolai Ivanovich Yezhov headed Soviet State Security for only two years, but they were the bloodiest and most irrational years of the Great Purge. The period is called by Russians the *yezhovshchina*, just as Americans applied the name of Senator Joseph McCarthy to the political witch-hunt known as McCarthyism.

To Russians, Yezhov was a mysterious and fear-inspiring figure. Dwarfish and ferret-faced, he bore a certain resemblance to Joseph Goebbels. Instead of a clubfoot, Yezhov had a lame leg, but like Goebbels, he was also a womanizer.

Yezhov was born in 1895 in St. Petersburg. He had little schooling and began to work in a factory at the age of fourteen. Before the revolution he was a metalworker, probably in the Tupolev works, one of the few real proletarians who ultimately succeeded in rising nearly to the top of the Soviet regime. He joined the Bolsheviks in March 1917, and soon abandoned his occupation to engage exclusively in party work.

During the civil war, he served with a number of Red Army detachments—as a political commissar. Beginning in 1922, he was appointed to responsible posts in various local party organizations, such as secretary of the Semipalatinsk provincial committee and secretary of the Kazak territorial committee.[19]

His big breakthrough came in 1927, when Yezhov was summoned to work in the Bolsheviks' central party apparatus in Moscow and joined Stalin's personal secretariat. This secretariat carried out the personal will of Stalin and drafted proposals and instructions to be approved officially by the higher party bodies. In addition, the secretariat also performed tasks secretly assigned by Stalin. It was built for the most part around young men who were unknown to the party at large and the country, but who came to wield enormous power in Stalin's name.

The personal secretariat was headed by Ivan Pavlovich Tovstukha, a Ukrainian, under whose direction Yezhov worked with Alexander Poskrebyshev, Georgi Malenkov, and Peter Pospelov. Each was given an official title that provided a cover for his secret activities. Since Stalin was often dissatisfied with Menzhinsky's and Yagoda's leadership of State Security, he ordered Tovstukha to set up, under Poskrebyshev's supervision, a "special Secret Political Section of State Security" to oversee the organization. Yezhov, who handled party personnel questions for the secretariat, maintained close cooperation with the Special Section.[20]

After Stalin launched his collectivization drive, Yezhov was given a temporary assignment as Deputy People's Commissar for Agriculture, a mark of his master's growing confidence in him. Yezhov must have displayed the requisite cold-bloodedness, ruthlessness, and determination to deal with millions of recalcitrant peasants, for he held the job during the critical years of 1929 and 1930.

Yezhov had become so indispensable that he was soon returned to full-time work in Stalin's personal secretariat. At the Seventeenth Party Congress in 1934 he was elected a full member of the Central Committee and a member of the Orgburo (Organizational Bureau). When the Central Control Commission was reorganized and renamed the Party Control Commission, stripped of all but its disciplinary powers, Yezhov became its deputy chairman and later, in 1935, chairman. Stalin approved of this reorganization because the commission's former responsibility for state security in the party was transferred to the Special Section of his secretariat, where Poskrebyshev handled it with the cooperation of Yezhov and Malenkov.

In early 1936 Stalin worked out a plan with Yezhov to prepare for the elimination of Grigori Zinoviev and Lev Kamenev at a staged trial. Forty top officials of State Security were summoned to a meeting at which they were told that a vast conspiracy led by Trotsky, Zinoviev, Kamenev, and other prominent members of the Right Opposition had been uncovered. The conspirators planned to kill Stalin and other Politburo members in order to regain power. Although it may have seemed odd to the officials that they, of all people, were hearing about this for the first time, none of them had the slightest inclination to question Stalin's secret orders.[21]

In the scheme drafted for Stalin by Yezhov, about three hundred members of the opposition then in prison or exile were to be brought to Moscow and "worked over" by KGB interrogators. Those who proved to be the most tractable would be induced to sign confessions incriminating Kamenev and Zinoviev as leaders of the conspiracy. But Yezhov's plan was only partially successful. Many of the arrested men withstood great pressure, and some of the confessions obtained in this way turned out to be unsatisfactory. Nevertheless, the "evidence" together with confessions also obtained under duress from the two former Soviet leaders were used at a show trial in July 1936. Kamenev and Zinoviev were duly convicted and executed.

Meanwhile Stalin had decided to get rid of Yagoda, who knew too much, and he ordered Yezhov to prepare for this step as well. Yezhov's position in charge of the Department of Cadres facilitated this action, and he secretly recruited a group of men ostensibly to work under his direction in the Central Committee. In reality, they were to take over the key jobs in the KGB, replacing Yagoda as well as most of the veteran officials there, many of whom went back to Dzerzhinsky's day.

Yezhov set about doing Stalin's housecleaning in Soviet State Security when he replaced Yagoda as People's Commissar for Internal Affairs in September 1936. The purge of the Intelligence organizations, including Soviet Military Intelligence, became one of the bloodiest of them all. Thus the man whom Stalin called "Our Mailed Fist" and "Our Blackberry" (both puns on Yezhov's name)[22] had reached the pinnacle of his power.

Naturally, the *yezhovshchina* was not limited to the security cadres, the party, or the armed forces, but soon extended to the entire Soviet population. That it involved the deaths or long imprisonments of millions of citizens has been amply documented, most graphically of all by Alexander Solzhenitsyn. By the summer of 1938 the Great Purge had served its purpose. Stalin's position was impregnable, and it was time to call a halt to the disruption and demoralization that the whole process entailed.

Yezhov had also served his purpose. He had been Stalin's willing tool, never making a move without his boss's orders, repeating Stalin's instructions to his subordinates word for word. According to Nikita Khrushchev, he was "diligent and reliable."[23] But only an accident of fate had raised him to one of the highest positions in the Soviet regime. In other circumstances Yezhov would have remained a worker and advanced to foreman as the culmination of his ambitions.

Yezhov's imminent downfall was signaled by the appointment of Lavrenti Beria, the head of the secret police in Georgia, as his deputy in July 1938. Not long afterward, Yezhov was appointed Commissar for Inland Water Transport. He disappeared a few weeks later and was never seen in public again.

Yezhov, however, did not owe his ouster to any particular sin, either of omission or commission. Stalin needed to put a stop to the bloodbath, and Yezhov provided an ideal scapegoat. "A scoundrel!" Stalin later said of him, explaining the *yezhovshchina*'s excesses.

According to some sources, Yezhov died in an asylum for the criminally insane. Purportedly he had been shot or was found hanging from a tree. A sign with the inscription "I am filth!" was attached to his clothes. Some wags familiar with the story joked that this inscription represented Yezhov's "spontaneous confession."[24]

Lavrenti Pavlovich Beria, the next boss of Soviet State Security, became in many ways the most powerful man to fill that office. Although Yagoda and Yezhov had also wielded the power of life and death over millions of citizens, they never held positions at the very top. Beria not only directed State Security for fifteen years, but was one of the most influential and feared members of the ruling Politburo. He controlled all aspects of State Security, including the vast network of labor camps, the militia or police, the separate army subordinate to the Ministry of Internal Affairs, the border guards, the Cheka internal security apparatus, and foreign espionage. In addition, he supervised the USSR's development of nuclear energy, which held a top priority in the Soviet economy.

On May Day and the October Revolution celebrations Beria stood on top of the Lenin mausoleum, never far from the master, Stalin. Among the large pictures of the leaders prominently displayed on such occasions, his picture sometimes followed close behind Stalin's. When it fell to fifth or sixth place, the Kremlin watchers abroad could speculate about his ranking in the top leadership, wondering whether he had fallen into disfavor or if his star would rise again.

Despite this prominence, Beria remained a mystery. Although Beria, like Stalin, came from Georgia, he was a Mingrelian belonging to a minority group closely related in culture and language to the Georgians.[25] While Stalin's strong Georgian accent sometimes made him difficult to understand in Russian, Beria spoke it well with no pronounced accent. In a Politburo of heavy drinkers, Beria was one of the heaviest and sometimes appeared drunk in public; but Stalin, who encouraged heavy drinking among his colleagues, was comparatively abstemious.

Beria was born in a village near Sukhumi in Georgia on March 29, 1899. His official biography in the *Great Soviet Encyclopedia* (2nd edition) claims that he came from a poor peasant family—a standard claim for Soviet leaders of the 1950's. In any case, Beria seems to have had an unusual education for a peasant, particularly during the czarist regime. He graduated from the Sukhumi high school in 1915 and entered a technical college in Baku. In March 1917 while still a student, he joined the Bolshevik party. Called up for military duty three months later, he served on the Rumanian front but seems to have spent most of his time in political work without seeing action. After his discharge, he went back to the technical college and received a diploma in 1919. But his main activity continued to be Bolshevik propaganda work. From the beginning of 1919 until the conquest of Azerbaijan by Soviet troops in April 1920, he was active in the Bolshevik organization in Baku. Then he was sent to Georgia, where he worked against the short-lived Menshevik regime until he was arrested and exiled.

Beria found his life's work when he joined the Cheka in April 1921. For the next ten years he engaged in espionage and counter-espionage work in the Transcaucasus. His State Security training remained with him long after he had risen to the top, when he would say to his Politburo colleagues about anyone who had fallen under suspicion: "Listen, let me have him for one night, and I'll have him confessing he's the king of England."[27]

State Security work, however, is also good training for Soviet politics. Beria received an important promotion in his political career in November 1931. At that time he became first secretary of the Central Committee of the Communist Party of Georgia as well as a secretary of the Transcaucasus Territorial Committee of the Bolshevik party.

Meanwhile Beria continued to direct State Security's operations in Georgia, never losing sight of the main chance. In July 1935 he curried favor with Stalin by delivering a series of four lectures to party workers in Tiflis on Stalin's leading role in the Bolshevik underground throughout the region. The lectures, published as a book later that year, presented Stalin as a close and highly esteemed comrade of Lenin. It gained Stalin's wholehearted approval.

In 1938, when Stalin decided that the Great Purge had gone far enough, he replaced Yezhov with Beria. His talents were well-suited to the KGB. He was a first-class organizer and planner, and after the rough treatment that intelligence officers had been subjected to by Yezhov, he reversed the process and won the loyalty of his men by supporting their personal well-being in every way he could, even against the rest of the bureaucracy.

Soviet State Security had already developed techniques for use against large numbers of people, compiling lists of those to be arrested, rounding up and processing them, transferring the prisoners to remote destinations, and putting them to work on giant construction and mining projects. Beria refined the same techniques for application during World War II in mass transfers of the population from Soviet-occupied regions in Poland and from the Baltic states, and later to the evacuation of areas of the Soviet Union threatened with German occupation, especially of those nationalities like the Volga Germans or the Crimean Tatars whose loyalty was suspect. As a member of the Defense Committee, Beria also organized the transfer of industry from European Russia to safe areas beyond the Urals as well as the mobilization of all remaining industry for the war.[28] Beria's control of many of these commissariats added considerably to his personal power.

Beria's powers, unprecedented even for the KGB, became even more awesome due to his hard work and efficiency. He handled all sorts of emergencies, at the same time exercising overall responsibility for public morale and security, even in the armed forces, where KGB officers, attached to an organization called SMERSH,* kept a strict watch for the slightest sign of defeatism or dissent among those in uniform. Moreover, Beria continued to direct the KGB's foreign espionage operations as well.

When the war ended, Beria was promoted to Politburo membership. Although some of his colleagues liked him because he could be friendly and enjoyed telling jokes, they considered him treacherous and two-faced and feared him, sometimes speaking among themselves about "Beria's ears" (listening devices).[29] They suspected that he not only kept them under observation secretly, but also had access to incriminating material about them in the KGB files.

Beria carried on even greater work in those immediate postwar years. It was necessary to round up all the German collaborators in areas occupied by the Soviet army and to root out "unreliable elements" as a preliminary to the setting up of Communist regimes. This action again involved the compilation of lists of people, by name or even by social category, and the transfer of masses of the population to largely uninhabited regions in Siberia, the far north, or the southern deserts. With the aid of "worthy" assistants like Sergei Nikiforovich Kruglov and Ivan Aleksandrovich Serov, Beria

---

* SMERSH is usually described as an acronym for *smert shpionam* (death to spies), but one source asserts that the acronym was derived from the expression *spetsial'nie metodi razoblachenia shpionov* (special methods for exposing spies). See Kirill Khenkin, p. 105.

took care of these and other tasks. State Security had to process all the Soviet prisoners of war returned from German captivity as well as the so-called displaced persons among Soviet citizens who had worked in Nazi-occupied Europe and were being returned—often against their will—to the USSR. The great majority were sent off to serve terms in forced-labor camps. In addition, State Security carefully screened members of the Soviet armed forces who had served in areas of Europe occupied at the end of the war for those considered unreliable or disloyal. Finally, internal security troops were obliged to carry out large-scale combat operations with tanks and planes against armed partisans seeking national independence in such areas as the Ukraine, Belorussia, and the Baltic states.

Beria's important assignments did not stop there. On August 7, 1946, the day after an atomic bomb exploded at Hiroshima, Stalin placed Beria in charge of nuclear arms development under a Soviet version of the Manhattan Project. Stalin's reasons for this appointment are unknown. The mining of uranium seems to have been a Gulag responsibility as early as 1934. It seems probable, however, that one important reason must have been Beria's responsibility for nuclear espionage against the West.

As Stalin aged and his paranoia grew, Beria and other colleagues shared periods of his disfavor or suspicion. On one occasion, Stalin told his daughter, Svetlana, "I don't trust that man."[30] Despite his difficulties, Beria managed to retain overall control of State Security, at least on the Politburo or Presidium level, but several administrative reorganizations may have been aimed in part at reducing his power. Certain moves, most likely made at Stalin's initiative or with his concurrence, seemed designed to undermine Beria's position, if not to dispose of him altogether. Stalin's death in 1953, however, put an end to that and temporarily allowed Beria to regain his ascendancy.

All available evidence indicates that Beria believed he could seize control of the regime after Stalin's death. He failed to reckon with the fact that his colleagues in the leadership, despite disagreements among themselves, became united in their opposition to him through their fear of him and combined to overthrow him only three months later.

Beria's fall took place at an expanded meeting of the Central Committee Presidium (Politburo) on June 26, 1953, when, by previous agreement among the conspirators, he was accused of being an enemy of the Communist Party. The conspirators had already made arrangements for eleven marshals and generals, all armed, to wait in an adjoining room, while Beria's bodyguards remained outside, ignorant of what was going on. After a secret button was pressed, the generals, led by Marshal Zhukov, came in. Zhukov pointed a gun at Beria and ordered, "Hands up!"[31]

Many of the conflicting stories about Beria's subsequent fate originated with Khrushchev. According to one version, he was placed on trial with other high-ranking KGB officers and executed in December 1953. Khrushchev also told a French visitor to the Soviet Union in May 1956 that Beria had been shot immediately after his arrest.[32]

Since the other top Soviet leaders considered Beria very dangerous, fearing an effort to free him by his own security forces, it seems probable that he was killed on June 26, 1953, or very soon thereafter. If a trial actually took place in December, it is doubtful that Beria ever sat on the same bench with his codefendants.

It became necessary to find a replacement for Beria without delay, and, fortunately, the right man was at hand.

Sergei Nikiforovich Kruglov, Beria's first deputy, had owed his advancement more to the favor of Stalin than of Beria. Moreover, Kruglov had the reputation of carrying out orders without question and finding the most efficient, if not the least brutal, methods for carrying them out. Even among Chekists, "he had a reputation for outstanding vengefulness and cruelty."[33] A figure of the second rank, he was not in any sense a "policymaker": he had to be considered primarily an executive (some would have said an executioner). This suited the needs of the moment, as the Soviet leadership wanted nothing more than compliance from the secret police. Appointed on June 26, 1953, the day of Beria's arrest, Kruglov exercised command of State Security for less than a year.

A bear of a man, six feet two inches tall, with a crop of thick black hair partly hanging over his eyes, Kruglov had not become a leading Chekist by accident or luck. His talents were formidable.

Born in 1900, he came from a peasant background, but details of his early life are lacking. By his own account, which perhaps reflected a self-created revolutionary past, he became a Red Guard during the revolution and served in a mounted reconnaissance unit. At the end of the civil war he was transferred to the Special Service Troops (Chon), State Security's own army, and continued to fight against "counterrevolution." Later he was sent to study at the Industrial Academy. After graduation, instead of being put to work in industry, he was assigned as a security officer under the general supervision of State Security's Economic Administration. He served in the so-called "special departments" of various construction projects, with the task of guarding against sabotage and malfeasance and simultaneously protecting "state secrets" from the USSR's enemies. Beginning with the first Five-Year Plan (1928–1932), Kruglov served at one time or another at all the largest construction sites in the country.

The role of the "special departments" was particularly significant at those construction sites where prisoners were employed. Kruglov soon acquired a reputation for firmness and persistence, insisting that orders be carried out to the letter and tolerating no excuses.

In 1934 he was brought back to Moscow and attached to the People's Commissariat of Heavy Industry. At first he worked in State Security's Second Department inside the commissariat; later he worked out of the office of Sergo Ordzhonikidze, the People's Commissar himself. Not content to sit in Moscow and issue orders, he traveled constantly to all parts of the Soviet Union, spreading fear and demoralization in his wake. Armed with the full powers he had obtained in Moscow, he made it his business to visit the enterprises that were failing to fulfill quarterly or annual plans, find out the reasons for this failure, and take measures on the spot to rectify the situation, having people arrested or fired or seeing to it that official reprimands were issued.

Since millions of prisoners were forced to work on these projects, Kruglov showed ingenuity in devising methods to squeeze more labor out of them in order to meet or exceed production targets. One of his most ingenious measures was to offer premiums to the guards who accompanied prisoners to work sites. To the extent that the prisoners fulfilled or overfulfilled production quotas, the guards received extra pay and extra time off or leaves. This special inducement to maintain pressure on prisoners and to punish them for slack work proved phenomenally successful in increasing output.

Another method was to offer to reduce the sentences of prisoners who overfulfilled their quotas.

At the same time Kruglov gained favor with Stalin by devoting special attention to the latter's pet construction projects. In his travels to these sites, the following type of dialogue frequently recurred:

KRUGLOV: Comrade X, even if you have to take a shovel yourself and start digging, the planned construction deadlines must be met.

COMRADE X: Comrade Kruglov, we're doing the best we can, but the winter conditions—the permafrost . . .

KRUGLOV: Comrade Stalin himself knows that it's December and not July. In my report to him, I can't explain your failures by the fact that this is wintertime. Construction plans must be met on time. The Party does not set tasks that cannot be fulfilled, and I'm going to prove to you that the winter plan for construction work can not only be fulfilled but overfulfilled!

And invariably Kruglov proved that this could be done.

In 1938, after Beria succeeded Yezhov, Kruglov was appointed deputy chief of Gulag's Capital Construction Administration, to which all the USSR's giant construction projects built with forced labor were subordinated. With his usual energy, Kruglov proceeded to extract the last ounce of strength from the camp inmates on such projects as the Moscow–Volga Canal, which took numerous lives.

Kruglov often reported personally to Stalin and pleased him so well that he was elected a candidate member of the CPSU Central Committee at the Eighteenth Party Congress in March 1939. Soon afterward, Kruglov became deputy chief of Gulag, but he did not remain there long, receiving a still more responsible post in the State Security counterespionage establishment. Kruglov knew nothing about counterespionage, but he learned the business quickly and demonstrated that ruthlessness combined with inexhaustible energy could go a long way in this sphere, too.

In the second half of 1942 Stalin personally assigned Kruglov to command a new counterespionage organization, SMERSH, composed of State Security counterespionage, military counterespionage, and the Border Guard's counterespionage, withdrawn from the western frontier after the German attack. This powerful organization under Kruglov's leadership was directly subordinated to the Defense Council, of which Stalin and Beria were members.

Kruglov's first big job was to halt the retreat of the Soviet Army, which had turned into a panicky flight of whole units, deserters, and stragglers. Kruglov established a cordon of internal security troops behind the lines to sweep up all such elements. SMERSH meted out harsh treatment, shooting some and sending others, under sentence of death, to serve in penal battalions.

Once the fronts had been more or less stabilized, SMERSH turned to those groups of the population considered disloyal or unreliable. It also began to run operations against German organizations that dispatched spies and infiltrators behind the Soviet lines, making extensive use of double agents. Finally, when the Soviet forces began to recapture lost territory and advance into Eastern Europe, SMERSH caught in its net the multitude of Soviet citizens, many of them soldiers, who had been in German captivity or merely worked or remained in hiding under the German occupation.

Kruglov's wartime activities were not limited to SMERSH. Enjoying Stalin's favor, he handled the security of Soviet leaders at the Teheran, Yalta, and Potsdam conferences, where he impressed foreign representatives as well as his own bosses with his efficiency. At the conferences of San Francisco and London in 1945, he organized the protection of Foreign Minister V. M. Molotov.[34]

After the war Kruglov took charge of the secret police operations against partisans in the Baltic states, particularly in Lithuania, where they were most active. He conducted these operations with notable ruthlessness, not only treating the partisans themselves with great cruelty but also using family members as hostages and burning down settlements and farms.

Kruglov's climb continued, although his privileged status would last only another decade. In 1945 he was one of a number of high-ranking Chekists promoted to Colonel General of State Security. On January 14, 1946, he replaced Beria as People's Commissar of Internal Affairs. This appointment, however, was only part of a subsequent reorganization of the security apparatus into the MVD and MGB, with Beria retaining overall responsibility for both ministries.[35] After Stalin's death, Beria reassumed direct control over Soviet State Security, merging the MVD and MGB into a single Ministry of Internal Affairs, which he headed. As Beria's first deputy, Kruglov was in a position to replace him when he fell.

In 1952 Kruglov had become a full member of the CPSU Central Committee. Nevertheless, his fortunes began to decline soon afterward. In March 1954, when the KGB was created with Ivan Serov as its chief, Kruglov lost control of State Security, although he remained for a time Minister of Internal Affairs.

The rest was anticlimax.

As Nikita Khrushchev sought to strengthen his position as First Secretary of the Party by a liberalization of the regime, culminating in his denunciation of Stalin in February 1956, Kruglov, the favorite of Stalin, became more and more of a liability, particularly in view of his close connection with the slave labor system. On the eve of the Congress, Kruglov lost his post as Minister of Internal Affairs.[36]

Thus ended Kruglov's long career. After his dismissal, he vanished into the limbo reserved for former heads of Soviet State Security. Even if he escaped physical extermination, he was already dead from the standpoint of the Soviet regime.

Just as Kruglov owed his career to Stalin, Ivan Aleksandrovich Serov owed his rise to Khrushchev.

Unlike his predecessors, Serov was a professional army officer. Nevertheless, he shared with them certain qualities that had helped them to excel in their secret police work. "He was not an enthusiastic killer," wrote one observer. "He was essentially an organization man and a gifted administrator, detached, cynical, wholly ruthless, killing without turning a hair when required to do so . . . then going home from his office and emerging on social occasions as an amiable, kindly, and amusing companion."[37]

Serov became an eminent specialist in one field that was of particular interest to Soviet State Security: mass deportations.

Ivan Serov was born into a peasant family on August 26, 1905, in the village of Afimskoye in the Ukraine. The family later moved to a larger town, where he attended middle school and joined the Komsomol, the Communist youth organization. While still a member, when he was only seventeen or eighteen, he became chairman of a village soviet. In 1926 he was formally admitted to the Communist Party.

With the aid of the Komsomol he secured admission to a Leningrad military school and, after graduation, began his military career as a platoon commander. Within seven years he was promoted to command of an artillery battery, later commanded a battalion, and by 1935 became chief of staff of a regiment.

From 1936 to 1939 he attended one of the USSR's most prestigious military schools, the Frunze Academy, where he received general-staff training. Logically, it seemed, he would have gone on to become a top artillery commander with a distinguished World War II record. But with the Great Purge winding down after Beria replaced Yezhov, there was not much logic about those times in Russia.

Soviet State Security had been decimated by the purge, which Yezhov turned against the Chekists themselves. So it was decided, under Beria, to fill their ranks with military men, and Serov was among those chosen for assignment to State Security.

Speaking of Serov in his memoirs, Khrushchev commented:

> He was a simple person, simple to the point of being naive. When I first knew him, he was still young and inexperienced. He had just graduated from an artillery academy. He was among those mobilized when we started drafting military men into the service of the NKVD. Naturally he had no experience in security operations. This was both an advantage and a disadvantage to him.[38]

In 1939 Serov was dispatched to the Ukraine, where Khrushchev held the top post of First Secretary of the Ukrainian Communist Party. After a brief interval as deputy to the head of the Ukrainian NKVD, Serov succeeded his boss and began to work closely with Khrushchev. Despite his inexperience in the security field, he impressed Khrushchev as a hard-working and dependable chief of local State Security. Before long, Khrushchev entrusted a number of important assignments to him.

The most important came about in September 1939 as a result of the Nazi-Soviet pact and the partition of Poland. Soviet forces occupied eastern Poland and proceeded to annex this territory. As an extension of his rule in the Ukraine, Khrushchev had the job of setting up a civilian administration with its capital at Lvov and carrying out the sovietization of the newly occupied Polish territory. Khrushchev in turn assigned Serov to do the dirty work.

First, Serov had to arrange for the processing of Polish Army formations rounded up by the Red Army and their transportation to prisons and labor camps in the Soviet Union. It is not known precisely what orders Serov received, but there is no question that fifteen thousand Polish officers vanished and were never heard from again, except for four thousand later found in a mass grave in the Katyn Forest who had been executed by the NKVD. More than two hundred thousand Polish prisoners of both sexes were sent to labor camps, where many of them died. Khrushchev had reason to be satisfied with his neophyte Ukrainian Commissar of Internal Affairs.

Serov worked closely with Khrushchev until February 1941, when he went to Moscow. By this time the NKVD had been divided into two commissariats (both subordinate to Beria): State Security, responsible for espionage and secret police functions, and Internal Affairs, responsible for the regular police force and the labor camps. Serov was appointed Deputy Commissar of State Security under V. N. Merkulov.

Having shown in Poland what he was capable of, Serov received a similar assignment after the USSR seized control of the Baltic states. In the summer of 1941, he organized mass deportations from Lithuania, Latvia, and Estonia. In a secret order signed by Serov, it was stated: "The deportation of anti-Soviet elements from the Baltic Republics is a task of great political importance." The same order gave detailed instructions for preparing lists of those to be arrested, carrying out the arrests, loading prisoners into freight cars, separating family members, avoiding unnecessary friction with the population, and the like.[39] "Under this order," observed Associated Press foreign news analyst Tom Whitney, "thousands of Baltic citizens were exiled to Siberia."[40]

As a rule, Serov's security forces operated behind the Soviet army's combat troops, cooperating closely with SMERSH in consolidating reconquered territory and rounding up collaborators. In this regard, Serov again resorted to his proven methods of mass deportation, exiling in a body such nationalities as the Crimean Tatars, the Chechen-Ingush, and the Kalmucks, who had taken advantage of the German invasion to revolt against the Soviet regime.[41] For these efforts Serov was decorated in March 1944 with the Order of Suvorov First Class, one of the Soviet Union's highest military honors. Like Kruglov, Serov was promoted to Colonel General of State Security.

During the last phase of the war, from 1944 until the capture of Berlin, Serov was deputy commander of the Belorussian front. Then he became a deputy of Marshal Georgi Zhukov, the commander-in-chief of the group of Soviet forces in occupied East Germany. He also functioned as the right-hand man of V. S. Abakumov, who ran State Security in the Soviet zone of Germany. Over glasses of vodka, Serov was fond of telling Allied officers that it had been his dream to torture German leaders until they wished for death ten times before he let them die.

Recalled from Germany in February 1947, after separate ministries of State Security and Internal Affairs had again been created, Serov was named first deputy of Kruglov, the new Minister of Internal Affairs. In this position he appears to have been responsible for the forced labor employed in the construction of the Volga–Don Canal.

After Stalin's death the two ministries were once again combined into a single Ministry of Internal Affairs under Beria. As a deputy, Serov then followed Beria and Kruglov in the hierarchy of the ministry. When Kruglov replaced Beria, Serov became first deputy; when Kruglov had the State Security apparatus taken away from him in March 1954, Serov was appointed chairman of the newly organized Committee of State Security (KGB). He had reached the zenith of his career.

As Kruglov had done earlier for Stalin, Serov went abroad to handle security arrangements for Khrushchev in his travels. Foreigners who came in contact with him remember a sinewy, shadowy man with gray-blue eyes, a high forehead, a firm mouth, and slightly graying brown hair. He wore conservative blue-gray suits and the thick-soled shoes of a policeman.

Serov accompanied Khrushchev to Yugoslavia in May 1955 to take charge of the security arrangements for the Soviet delegation seeking to patch up relations with Tito after his rift with Stalin. Soon afterward, on his fiftieth birthday, Serov was awarded his third Order of Lenin and was promoted to the rank of General of the Army.

In November 1955 Serov also handled the security arrangements during the trip of Nikita Khrushchev and Nikolai Bulganin to India, Burma, and Afghanistan. When enthusiastic crowds almost mobbed the two Soviet leaders, Serov, keenly aware of his responsibility for their security, became involved in disputes with newsmen seeking stories and pictures and received a good deal of unwelcome publicity.

In March 1956 he flew to England to complete security arrangements for the visit of Khrushchev and Bulganin. There was an immediate uproar in the British press because of his notorious record, and Serov responded to the criticism by saying that the newsmen "spoke without knowing the true facts." With a broad grin and thumping himself on the chest, Serov said, "Look at me— would you call me Ivan the Terrible?"[42] Serov still expected to remain in charge of security during the visit, but when the time came his name was omitted from the list of delegation members. Khrushchev could not understand why the British disapproved of Serov.[43]

Seven months later, when the Hungarian Revolution erupted, General Serov was back in the news. After the revolution had been crushed by Soviet troops, it was reported that Serov himself arrived in Budapest on November 18.[44] The deportation of Hungarians of military age to the Soviet Union was already under way.[45] According to Japanese prisoners of war repatriated from Soviet labor camps, deported Hungarians were expected to arrive in the camps shortly.[46] On November 23 the Yugoslav press reported the kidnapping of former Hungarian Premier Imre Nagy by the Soviet secret police.[47] While Serov's direct involvement in these affairs remained unclear, as chairman of the KGB he must not only have been aware of but also approved all such matters.

Despite Khrushchev's protection, Serov apparently forfeited Khrushchev's confidence at some point and was fired from his post, presumably in December 1958. Khrushchev said: "Serov was punished during my time. I think he was careless, but he was an honest, uncorruptible, reliable comrade despite his mistakes."[48] Precisely how Serov was "careless" or made "mistakes" no one outside the Soviet leadership knows. Perhaps Khrushchev was thinking of Serov's failure to warn him in time about the "antiparty" group that outvoted him in the Central Committee Presidium in June 1957. In any event, once Khrushchev had again tightened his grip on power he probably felt that he could get rid of a man like Serov, who was tainted with so many of the crimes committed by the professional Chekists.

Demoted to head of the GRU, or Soviet Military Intelligence, Serov was obviously compromised by the case of Colonel Oleg Penkovsky, a veteran GRU officer, who spied for the CIA and MI6 and was placed on trial in May 1963 and subsequently executed. The leadership allowed him to retain his post until March 1964, when he finally had to step down. After Khrushchev was forced to retire from the leadership, Serov was reportedly expelled from the Communist Party in 1965 amid rumors that he might even be placed on trial. The man who was notable chiefly for his loyalty to Stalin and Khrushchev, as well as his expertise in genocide, ended in disgrace, becoming a nonperson under the regime he had served for years.

The excesses of the Soviet secret police in the Stalin era had made an indelible impression on the post-Stalin leadership of the Communist Party. To be sure, these leaders were concerned only about the excesses committed against the party. In his speech denouncing Stalin, Khrushchev spoke at length about the crimes of the secret police committed against innumerable innocent and loyal party members. Khrushchev's successors have not been more concerned with the KGB's arbitrary and frequently illegal abuses directed against the Soviet population in general, but at most have attempted to limit the more flagrant excesses liable to arouse widespread popular resentment. The determination to keep State Security under party control resulted in the replacement of Ivan Serov by a career party functionary.

Aleksandr Nikolaevich Shelepin was an eager and ambitious young *apparatchik*—an "organization man"—who had made his name in the Komsomol, the Communist youth organization. He had followed the classic pattern of using people until they could no longer help him and then casting them off. Friends from his student days who contacted him when he reached more exalted positions found that he no longer "knew" them. He was only forty when he was appointed chairman of the KGB.

By then he could have been easily taken for an American businessman. His heavy, dark good looks just missed being handsome in his youth and became full and jowly as he grew older; with a day's growth of beard he resembled a bandit more than a banker. He had short-cropped thick black hair, a high forehead, crooked eyebrows surmounting hooded eyes, and a straight hard mouth, revealing his Slavic origin only in his broad nose. He had the proud bearing of a leader, accustomed to being surrounded or followed and conducting himself with the self-assurance that went with it.

Born on August 18, 1918, in Voronezh, in the central part of European Russia, Shelepin was entirely a product of the Soviet system. His father was a railroad employee, an office worker, but the family must have enjoyed certain privileges, since Shelepin received an excellent education. Considered promising by those who exercised "Soviet power" in Voronezh, Shelepin received the opportunity to attend the Institute of History, Philosophy, and Language in Moscow, where he studied from 1936 to 1939. While still a student, he attracted notice, becoming very active in those years of the Great Purge in exposing "enemies of the people." Not surprisingly, he was appointed secretary of the institute's Komsomol organization.

Indeed, Shelepin's entire career provides almost a textbook model for a successful Soviet bureaucrat. After graduation he managed to display his patriotism by taking part in the war with Finland in 1939–1940—not as a soldier but as a political commissar of the type attached to all military units. Having done his stint of military service, he subsequently avoided all direct involvement in the "Great Patriotic War." From 1940 to 1943 he was a so-called instructor, then a section chief, and, finally, secretary for propaganda of the Moscow city Komsomol organization, the most important branch in the USSR. From 1943 to 1952 he was a secretary of the All-Union Komsomol Central Committee and, simultaneously, a member of the Committee for Affairs of Physical Culture and Sport. During the war he was responsible for Komsomol work in the armed forces as well as personnel and organizational questions. After the war he dealt with ideological questions and international contacts.[49]

Continuing to bolster his position, Shelepin pushed himself forward to become a key figure in the organization of the World Youth Festival in East Berlin in 1951. In 1952 he ascended to the top of the Komsomol as first secretary, a post he retained until 1958. As a Komsomol leader, he made numerous trips abroad, taking a prominent part in international Communist-front organizations. As early as 1949, he was elected a vice-chairman of the Executive Committee of the International Union of Students (IUS), a decade after he had ended his own student career. From 1953 to 1958 he was a vice-chairman of the World Federation of Democratic Youth (WFDY).

His election as a member of the CPSU Central Committee at the Nineteenth and Twentieth Party Congresses augured well for his advancement.

He was thirty-four when Stalin died and favorably situated to move farther up in the hierarchy, for he was the kind of functionary needed just then. He had acquired considerable political experience and displayed great organizational talents, yet he had not been overly compromised during the Stalin era. No one could doubt his party loyalty.

As leader of the Komsomol, which had more than eighteen million members, Shelepin affected the same rough, down-to-earth language of the CPSU's emerging chief, Nikita Khrushchev, scolding Soviet youth roundly and urging them to do better. He was scornful of white-collar workers (his father had been one) and denounced those who avoided factory or farm work, although he had never dirtied his own hands except in a figurative sense. He accused many Komsomol members of being shirkers and idlers, attacking young people with "alien" tastes for "vulgar dancing, abstractionist paintings, and sculpture." Shelepin, however, came up with a solution for such problems: he mobilized the country's youth for work in the USSR's most remote regions. In 1954, for example, he mobilized three hundred and fifty thousand young Komsomol members for Khrushchev's pet Virgin Lands scheme, intended as a permanent solution for lagging Soviet grain production. Two years later he mobilized another three hundred thousand young people to "build communism" in Siberia, northern Russia, and the Soviet Far East. Finally, just before he gave up leadership of the Komsomol, Shelepin organized a campaign in 1957 involving the participation of some six hundred and fifty thousand middle-school graduates in cattle raising.

Another area in which Shelepin was notably active was in militarizing the Komsomol. He insisted that every member join the so-called Voluntary Society for Cooperation with the Army, Air Force, and Navy (DOSAAF). Another original idea was to push "voluntary" fund-raising drives among members on behalf of the state. In this way, the Komsomol "donated" three billion rubles to the state in 1957, on the occasion of the fortieth anniversary of the October Revolution, and five billion rubles at the time of the Thirteenth Komsomol Congress in 1958.

At the Twentieth Party Congress in 1956, Shelepin sounded even more like an echo of Khrushchev. During a debate on problems of Soviet industry, he scathingly criticized the USSR's toy industry (presumably because of the connection between youth and toys). He aroused laughter when he commented: "A chicken made of plastic costs more than three live suckling pigs." Shelepin's future looked brighter than ever when he was chosen a member of a special commission with responsibility for drafting a new party program.

In April 1958 Shelepin gave up his post as first secretary of the Komsomol to a devoted follower, Vladimir Semichastny, and became head of the influential CPSU Central Committee Department of Party Organs in the Union Republics. Eight months later, on December 25, 1958, he replaced Serov as chairman of the KGB.

It was Khrushchev's intention to redeem his pledge at the Twentieth Party Congress to place the secret police again under firm control of the party. Having ousted the "antiparty" group from the Central Committee Presidium and strengthened his own power in the party, he decided that the time was right to select his own man from the party ranks for the top job in the KGB. His choice fell on Shelepin, whom he considered a personal protégé and who had impressed him as an organizer and mobilizer of Soviet Youth. In addition, Shelepin's credentials as a manipulator of international Communist-front organizations may have recommended him to Khrushchev.

Shelepin's tenure lasted less than three years. Obviously he viewed the job only as a stepping-stone to the top of the party pyramid. He did not stay long enough in the KGB to leave any lasting imprint, although this period must have increased his taste for power.

As KGB chairman, Shelepin inevitably acquired some of the

odium caused by State Security's dirtier deeds during his tenure. When a KGB agent named Stashinsky, who had murdered two Ukrainian emigrés in West Germany, confessed that Shelepin had personally decorated him for his deeds with the Order of the Red Banner, it created such a scandal that Shelepin was later threatened with possible prosecution if he traveled to that country. At the time of Khrushchev's trip to the United States in 1959, the job of supervising arrangements for his security, which normally devolved on the KGB chairman, was handled by a lower-ranking official. Perhaps Khrushchev feared that Shelepin's inclusion in the Soviet delegation would create a storm like that which had broken around Serov in England. In any case, since Shelepin lacked the security experience of Kruglov or Serov, his presence was not essential.

Shelepin appeared briefly in the limelight in 1960 when he signed the indictment of U-2 pilot Francis Gary Powers after the latter's plane was downed in the Soviet Union. By then Shelepin's service was approaching its end, and on November 13, 1961, he relinquished his position as KGB chairman to Vladimir Semichastny, probably on his own recommendation.

Shelepin's departure from the KGB had been foreshadowed by his election as a secretary of the CPSU Central Committee at the time of the Twenty-second Party Congress. This was one of the top positions of authority in the party, continuing his upward progress.

In November 1963 Shelepin was appointed chairman of the newly formed, combined Party-State Control Commission, created as a part of Khrushchev's reorganization of the party. At the same time, Shelepin retained his post as secretary of the Central Committee and became a deputy chairman of the USSR Council of Ministers. As head of the Party-State Control Commission, Shelepin commanded a vast network of "controllers" at all levels of the party and government; their number was estimated at one hundred and thirty thousand functionaries and over four million activists.

Nevertheless, the fiercely ambitious Shelepin joined the opposition to Khrushchev and, together with his follower Semichastny, helped to seal off Khrushchev (through the State Security apparatus) when Brezhnev, Kosygin, and others made their move in the Presidium to unseat him. In this way, Khrushchev's opponents sought to prevent him from repeating his appeal to a plenum of the

Central Committee, as in the case of the "antiparty" group in 1957, although there was little danger of this in reality. Khrushchev had alienated most of the foremost republican and provincial party bosses, all members of the Central Committee, with his radical plans for reorganizing the party structure into separate agricultural and industrial apparatuses. At any rate, Khrushchev, who was vacationing in the south at the time, first learned about the plot against him when an airplane was sent to bring him back to the Presidium session that resulted in his ouster.

Although Shelepin showed an abiding fondness for foreign travel, he never neglected his career. After Khrushchev's ouster, his reward for betraying his mentor was full membership in the Presidium, to which he was elected in mid-November 1964, a month later. Thus, it appeared that Shelepin was likely to play a still more prominent role in the new leadership.

Nevertheless, Shelepin soon overreached himself in his new position. Evidently he regarded his older colleagues like Brezhnev and Kosygin with a certain contempt and made no effort to hide his attitude. His outspoken criticism of the new policies and his overweening ambition soon alarmed other members of the Presidium. This proved to be a serious mistake. In December 1965, slightly more than a year after the new leadership had taken office, he was forced to give up his positions as deputy chairman of the Council of Ministers and chairman of the Party-State Control Commission.

Shelepin's assertiveness had cost him dearly. Thereafter his path turned downward.

The next setback came in July 1967, when Shelepin was named chairman of the All-Union Central Council of Trade Unions (AUCCTU), a job of little political influence. By September he formally gave up his position of secretary of the Central Committee. His political position was also gradually undermined as his former associates (like Semichastny) were removed from key posts. Waging a losing battle against Brezhnev on policy toward China, Shelepin was finally ousted from the Presidium as a result of the Central Committee plenum in April 1975.

Just before the plenum, Shelepin was mousetrapped when he went on a trip to England only to encounter demonstrations and protest actions against him on the basis of the Stashinsky case. This could have been easily foreseen, and it was used as a pretext to oust him from the Politburo. Not long thereafter, Shelepin was dismissed from his post as chairman of the AUCCTU.

A measure of Shelepin's fall from grace is the elimination of his official biography, published in 1957 in the second edition of the *Great Soviet Encyclopedia*, from the corresponding volume of the third edition, published in 1978.

Thus the fear and suspicion every State Security chief inevitably aroused among his colleagues at the summit also turned out to be a jinx for Shelepin. This seemed to be further confirmation that no KGB chairman could ever become a successor to Lenin, Stalin, Khrushchev, or Brezhnev.

The appointment of Vladimir Yefimovich Semichastny as KGB chairman was a continuation of the policy of keeping State Security under tight party control. But since Semichastny was one of the young men Khrushchev had advanced through the Komsomol, it could also be viewed as an effort by Khrushchev to further solidify his power.

Semichastny was a second-rate figure who tried to ape Shelepin in staking out a position as a hard-liner. His essential mediocrity is evinced in the fact that his career was contained within and dwarfed by Shelepin's.

Semichastny was born in 1924 into a Ukrainian working-class family. Details of his early life are unknown. He became a student in the Chemical-Technical Institute at Kemerovo in western Siberia, where his family probably lived. He began his career as a Komsomol activist in 1942, possibly as a student at the institute. In 1944 he was accepted as a Communist Party member. Shifted to Komsomol work in the Ukraine, he served as secretary for cadres (personnel) in the Ukrainian Komsomol Central Committee from 1946 to 1947 and was named Ukrainian Komsomol first secretary in 1947. He must have caught the eye of Khrushchev, then Ukrainian CP first secretary and Union Republic prime minister, for he rose rapidly thereafter. He was elected a member of the Ukrainian CP Central Committee and a candidate member of its Organizational Bureau. In 1950 he was shifted from his Komsomol post to Moscow, where he became a secretary of the All-Union Komsomol organization. At last, in 1958, he succeeded Shelepin as first secretary and reached the top of the Komsomol. In that year, emulating Shelepin, he was credited with the formation of thirty-four thousand "voluntary" youth brigades for the purpose of over-fulfilling industrial production plans. He also mobilized three hundred and fifty thousand young people and sent them to work in the Virgin Lands of Kazakstan and Siberia.

Boorishness designed to outrage international public opinion in order to demonstrate Communist orthodoxy was an earmark of the Khrushchev era. As Khrushchev had once pounded his shoe on the desk at the United Nations, Semichastny came up with his own version of this act on October 29, 1958, during his keynote speech at the Komsomol's fortieth anniversary meeting. His outburst was inspired by the award of the Nobel Prize to Boris Pasternak for *Doctor Zhivago*, a work that had met with the stern disapproval of the Soviet regime. Diverging suddenly from the theme of his speech, the history of the Komsomol, Semichastny cast aside the prepared text and launched into a tirade against Pasternak and his book. With Khrushchev nodding approvingly, Semichastny called Pasternak a "mangy sheep" and a "pig," asserting that although he "has lived in our midst . . . [he] has decided to spit in the face of our people." At this point, Semichastny demanded that the aged Pasternak be exiled from the Soviet Union.[50] By renouncing the Nobel Prize, Pasternak escaped this fate, but another Nobel Prize winner whose work was frowned on by the Soviet regime, Alexander Solzhenitsyn, had the misfortune to be exiled from his native country some years later.

Semichastny, whose physical resemblance to a bull was reflected in his nature, prospered as he cracked down on independent-minded youth accused of contaminating Marxist-Leninist ideology with "alien" influences. In March 1959 he left the Komsomol to take up a career in the CPSU apparatus. Five months later he was named second secretary of the Azerbaijan CP Central Committee, a position that made him the de facto party boss in Azerbaijan. Semichastny remained in Baku until November 1961, when he was recalled to Moscow to become chairman of the KGB.

Semichastny's tenure in the KGB coincided with a period of transition for Soviet State Security. Within the USSR the KGB was obliged to cope with a tiny but growing dissent movement and the appearance of the *samizdat* (self-publishing) phenomenon, in which authors denied publication because of official condemnation circulated their works in carbon copies from hand to hand. Since the post-Stalin leadership was unwilling to give the secret police a free hand in dealing with dissent, the KGB selectively restricted such measures as incarceration in a forced-labor camp only to the most blatant offenders. A "moderate" solution entailed putting some dissenters in psychiatric hospitals, from which they could be released only by convincing the doctor-jailers that they had recovered their "mental health."

In its foreign espionage activities, the KGB made some adjustments to the international situation, shifting its covert struggle with Western intelligence services waged across the Iron Curtain or other East-West borders to a global struggle waged country by country. The KGB also turned from a use of direct terror to indirect terror and guerrilla warfare through proxies.

Semichastny personally had little to do with these changes, and even in a representational sense he did not make much of a showing. His main function in the KGB was apparently exercised in October 1964, in close consultation with Shelepin, to bring about Khrushchev's downfall. He knew that the old man had lost the support of most of the party bosses, the generals, and the managers; the time had come for him and Shelepin to join the opposition. Together, they sealed off Khrushchev from the outside world in the state dacha at Pitsunda, where he was on vacation, so that his supporters could not warn him about plans for the coup. The two men also arranged for Khrushchev's transportation by plane directly from Pitsunda to the Presidium session at which he received notice of his forced retirement.

As Shelepin's star waned, Semichastny faded away. In May 1967, while Brezhnev and Kosygin were disposing of Shelepin, Semichastny lost his job as KGB chairman to Yuri Vladimirovich Andropov and was simultaneously appointed first deputy chairman of the Ukrainian Council of Ministers. Exiled to Kiev, he gradually sank into the obscurity that had already overtaken some of his immediate predecessors.

Of all the heads of the KGB up to 1967, Yuri Vladimirovich Andropov was by all odds the most seasoned and formidable.

Tough, steely-eyed, and white-haired, Andropov had come up through the party ranks the hard way, demonstrating his ability in a series of challenging assignments. His only previous connection with intelligence seems to have been during World War II, when he organized partisan detachments in Karelia, presumably under Soviet State Security's Fourth Administration.

A man of the *nomenklatura*,* Andropov represented Soviet conformism with a vengeance, dedicating himself to stamping out dissent inside the country and to keeping the "fraternal" states in line within the much-vaunted Socialist Commonwealth.

Although younger than most Politburo members, Andropov possessed perhaps the widest experience. For eight years he was a Komsomol functionary, and he had nineteen years of service in the Communist Party apparatus. For four years he was in the diplomatic service. Between 1967 and 1982, he had headed the KGB for fifteen years. Since he had apparently avoided making any major mistakes, he was still a man to be reckoned with.

Andropov was born on June 15, 1914, at Nagutskaya, a railroad settlement in the North Caucasus. His father was a railroad worker, presumably Russian; his mother, like Beria's, was rumored to be Jewish. In 1930, the year he joined the Komsomol, he obtained employment as a telegraph worker in the city of Mozdok. Later he became an apprentice to a movie projectionist and then a sailor on the Volga.[51]

His work as a sailor probably led him to seek to improve himself by enrolling in a water-transport technical school at Rybinsk, and Komsomol membership undoubtedly facilitated his acceptance. He attended this school from 1932 to 1936, serving as a secretary-at-large of its Komsomol organization.

After graduation, Andropov worked as a Komsomol organizer at a shipyard in Rybinsk. In 1937 he was elected a secretary and a year later first secretary of the Komsomol's Yaroslavl Oblast Committee. He owed his rapid advancement to the Great Purge, which created numerous vacancies in higher positions. After surviving a

---

* The word *nomenklatura* applies to a listing of the whole Communist elite, career workers subordinate to the party apparatus, for whom all key positions of the Soviet Union are reserved and to which they are assigned by the Central Committee apparatus. The number of *nomenklatura* workers amounts to about two hundred and fifty thousand; they are the real rulers of the Soviet Union.

widescale purge of the Komsomol in 1938, he had a clear path for his rise in the hierarchy. He also became a Communist Party member in 1939.

Joined by Finnish forces hoping to regain territory in western Karelia ceded to the USSR, Germany invaded the Soviet Union in June 1941. Andropov now took part in organizing partisan warfare behind the lines in Karelia. As the Soviet Army retreated, with Leningrad under siege, he was forced for a time to operate from Murmansk. In 1944, as the war drew to a close, Andropov commenced his party career, becoming second secretary of the CPSU's Petrozavodsk City Committee.

He remained in the same area during the first postwar years, evidently performing very effectively, since he was promoted in 1947 to the post of second secretary of the Karelo-Finnish CP Central Committee. While working in Petrozavodsk, he took courses at the university there but did not graduate.

In 1951 Andropov was transferred to the CPSU's central apparatus in Moscow. He began as an inspector and then became chief of a section of the Central Committee. Meanwhile he was studying at the Higher Party School.

In 1953 Andropov began a new phase of his career when he was reassigned to the Ministry of Foreign Affairs, where he served briefly in the Fourth European Department, which dealt with Poland and Czechoslovakia, before being sent to Budapest as counselor and chargé d'affaires ad interim at the Soviet Embassy. It was understood that he would succeed the incumbent ambassador, and this came about in July 1954.

Andropov was still in Budapest when the Hungarian Revolution broke out. Evidently Moscow did not hold him responsible for this enormous foreign policy failure, possibly because his warnings had been ignored or because the real cause of the revolution was the shock wave discharged through the Communist world by Khrushchev's secret speech denouncing Stalin. In any case, Andropov played a leading role in the suppression of the uprising by Soviet troops in October 1956. One of his contributions was the arrest of Hungarian Defense Minister Pál Maléter, a symbolic figure of the uprising, while dining with the ambassador at his residence.

Andropov was recalled to Moscow in March 1957 and rewarded with an even more responsible job. As head of a key CPSU Central

Committee body, the Department for Liaison with Communist and Workers' Parties of Socialist Countries, he was charged with supervising the ruling parties of Communist states, particularly those in Eastern and Central Europe. He was elected to the Central Committee at the Twenty-second Party Congress in 1961, and in 1962 was appointed secretary of the Central Committee, placing him on the same level with Boris Ponomarev, who headed another department responsible for relations with the nonruling Communist parties.

During the ten years he headed the Central Committee department for relations with Communist parties in Socialist countries, Andropov traveled abroad frequently, visiting every country of the Soviet bloc as well as Yugoslavia, Albania, China, Mongolia, North Korea, and North Vietnam. Moreover, he was a member of the CPSU delegation that engaged in difficult and unsuccessful negotiations in Moscow in July 1963 with representatives of the Chinese Communist Party.

Andropov became the spokesman for the doctrine of "proletarian internationalism," which provided a theoretical basis for Soviet military intervention anywhere in the Soviet bloc. "Marxism-Leninism is the doctrine of the victory of Socialist revolution and the construction of a new society in all countries of the world," he said on the occasion of the First Socialist International's centenary in September 1964. "And its founders naturally proceeded on the assumption that relations among peoples under Communism would be built on a completely new foundation."

Andropov had a facile pen, writing numerous articles on questions pertaining to relations among the ruling Communist parties. He was coauthor with B. N. Ponomarev and F. V. Konstantinov of an article that appeared in the CPSU Central Committee journal *Kommunist* in May 1960, launching a major attack on Yugoslav revisionism. After Enver Hoxha, the Albanian party boss, made an anti-Soviet speech, Andropov wrote an article for *Pravda* published on December 2, 1961, in which he sharply criticized the Albanian party for its deviations from Communist doctrine. His other newspaper and journal articles treated such themes as the building of Communism and the significance of Soviet aid to Socialist countries.

On May 18, 1967, Andropov was appointed chairman of the KGB, replacing Semichastny, who had been held responsible for the spectacular escape, Svetlana Alliluyeva (Stalin's daughter), although this amounted only to a pretext for dismissal. In fact, Brezhnev and his associates wanted someone in that job who was no threat.

A month after his new appointment, Andropov was elected a candidate member of the Politburo and simultaneously released from his position as secretary of the Central Committee. In April 1973 he was elected a full member of the Politburo. No head of State Security had become a full member of the Politburo since 1953, when Beria was expelled from the party and executed.

As KGB chairman, Andropov had under his command an estimated twenty-five thousand intelligence officers at home and abroad as well as three hundred thousand border guards. He controlled a budget in the neighborhood of five billion dollars. Foreign espionage proceeded as usual, although it was based largely on "legal" residencies (KGB officers in embassies, consulates, the UN, TASS, Novosti, Aeroflot, Amtorg, and the like). No blame seems to have attached to him for the "Prague Spring" of 1968, which brought about Soviet military intervention in Czechoslovakia, or the expulsion from London of one hundred and five Soviet officials on espionage charges in the fall of 1971. At home, the principal preoccupation of the KGB was the combating of dissent in various forms—among Russians seeking democratization of the regime, national minority groups seeking greater rights, and religious groups seeking freedom of worship.

Beyond doubt, Andropov enjoyed the confidence of General Secretary Leonid Brezhnev. They both lived in the same building at Kutuzov Prospekt 26, Brezhnev on the fifth floor, Andropov on the sixth. Andropov was one of the privileged few who could visit Brezhnev in his apartment without making an appointment.

Andropov carefully avoided the limelight. After becoming KGB chairman, he no longer accompanied Brezhnev on foreign trips, leaving security arrangements to lesser officials. In April 1976 Andropov delivered the principal speech on the one hundred and sixth anniversary of Lenin's birthday, one of his rare public appearances. A book of his speeches and articles devoted to attacks on dissidents appeared in 1980.

Eight years younger than Brezhnev, and one of the youngest members of the Politburo, the mercurial Yuri Vladimirovich

Andropov, with his challenging glance behind horn-rimmed glasses, seemed in 1982 to have a good chance of becoming Brezhnev's successor. It remained to be seen whether he would excel his predecessors as head of Soviet State Security and escape the jinx that cut them down short of the summit.

In late May 1982 Yuri Andropov was appointed (for the second time) a secretary of the CPSU Central Committee and relinquished his position as chairman of the KGB after serving for fifteen years. His appointment to the Secretariat of the Central Committee came about partly as a result of the death of Mikhail Suslov, who had been a leader in the Central Committee apparatus for many years, and partly in anticipation of the demise of Leonid Brezhnev, head of the Soviet state and party, who was increasingly showing signs of mental and physical debility. If Andropov hoped to succeed Brezhnev, with whom he had been closely associated, it was important for him to occupy a transitional position before Brezhnev passed from the scene, for he needed to rid himself of the stigma of secret police chief that had been fatal to the ambitions of his predecessors.

The man chosen to succeed Andropov was a relatively unknown but veteran secret-police officer named Vitali Vasilievich Fedorchuk, who had served for twelve years as the head of the KGB in the Ukraine but had never held a central party or government post in Moscow. Since Fedorchuk's tenure in the Ukraine more or less coincided with Andropov's service as head of the KGB, it could be assumed that they had worked together closely and that Fedorchuk was appointed on Andropov's recommendation.

Many observers were surprised by Fedorchuk's appointment because it apparently reversed the policy initiated in 1958 with Shelepin's appointment of installing an active party leader as KGB chairman. Yet this departure was not as surprising as it appeared at first glance. Neither Andropov, who felt the need to relinquish the position, nor his Politburo colleagues could wish to place a political rival at the top of the KGB at a time when the jockeying for supreme leadership in the USSR seemed about to resume. At the age of sixty-three, Fedorchuk was not likely to turn the KGB into a personal power base that would make him an important figure in the political maneuvering expected at the end of the Brezhnev era.

Fedorchuk was born in December 1918[52] in the Ukraine, not far from today's Polish border.[53] According to his official biography, he went to work at the age of sixteen for local newspapers in Zhitomir and Kiev oblasts and then attended a military academy for three years. Like his predecessor Serov, he was moved into State Security in 1939,[54] when many people with military backgrounds were called upon to replace KGB officers who had vanished during the Great Purge.

Fedorchuk reportedly served in the armed forces during World War II, but since there was no break in his connection with State Security, he probably served in SMERSH under Kruglov's command and was involved in eradicating supposedly disloyal or unreliable elements in the Soviet population. Following the war, Fedorchuk worked in the occupation regimes in East Germany and Austria,[55] where State Security supervised a purge of the population and the dismantling of industry and its shipment in the guise of "war reparations" to the USSR.

Although he became a member of the Communist Party in 1940, the pudgy Fedorchuk exercised purely State Security functions and held essentially ex officio party positions. For example, after being appointed head of the Ukrainian KGB, he became a candidate member of the Ukrainian CP Politburo in September 1973 and a full member three years later.[56] His education was limited to the military academy and, later, the Higher KGB School, from which he graduated. Eventually he achieved the rank of KGB colonel general, managing to look the part with his bulldog face and incipient double chin, with a full head of gray hair brushed straight back.

Through the 1950's and 1960's, Fedorchuk served in a series of provincial KGB posts and was said to have won the approval of his superiors by his vigorous leadership of security organs in the eastern regions of the RSFSR, where many of his fellow Ukrainians lived. In July 1970 Fedorchuk became chairman of the Ukrainian KGB. Andropov was in the process of cracking down on the dissent movement, and it was felt in the Kremlin that Pyotr E. Shelest, the Ukrainian CP boss, had been lax in dealing with manifestations of Ukrainian nationalism and with dissidents. Fedorchuk had no compunction in crushing dissent among his compatriots, and within two years after his appointment, he launched a wave of arrests that swept up hundreds of human rights activists. Fedorchuk was not troubled in his crackdown by legal niceties. He told members of a KGB club in April 1981: "Last year a major job was done—forty Ukrainian nationalists were rendered harmless. In order to preclude unnecessary international friction, the majority of them were convicted on criminal charges."[57]

During his last years in the Ukraine, Fedorchuk was worried about the possible effect that the Polish trade union Solidarity might have on Ukrainian workers and the influence in general of events in Poland on the situation in the Ukraine. Arguing against any relaxation of party and police control, Fedorchuk wrote in *Pid praporom leninizmu,* a journal for Ukrainian party propagandists, in October 1981:

> These events plainly confirm the incontrovertible truth that any kind of belittlement of Marxist and Communist ideology, any mistake, shortcoming, or violation of the economic laws of socialism, any relaxation of ideological and political education of the masses boomerangs, with the inevitable onslaughts of bourgeois ideology. They graphically illustrate that the primary objective of counterrevolutionary forces, supported morally and materially from outside, is to disorient the masses, ideologically disarm and disorganize the Communist Party, and remove it from the leadership of society with the aim of seizing power in the country and creating conditions for the restoration of capitalism.[58]

In appointing a lowbrow Chekist as chairman of the KGB, ignoring his lack of experience abroad (except for the occupation period in East Germany and Austria), the Soviet leadership obviously wanted Fedorchuk to expand his repressive measures to the Soviet Union as a whole, with the object of keeping the population under firm control.

Fedorchuk was an unreconstructed Stalinist like his predecessors Kruglov and Serov. Nothing could better illustrate the fact that the primary task of Soviet State Security has remained the same since the days of Dzerzhinsky: to protect the power of a tiny "Communist" elite under the totalitarian Soviet system.

The next change in the top leadership of the KGB came about with surprising suddenness in December 1982, when a compara-

tively unknown official named Viktor Mikhailovich Chebrikov succeeded Fedorchuk, who had been in office only since May of that
year.

Fedorchuk had not fallen into disgrace, however. On the contrary, he was appointed to a cabinet-level position as Minister of
Internal Affairs, replacing Brezhnev's old friend and neighbor
Nikolai A. Shchelokov. Both Chebrikov's elevation to the post of
KGB Chairman and Fedorchuk's new appointment were obviously
part of a wide-ranging plan implemented by Andropov after
Brezhnev's sudden but hardly unexpected death in November, after
which Andropov took over as CPSU General Secretary. An-
dropov's use of KGB connections to solidify his position as the new
"first among equals" had already been seen in the promotion of
Geidar Aliyev, a former head of the KGB in Azerbaijan, to First
Deputy Chairman of the USSR Council of Ministers (or deputy
prime minister), with the task of keeping an eye on Chairman
Nikolai Tikhonov.

Viktor Mikhailovich Chebrikov, the new KGB Chairman, was
undoubtedly smart, able, and still relatively young for a high-ranking Soviet official, though he looked a good ten years older. Born in
1923 of Russian parentage,[59] he came from Dnepropetrovsk in the
Ukraine, which had been a stronghold of Brezhnev's in earlier
years. He served with the army in the field from 1941 to 1946
during World War II and its aftermath.[60] After the war, he completed his higher education when he graduated from the Dnepropetrovsk Metallurgical Institute in 1950 and qualified as an
engineer.[61] Chebrikov's sister, Z. M. Chebrikova, worked as a
chemist in a research institute in Dnepropetrovsk.[62]

Nevertheless, Chebrikov, who became a CPSU member in
1944,[63] did not practice his profession as an engineer but went
instead into full-time party work from 1951 on. He first came to
public notice at the Nineteenth Ukrainian CP Congress in 1956
when he was elected to membership on the Auditing Commission of
the Ukrainian CP. In 1960 he became First Secretary of the
Dnepropetrovsk City Party Committee. After holding other party
posts in the same area, he was promoted to the post of Second
Secretary of the Dnepropetrovsk Oblast Party Committee in
1965.[64]

After some fifteen or sixteen years as a local party official,

Chebrikov had his party career interrupted in 1967, just at the time Andropov assumed his duties as KGB Chairman. Summoned to Moscow to become head of the KGB's personnel department,[65] Chebrikov reportedly soon became Andropov's "favorite aide."[66]

Only a year after his arrival in Moscow, Chebrikov was named a deputy chairman of the KGB, becoming one of six top officials holding that title. Appointed in September 1968,[67] he worked for the next thirteen and a half years in close proximity to Andropov on the third floor of the KGB headquarters in central Moscow.[68] In April 1982, as Andropov was preparing his own transfer to a post as Secretary of the CPSU Central Committee, Chebrikov received still another promotion. He became one of only two First Deputy Chairmen directly subordinate to Andropov.[69]

While climbing to the summit of the KGB in a career that spanned no more than fifteen years, Chebrikov continued to advance within the party hierarchy. He became a candidate member of the CPSU Central Committee and a full member in 1981.[70] His growing status in the CPSU held the promise of further advancement, barring some serious error on his part or the downfall of his patron, who was probably Andropov.

The appointments of Chebrikov as KGB Chairman and Fedorchuk as Minister of Internal Affairs appear to have fit into a general plan for a war on corruption and economic crime of which Andropov was the author.

Over the years, Chebrikov had written a number of articles for the press. During his involvement as a party official in Dnepropetrovsk's economic affairs, he wrote articles on such subjects as improving the quality of steel and on the electrification of agriculture in Dnepropetrovsk Oblast.[71] In April 1981, while a deputy chairman of the KGB, Chebrikov wrote an article entitled "Vigilance Is a Well-Tried Weapon" for the Soviet youth journal *Molodoi Kommunist* (Young Communist).

In this article, Chebrikov expressed concern, presumably on behalf of the KGB, that youth might be infected by foreign ideas and begin to question Soviet norms of behavior. Calling for increased vigilance against alleged subversion from the West, Chebrikov wrote: "The strategists of imperialism are making use of the vast machinery of modern bourgeois propaganda, their own intelligence services, numerous ideological sabotage centers, and a variety of foreign anti-Soviet organizations to perniciously influence the minds and hearts of young people."

Chebrikov's appointment as KGB Chairman, like that of Fedorchuk earlier, ignored the new chairman's lack of foreign experience, suggesting that the post-Brezhnev leadership was far more concerned about such internal problems as subversion, dissent, and nationalist ferment, in addition to state corruption and economic crime, although the foreign branch of the KGB could be counted on, as always, to pursue vigorously its own subversive goals abroad.

3

On the Firing Line

FOR THE KGB CHIEFS, Soviet spy rings are the front line of foreign espionage. Despite the intricate plans devised in Moscow, it is in some foreign setting—a Paris café, a hut at the top of a ski lift in Austria, or a park in Buenos Aires—that secret information changes hands, with no one else the wiser, even an arm's length away. The chain of agents and cutouts (intermediaries between spies and their agents) may be very long, but sooner or later that information will reach Moscow, to be studied and evaluated and, if deemed important enough, passed on to a select group of leaders who are, in effect, cleared for top secret information.

Life must have seemed comparatively simple to State Security in the 1920's. Most of the leading Chekists were Old Bolsheviks and the agents they recruited were foreign Communists; the circles in which the Chekists moved, such as Marxist clubs and workingmen's bars, received all outsiders with hostility and suspicion. To recruit among Communists on behalf of the "first socialist state" was no great trick. It was simply necessary to emphasize that only by defending and strengthening communism in Russia would it be possible to spread the revolution to other countries.

By the 1930's the KGB could take advantage of the world economic crisis by pointing out to prospective agents—particularly those shocked by the abuses and inequities of capitalism—that its collapse was imminent and that only the Soviet variety of socialism offered a permanent solution to the world's ills.

Moreover, the KGB found itself at home among anti-Fascists, and since antifascism had become fashionable in upper social circles, the possibility of recruiting high-level agents with excellent access to the secrets of other governments increased by leaps and bounds. With Fascist regimes in Italy and Germany proclaiming themselves bulwarks against communism, the Soviet Union could claim to be in the forefront of the struggle against fascism. At the same time, the KGB pointed to the weakness, confusion, and pusillanimity of the Western democracies and their contemptible attempts at appeasement, arguing that the only effective resistance against fascism came from the USSR and that those who sincerely wished to participate in this struggle must help Moscow.

The KGB's blandishments often proved effective with people who had become disillusioned by capitalism and, opposing fascism on idealistic grounds, were already disgusted with their own governments' policies. In this way, many Western intellectuals were influenced by direct or indirect sales pitches of the KGB. If they were not much good as spies they could always be used to spread propaganda, either in favor of communism or against fascism.

While seeking to recruit agents among anti-Fascists, the KGB also hit on a useful cover for agents who had already been recruited —as Fascists. For example, Kim Philby, a Soviet agent, established his credentials in the British conservative establishment by associating himself with the Anglo-German Fellowship, a pro-German association.[1] He also became a correspondent reporting the Spanish Civil War with a definite bias toward the Fascists.

The Nazi-Soviet pact, concluded in August 1939, briefly tarnished the Soviet image and even brought about the defection of a few KGB agents, but as Soviet leaders learned long ago, people in the West have short memories. After the Nazi invasion of the USSR in 1941, the Soviet Union regained a measure of respectability by becoming an ally of the West—not exactly by choice, since that alliance was crucial to the USSR's survival.

During the 1940's the KGB developed two effective recruitment tactics for people in such countries as England and the United

States. The first, which was useful until 1944, was based on the complaint that Allied leaders had deliberately delayed opening a second front in Nazi-occupied France, as Moscow kept demanding, in order to aid the "heroic" Red Army, which had absorbed the brunt of German military might. Thus the USSR was presented as fighting the West's battle. In view of the perfidious behavior of those Allied leaders, it was all the more incumbent on people of good will to assist the Soviet government in every way they could, including spying for the Soviet Union. As Allied research on the atom bomb became known to Moscow, the KGB expounded a second line to those working on or having access to the project: world peace could be assured only by providing the USSR with the secrets of the atom bomb, thereby guaranteeing military equality in the postwar period. Such arguments carried conviction with Klaus Fuchs and other scientists working on the combined U.S. and British program and induced them to become Soviet spies.

The KGB's work was immensely complicated by circumstances that took firm shape in the aftermath of World War II. Before the war, the United States had not possessed an Intelligence establishment worthy of the name. Collection of secret information was limited to military and naval Intelligence and depended largely on attachés stationed abroad. During the war an extensive Intelligence establishment came into being, including a completely new organization, the Office of Strategic Services (OSS), which was under civilian rather than military control. Although the OSS was abolished after the war, the vastly altered world situation compelled American political leaders to establish the Central Intelligence Agency (CIA), which soon began to offer a serious challenge to the KGB. No longer could the KGB conduct espionage with complete contempt for the citizens of other countries and their governments.

The KGB, however, did gain some important advantages as a result of the establishment of Communist regimes in Europe and Asia. The Intelligence services created by these regimes were modeled on the KGB and set up by Soviet Chekists; they not only operated under the general guidance of the KGB but observed a "division of labor" determined by Moscow. According to a former Polish military attaché who defected, Polish Intelligence had the special task of reporting on the NATO forces in all areas.[2] Soviet

Intelligence also set requirements for the satellite Intelligence services that expected them to collect information related to specific
subjects.[3]

While the KGB did not suffer in the postwar years from a dearth
of agents, Soviet Intelligence officers no longer enjoyed a field day
in their recruitment activities. In Western Europe the KGB was
able to exploit the fear and resentment—if not outright envy—of
American hegemony, which made these nations appear hopelessly
dependent on the United States both economically and militarily.
Although the ideological appeal of communism had waned among
Americans, and there was no antifascism to exploit, the KGB found
that a few Americans would betray their country for money.

Certain groups, of special interest to the KGB, offer a pool from
which agents can be drawn on the basis of ideological or idealistic
motivation. Since these groups tend to unite internationally as well
as nationally, the KGB can obtain information about them in one
part of the world and use it for recruiting in a country far removed
from the original source of information.

There are three principal groups of interest to the KGB. The first
consists of the peace, antinuclear, and the so-called green or ecological movements. The second group is made up of the "national
liberation" movements, such as the PLO and similar groups in
black Africa, as well as Marxist revolutionary groups, particularly
in the Third World. The third is the radical "student" groups, which
tend to overlap with the first two categories but sometimes have an
independent existence; here the goals seem to be primarily an-
archistic, as with the Red Army Faction in West Germany and the
Red Brigades in Italy.

The antinuclear movement has recently broadened its base because of a growing fear stimulated by the stationing of Soviet
medium-range rockets in the USSR aimed at NATO countries and
NATO plans to match this buildup in Western Europe. Adding size
and influence to the movement is a substantial opposition to nuclear
power plants and the struggle on behalf of ecological or environ-
mental goals, all of which has tended to coalesce into massive demonstrations that sometimes become quite violent.

The KGB has naturally endeavored to infiltrate these movements, hoping to influence both their strategy and tactics. The
movements indeed threaten to overturn West European govern-

ments already overwhelmed with economic problems and, consequently, to weaken NATO—precisely what the KGB wishes to achieve. In recruiting within the peace movement, the KGB has effectively used the argument that the United States—not the USSR —is the major threat to world peace.

Although disturbed by these movements, Washington and West European capitals find it difficult to cope with them because any effort to satisfy their demands tends to weaken the West's position in some way. In U.S.-Soviet negotiations on reduction of strategic arms, which recommenced in 1981, the Soviet strategy was aimed at showing that the United States had no serious interest in an agreement and wished only to stall in order to carry out a nuclear rearmament. The KGB can be expected to use the same line in recruiting agents in the peace movement. As in the case of terrorism, however, the KGB does not need to control such groups in order to achieve its objectives.

In the case of "national liberation" and Marxist revolutionary groups, the USSR furnishes diplomatic and moral support, while the KGB furnishes training, weapons, and tactical advice. The KGB may also find it worthwhile to infiltrate these groups with agents who collect intelligence of interest to the USSR that is received through each group's independent channels.

Similarly, the KGB provides help to radical student groups, usually through the PLO or other "liberation" movements already benefitting from Soviet support. Although the KGB may place its own agents in such groups, they are generally less valuable than the other groups, and for purposes of disruption—their chief attraction —they can be better aided from afar.

The KGB's front line abroad is manned by its stations, to each of which the name *rezidentura* (residency) is applied. The residencies are of two types.

The "legal" residency is always based on a Soviet official or semiofficial status. Such a residency exists under cover of a Soviet embassy, consulate, UN delegation, trade representative, a news agency like TASS or Novosti, a Soviet bank, Aeroflot, and so forth. KGB employees under this type of cover frequently enjoy diplomatic immunity and special privileges accorded them by the host government. The designation "legal" does not mean in any sense that these activities are legal under the laws of the country where they take place, except in a superficial way. It implies only that the KGB employees are openly identified as Soviet citizens on an official mission abroad. But their true rank, and hence importance, may be hidden by the cover job, and the Soviet passports they carry may be issued under a false identity. (The same cannot be said for the U.S. State Department, which, as one former CIA official noted, "had an unyielding policy against the issuance of false passports or, indeed, their use by official or unofficial personnel under any circumstances."[4])

In countries like the United States, a major Intelligence target, such "legal" residencies sometimes have hundreds of employees for one simple reason: in general, this personnel can be sent to foreign countries, set up there, and provided with logistical support with complete legality. Nevertheless, the "legal" residencies and their personnel are never acknowledged as belonging to the KGB. Former KGB employees have asserted that many Soviet embassies have more KGB people than diplomats on their staffs. When the non-Soviet press reports that Soviet diplomats have been expelled from a country, the reader can be sure that the "diplomats" are in reality KGB personnel who have been caught.

The second type of station, the "illegal" residency, may be staffed by only one KGB intelligence officer or, at most, several officers. "Illegal" residencies must not have any overt or traceable connection with the Soviet Union. The *rezident* (resident) who heads such a station may carry a passport of the country where he is "residing" and even appear to be a citizen of that country. The passport itself can be genuine (in the sense of having been officially issued in the name of a real person whose identity has been appropriated by the KGB agent) or forged (in that the photograph or other personal data have been altered so as to make it usable by the intelligence officer). Although a *rezident* may have a foreign nationality (never Soviet), he does not identify himself directly or indirectly with the Soviet Union.

An "illegal" resident (or any of his assistants) employs the cover of some civilian pursuit consistent with his purported background —his "cover story" or "legend"—and offers a convincing explanation for his presence in a country and activities. If, for example, he claims to be an automobile mechanic by trade, he works in a garage or runs a garage of his own.

In contrast to "illegal" residencies, which encounter formidable logistical and communications problems, the Soviet "legal" residencies possess many advantages.

It is comparatively simple for a "legal" residency to bring personnel into a country and establish them there. As a rule, the host government gives pro forma approval for the stationing of Soviet representatives. The size of the KGB residency can be determined by Moscow, according to its own requirements, although the size of the official establishment as a whole is sometimes restricted by the host government on the basis of the size of its own official representation in the Soviet Union.

Once established in the country, KGB employees can function with considerable ease. To begin with, they can rely to some extent on assistance from the host government in obtaining information through official channels, interviews with officials themselves, or official, nonclassified documents, which are often valuable. They take advantage of officially sponsored tours for foreign diplomats, official briefings for newsmen,* and invitations to receptions and ceremonial gatherings.

The premises of a "legal" residency—almost invariably protected against hostile audio surveillance—make it possible to hold operational meetings in perfect safety. Because an embassy or consulate has the protection of extraterritoriality, there is no possibility of interference or arrest by a local security service like the FBI or Scotland Yard's Special Branch. Other Soviet installations, even without extraterritoriality, remain more or less sacrosanct. Naturally, the "legal" residency has no problem about storage of files, although the real repository of operational correspondence is in Moscow. The residency maintains only skeleton files; copies of cables are destroyed almost immediately, while other correspondence, which travels via diplomatic pouch on microfilm negatives, is retained only for a strictly limited period in the case of "Moscow

---

* TASS and Novosti correspondents are almost invariably KGB officers. In the United States they attend top-level government press conferences—where they are quick to ask questions—and congressional hearings.

letters."[5] The residency also possesses, in many cases, its own radio communications, as well as ample photographic facilities. Equipment of all kinds can be forwarded through the diplomatic pouch or even in the baggage of "diplomats," which crosses the border with no customs inspection.

Moreover, it is no trifling advantage to be able to transfer funds freely for the residency's operations. Large amounts of cash, in all currencies, can be moved back and forth between Moscow and the residency without a trace.

Of course, "legal" residencies have their disadvantages too. It is easy for the local security service to identify KGB personnel within a short time and to keep them under surveillance outside an embassy. Diplomatic license plates are a dead giveaway, and if ordinary plates are issued to nondiplomats they are also registered by the local security service. KGB personnel engage in every conceivable maneuver to throw off surveillance when traveling by public transportation, but in theory, if not in practice, there is no limit to the resources that can be applied to the job of following their movements.

All of these factors considerably inhibit the recruitment of agents and covert meetings with them. KGB case officers working out of "legal" residencies sometimes succeed in overcoming the difficulties, but the risks of getting caught are so great that they are hardly worth taking unless a big payoff can be expected.

Nevertheless, the KGB's professional apparatus does not have to rely exclusively on agents for intelligence collection. Aside from the official channels, other opportunities develop while a KGB case officer is going about his "normal" duties. If he is attached under diplomatic cover to an embassy in an Asian or Latin American country, for example, he circulates at cocktail parties—as all diplomats do—and picks up interesting tidbits from non-Communist diplomats. But he does not stop there. He proceeds to develop certain contacts, especially when he senses a vulnerability in one of them. An excessive fondness for alcohol, for example, the use of drugs, a weakness for sex (above all, if it is homosexual), reckless gambling, extravagance, serious indebtedness, greed, involvement in smuggling—these and other factors may afford the KGB a potential means of extortion.

The same techniques can be exploited with local officials who have similar vulnerabilities. In such cases, it may be deemed preferable to extract intelligence on a "friendly" basis, without attempting to recruit the subject formally as an agent; this step could bring about a crisis of conscience that would make him confess everything to his superiors. The intelligence thus obtained might concern important policy decisions, diplomatic moves, economic problems, military preparations, and the local political situation, but it could well go beyond that country and provide a glimpse into the policies of governments in Washington, London, Paris, Bonn, Tokyo, and other world capitals.

Direct observation by a KGB officer also frequently yields intelligence, such as a view of a factory, power installation, or military airfield from a train or car window or while out walking. But there are other possibilities. In Washington, KGB officers have been known to visit federal buildings and congressional offices, where they sit in snack bars and restaurants to eavesdrop on conversations, circulate through the corridors to read official announcements and private notices on bulletin boards, and even steal documents off desktops in a temporarily unguarded office.

Like Intelligence people the world over, KGB officers prefer to serve in "legal" residencies, where they enjoy diplomatic immunity, good housing, and the opportunity to be accompanied by their wives and children. To exchange these perquisites for the precarious status of an "illegal"—cut off from home, family, and friends while surrounded on all sides by enemies, with prison or execution looming at the end of the road—calls for a degree of motivation that even well-schooled and well-indoctrinated KGB officers lack. The choice, however, is not always theirs.

One can much more readily perceive the advantages of the "illegal" residency by considering the disadvantages of the "legal" residency.

First and foremost is anonymity and freedom of movement. Since none of the personnel of an "illegal" residency has been identified as a spy, and all connection with the Soviet Union remains unknown, it can function without time-consuming efforts to shake off surveillance or the necessity to conduct meetings under strictly conspiratorial rules.

These circumstances also facilitate the cultivation and recruitment of prospective agents. There is no need for haste. It is possible to establish a normal friendship, develop the relationship, and avoid prematurely committing oneself. If the friendship does not lead to recruitment, the prospective agent never finds out that he has been the prey of a Soviet spy. And for the KGB man himself, the loss of time is negligible.

Once established in a country, the "illegal" resident can look forward to a long period of service unless he makes some inexcusable blunder and is exposed. If all goes well, he can penetrate ever deeper into the fabric of society, and the longer he is there the more trust he can win among unsuspecting citizens. With a minimum of precautions, he is in little danger of exposure. If the country in which he resides is not far from the Soviet Union, he may be able to visit home secretly every year.

Examined from the opposite point of view, the disadvantages of the "illegal" residency are the advantages of the "legal" residency. Where the latter benefits from all sorts of logistical aids and special privileges, the former lacks nearly all of them.

At the very outset, there is the problem of getting the "illegal" resident or an assistant to his post. The KGB apparatus must work out all the details, beginning with the resident's passport and cover story. In most cases, the department responsible for such details can supply a genuine passport that requires only some minor doctoring, by replacing the photograph or changing the physical description. (The KGB is constantly engaged in collecting genuine passports, which are often obtained from foreigners who die or disappear into concentration camps. An unusual example comes from the Spanish Civil War, when passports were collected from volunteers in the International Brigades, which included two thousand Americans. When they were killed, the passports went straight to the Foreign Administration of the KGB in Moscow.[6])

Then there is always the risk that the spy will be caught at the border, perhaps by some freakish accident, or a subsequent investigation brought about by involvement with the authorities may prove the passport to be false.

Entering the United States with a forged passport has usually been accomplished with ease, but some borders are friendlier than others. The KGB knows that entry via New York is apt to be more hazardous than one from Canada, which offers numerous crossing points where passport checks tend to be less strict.

Having reached his post, the "illegal" resident must find a place to live, obtain a cover job or occupation (to account for his income), open up a bank account, and provide himself with supporting documents. His background story must be letter-perfect. If he claims to have lived in another city, he is obliged to familiarize himself with it, even studying files of its principal newspaper in the public library for the period he supposedly lived there.

Establishing a residence in the United States offers no problem because the formalities involved in its rental are minimal. But in many countries of Western Europe housing is scarce and expensive, and negotiations for its rental can become complicated. Residence in Europe usually requires registration with the police, and every change of residence must also be recorded.

There are other serious problems. The "illegal" resident needs to communicate with the Center in Moscow. He has basically three means at his disposal: two-way radio contact, messages exchanged through dead drops or cutouts (live drops), and postal channels that involve secret writing (inks) or microdots containing encrypted messages. All of these are unreliable, and only radio communication affords direct contact. Most "illegal" residents have been trained to handle their own radio communications, which is of the shortwave variety, but in the case of busy spy networks, the KGB will frequently assign a radio operator for this task alone.

Another problem is the supply of funds. Obviously an "illegal" resident cannot run a spy ring without regular transfers of funds, which normally must take place in such a manner that the original source is concealed. Moreover, transfers must not create problems with the tax authorities. Sometimes transfers can be safely arranged through normal banking channels, but as a rule they must be made in cash, through a dead drop or a courier.

Finally, the psychological problems should never be underestimated. Long absences from home and family are bound to affect morale. The "illegal" resident finds himself almost completely isolated, except for his association with others in the spy ring. Even then, he may be known to them only by a pseudonym and be unable to confide anything but the immediate details of his work. Consequently, with no one to trust completely, no one with whom he can talk about the past and mutual friends, he can never feel completely relaxed.

At the same time the "illegal" resident remains in constant fear that either by his own mistakes or, still worse, through circumstances of which he can have no knowledge, he will suddenly be discovered and arrested. As the pressure increases, he begins to show the strain. Every step behind him in the street, every unexpected occurrence, even the ringing of a doorbell, seems to herald doom. In such circumstances, the Moscow Center's effort to boost his morale with an enciphered shortwave message is apt to appear ironic rather than comforting. William Fisher—"Colonel Abel"— related the story that while living his underground existence in New York City, he went to a certain delicatessen just before November 7, purchasing a grilled chicken to take home with him. At his dining room table he extracted the bone of the chicken leg, unscrewed it, and removed a microfilm. In it there was a message in his own cipher. After deciphering it, he found that it contained the following text: "Our heartiest congratulations to you on the anniversary of the October Revolution!"[7]

What the "illegal" resident most appreciates are the microfilmed letters he receives from his wife or children with personal news from home, though these, too, are carefully censored to eliminate any information that could be helpful to the "enemy."

From the standpoint of the KGB leadership, however, one unique advantage of the "illegal" residency makes all the effort and trouble worthwhile. In wartime, when Soviet diplomats and other official representatives are either interned or repatriated, thus shutting down the "legal" residency, the "illegal" residency continues to function. Controls such as postal censorship, increased detection of unidentified radio transmissions, and government restrictions on international transactions and shipments might hamper operations, but would hardly stop them. And the direct involvement of millions of the target country's citizens in the war effort would greatly expand the potential scope of these operations.

The traditions of an Intelligence service embrace, among other things, its operational structure and functions. Therefore it should not be surprising that in both respects Soviet "legal" and "illegal" residencies considerably resemble each other.

Both types are headed by a *rezident*. Under the "legal" residency, however, he has a number of KGB intelligence officers under his command, while in the "illegal" residency he may be entirely alone or have at most one intelligence officer as his assistant. Immediately below the Intelligence officers in both residencies are the professional, full-time agents who are equivalent to non-commissioned army officers. These agents, usually trained in Moscow, have made a career as KGB spies and may be transferred from one country to another, as the need arises. Finally, there are the agents recruited for specific operations because of their positions or access to certain information. They may also become life-long KGB spies, because of the positions they occupy, or they may be dropped when their usefulness ends.

The "legal" resident has a cipher clerk, or communicator, on his staff who is responsible for sending and receiving messages, including encoding and decoding. In many cases, the "illegal" resident has to handle his own communications but, if the network is important enough, he may have a radio operator assigned to him.

To the extent that the "illegal" residency can be said to have an independent existence, it may be situated in an antique shop, photographic studio, radio store—wherever the resident allegedly works or lives. The "legal" residency boasts a code room, darkroom, and radio facilities (the antennae can be seen on the embassy roof) and secure file space. Everything of this nature that the "illegal" residency possesses must be cunningly concealed so that nothing will come to light during a routine search. It is not necessarily all in one place; a radio operator assigned to the network will have his radio equipment hidden somewhere close to him.

Both residencies may use safe houses or apartments for meetings with agents. One "illegal" resident employed the office of a dentist, who was his agent. When the resident and an agent appeared among the patients, they were ushered separately into an inner room where the dentist's chair was a mute witness of their meeting. As soon as they had concluded their business, they left at different times and went their separate ways.

The KGB operates in the espionage field abroad under a sound doctrine that strictly forbids any contact or overlapping between "legal" and "illegal" residencies, including their respective net-works. One does not have to search far for the reasons. When KGB case officers in the "legal" residency are identified and observed in meetings with their own agents, the worst that can happen is the loss by the "legal" residency of some of its agents. On the other hand, if a KGB officer belonging to a "legal" residency is spotted during a meeting with the "illegal" resident or one of the latter's assistants—even if it is only a meeting between an agent of the "legal" residency with another agent of the "illegal" residency—the entire clandestine "illegal" residency could be rolled up as a result.

Yet this doctrine is sometimes violated. Why? Because it is believed that the exception proves the rule? Our of sheer ignorance? Hardly. Occasionally the KGB personnel may have such contempt for the local security service that they see no reason to take these precautions. But, in most cases, breaching the doctrine results from necessity, from an urgent need to provide money, deliver equipment, or pass an important message to the "illegal" resident, without which an even more serious situation might develop.

One other difference is worth mentioning. KGB officers attached to a "legal" residency, openly identified as Soviet citizens, can get by with only a working knowledge of the local language or speak it with a marked Russian accent. When an "illegal" officer has little or no knowledge of the local language, it is usually because he pretends to be an immigrant and speaks some other language—not Russian—with native fluency. In general, however, he has been selected for service in a particular country because he has complete and, in many instances, native command of the language. Without it he could not be expected to function effectively.

All in all, the individual capabilities of Soviet spies determine where and how they are employed, and the KGB makes a careful study of its personnel before giving them foreign assignments. Therefore, to understand its espionage operations, it is essential to study the spies themselves and to learn about their origins and background, and about the kind of work they undertook as spies. But it is equally important to know something of their essential character, to obtain some insight into their motivations, dreams, and aspirations as well as their frustrations, disappointments, and failures.

At that point, we may finally achieve a genuine understanding of the nature of Soviet State Security.

4

The Spy Who Reported to Stalin

DREAMERS, IDEALISTS, AND FANATICS do not long survive any revolution. Those who sacrificed everything—health, happiness, and families and loved ones—are themselves destroyed by the revolution they helped to bring about. The true heirs of the revolution are not the revolutionaries but, rather, are hardheaded, selfish, amoral realists who are quick to grasp the chance that the revolution has opened up for them.

Alexander Orlov was one of these opportunists. His true name was Nikolsky, but he used a number of aliases, such as Shved ("Swede") and Lyova.[1] The nickname "Swede" may have stuck because of his resemblance to people of that nationality: he was big, broad-shouldered, blond, with a flushed face (as if from drink) and blunt features. The process of natural selection in Soviet State Security, in his case, was helped along by character. Here was a man who kept his own counsel and remained unmoved by any of the horrors that surrounded him, who did what was expected of him without forming any enduring loyalties, and who had his own deep plans that he followed unswervingly to their fruition. He was, in short, a careerist of the most unscrupulous type.

———•———

Alexander Orlov always remained reticent about his origins in Russia. He must have been about twenty-one at the time of the revolution and evidently studied law at some university. He joined the Communist Party and became involved with the Cheka. During the civil war he ran partisan operations behind enemy lines on the southwestern front and engaged in counterespionage.

In late 1920, at the end of the civil war, Orlov was assigned to the Supreme Tribunal, which had close ties with the Cheka, and served as an assistant prosecutor. In this capacity Orlov took part in the drafting of the the first Soviet criminal code. Orlov's share in this accomplishment, such as it was, reflected the interests of Soviet State Security and not those of the people.

Orlov's colleagues on the Supreme Tribunal and the Supreme Court, where he later worked, included such men as Nikolai Krylenko and Otto Karklin, whom Orlov called "venerated members of the Soviet old guard." He went on to say: "They were men who had spent in czarist prisons, in the *katorga* [penal colony] and Siberian exile a considerable part of their lives and who did not regard the October Revolution as a source of high posts or personal gain. The characteristic trait of these men was their extreme modesty and simplicity."[2] In truth, Krylenko and Karklin were a despicable team. With Krylenko as prosecutor and Karklin as presiding judge, they conducted the early "show trials" of the Soviet regime.

Another person whom Orlov described in respectful terms in his memoirs was Georgi ("Yuri") Pyatakov, a leading figure of the Soviet state. Orlov first met Pyatakov in 1924, after being appointed deputy chief of Soviet State Security's Economic Administration. In his new job, Orlov had the task of uncovering corruption, embezzlement, and other misdeeds in Soviet economic enterprises. Also in 1924 Orlov and his wife, who had also taken part in the civil war, became the parents of a daughter, whom they named Vera.

Some patron must have decided that Orlov had a promising future and, to demonstrate his prescience, gave him another push up the ladder. Since Stalin, as General Secretary of the party, controlled and supervised all personnel assignments of party members, it is hard to avoid the conclusion that Orlov owed his new appointment, as commander of border troops in the Transcaucasus, to him. In that remote region he became still more accustomed to command. Although smuggling still went on across the border around Mount Ararat, impossible to stop completely due to the mountainous terrain, Orlov soon discovered that his job was not so much to stop the smuggling as to prevent Soviet citizens from escaping to Georgia.

Orlov was a stern commander and kept his men alert and vigilant. Whether through his own efforts or luck, no prominent "enemy of the people" succeeded in fleeing across that border during his period of service, Moscow was pleased with him and recalled him in 1926.

Orlov now learned that he was being transferred to the Foreign Administration of State Security in preparation for a permanent assignment abroad. He became chief of the Economic Department with responsibility for security aspects of foreign trade—assigning KGB officers to Soviet trade delegations abroad and using those organizations for espionage and counterespionage, as well as for investigating corruption and embezzlement by Soviet trade representatives. The experience that he gained in this job stood him in good stead in a series of KGB posts in Soviet trade delegations abroad over the next decade.

Early in 1929 Orlov was given his first permanent post, an assignment to which he had eagerly looked forward since he was recalled to Moscow. An assignment abroad would not only provide Orlov and his wife with many material advantages but would make it possible to take better care of their ailing daughter, who was allowed to accompany them.

Orlov was named to a leading post in the Soviet Trade Delegation in Berlin, where he worked for the next two years. His cover job was to approve the contracts for Soviet imports and exports, including the secret purchase of arms manufactured by the Germans in contravention of the Versailles Treaty, to which the USSR was not a party. In reality, he was the resident in Germany, with a group of intelligence officers and agents under his direction. In addition, he traveled to neighboring European countries for meetings with top-level agents who had been recruited in Germany and continued to work for him.

In 1931 Orlov was reassigned to a post in England. Once again he functioned as a State Security resident. One of the intelligence officers who served under him there would later become celebrated as Colonel Rudolf Ivanovich Abel.

While in England, Orlov implemented a strategy that had serious long-term repercussions. He attributed the strategy to "one of the chiefs of the NKVD intelligence," although he may have had a hand in originating it. Orlov himself described the strategy:

> In the early 1930s, the NKVD *rezidenturas* concentrated their energy on recruitment of young men of influential families. The political climate of that period was very favorable for such an undertaking, and the young generation was receptive to libertarian theories and to the sublime ideas of making the world safe from the menace of Fascism and of abolishing the exploitation of man by man. This was the main theme on which NKVD *rezidenturas* based their appeal to young men who were tired of a tedious life in the stifling atmosphere of their privileged class. And when the young men reached the stage when their thinking made them ripe for joining the Communist Party, they were told that they could be much more useful to the movement if they stayed away from the party, concealed their political views, and entered the "revolutionary underground."[3]

Of the bright young men recruited at Cambridge, Kim Philby and Donald Maclean became Soviet spies in 1933. Guy Burgess was certainly approached at the same time but may not have been formally recruited until 1934, when he visited Moscow. In describing these men as "Soviet spies," it should be stressed that they were "sleepers" or "moles" in intelligence parlance; they were not expected to provide information for a number of years, until they had worked their way into highly confidential positions. The evidence indicates that Orlov directed these recruitments, which were in all likelihood effected through Britons working as Soviet agents. The "spotters" or "talent scouts," if not the recruiters themselves, must have included a couple of university dons.

In 1933, Orlov went to Vienna, again accompanied by his wife and daughter, and assumed a cover job as a Soviet commercial representative. His work obviously satisfied Stalin, who paid close attention to State Security's spy activities, and when Orlov was recalled to Moscow in the fall of 1935, he received a top job at the

KGB headquarters. If his own memoirs can be believed, he was merely an interested observer while the KGB was preparing the first purge trials of Old Bolsheviks.

Then, in September 1936, Orlov received the most important appointment of his career. After the outbreak of the Spanish Civil War, Stalin ordered Yagoda, the KGB chief, to set up a major operation in Republican Spain. The man selected to head it, clearly on Stalin's recommendation or at least with his concurrence, was Alexander Orlov.

When the Spanish Civil War erupted in July 1936, the calculating Stalin watched and waited while the world wondered about Moscow's silence. Stalin, however, was determined to avoid any risk of direct Soviet involvement in a war with Germany and Italy. But by September he had decided on secret intervention on the side of the Loyalist regime, hoping that Franco's defeat would have a devastating psychological effect on the two Fascist nations.

In response to Stalin's orders, Yagoda held an emergency conference on September 14 in the Lubyanka to which Mikhail Frinovsky, then commander of the KGB's security troops, Abram Slutsky, chief of the Foreign Administration, and General Uritsky of the Red Army's General Staff were invited.

"From Slutsky, whom I met frequently in Paris and elsewhere," wrote Walter Krivitsky, a KGB resident abroad, "I learned that at this conference a veteran officer of his department was detailed to establish the OGPU in Loyalist Spain. He was Nikolsky, alias Schwed, alias Lyova, alias Orlov."[4]

Orlov received extraordinary powers as a result of the conference. He was to head up the whole OGPU-KGB headquarters in Spain, to which all Comintern operations there would be subordinated, and to "coordinate" all activities of the Spanish Communist Party. He would also be responsible for secretly checking all the volunteers who came to Spain and placing informers among them—after the applicants had been screened by OGPU control points in their own country. He would also keep close tabs on the Spanish government and political parties.

Accompanied by his wife and daughter, Orlov arrived in Spain that month and immediately set up his headquarters in Valencia, the temporary capital of the Spanish Republic. Largo Caballero, who headed the government, knew about Orlov's mission and had reluctantly acceded to it, recognizing that this was a down payment on Soviet aid. Without it his government would have little chance of survival.

Orlov commandeered Valencia's newest and most luxurious hotel, the eight-story Metropole, taking it over completely for the Russians. Guards were posted at the door, and only the Russians themselves or authorized visitors were allowed to enter. In this way, Orlov began the life of a proconsul, occupying an entire suite on an upper floor. He enjoyed lavish food and drink; he was always well-groomed, with finely manicured nails, and favored flannels and silk shirts in his day dress, apart from the odd touch of a 7.65 caliber Walther automatic pistol in a holster at his waist.[5]

Orlov lost no time in getting to work. Within a couple of months he had created a secret police organization modeled on Soviet State Security that covered all of Loyalist Spain and extended to all its major cities, with its major thrust on Catalonia, where syndicalists, anarchists, and Trotskyites were concentrated. Orlov's organization soon had its own special prisons, where numerous executions and torture took place. The prisons were filled as a result of mass arrests of dissidents and independents, anti-Stalinists, and especially Trotskyites, and kidnap victims were spirited away to the Soviet Union for final disposition. Orlov operated with a free hand. The Loyalist government's Ministry of Justice found itself completely circumvented and was helpless to intervene.

While the secret police under his direction was spreading its tentacles across Spain, Orlov began to conduct broad-scale espionage and counterespionage operations. He directed paramilitary activities, organizing partisan detachments. He had the overall responsibility for large numbers of agents operating behind the Franco lines, spying on the enemy and reporting information by radio. He placed in the International Brigades not only hardened Communists as commissars, but secret police informers who reported any criticism of the leadership in Spain or of the Stalin dictatorship.

The successful defense of Madrid in November and December

1936, masterminded by General Jan Berzin, former chief of Soviet Military Intelligence, and based on Soviet pilots, planes, and tanks, strengthened the position of the Soviet secret police even more.

The terror spread, with thousands being arrested, including many volunteers who had come to Spain to fight against Franco. Sometimes they simply disappeared and, if they were lucky, turned up in the USSR to be incarcerated in forced labor camps.

"There were countless such disappearances," Krivitsky wrote. "One of the most celebrated cases is that of Andrés Nin, the leader of the revolutionary party of Marxist Unity (POUM). Nin had once been a Trotskyist, and years before one of the leaders of the Comintern. With a group of his associates, Nin vanished from the prison where they had been confined by the OGPU. Their bodies were found only after a commission of British Members of Parliament had come to Spain to investigate their disappearance."[6]

On the recommendation of his doctor, Orlov went to Paris for an operation in February 1937 and was visited by Slutsky in the hospital. He had formed his own impressions of what was going on in Moscow, but he listened with interest as Slutsky described in detail how Yezhov had taken control of State Security, bringing in hundreds of people from the Central Committee to replace old State Security chiefs. Slutsky also informed him that Yezhov had organized "mobile groups" to go abroad to assassinate those whom Stalin wanted to get rid of.[7]

By the time Orlov returned to his post in Spain, serious trouble had developed among top Soviet leaders there who objected to the KGB's high-handed methods, and the Largo Caballero government was also split on the issue as Spanish leaders felt more and more that Spain was being turned into a Soviet colony in the iron grip of the KGB.

The trouble came to a head in March and April 1937.

First of all, General Berzin, who was in charge of Loyalist Spain's entire military effort, wrote a report to Commissar of War Klim Voroshilov, with a copy to Yezhov. In this report Berzin stated that there was growing resentment against the KGB in high Spanish circles, and this had already taken the form of vociferous protest against the KGB's activities. Berzin expressed his own opinion that KGB personnel were compromising the Soviet government in Spain by their unwarranted interference in the affairs of the

Spanish government and by spying in all spheres of Spanish life. He called for the immediate recall of Orlov from Spain.

"Berzin is absolutely right," Slutsky said to Krivitsky after the latter had read Berzin's report.

"Will anything be done about Orlov?" Krivitsky asked.

Slutsky shrugged. "That depends on Yezhov."[8]

Regrettably, any report by Berzin was bound to be viewed with suspicion at this point, as Berzin's old army comrades were being arrested left and right in the ongoing purge in Russia.

In April, Arthur Stashevsky, Stalin's chief political representative in Spain returned to Moscow to report in person on the situation. A solid supporter of Stalin, Stashevsky had no objection to the methods used by the KGB against Trotskyites and other dissenting Communists. In his discussion with Stalin, however, Stashevsky said that the KGB should not interfere with the regular Spanish political parties and cautiously suggested that Stalin might wish to instruct the KGB to change its approach in Spain.

Stalin may have allowed Stashevsky to think that he agreed with him on this matter, keeping his real views to himself. But Stashevsky was probably guilty of a serious error in judgment when he then called on Marshal Tukhachevsky and repeated his criticisms of the KGB, complaining of its disgraceful behavior in Spain. The meeting inevitably became known to members of the inner circle and aroused amazement among them. As one writer has observed: "Bureaucracies are quick to perceive when one of their own has slipped and fallen. . . . And by approaching the fallen, one can be identified as friend or ally. This is not desirable or practical."[9] Stashevsky had either lost sight of this reality or chosen to ignore it, with fatal consequences to himself.

Apart from that, Stalin unquestionably approved of the steps being taken, if he had not initiated them in the first place. Stashevsky should have known this better than anyone else. He was directly involved in the scheme to replace Largo Caballero with another man considered more responsive to Soviet control. Stashevsky had also been instrumental in shipping the gold reserve of the Bank of Spain to the Soviet Union. Direction of the Spanish army was in Berzin's hands. The KGB juggernaut was rolling over all opposition in Loyalist Spain. The Comintern had been removed from the picture. All of these moves were completely consistent with Stalin's policy of turning Spain into a Soviet province without any risk of a head-on collision with Germany and Italy. The Soviet representatives had obeyed Stalin's dictum, "Stay out of the range of artillery fire!"

The only area of the Spanish Republic that still held out against Stalin was Catalonia, where anti-Stalinists held a strong majority. It was also the region in which Largo Caballero, whom Stalin was determined to oust, had the bulk of his support.

For that very reason, Orlov made it his first priority to undermine the fragile unity in Catalonia. It was endangered by conflicts among the Trotskyites, anarchists, socialists, and syndicalists, and Orlov planned to take advantage of these conflicts to inflame the antagonisms among them and bring them to the point of explosion.

The KGB had already infiltrated its agents into Russian groups in Paris that maintained close links with ideologically allied groups in Barcelona. Many such agents had gone to Spain ostensibly to fight Franco but with the real mission of carrying out tasks assigned to them by the KGB.

Orlov's idea, based on his experience in Austria, was to provoke the Catalonians into rash and ill-considered actions, thus providing the KGB with an excuse to smash the opposition, made up of violently anti-Stalinist workers, once and for all. In this way, it would be possible to solidify Stalin's control.

One of the leaders of a Russian anarchist group in Paris, himself a KGB agent, was dispatched to Barcelona, where he established contact with anarchist and syndicalist officials in the government. His mission was to act as an agent provocateur, encouraging them to overreach themselves in a crackdown on their political rivals. In line with Orlov's scheme, this would be presented as an uprising to justify the Spanish army's intervention.[10]

With all the dexterity of a juggler, Orlov coordinated these provocations to take place in May. Wishing to make certain that there would be no interference with his plans, he arranged an invitation to the May Day celebration in Moscow for a man named Garcia, who was the head of the Spanish secret police. Orlov sent word to his colleagues in Moscow that Garcia should be prevented from leaving Russia for the entire month, using whatever pretexts were necessary. Due to the disorganization brought about by the purge, Orlov's telegram notifying them of Garcia's arrival was overlooked. Slutsky, chief of the Foreign Administration, asked Krivitsky to call on Garcia at the New Moscow Hotel and soothe the Spaniard's ruffled feelings.

Later Krivitsky asked Slutsky, "What's the idea of bringing that Spaniard over here?"

"Orlov wants him out of the way," Slutsky explained. "We have to keep him amused here until the end of May."[11]

Krivitsky, who had read the reports of the KGB agents, did not have to ask what was going to happen in Spain during the month of May.

Orlov's plans went through without a hitch. Soon the headlines of the world press exploded with the news of an uprising in Barcelona, of fratricidal fighting, of an attempt to seize the telephone exchange, of rioting in the streets, the construction of barricades, and impromptu executions. In due course, the Spanish army was called in to restore order. By the time the fighting ceased, a few days later, the KGB had destroyed the opposition groups. The "revolt" was put down at a cost of five hundred dead and over one thousand wounded, mostly among the workers.

The Spanish Communist Party, which was under Orlov's thumb, made various demands: the suppression of all anti-Stalinist trade unions and parties in Catalonia; imposition of KGB control over all newspapers, radio stations, and meeting halls; and the complete extirpation of anti-Stalinist movements throughout Loyalist territory.[12] When Largo Caballero resisted these demands, he was forced to step down on May 15. His successor was Dr. Juan Negrin, Moscow's handpicked candidate, who remained in office until the Spanish Republic's defenses collapsed in March 1939.

Meanwhile, the Great Purge, like a gigantic scythe, was mowing down more and more people in the USSR, and Orlov did not fail to follow what was happening at home with keen interest, well aware that he himself might soon be affected. In June he learned of the arrest and execution of Marshal Tukhachevsky and seven other leading generals of the Red Army.

The purge of the Red Army soon spread to Spain, resulting in the recall of many Soviet officers. By July two of Orlov's most dangerous enemies, Jan Berzin and Arthur Stashevsky, were summoned home. They hurriedly made their way back via Paris, stopping there only between trains, and disappeared immediately after their arrival in Moscow.[13] It seems a reasonable assumption, however, that any concern the experienced Chekist Orlov felt about the purge in general was outweighed by the secret satisfaction he must have taken in the elimination of enemies like Berzin and Stashevsky, whose attacks on him at home could not have remained unknown to him.

That summer Orlov received other news from the Soviet Union. An important change of policy had taken place in Moscow. Up to that time, it had been the Politburo's policy to furnish the Spanish Republic with arms, pilots, and tank detachments as speedily as possible in the hope of defeating Franco. Now, however, the bosses in Moscow had decided that it would be more in the USSR's interest to prolong the war, keeping either side from gaining a preponderance of strength, so that Hitler would be bogged down indefinitely in Spain.[14]

From Orlov's point of view, this meant that partisan warfare and other offensive operations should be scaled down in favor of secret police activities designed to deal promptly with dissatisfaction and poor morale in the population on Loyalist territory.

Nevertheless, while he continued his work, he became aware, on the basis of private reports from KGB officers who traveled in France and Spain, that the purge of the KGB apparatus was making ever wider circles. He already knew about some defections of intelligence officers abroad. Since he had worked directly under Yagoda and in close collaboration with other high-ranking Chekists purged since Yagoda's arrest, he could not help wondering what he would do if he was recalled to Moscow. True, he had enjoyed the patronage of Stalin, but others who were reputedly Stalin's favorites had fallen. Still, he might come through unscathed, and he had good reason to hesitate about any rash action, since both his mother and mother-in-law were in effect hostages and would probably be executed if he defected.

"While visiting the fronts in Spain on many occasions, especially when an offensive was to begin," he recalled, "I frequently came under severe bombardment, and at those tense moments I often caught myself thinking that if I were killed while carrying out my duty the threat which hung over my family and our mothers would immediately dissolve, and those thoughts loomed before me as a welcome alternative to an open break with Moscow."[15]

It is not surprising that Orlov quickly scented danger to himself. He knew all the tricks and was not to be caught off guard so easily.

In August 1937, shortly after Berzin and Stashevsky had vanished into State Security's dungeons, Orlov received a telegram from Slutsky warning of an alleged plot by the intelligence services of France and Germany to abduct him. The purpose of the abduction, Slutsky said, was to extort from Orlov information concerning the extent of Russian aid to Spain. What really made Orlov take notice, however, was Slutsky's statement that State Security intended to send him a squad of twelve men to see to his personal safety and accompany him everywhere he went.

The pretext for sending these bodyguards was so transparent that Orlov's suspicions were instantly aroused. What if their real mission was to liquidate him? Orlov responded at once with a telegram informing Slutsky that he had no need of this squad since he was already well-protected. His offices were guarded around the clock by the Spanish Civil Guard, and he was accompanied by armed agents of the Spanish secret service on all his travels. (This happened to be true.) Nevertheless, Orlov had no intention of accepting State Security bodyguards under any circumstances.

Although Slutsky dropped the matter, Orlov remained uneasy, sensing more behind Slutsky's proposal than appeared on the surface. Orlov began to wonder whether Yezhov might not give orders to one of the State Security "mobile groups" to assassinate him in Spain.

Turning over the question in his mind, he remembered how Kirov was murdered in 1934 while his guards looked the other way. He had always had confidence in the Spaniards who guarded him, but it occurred to him now that they too could be bribed to look the other way. Then he had an inspiration. He sent an assistant to the German International Brigade at the front with instructions to select ten dedicated Communists who had been fighting uninterruptedly and badly needed a rest. These men became his personal bodyguards. Armed with submachine guns and with grenades dangling at their belts, they gave him a degree of security that he had never felt before.

In October, Shpigelglas, Slutsky's deputy, made an unexpected appearance in Spain. Orlov had known him for years as able and ruthless and therefore considered him very dangerous. He had also heard that Shpigelglas organized the murder in Switzerland of Ignace Reiss, a KGB defector, only a month earlier. Shpigelglas' agents in Paris were maintaining surveillance of Walter Krivitsky, another suspected defector, at that very moment.

Traveling by car from Valencia to Barcelona, Shpigelglas told Orlov about the mass arrests in the Soviet Union, mentioning several State Security officials who had committed suicide. One patrol had come to the apartment of Chertok, an interrogator, known for his special cruelty to Kamenev. When they called on him to open the door, he shouted, "You won't get *me!*" and plunged to his death from the twelfth floor. Since the headquarters of State Security was located in the heart of Moscow, the suicides of officers who threw themselves from its upper floors took place in the sight of numerous passersby, and the news spread all over the capital, increasing the panic of the population.[16] Both Orlov and Shpigelglas understood what was going on and could speak to one another about it, but neither dared to speak about what was in his own heart.

Shpigelglas hinted to Orlov that he would like an assignment in Spain. When Orlov failed to react, he finally came straight out and said that he wished to become Orlov's deputy, if Orlov would just take the initiative by asking Moscow to give him the assignment.[17]

Orlov did not allow himself to be misled. He still did not trust Shpigelglas, even though the latter obviously feared for his own life and was seeking to get away from Moscow, where his wife and daughter were virtual hostages. Orlov was aware that Shpigelglas had no real business in Spain. Later, when he found out that Shpigelglas had met in Madrid with a man named Bolodin, his suspicions sharpened, for he had already been tipped off that Bolodin belonged to one of the "mobile groups" organized by Yezhov for assassinations abroad.

"Shpigelglas and Bolodin must have realized that I was well protected by my guards," Orlov wrote, "and that an attempt on my life might backfire and cause more trouble than they cared for."[18]

But Orlov was too wise to think that they would give up in the face of one or two setbacks. The notion suddenly struck him that Bolodin might try to kidnap his fourteen-year-old daughter, Vera, who was living with her parents in the country, as a means of blackmailing him into returning to the Soviet Union. He was so alarmed by this idea that he immediately returned home, had his wife and daughter pack their things, and drove them across the border into southern France, where he found a small villa and left them in the care of his chauffeur, a trusted officer of the Spanish secret service. Then he returned to work in Barcelona.

Orlov's actions were bound to seem provocative to Moscow, no matter what the intentions of State Security. If his superiors were going to use such methods against him, he thought, they obviously did not expect him to obey a summons to return to Moscow. They feared that he would defect but, moreover, apparently believed that the knowledge he possessed was extremely harmful to them. That was both the strength and the weakness of his position; he had a hold over them, but it made it all the more necessary to act against him. At any rate, it afforded him time, while they tried to work out how to remove him without any risks.

Although the months passed and nothing happened, Orlov was not lulled into a false sense of security. Early in March 1938, he was startled to receive a routine dispatch from Moscow announcing the death twelve days earlier of Slutsky, a "faithful Stalinist who had been consumed by hard work." Yet in the twelve days since Slutsky's death, Orlov had received replies to cables over Slutsky's signature.[19] Although he did not learn until later that Slutsky had been poisoned by his own colleagues, his apprehension was increased by the way he had heard about this death and the fact that Slutsky was succeeded by Shpigelglas as acting chief.

Despite everything, he still clung to the hope that by doing nothing he might prolong the lives of his mother and mother-in-law. In any case, there was always the chance that something would happen to change the situation.

On July 9, 1938, a long telegram signed by Yezhov arrived from Moscow, ordering Orlov to proceed to Antwerp and board the Soviet ship *Svir* on July 14 for a conference with a "comrade whom you know personally." The telegram suggested that he travel to Antwerp in a car with diplomatic plates from the Soviet Embassy in

Paris, accompanied by Birukov, the Consul General, who "might come in handy as a liaison man in connection with the important task that lay ahead."

Orlov, however, was not deceived. "The telegram was long and tricky," he recalled. "Yezhov and the men whom he brought with him to the NKVD . . . tried so hard to allay my suspicions and did it so clumsily that they betrayed their purpose. It was clear to me that the ship was to become my floating prison."[20]

But realizing that disobedience would immediately lead to his arrest, Orlov replied without delay, saying that he would arrive on the appointed day. After sending off the reply, he sat in his office thinking about everything he had done to satisfy his bosses. "And this is the thanks I get!" he told himself bitterly.

On July 12 Orlov's staff came to bid him farewell. He had no difficulty in reading their thoughts. Before leaving, Orlov seems to have taken certain precautions. He had no intention of going like a sheep to the slaughter, and his suspicions had given him sufficient warning to consider his course. What alternative did he have but defection? Yet as soon as he deviated from the itinerary laid down for him, within forty-eight hours at most, Yezhov's "mobile groups" would be put on his trail. And to escape with his family he needed money—more money than he possessed in personal funds, but, he knew where it could be found—in his own safe, which held all the KGB's operational funds.

Orlov did not clear out the entire safe, but removed thirty thousand dollars, and "inadvertently" took the key to the safe with him. In the excitement of his leavetaking, no one thought to ask him for it. When his colleagues discovered it was missing, they assumed he had taken it by accident and sent an enciphered message to the Soviet Embassy in Paris, suggesting it be retrieved from Orlov on his arrival. Orlov, however, never appeared at the Soviet Embassy. The missing funds came to light only when the safe was finally opened by a technician.[21]

Two hours after leaving Barcelona, Orlov crossed the French border, where he parted from his personal bodyguards and Spanish secret service escorts and went on to Perpignan to meet his wife and daughter at the Grand Hotel. They took the night train to Paris, arriving on July 13.

But time was precious. Orlov went straight to the American Embassy, where he asked to see Ambassador William C. Bullitt. To his disappointment, he found out that Bullitt was out of town, since it was the eve of Bastille Day.

Orlov began to get panicky. With the American ambassador absent, no one else was likely to take on the responsibility for helping a Soviet defector. Moreover, the Soviet Union had powerful friends in France who were willing—even eager—to provide assistance. The French authorities could very well pretend to see nothing while the KGB disposed of him.

Then Orlov's wife thought of the Canadian Legation. Canada was also far enough away to provide refuge. At the legation, Orlov showed their diplomatic passports and requested visas, ostensibly for the purpose of a vacation in Quebec. Since the Soviet Union did not have diplomatic relations with Canada, it seemed possible that their request would be turned down. But luck was with them. The minister who headed the legation had been commissioner of immigration in Canada. He not only issued the visas but provided a personal letter to immigration officials in Quebec.

But that was not all. At the legation the Orlovs met a Canadian priest who informed them that the *Mountclair*, a passenger ship, was leaving from Cherbourg that day and that there were still empty cabins. Orlov hastily arranged for the tickets, while his wife rushed back to their hotel to get their daughter. They nearly missed the train to Cherbourg, but they arrived at the port and boarded the *Mountclair* on time.

When he reached Canada, Orlov wrote a letter to Stalin with a copy to Yezhov. He knew perfectly well that KGB executioners would soon be after them.

Describing the letter, Orlov said in his memoirs:

> I warned him with all the determination at my command that if he dared to revenge himself on our mothers I would publish *everything* that was known to me about him. To show Stalin that I meant business I wrote down an account of his crimes and attached it to my letter.
>
> I warned him also that if I were murdered by his henchmen the record of his crimes would be published by my lawyer at once. I knew Stalin well and I was sure that he would heed my warning.
>
> It was a dangerous game for me and my family. But I was confident that Stalin would have to postpone his revenge until he had succeeded in kidnapping me and forcing me to yield my hidden memoirs, thus

making sure that the secrets of his crimes would not be published. Only then would he take the full measure of vengeance.[22]

Vladimir Petrov, on duty in Moscow as a code clerk at the time, told a significantly different story—after his own defection from the KGB. "There was one dramatic cable from Madrid in July 1938, which I can still visualize as it lay decoded on the table before me," Petrov related. "In laconic official language it reported that our OGPU resident 'X' had deserted the Soviet service and had fled to Paris with his wife and daughter. . . . In Paris, the cable continued, 'X' had instructed a lawyer, if he should be assassinated or meet with any mishap, to publish his memoirs which contained the names of all his agents and contacts in Spain, and a description of his important and highly secret work on behalf of the Soviet gov-enrnment."[23]

The "secret history of Stalin's crimes," which Orlov did not publish until 1953, was not precisely secret during the 1930's. Indeed, Walter Krivitsky, another high-ranking KGB defector, not only could but did tell about them in a book published in 1939. There is good reason to doubt that any threat by Orlov to reveal Stalin's crimes would have had much impact on Stalin, who could rely on Soviet and worldwide Communist propaganda to deny, distort, and ridicule such information.

What, in fact, Orlov could threaten was to exchange his silence about State Security's espionage operations for safety of himself and his family. As long as the Kremlin remained convinced that he had not violated his promise to remain silent, he would have little to fear, especially if his former bosses believed that he had made good on his threat to write down the information and conceal it in a safe place.

This seems to have been the true substance of Orlov's letter to Stalin.

Orlov stayed in Canada only long enough to obtain visas from the American Legation in Ottawa permitting him and his family to enter the United States. In New York he contacted a lawyer, who accompanied him to Washington, where he presented himself to the commissioner of immigration to announce his break with Stalin and ask for political asylum.

With thirty thousand dollars, he had no trouble about money. He cleverly avoided publicity, for he did not need to peddle his knowledge to the press, nor would it have been advisable in view of his undertaking to Stalin.

Nevertheless, he found it useful to establish ties with Russian Social Democratic and other emigré circles in New York, revealing a certain amount of information that would give him standing without jeopardizing his safety. Ironically, the Russian socialists apparently accepted him, although his hands were stained with the blood of socialists killed in Spain by his minions.

Possibly during World War II or in the postwar period, Orlov succeeded in selling himself to the FBI as a "consultant" on Soviet intelligence matters. How much did he tell the U.S. government about the KGB's secrets before publishing his book?

 It seems significant that Philby, Maclean, and Burgess continued to operate as Soviet agents until 1951, although Orlov had been the resident in England at the time of their recruitment.

There are other mysteries about Orlov's involvement with official Washington.

 Curiously enough, Orlov omitted from his catalog of Stalin's crimes the assassination of Leon Trotsky in 1940, about which Orlov was extremely well-informed. As the KGB chief in Spain, Orlov had as his assistant Leonid Eitingon, the very man who planned the assassination. Moreover, Caridad Mercader, the mother of the killer, Ramon Mercader, was Eitingon's mistress and a member of Orlov's own circle. Ramon had served in one of the special units under Orlov's command in Spain and carried out missions behind the enemy lines. Testifying before the U.S. Senate subcommittee on internal security in 1957, Orlov said that Eitingon had been assigned by Beria or Stalin to organize Trotsky's assassination. Since Orlov had defected before Beria's time, his testimony on this point seemed designed to exonerate himself. But there can be little doubt that Eitingon received the assignment while Orlov was still the top man in Spain.

This is shown by Orlov's warning to Trotsky, which he admitted sending anonymously from New York shortly after his defection. In a letter dated December 27, 1938, the anonymous correspondent warned that a dangerous provocateur named "Mark" had penetrated the Troskyite organization in Paris. From the description in the letter, it was easy to identify the provocateur as Mark Zborowski, who had become the right-hand man of Leon Sedov, Trotsky's son, and was later implicated in Sedov's murder. In addition, the letter warned of plans afoot for Trotsky's assassination, which would be carried out either by Zborowski or by a Spaniard pretending to be a Trotsky supporter.

This letter provides evidence that as early as 1938 Orlov knew about an assassination plot against Trotsky. Orlov was very well acquainted with Zborowski, a Soviet agent among the Trotskyites; the "Spaniard pretending to be a Trotsky supporter" was obviously Ramon Mercader, who posed as a Belgian journalist when he turned up in Trotskyite circles in Paris in 1939, at the beginning of his road to Mexico.

Trotsky probably took the letter for a provocation or assumed that the writer was a crank. Did Orlov really mean it to be taken seriously as a warning? Or was he just trying to establish his bona fides with the letter if it later became expedient to do so?

In 1955 Orlov testified before the same Senate subcommittee to the effect that Zborowski, who had come to the United States in the meantime, was a Soviet agent. In 1962 Orlov was prepared to testify as a witness at a second perjury trial of Zborowski but did not appear because the premature release of his 1955 testimony might have provided a basis for the defense to move for a mistrial.[24]

Except for Zborowski, who might have been considered expendable, Orlov's testimony against Soviet spies was limited to Chekist officials like Slutsky and Shpigelglas, who had long since disappeared from the ranks of Soviet State Security, and Leonid Eitingon, who was then in a Soviet jail. Did Orlov tell about any active Soviet agents? When William Fisher, who had worked for Orlov in England, was arrested in the United States as a top Soviet spy in 1957, Orlov could not have failed to see his photographs in the American press—apart from being questioned about him by the FBI—but there is no indication that he ever identified Fisher. (Possibly the information was suppressed in order to deceive Moscow.) On the other hand, if the FBI and the federal prosecutors had wished to obtain the conviction of "Abel" on the first count of conspiracy to transmit atomic and military information to Soviet Russia, which carried a death penalty, it would have been helpful to have Orlov testify about Fisher's earlier association with the nuclear physicist Kapitsa.

Alexander Orlov may have been that type of defector who has broken only outwardly with the Soviet system and withholds information more significant than any he chooses to give. Or he can be seen as a double agent. In either case Orlov seems to have been more faithful to the Soviet system than to the country that gave him political asylum.

5

The Neighbors

BECAUSE OF THE AURA of fear and mystery that has surrounded Soviet State Security, acronyms like the GPU, NKVD, and KGB have seized the imaginations of people all over the world. But few people outside Russia realize that there is another Soviet Intelligence service with many notable coups to its credit.

When KGB officers speak of the "neighbors" (*sosedy*), they are referring to their competitors, Soviet Military Intelligence. Formerly known as the Fourth Department, and now the Main Intelligence Administration (*Glavnoe Razvedyvatelnoe Upravlenie*, or GRU), is attached to the General Staff of the Soviet Army. Such people as Whittaker Chambers and Richard Sorge, who have become famous in the West, worked for the Fourth Department.

Soviet Military Intelligence was already involved in foreign espionage before State Security moved into the field. In most respects, the foreign operations of the two organizations closely resemble one another. In actuality, the GRU does not focus exclusively on Military Intelligence, but works in the same areas as its more important rival. Indeed, Moscow values more highly information on government policies and high-level diplomacy than run-of-the-mill blueprints of weapons. Much depends on the access enjoyed by the GRU's agents; if those agents can obtain high-level political intelligence, the GRU clearly will be glad to accept the product and forward it to the Kremlin. The very freedom of competition despised in the economic sphere is endorsed by the Soviet leadership in espionage, where the leaders are reluctant to place exclusive reliance on any one Intelligence service.

From the outset Military Intelligence found itself enmeshed in political questions. In the early 1920's it was obliged to work closely with the Comintern, in the expectation that workers' revolutions would soon spread throughout Europe. Since revolution was to be brought about through armed uprisings, it appeared logical to use Soviet military officers with Intelligence backgrounds to prepare them. This in turn required further cooperation with the Communist parties of such countries, which were subordinate to the Comintern.

Having no responsibility for internal security, Military Intelligence never acquired the evil reputation of State Security among Soviet citizens. Quite the contrary: GRU officers acquired the reputation of carrying out daring feats against the enemies who surrounded the Soviet state and plotted its destruction. Throughout the history of Soviet Military Intelligence, its officers retained an image of decency and honor, even during the years when State Security was steeped in the blood of millions.

Today the GRU remains a separate, much smaller organization than the KGB, but it is also inferior in the sense that, like the great masses of the Soviet population, its personnel are subject to the surveillance of the KGB both at home and abroad.

One of the most remarkable of the Military Intelligence officers, one who worked unremittingly with revolutionary fervor on behalf of Bolshevism, was named Walter Krivitsky. Like Alexander Orlov, Krivitsky was an assumed name, derived from the word *krivit* (to bend or twist).

Krivitsky was born Samuel Ginsberg on June 28, 1899. His birthplace, Podvolochisk, in the western Ukraine, was close to the line at which two great empires—the Russian and the Austrian— collided. Podvolochisk stood on territory that passed from Russia to an independent Poland after World War I. Growing up in this strategic no-man's-land, Ginsberg learned Russian, Polish,

Ukrainian, and German—linguistic as well as cultural advantages that were to make him an invaluable Intelligence agent.

As a boy, Ginsberg was small and deceptively frail, and of a sensitive, nervous nature. He came from a family of merchants, but circumstances did not favor a continuation of this heritage. In the Jewish community he knew—forced to accept the buffeting of a hostile environment—one promising weapon against czarist persecution was to take part in the revolutionary politics of the time. There were strong socialist currents in his homeland: the Bolshevik and Menshevik factions of the Social Democratic Party; the Social Revolutionaries, strongly supported by the peasants of the Ukraine; and the Jewish Bund, socialist in its views but determined to eliminate discrimination against Jews.

The region where he lived was occupied by the Central Powers during the last years of World War I, and the teenage Ginsberg's contact with occupying German and Austrian troops probably had some importance for his future work as a spy. But the event that fired his imagination was the Russian Revolution, above all the ascent to power of the Bolsheviks, with their slogans of brotherhood, racial and national equality, social and economic justice, and their demand that factories be given to the workers and land to the peasants.

Krivitsky wrote:

> At the age of thirteen I had entered the working-class movement. It was a half-mature, half-childish act. I heard the plaintive melodies of my suffering race mingled with new songs of freedom. But in 1917 I was a youngster of eighteen, and the Bolshevik Revolution came to me as an absolute solution of all problems of poverty, inequality and injustice. I joined the Bolshevik Party with my whole soul. I seized the Marxist and Leninist faith as a weapon with which to assault the wrongs against which I had instinctively rebelled.[1]

The circumstances under which young Ginsberg was recruited into Soviet Military Intelligence remain unclear, but the timing of his recruitment can be placed in the second half of 1919, probably on his arrival in Moscow after a brief sojourn abroad.

When the German troops withdrew from the area following the armistice, the Bolsheviks attempted to move into the vacuum of power by setting up a West Galician People's Republic. At the age of nineteen, Ginsberg took an active part in this political coup, but the People's Republic was short-lived, and under the terms of the Versailles Treaty the territory was incorporated into a newly independent Poland. Instead of returning to the USSR, the leaders of the West Galician People's Republic chose exile in Germany under the guise of returning prisoners of war. Their assignment from the Bolshevik Party, however, was to spread revolution in Central Europe.[2]

This was Ginsberg's baptism by fire. In June 1919 he joined members of the embryo Austrian Communist Party in Vienna in a demonstration aimed at forcing the Social Democratic government to support a Communist Hungarian Republic established by Béla Kun. The demonstration ended in bloodshed, but Ginsberg, who marched in the front ranks of the demonstrators, escaped unharmed.

Ginsberg was presumably already in touch with the GRU, and, on his arrival in Moscow, began his career in Military Intelligence. For a time he apparently served in the civil war behind the White lines in the Ukraine, gathering intelligence, organizing guerrilla bands, and engaging in sabotage. He must have distinguished himself in this work, for when the Soviet-Polish War broke out in 1920, he was assigned to Military Intelligence for the Western Front, whose headquarters was in Smolensk. Assigned to prepare the way for the Red Army under Tukhachevsky in its drive on Warsaw, Krivitsky and his colleagues carried out diversions behind the lines, sabotaged arms supplies destined for the Polish Army, disseminated propaganda against it, and—as usual—collected intelligence.

Krivitsky, who easily passed as a Polish citizen, worked behind the enemy lines on many such missions. A man of keen intelligence, he took very seriously the conspiratorial discipline at which others, who considered themselves equally intelligent, often sneered. His life had been saved more than once by observing those rules. He never emptied a dead drop without feeling a tightening in his stomach. Yet he would proceed with icy calm, carefully noting the chalk mark on a lamppost that told him the dead drop had been filled, then approaching, with due caution, the loose brick in a wall behind which a roll of film had been hidden. Considering how the oposition could be watching the drop and waiting for him, he mentally selected the points at which he would have posted his own men for such surveillance. Only when he felt certain he was not walking into a trap did he remove the brick and pick up the film, erasing the chalk mark so that the agent would know the drop had been emptied.

At meetings with an agent, he was also careful to observe the proprieties. He would wear a black hat and carry a copy of a book in his left hand and a brown wooden cane in the other. If he thought he was under surveillance, he pulled the hat brim down. The other man would wear a red tie and carry a half-dozen roses in his left hand. Shifting the roses to his right hand indicated that he was being followed, and Krivitsky would not approach him. When they came together, they exchanged apparently harmless remarks that represented recognition signals:

Krivitsky: "There's supposed to be a hospital around here. Can you tell me where it is?"

Agent: "No. It's my aunt's birthday, and I'm bringing her these flowers."

Silly as it seemed to some people, the system worked.

Krivitsky's activities took him to all parts of Poland, meeting Polish Communists who cooperated with him against their own government. Together, they engaged in sabotage and organized strikes against arms shipments. "I organized a successful railway strike in the Czech railway junction of Oderberg," he wrote later, "persuading the Czech railway to walk out, rather than handle Skoda munitions for the Poland of Pilsudski."[3]

The Soviet forces under Tukhachevsky's command marched to the gates of Warsaw, closely followed by a Polish Soviet government led by Felix Dzerzhinsky that was to be installed after the anticipated victory. At that time Dzerzhinsky, a native Pole, was still the head of Soviet State Security.

But Lenin's dream of capturing Poland as a bridge to Germany, where the real revolution was to take place, failed to materialize, and the exhausted Red Army was forced into retreat.

Since Communism could not then be carried to Germany by Soviet arms, the Kremlin leaders decided to try to bring about a revolution in Germany with the asssistance of an armed uprising from within. This assignment was to absorb all of Krivitsky's energies during the next few years.

In January 1923, while Krivitsky was working in the Third

Section at Military Intelligence headquarters in Moscow, an elec-
trifying report arrived: the French Army was about to occupy the
Ruhr in order to enforce German reparation payments. It immediately became apparent to the Soviet leaders that the French action
would have a devastating effect on the situation in Germany, which
was already nearly catastrophic. The economy was prostrate, infla-
tion raged, and there was widespread unemployment. With discontent rife, hardly a day passed without pitched battles in the streets
between workers and police or workers and nationalists. What the
Kremlin saw was the ripening of a revolutionary situation in which
the Comintern could hope to intervene decisively.

The chief of Military Intelligence, General Jan Karlovich
Berzin, ordered five or six Red Army officers, including Krivitsky,
to leave immediately for Germany. They had strict instructions to
reconnoiter the situation, organize resistance in the Ruhr, and
make underground preparations for military action when the time
came.

Arriving in Berlin, Krivitsky quickly confirmed the seriousness of
the situation. He witnessed bitter fighting in the streets, observed
pedestrians with suitcases bulging with worthless money, while
prices tripled and quadrupled daily, and he saw factories that had
closed their gates due to the lack of raw materials. Confronted with
this bleak picture, Krivitsky became convinced that the Comintern
at last had an excellent chance of bringing about a revolution.

Krivitsky and his comrades wasted no time in getting to work. In
the name of the German Communist Party, they created a political
intelligence network under the general supervision of Soviet Military Intelligence, organized military formations as a nucleus of the
future German Red Army, and pushed through a *Zersetzungsdienst*,
small units of picked men whose task was to subvert the Reichswehr
—the army—and the police. To achieve the latter goal, they established "T" (terror) units that were to asssassinate certain officers.

In the Ruhr, Krivitsky and his fellow officers found widespread
passive resistance to the French occupation. Factories were operating with skeleton maintenance crews, shops and offices remained
closed, the railroads had stopped running.

Meanwhile the Red Army officers working underground continued to plan for an armed uprising. German Communists were
organized into military units of one hundred men each; lists of

Communists with wartime service were drawn up for eventual recruitment as officer cadres of a future German Red Army; and
military specialists with a background in artillery, engineering,
aviation, and communications, as well as women to serve as nurses
and hospital workers, were also enlisted.

By the end of that summer the atmosphere had reached the level
of tension before an electrical storm, when silence itself becomes
ominous. September gave way to a still more threatening October.
Boris Souvarine was working for the Comintern in Moscow at the
time:

> In October 1923 a revolution in Germany appeared inevitable. In the
> Politburo Trotsky proposed to set a date for the uprising, but other
> Politburo members objected. Trotsky published an article in Pravda:
> "Should a Date Be Set for the Uprising?" He maintained that the date
> of the revolution could not be set but that it was possible to set a date
> for the uprising. He proposed a date—November 7. He wanted to re-
> peat once again what had succeeded six years earlier.[4]

On the military side, Krivitsky and the other Red Army officers
had worked out a strategy that called for Communist fighting units
to avoid a clash with the French Army in the Ruhr at the time of
the uprising by withdrawing into central Germany. While they
awaited a final decision in Moscow setting the date of the uprising,
they conducted night maneuvers in the Rhineland with thousands
of armed German workers. Determined to do the job thoroughly,
the Kremlin dispatched many of its best men to Germany.

Grigori Zinoviev, president of the Comintern, kept setting dates
for the uprising and then canceling them. Finally he dispatched
couriers throughout Germany setting November 9 as the definite
date. The idea was to use the workers' demonstrations on the sixth
anniversary of the revolution to provoke battles with the police that
would lead to a full-scale uprising.

With the Communist forces alerted and ready, the Politburo got
cold feet at the last minute. Reports from the Soviet representatives
in Germany expressed alarm about the chances of success, since the
mood of the workers was unfavorable and the concrete preparations
for a revolt were considered inadequate. Zinoviev sent off an urgent
message canceling the uprising. Once more couriers rushed to the
local Communist organizations with the news.

But the party organization in Hamburg, one of the Communist strongholds, did not receive word in time. At the appointed hour, the Communists of Hamburg carried out their long-assigned military tasks, attacking police stations and seizing central points in the city. When the anticipated uprising in other parts of Germany did not take place, the Hamburg Communists desperately continued their battle, holding out for several days. Inevitably, they were overwhelmed.

To Krivitsky himself, who had personally known and worked with many of these workers, the outcome of the 1923 events was more than a disappointment—it was a tragedy. The memory would remain with him until the end of his life. Never again, as a professional Soviet intelligence officer, would he have such direct and intimate contact with the workers in whose name he was trying to bring about world revolution. From that time on he ceased to be an idealist and became a realist.

Out of the wreckage of the German "Red Army," Krivitsky and his colleagues foresightedly salvaged assets that would enable Soviet Intelligence to penetrate the Nazi regime. "We took the best men developed by our Party Intelligence and the *Zersetzungsdienst*," said Krivitsky, "and incorporated them into the Soviet Military Intelligence. Out of the ruins of the Communist revolution we built in Germany for Soviet Russia a brilliant Intelligence service, the envy of every other nation."[5]

Krivitsky spent the next couple of years in Germany, occupied with building up the German networks. At the beginning of 1926, however, he served again in Moscow in the Third Section, this time as the chief for Central Europe, but he was reassigned to foreign work during that year. Journalist Paul Wohl, who had first met Krivitsky in December 1925, before the latter went back to Moscow, wrote: "All I knew of him then was that he was an important emissary of the Bolsheviks." Wohl continued:

It was . . . in 1926, when I returned to Berlin for a brief visit and met, in the Soviet Embassy, an unrecognizable Krivitsky. . . . I was very much intrigued by this mysterious Russian. Never in the course of my international career did I meet a man of such unusual qualities. The information he possessed was vast, his understanding of political events unique.[6]

This meeting took place perhaps during the time Krivitsky was hiding in the Soviet Embassy. For two months he remained in this refuge in order to avoid arrest by the Berlin police, which knew of his efforts to organize a German Red Army.

Immersing himself completely in his career, Krivitsky attended a military academy and even took part in maneuvers as a means of improving his qualifications in the Red Army. To what extent he became aware of the secret Soviet cooperation with the German Reichswehr, which helped Germany to rearm in violation of the Versailles Treaty, has not been recorded. In view of his close connection with German affairs, however, it seems likely that he would have become involved in arrangements for training Reichswehr officers as pilots or in tank warfare.

Krivitsky never remained at home for long. Soon he went abroad again, running his German networks from the periphery as he traveled to Austria, Switzerland, France, and Holland. Toward the end of the 1920's he ranged farther afield, into Fascist Italy, which had developed into an important Soviet Intelligence target.

He found a venal Italian officer who was willing to sell the plans of a new submarine. But it took more than year and a several trips to complete the operation. Once, on his way to a meeting with this agent, he came face to face with a man whom he had known all his life. The other man greeted him like a long-lost brother, but he did not forget his training as a spy.

"I just stared blankly at him," Krivitsky recalled, "as though I didn't even speak his language."[7]

On another occasion, early in 1930, Krivitsky obtained the first clue to a large counterfeiting operation pushed by Stalin himself and involving both the GRU and KGB. He happened to read in a newspaper that a man he knew to be a GRU agent was being sought by the Berlin police in connection with the passing of counterfeit U.S. hundred-dollar bills. Lacking foreign exchange for the purchase abroad of machinery and other equipment essential for the first Five-Year Plan (1928–32), Stalin had established a refined counterfeiting plant in the Soviet Union under KGB supervision that was producing American banknotes nearly as "good" as the originals. Over a period of several years, using the GRU for this purpose, some ten million dollars worth of forged currency was passed.

Once Krivitsky learned about this operation, he attempted to convince his superiors that counterfeiting could not produce the vast amounts of foreign exchange needed by the Soviet Union, while it was sure to be discovered and result in a serious loss of prestige for Moscow.

Eventually Stalin came to the same conclusion, but by then it was too late. Moscow's involvement became known to the U.S. government. The damage might have jeopardized negotiations for diplomatic recognition of the USSR, had President Franklin Delano Roosevelt chosen to make an issue of Stalin's counterfeiting.

Krivitsky was recalled to Moscow in 1933 and appointed director of the Soviet War Industries Institute. Although ostensibly unrelated to Military Intelligence, this institute had the function of utilizing plans and blueprints stolen by Intelligence agents from foreign powers and applying them to the Soviet war industry. Krivitsky's institute also produced requirements for the Intelligence services for the procurement of other plans and blueprints urgently needed by Soviet industry.

In those same years, however, Military Intelligence was steadily losing ground to State Security, which was jealous of the former's relatively autonomous status and now able to profit from Stalin's increasing reliance on it. As his distrust of the military grew, Stalin became willing to allow the KGB to take over the GRU's assets abroad. In 1935 General Berzin, who had headed the Military Intelligence set-up from the beginning, was relieved of his duties and sent by Stalin to organize and direct the Loyalist Army during the Spanish Civil War. That September, Krivitsky was summoned to work in the State Security apparatus and sent to Holland as the KGB "illegal" resident there.

Whether he liked it or not, he had no choice but to leave the "neighbors" and join the hated competition. Yet whatever reluctance he felt was certainly tempered by relief at leaving behind the fears and hazards of Russia during those purge years, even though safety abroad was an illusion. He was accompanied by his wife, Antonina, and their one-year-old son, Alexander.

True to his status as an "illegal," Krivitsky established himself in The Hague as an Austrian art dealer, Dr. Martin Lessner, with a shop at Celebes Straat 32.[8] Operating from the Dutch capital, he assumed control of some of his old German networks. Although he had to direct them from the periphery, Krivitsky could take satisfaction in working directly against Hitler, whom he clearly saw as the greatest menace the Soviet state had ever faced.

Krivitsky had been at his post barely a month when he found it necessary to rush back to Moscow. He had learned from one of his German agents that highly confidential and sensitive negotiations were being conducted in Berlin between Baron Joachim von Ribbentrop, Hitler's personal diplomatic representative, and the Japanese military attaché, General Hiroshi Oshima. The negotiations were so secret that neither the German Foreign Ministry nor its Japanese counterpart had any knowledge of them. Krivitsky suspected that these negotiations were laying the groundwork for future German-Japanese cooperation.

Stalin himself agreed to make available additional agents and technical support and to furnish Krivitsky with ample funds for this operation. The target: complete information about the secret German-Japanese negotiations.

Back in The Hague, Krivitsky set about this task with renewed vigor. Certain that the Gestapo would not long remain in the dark about the negotiations, Krivitsky instructed his agent to find out what the S.S. men around Himmler knew about the negotiations. His success was greater than he had dared to hope. Not only were they aware of them, he learned, but they already possessed a complete file of Oshima's encoded reports to Tokyo on the progress of the negotiations.

The high-ranking S.S. officer who had been so cooperative with Krivitsky's agent badly needed money to support his affair with a young actress. He would be willing to turn over copies of the message file—for a price.

The messages themselves would have been of little value without the code book, but this was available from another source. In late July 1936, Krivitsky received word that the material was in the hands of his agents in Germany. On August 8, while in Rotterdam, Krivitsky heard that the courier was expected at any moment in Amsterdam. He drove at top speed toward Amsterdam and stopped along the highway for a few minutes.

"Here it is. We've got it," the courier said to Krivitsky, handing him several rolls of undeveloped film.[9]

Krivitsky rushed the rolls of film to Haarlem, where an agent maintained a secret photographic laboratory. While the film was being developed, Krivitsky called in a Japanese-language expert, who translated the messages as each print became available.

Assured that the messages provided a complete record of the Ribbentrop-Oshima talks, Krivitsky had to find a way to send the translations to Moscow. Since he had no radio facilities in Holland and did not wish to keep Moscow waiting for a courier, he ordered an assistant to fly to Paris, where facilities existed for sending off a long message.

Thereafter the Soviet government followed the progress of the secret negotiations until a final agreement was initialed in Berlin.

"The pact was so worded," Krivitsky wrote, "as to extend the field of cooperation between Japan and Germany to include interests beyond China and Soviet Russia."[10]

As camouflage, however, the two governments drafted the anti-Comintern pact, which consisted of a couple of grandiose but meaningless paragraphs. The pact was signed on November 25 with great fanfare before members of the diplomatic corps. Thanks to Krivitsky's efforts, Soviet leaders were not at all misled by the published agreement.

Stalin now decided to let Hitler know that Moscow was fully aware of what was going on.

During the Extraordinary VIIIth Congress of Soviets in Moscow a few days later, People's Commissar for Foreign Affairs Maksim Maksimovich Litvinov included the following remarks in his speech:

> Judging from press reactions, it is no wonder that the reports about these treaties have met with hardly restrained polite laughter in all non-fascist countries. Well-informed people refuse to believe that it was necessary to conduct negotiations over a period of fifteen months in order to draft the two meager articles of the Japanese-German agreement; that for the conduct of these negotiations it was absolutely neces-

sary to entrust them to an army general on the Japanese side and a
superdiplomat on the German side; and that these negotiations had to
be carried on in a situation of extraordinary secrecy, kept secret even
from the German and Japanese official diplomacy. It is no wonder that
assumptions are made that the Japanese-German agreement was written in a special code in which anti-Communism signifies something entirely different from what is written in dictionaries, and that people
decipher this code in various ways. . . .

As far as the published Japanese-German agreement is concerned,
I would recommend not to seek any meaning in it because this agreement really has no meaning at all, for the simple reason that it is only
a cover for another agreement that was under consideration at the same
time and initialed and also probably signed, and that has not been published and will not be made public. I assert, with full awareness of the
responsibility I bear for my words, that it was preceisely to the drawing
up of this secret document, in which the word communism is not mentioned, that fifteen months of negotiations between the Japanese military attaché and the German superdiplomat were devoted. . . .

This agreement with Japan will tend to extend any war that breaks
out on one continent to at least two, if not more than two continents.[11]

Litvinov's remarks, which demonstrated how well-informed the
Soviet government was, aroused consternation in Berlin. Yet Stalin
clung to the belief that an agreement could be reached with Hitler.
Shortly afterward he instructed the Soviet trade envoy in Berlin to
act as his personal emissary in secretly approaching the Germans.

Krivitsky, who considered Hitler a deadly enemy with whom
compromise was impossible, was unhappy with Stalin's attitude,
and he became still more unhappy in December, when he received
orders to suspend his operations in Germany until further notice.

Krivitsky's exploit in penetrating the negotiations was regarded
in Moscow as a great triumph, and he was recommended for the
Order of Lenin. The award would elude him to the end.

Within a year he would become a fugitive, a man without a
country, pursued all over the world by KGB assassins.

On July 19, 1936, the day General Franco began his revolt
against the government in Madrid, thereby beginning the Spanish
Civil War, Krivitsky was in The Hague, where he still carried on his
overt occupation as an antiquarian and dealer in rare books.
Acting on his own initiative, without waiting for instructions from

Moscow, he sent one agent to Hendaye on the French-Spanish border and a second agent to Lisbon to report on developments in Spain.

The reports from Krivitsky's agents soon revealed that Italy and Germany were sending substantial military aid to Franco's insurgent forces. Nevertheless, Moscow remained silent. Krivitsky received no instructions and could only guess at the reasons for this silence. The Soviet press also failed to give him any clues.

Late in August, however, Stalin made his first move in the intricate chess game that the great powers had made out of the Spanish Civil War.

The Soviet media—press and radio—announced to the world a decree of the Commissar for Foreign Trade dated August 28, 1936, banning "the export, reexport, or transit to Spain of all kinds of arms, munitions, war materials, airplanes, and warships."[12] This was a tremendous disappointment to liberals abroad who supported the Spanish Loyalist government, including those "progressive" elements mobilized by the Comintern to take part in meetings and demonstrations and to collect funds for what was billed as the struggle of democracy against fascism. But these temporarily disappointed liberals did not understand Stalin, who had no intention of running the risk that the Soviet Union might become directly involved in a war with Germany and Italy. At the same time he was preparing to do unofficially and covertly the very things he had prohibited in this decree.

Immediately following a Politburo meeting at which Stalin's proposed policy in Spain was routinely approved, a courier came by plane from Moscow to deliver instructions to Krivitsky: "Extend your operations immediately to cover the Spanish Civil War. Mobilize all available agents and facilities for prompt creation of a system to purchase and transport arms to Spain. A special agent is being dispatched to Paris to aid you in this work. He will report to you there and work under your supervision."[13]

Meanwhile Yagoda was moving to establish a separate KGB organization in Loyalist Spain in accordance with Stalin's instructions. This was the organization headed by Alexander Orlov. Moving to implement other aspects of Stalin's policy of covert aid to the Loyalists (all designed to gain Soviet control of the Spanish Republican government), Yagoda called a meeting on September

14 in the Lubyanka, the KGB headquarters in Moscow. At this meeting a number of decisions were made: all Comintern activities in Spain would be placed under KGB supervision; the activities of the Spanish Communist Party would be coordinated with those of the KGB; and the volunteers being recruited in foreign countries to fight in Spain would be secretly checked by the KGB in order to screen out those who were anti-Communist or anti-Soviet and might strengthen the opposition to Soviet policies within Loyalist Spain.

One other decision concerned Krivitsky directly. The covert arms shipments to Spain ordered by Stalin had two sides: the first involved arms procured through clandestine channels abroad; the second was the unofficial shipment of arms from the USSR itself. Krivitsky received the assignment of organizing the foreign arms shipments, while Yagoda was to oversee those from the USSR.

All this time Krivitsky was continuing to run his German networks and following the secret Ribbentrop-Oshima talks with remarkable success. From his agents in Germany he was also receiving voluminous reports on German plans and preparations for operations in Spain.

Responsibility for these arms shipments placed an enormous additional burden on him. Nevertheless, the physical strain was nothing compared to his disturbed mental state as he read in the Soviet press about the trials of the Old Bolsheviks charged with treason. The first of these trials, involving Kamenev and Zinoviev, had already taken place in August 1936. The second trial had as its defendants Radek, Pyatakov, and Grigori Yakovlevich Sokolnikov. When Krivitsky read Radek's testimony at his trial in January 1937, he was shocked that Radek mentioned by name Krivitsky's hero, Marshal Mikhail Nikolayevich Tukhachevsky. The reference was innocuous enough, but Krivitsky knew that such references were not made without a reason. With a sinking heart, he turned to his wife, handing her the newspaper, and said: "Tukhachevsky is doomed!"[14]

Only a week after Yagoda's Lubyanka conference, on September 21, Krivitsky arrived in Paris to meet with the agent sent from Moscow. At this clandestine meeting, to which he had summoned three of his own subordinates from London, Stockholm, and Switzerland, he led an urgent discussion of the steps to be taken in organizing the arms shipments.

The agent from Moscow was Zimin, an arms expert who worked in the KGB's military section. Zimin transmitted to them categorical and emphatic instructions: the Soviet government was to be in no way associated with the arms supplies. All purchases and shipments had to be handled by private import-export firms set up for this purpose. The trail must not lead back to the Soviet Union.

This was Krivitsky's introduction to the shady world of munitions makers and gun runners. He had no difficulty in finding people already engaged in the business who would have gladly taken on this new assignment, caring nothing about the identity of their employers and asking no embarrassing questions. But neither the KGB nor Krivitsky wanted to become involved with adventurers or purely criminal types.

Krivitsky found other people who had been associated with Communist fronts and were prepared to work with him out of idealism, having already proved their reliability and efficiency.

By the end of September, a number of completely new import-export firms had been established in a dozen or more European cities, including London, Paris, Brussels, Amsterdam, Copenhagen, Zurich, Prague, and Warsaw. In each of these firms he placed a KGB agent who handled all the funds and checked every transaction.

While these companies were exploring all conceivable markets for arms supplies both in Europe and America, Krivitsky turned his attention to the critical problem of transportation. Since countries like France and England had proclaimed their neutrality in the Spanish Civil War and prohibited shipment of arms to the warring sides in Spain, this problem could not be easily solved.

He had no difficulty in leasing the necessary shipping in Scandinavian countries, provided he was willing to pay the price the ship owners demanded for the risk of entering a war zone. The real problem centered on the documentation required to obtain clearance for the shipments from those countries where the arms had to be loaded.

In the beginning he hoped that the arms shipments could be consigned to France and transshipped to ports in Loyalist Spain. The French government, however, refused to grant clearance for such shipments, and he had to fall back on another expedient. He succeeded in making arrangements with some Latin American consulates to issue an unlimited number of certifications that the shipments were bound for their countries. Certain Asian and East European consulates also provided papers for shipments. With these documents, it was possible to obtain clearance, and the arms soon went on their way, not to ports in Latin America or Asia but to ports in Loyalist Spain.

At home his colleagues were forced to resort to trickier methods to ship Soviet arms to Spain. Since the Soviet government had officially banned arms shipments, State Security created a "private" company in a country where private companies do not exist. This dummy company sold the arms to Spanish representatives, who paid with gold from the Spanish government reserves.

But Stalin had also prohibited the transport of those arms in Soviet ships. Unfortunately, foreign bottoms were not available on short notice, so the KGB made excellent forgeries of the papers of real foreign vessels. Then the names of the foreign vessels were painted over the names of Soviet ships in their home ports, and these ships sailed under the appropriate foreign flag to Spain. After unloading the cargo in Spain, the names of the Soviet ships were repainted on the foreign ships, the Soviet flag was raised, and the ships returned to their home ports in the USSR.

By mid-October shiploads of arms originating from many countries began to reach Largo Caballero's government. One consignment of arms even came from Nazi Germany, reflecting the typical murkiness of the munitions business.

With these arrangements well in hand, Krivitsky could devote himself to other matters. Early in November, he flew to Barcelona from Marseilles. He went to the downtown Barcelona hotel that served as Soviet headquarters and where only Soviet personnel were permitted to enter the hotel. There he found General Ivan Alekseyevich Akulov, a former favorite of Stalin, who headed a group engaged in operations in the Franco-held areas of Spain. Agents equipped with shortwave radio sets were sending valuable intelligence to Akulov, who was nominally subordinate to Orlov, but since the latter spent most of his time in Valencia, temporary seat of the Spanish Republican government, Akulov ran his operations quite independently.

Krivitsky arranged to transfer to Akulov the direction of agents he had himself sent into insurgent territory. Once this was done, Krivitsky had a talk with Arthur Stashevsky, Stalin's top political emissary in Loyalist Spain, who filled him in on the situation. Stashevsky told him about plans to replace the radical but undependable Largo Caballero with Dr. Juan Negrin, a bureaucrat, at the head of the Spanish government.

To his regret, Krivitsky did not see his old boss, General Berzin, who had been sent to Spain to organize and direct the Loyalist Army. Berzin's presence in the country was so secret that outside Soviet circles only half a dozen of the highest Spanish Loyalist leaders knew about it.

Thus General Berzin and his staff silently directed the fighting while General Miaja remained publicly in command. It did not matter to most outside observers that Miaja was assisted by peasant and worker Spanish commanders, many of whom spoke Russian.

Stalin, who eventually became suspicious of all the Soviet officials who served in Spain, doubting their loyalty to him, had most of them purged later on.

General Berzin was recalled to Russia and shot in 1937.

In March 1937, not without considerable trepidation, Walter Krivitsky traveled back to Moscow, leaving his wife and small son in Holland. The ostensible reason for his trip was to report to his new chief, Yezhov, who had taken the place of the hated Yagoda, now under arrest.

Krivitsky decided to make the trip on his own initiative, supposedly on business, but he had a private reason as well. After reading the sensational reports of the purges in the foreign press and the surprising accounts in the Soviet press, he wished to see for himself what was happening and to test the psychological climate.

On March 16 he flew to Helsinki and arrived by train in Leningrad. Encountering an old friend at the railroad ticket office, he asked, "Well, how are things?"

The friend looked around carefully. "Arrests, nothing but arrests. In the Leningrad district alone they have arrested more than seventy percent of all the directors of factories, including the munition plants. This is official information given us by the party committee. No one is secure. No one trusts anyone else."[15]

Krivitsky's stay in Moscow confirmed what he had already heard. "Within the first five months of 1937, 350,000 political arrests were made by the OGPU, according to official figures of the special section in charge of the purge," he wrote. "The prisoners ranged from marshals and founders of the Soviet government to minor Communist officeholders."[16]

Even officers on the highest level of State Security did not escape the purge. Yagoda finally had to be eliminated because he knew too much, he was too intimately acquainted with Stalin's methods, and he also continued to rely on the old KGB brass. After Yagoda's fall, it was their turn.

On Stalin's orders, Yezhov had built up a parallel KGB apparatus composed of about three hundred handpicked men who were slated to take over the top jobs in the KGB after Yezhov replaced Yagoda.[17] Stalin told Yezhov: "Intensify the purge!" From Yezhov's point of view, the place to begin was in the KGB itself, where he decided to show that the old leadership had been lax, inefficient, and corrupt. In any case, the old KGB leadership had to be destroyed.

The day after his arrival in Moscow, Krivitsky attended a meeting called by Yezhov and convened in the Lubyanka annex ballroom. Yezhov began the meeting with a denunciation of Yagoda, who, he said, had sought to emulate Napoleon's notorious minister of police, Joseph Fouché.

Next the gray-bearded Artur Khristianovich Artuzov, formerly one of Dzerzhinsky's closest colleagues, rose to denounce Abram Slutsky, head of State Security's Foreign Administration, calling him Yagoda's closest accomplice. Slutsky fired back with an attack on Artuzov, charging that, as a member of the Collegium, he had been Yagoda's principal supporter.

After this meeting the purge of the KGB accelerated. Many KGB officers forestalled arrest by shooting themselves or jumping out of windows, even in the Lubyanka itself. Shaken by these events, Krivitsky realized that he had placed his head in the lion's mouth and could only hope that his voluntary return might have convinced Stalin and Yezhov of his loyalty. There was no chance for him to escape, since Yezhov had placed directly under his office the section that handled passports and other arrangements for foreign travel. Without his specific approval, no KGB officer was able to depart.

Nevertheless, Krivitsky was encouraged by several long conferences with Yezhov and had seen nothing in his small, sharp-angled face that revealed the slightest suspicion or distrust. Taking a strong line in his dealings with Yezhov, Krivitsky urgently pressed for the assignment of at least six additional officers to his staff abroad. The tactic appeared to work, and he was soon going through personnel files and interviewing the more promising candidates.

Since he had planned only a brief stay in Moscow, Krivitsky's optimism began to fade after two months had passed and he had still not been ordered back to his post. On May 22, as he was on the verge of sending a telegram to his wife and son in The Hague, instructing them to return home, he suddenly received word to take the train at ten o'clock that night. The Kremlin apparently had confidence in him after all.

"Although shaken by my experience in Moscow," Krivitsky said, "I was returning to my post, determined to continue to serve the Soviet government."[18]

He reached The Hague on May 27, greeted with joyful cries by his wife and son. All seemed well. He had returned to the bosom of his family, energy restored and brimming with plans for the future.

Only two days later he was plunged into the most serious crisis of his life.

One of the agents Krivitsky assigned to the KGB operation of arms shipments to Spain was a lifelong friend who came from his own hometown. Ignace Reiss, like Krivitsky, had changed his last name, to Poretsky. Krivitsky had not only sponsored Reiss's membership in the Communist Party but also recommended him to the KGB. For sixteen years he worked for the KGB abroad, known to his colleagues as Ludwig. For his services he had received the Order of the Red Banner.

Later, when Krivitsky began to work under the KGB, he became Reiss's boss. Each man felt that he had a trustworthy friend, someone to whom he could always unburden himself, and with this mutual trust they soon found that they could hold nothing back from each other. In these circumstances, it was natural that Krivitsky should confide his own misgivings. Reiss had been horribly shocked by the trials of Old Bolsheviks and the arrests of prominent generals on charges of treason, as well as by the great purge of thousands of Communists.

Two days after Krivitsky's return to The Hague, Reiss went to Holland and questioned him in detail about events in the Soviet Union. Reiss was traveling with a passport in the name of Hans Eberhardt, a Czechoslovak citizen. He had already made up his mind to sever his ties with Moscow. Krivitsky urged Reiss to reconsider, pointing out that even if Stalin was wrong, he would not live forever and the Soviet state would go on. But Krivitsky's replies to his friend's probing questions only shocked him still more and reinforced his determination to make a complete break with Stalin's regime.

When they parted, Krivitsky thought that he had convinced Reiss to await developments and not act precipitously. Nevertheless, he was deeply afraid that his past relationship with Reiss, which was already well known, could cause him a great deal of trouble if Reiss's hostility toward Stalin came to the attention of their superiors.

Krivitsky would have been still more disturbed had he known that Reiss had already established contact with the Trotskyites and revealed much of Krivitsky's thinking to them. For it was naive of Reiss not to realize that the Trotskyite organization had been thoroughly penetrated by Soviet agents.

Still, a deceptive calm prevailed until July, when Krivitsky traveled to Paris to meet with several of his agents. At a café he encountered Reiss. They talked for a few minutes, and Reiss seemed eager to have a private discussion with him. Krivitsky agreed, telling Reiss to call him the next morning at his hotel, when they would firm up arrangements for this meeting.

Only two hours later, Krivitsky received an urgent message to meet Shpigelglas, deputy chief of the Foreign Administration, who had been sent to Europe by Yezhov on a matter of great secrecy. Krivitsky met Shpigelglas at the Paris World's Fair and saw at once from his manner that something unusually important had happened. Shpigelglas showed him two letters written by Ignace Reiss that had been turned over by Reiss to a KGB employee at the Soviet trade mission, for dispatch to Moscow. Not realizing that he was already under suspicion, Reiss had no idea that the letters would be opened in France.

In one letter, addressed to the Central Committee of the Communist Party, Reiss wrote: "Up to now I have followed you. From now on, not a step farther. Our ways part! He who keeps silent at this hour becomes an accomplice of Stalin, and a traitor to the cause of the working class and Socialism."[19] To make matters worse, Reiss had also sent letters to his agents informing them of his defection. Krivitsky himself received a similar letter the next day.

Pointing to the letters in his hand, Shpigelglas said: "Yes, we even suspected *you* in the beginning. For we were told only that some high Soviet agent had appeared in Holland and established contact with the Trotskyites. We found out that Ludwig and not you was the traitor."[20]

Perhaps Shpigelglas thought that Krivitsky would be gratified by this exoneration and that it would put him in the right frame of mind. But as he had feared, the conversation soon took an unpleasant turn. Shpigelglas pointed out with exaggerated politeness that, as Reiss's sponsor, Krivitsky had a special responsibility to see that the problem was solved.

For a short time Shpigelglas skirted the subject, throwing out hints, seeking to convey his meaning by implication. When Krivitsky refused to be drawn into a discussion of how this "enemy of the people" was to be eliminated, Shpigelglas became more explicit. Action had to be taken tonight, he said, since he had information that Reiss intended to flee the next morning. Krivitsky needed to prove himself to Stalin and Yezhov by personally handling the "solution" of the case.

While Krivitsky sat in silence, Shpigelglas continued to insist that Krivitsky had to preside over Reiss's liquidation. Forced to reply, Krivitsky told Shpigelglas that he refused to take part in such an undertaking.

"At that moment I realized," Krivitsky wrote, "that my lifelong service to the Soviet government was ended."[21]

Quietly, Krivitsky asked whether Shpigelglas had the authority to take over his operations, as the situation obviously required him to return to Moscow. Shpigelglas answered that he did not have jurisdiction over this question, which Krivitsky should take up with his superiors through channels.

The conversation continued as if nothing had happened. From time to time Shpigelglas left Krivitsky to go to another pavilion, presumably to meet with some agent. Shortly after midnight, during one of Shpigelglas's absences, Krivitsky went to a pay telephone and called Reiss at his hotel. When he recognized Reiss's voice at the other end, Krivitsky hung up without uttering a word. In the next few hours, Krivitsky made a number of similar calls, all intended to warn Reiss that he was in danger. The warnings must have had some effect, for Reiss disappeared from his hotel early that morning.

Relief over Reiss's escape could not obscure for Krivitsky the fact that his own situation had become extremely hazardous. It was clear that Shpigelglas now suspected him of being a traitor as well. He wrote a letter telling his wife to join him in Paris as soon as possible, in preparation for their return to Moscow.

From the outset of the Reiss affair, Krivitsky had become aware of surveillance, which intensified after he moved with his wife and son to a pension in Passy. His wife also noticed it when she took the child to walk in the park. On August 10 word finally arrived from Moscow for Krivitsky's return. He was to book passage on the *Bretagne*, which made regular trips between Le Havre and Leningrad during the summer.

Meanwhile, Krivitsky introduced one of his most talented agents to Shpigelglas. A young Dutchman named Hans Bruesse, he had taken part with Krivitsky in sensitive and unconventional operations and had won his trust. Now Bruesse would be taking temporary charge of Krivitsky's operations, but this change in their professional relationship seemed to have no effect on their close friendship.

Worry over their situation affected Antonina's health, and matters became still more complicated when their son contracted whooping cough. As the date of departure approached, Krivitsky decided that he would have to return to Moscow alone. He therefore made arrangements for his wife and son to follow in a few weeks.

On August 21 Krivitsky boarded the train for Le Havre at the Gare St. Lazare. After disposing of his baggage, he seated himself in a coach to await the departure of the train. Ten minutes before the scheduled departure, while lost in his somber thoughts, he suddenly felt a tap on his shoulder. He looked up to see the KGB Paris resident's assistant, who told him that a telegram had just been received from Moscow ordering him to stay in Paris. At first he doubted this information, but then one of his own subordinates arrived with a similar message that had just been decoded.

Krivitsky managed to recover his baggage and leave the train just before it pulled out of the station. This incident, however, made him wonder whether the whole business had been a test of his willingness to return to the Soviet Union. Thinking this more and more likely, he could not help being filled with resentment. For the first time the thought crossed his mind that he would never go back to that country.

During the next two weeks, surveillance of both Krivitsky and his wife grew still more rigorous. Their social contacts were restricted almost entirely to Hans Bruesse and his wife, who accompanied them to the theater and other public places. The Bruesses expressed sympathy for them through small gestures of solicitude.

On the morning of September 5, Krivitsky bought a copy of *Le Matin* and came upon a distressing dispatch from Lausanne, concerning the mysterious murder of a Czech citizen named Hans Eberhardt. Krivitsky could have no doubt that Soviet State Security had succeeded in killing Ignace Reiss.

Months went by before many facts about the murder could be established. Years went by before the truth emerged, and what were only suspicions on Krivitsky's part hardened into fact. As Krivitsky had suspected, the organizer of the murder was Shpigelglas.

A KGB agent who had been a close personal friend of Reiss and his family was a German woman named Gertrude Schildbach. Reiss knew that she had been shocked by the purges in Russia and thought that he could convince her to defect as well. While hiding in Lausanne, he proposed a meeting, to which she agreed, but immediately betrayed Reiss by informing her KGB bosses.

Shpigelglas sent Schildbach to Lausanne in the company of an agent from Paris, Roland Abbiat. In Lausanne, Reiss called Schildbach at her hotel and made arrangements to have dinner with her. After dinner Schildbach suggested a short walk, and as they strolled along the dark road, a car drove up, men jumped out, and, after a brief struggle, dragged Reiss into the car and fired at him at point-blank range. A short distance farther on they threw him out of the car. When Reiss was found beside the road, he had five bullets in his head and seven in his body.

When he heard about Reiss's murder, Krivitsky now knew that his own turn was bound to come. While awaiting further word from Moscow, he brooded about the course he should follow. "I had before me now the choice," he noted, "between a bullet in the Lubyanka from Stalin's formal executioners and outside Russia a rain of bullets from a submachine gun in the hands of his informal assassins."[22]

Krivitsky's wife was slowly beginning to understand their plight. One day she asked: "What will happen to you in Moscow? What chance is there that they won't harm you?"

"None," Krivitsky replied. Then he went on: "There is no reason why you should be punished on account of me. When you get back, they will make you sign a paper repudiating me and denouncing me as a traitor. As a reward for this, you and our child will be spared. As for me, it's certain death over there."[23]

His wife broke into tears. She refused to part with her husband, but her parents and two brothers remained in the Soviet Union, and she could not bear to think of permanent separation from them.

But Krivitsky recognized their desperate position better than she. He had no legal documents, no money, and no confidant to turn to. Finally he made up his mind to get in touch with Paul Wohl, who lived in Paris and with whom he had been friendly for years. Wohl immediately set about helping Krivitsky. He found a villa in the south of France as a temporary refuge when the break came, as it inevitably would.

The moment of decision was approaching rapidly. Moscow informed Krivitsky that he could take a Soviet ship, the *Zhdanov*, sailing from Le Havre on October 6. This left only a few days for Krivitsky to complete his preparations, either for the return to Moscow or their flight.

There remained little doubt as to that decision. Krivitsky balked at the idea of going back to Russia like a lamb to the slaughter. He understood perfectly well what awaited him. His wife was determined to share his fate.

On the morning of October 6, 1937, Krivitsky took the last, irrevocable step. He paid the bill at the hotel to which he had moved and checked his baggage at the Gare d'Austerlitz. After leaving the station, he spent most of the next hour in maneuvers intended to throw off any surveillance. Satisfied that he was not being followed, he met Wohl at a café and gave his friend the baggage check. When they parted, Krivitsky went to another hotel where his wife and son were waiting, and Wohl reclaimed Krivitsky's baggage at the Gare d'Austerlitz. Finally, with a hired car and chauffeur, he called for the Krivitskys, and soon afterward the group was on its way to the rented villa in the south of France.

While still hiding out, Krivitsky established contact with the Russian socialist leader Theodore Dan, who sought help on Krivitsky's behalf from the French Premier Léon Blum. Appealing for political asylum, Krivitsky said: "I know that a price has been put on my head. The assassins are after me, and they will not spare even my wife and child. I have often risked my life for my cause, but I do not wish to die now for nothing."[24] In due course, he received a *carte d'identité*. Although the Krivitskys had around-the-clock police protection after their return to Paris, they still lived in fear of the KGB.

"I have no doubt that the OGPU could have kidnapped or killed Krivitsky in Paris in spite of the protection afforded him by the French government," wrote Paul Wohl at a later date:

> However, it would have been absolutely necessary that such an attempt succeed. A second failure would have called the attention of the entire world to Krivitsky and that was precisely what Stalin wished to avoid. . . . The principal impediment was Stalin's desire not to strain relations with a friendly French government which had warned the Soviet Ambassador that Krivitsky enjoyed the protection of the French Republic. It is not probable though that Stalin—had he considered the immediate death or the capture of Krivitsky of paramount importance —would have had so much regard for smooth diplomatic relations with France at a time when people were so forgetful of the most extraordinary incidents.[25]

Such considerations must have led Krivitsky to conclude that he needed to go farther away, where he had a better chance to live in peace. With Wohl's help and the backing of American Ambassador William C. Bullitt, he and his family finally received temporary passports allowing them to enter the United States.

Rounding out the circle of his life, Krivitsky resumed his real name of Samuel Ginsberg and sailed with his wife and son to the United States in December 1938. For a time, it seemed, he had succeeded in finding the anonymity he had sought for so long.

In New York, the most international of American cities, Walter Krivitsky felt lost. What he found in American society exceeded his worst prejudices and preconceptions, and was therefore profoundly disillusioning. Yet not everything displeased him. When he called the police about a Soviet agent and was told that no one could be arrested unless a crime had been committed, he said to a friend, "Imagine, what a wonderful country. People are free unless they actually commit crimes."[26]

But what hit him hardest was his loss of faith in the cause for which he had striven all his life.

Paul Wohl wrote: "No other Bolshevik ever left the Soviet world to become so lonely and desperate as Krivitsky. . . . Krivitsky's forces were exhausted. . . . The world into which he fled was a hostile world which originally he had set out to destroy and to which he could not now adjust himself."[27]

Despite his psychological problems, Krivitsky still had to make a living for himself and his family. Unlike Orlov, who reportedly got away with thirty thousand dollars, Krivitsky had nothing to show for all the years of danger and privation in an underground existence. He thought of doing research in history or political science; he even considered a study of slavery, interpreted from an economic point of view, which he had started in the Vatican library. But there was little money to be earned in this manner. Moreover, he could not compete with other researchers trained in a Western academic tradition. Finally, for all his linguistic gifts, he doubted his ability to become a writer in a strange language and a strange country.

When the journalist Isaac Don Levine approached him with a proposal to write a series of articles, Krivitsky was in a mood to accept. Levine had the right connections and knew how to write and market such a series. Levine talked the *Saturday Evening Post* into buying up to eight articles written with Krivitsky at a rate of five thousand dollars per article.

In the end, five articles were published in 1939 at the cost of great nervous strain for all involved. Levine knew what an American mass-circulation magazine wanted, but Krivitsky did not. Levine personalized and dramatized, providing details to whet the reader's appetite; Krivitsky wanted to generalize and theorize, in the turgid style of European academic journals. So they quarreled and parted company, although Krivitsky had most of his financial problems solved for some time to come from the proceeds of the articles.

But the articles also brought Krivitsky into a prominence that he had not sought and really wished to avoid. Although his sensational disclosures won him a wide audience, he became persona non grata to many people who wished to focus the hostility of the American people on Hitler and fascism. Krivitsky's denunciation of Stalin was therefore unwelcome to those influential elements who continued to view Stalin as a potential ally against Hitler.

The enemies that Krivitsky inadvertently made in the United States launched a counterattack against him. Persuading congressmen to demand information as to how he could have been admitted to the United States, they succeeded in getting the Immigration Service to begin deportation proceedings against him in July 1939. In despair, Krivitsky went to Louis Waldman, who had twice run for governor of New York on the Socialist ticket and won fame as a labor lawyer. With Waldman's help, the deportation order was dropped.

Nevertheless, Krivitsky was shaken by these developments. He also worried when he came under pressure from congressional committees and grand juries to provide evidence about Soviet espionage. Krivitsky was willing to testify about certain matters—particularly those exposing Stalinism—but was still loyal to his old colleagues and reluctant to expose the agents he knew. On other occasions, he discovered that the information he had provided became known to the Soviet side within a day or two. Such experiences made him still more reluctant to provide any sensitive information.

But on at least one occasion Krivitsky provided information of exceptional value. He told Levine in strict confidence about two Soviet spies—"moles"—who had gained access to England's greatest secrets. "One of them was a code clerk in the secretariat of the Cabinet," Levine related. "Krivitsky knew only his last name, King.

The other was on the inside of the Council of Imperial Defense. Krivitsky could describe his appearance, he knew something of his background, but did not know his name. Subsequently it appeared that this individual strongly resembled Donald Maclean. He and his friend Guy Burgess were later exposed as spies and fled to the Soviet Union."[28]

Worried that vital secrets shared with Britain might be passed on by Moscow to the Nazis, Krivitsky arranged to see Lord Lothian, the British ambassador in Washington, who was at first skeptical about Krivitsky's information. When Lothian checked with London, however, it developed that a man named King did indeed work in the Cabinet's code room, and further investigation established that he was a Soviet agent.

The British were so impressed that they invited Krivitsky to England. Krivitsky was hesitant about accepting the invitation. He had once entered the country illegally and carried out an intelligence mission there, and he feared that the British would bring charges against him. Moreover, he suspected that Prime Minister Chamberlain might make a deal with Stalin and turn him over to the Russians as an additional bonus. After assurances were received concerning his safety, including protection against Soviet reprisals, Krivitsky finally agreed and departed for England in December 1939.

The assistance he gave the authorities in London led to arrests all over England. The British government invited him to stay in England, but he still hoped to find a safer haven in the United States.

In January 1941, two months after his return, Krivitsky received an ominous warning from Paul Wohl; Hans Bruesse, Krivitsky's former assistant and closest colleague, had been seen boarding a bus in New York City. Since Bruesse had already participated in two attempts to kill or kidnap him, Krivitsky immediately concluded that there could be only one explanation for his presence in the United States.

Now Krivitsky grew very anxious to obtain a gun, which he said he needed for self-protection. Somehow he found out that he could purchase one in Virginia without a permit. He had this in the back of his mind before he came up with another reason for a trip there.

Eitel and Marguerite Dobert, refugees from Nazi Germany, had become very friendly with the Krivitskys soon after their arrival in

America. The Doberts then moved to Virginia, where they purchased a farm outside Charlottesville, struggling to establish themselves in this rural world. Dobert had also become a lecturer at the
University of Virginia. All of this appealed to Krivitsky, at least at a
distance, and he talked of buying a half-interest in the farm and
moving there with his wife and six-year-old son.

The visit to the Doberts was not a success. They remained as
friendly as ever, but it became more and more evident to them,
even as Krivitsky spoke with enthusiasm about life on the farm, that
he was totally unsuited to the atmosphere and had no aptitude for
the physical labor that a farm entailed. The Doberts made no effort
to discourage him, but they must have found it hard to conceal
their misgivings.

Nevertheless, Krivitsky did not tire that evening of talking about
the farm, questioning them about all the details—the costs involved, the work that had to be done, the possibilities for future
development. As soon as his wife saw the farm, he said, they would
come to a firm agreement.

Finally they all went to bed, but before long Krivitsky knocked
on the Doberts' bedroom door, saying he could not sleep. Marguerite Dobert gave him aspirins and writing paper—he wanted to
write some letters, he said—and went back to bed.

But Krivitsky still did not sleep. He told them the next morning
that, after writing letters, he left the house and walked in the woods.
He praised the peace and quiet in the countryside, yet what he was
obviously seeking was peace of mind. To his hosts, he looked as
nervous and tense as always.

The next day Marguerite drove Krivitsky into Charlottesville,
where he went into a hardware store and bought a .38 automatic.
For some reason, the clerk sold him 130-grain mushroom bullets
with a scooped head designed to make a larger wound.

At the end of his visit on Sunday, Marguerite drove Krivitsky to
Washington, where he intended to catch a train to New York. As
they were parting at Union Station, Marguerite asked if he wanted
her to mail the letters he had written at the farm. He said that he
would take care of them himself. She also inquired whether he still
had his "artillery." He patted the canvas bag that constituted his
only luggage and said that it was all in there. Krivitsky asked a
question of his own. Did she know whether there was any place, as

in European railroad stations, where one could bathe? The farm had no running water, and he wished to clean up before taking the train to New York.

Later, Marguerite Dobert was sure that Krivitsky had not indicated any intention of not proceeding directly to New York. Only once during the drive had he said anything out of the ordinary. "If anything happens to me, look after Alex and Tonya." Marguerite replied, "Don't be silly, Walter. Nothing will happen to you."[29]

But Krivitsky did not take a train from Union Station, as he supposedly intended. After he parted from Marguerite Dobert, he walked the short distance from Union Station to the Bellevue Hotel at 15 E Street N.W. At 5:49 P.M. Sunday afternoon Krivitsky signed the hotel register as "Walter Poref"—the name, according to his attorney, he proposed to adopt legally in the United States—and was assigned Room 532.

The bellboy, Randolph Thompson, saw Krivitsky between 6:30 and 7 P.M. that evening, when he brought a bottle of club soda to his room. Krivitsky gave him a dollar bill in payment; Thompson went downstairs and returned a few minutes later with the change. So far as any of the employees knew, "Mr. Poref" did not leave his room. Hotel records showed that he had made no telephone calls during his stay. No one knew of any visitors or incoming calls, although the hotel was large enough that they would not necessarily attract attention.

At 9:30 the next morning, after knocking on the door several times without any reply, the maid, Thelma Jackson, opened the door with a passkey and went in.

Krivitsky was lying with his feet at the head of the bed, fully dressed except for jacket and shoes. The maid asked what time she should come back to clean the room. The man did not answer.

A half hour later the maid told the police sergeant, "So I walked on over to the bed and looked and I saw he had blood all over his head. . . . Then I saw he wasn't breathing. . . ."[30]

A mushroom bullet of the type sold to Krivitsky in Charlottesville had blown his brains out. Fired at close range, it had entered his right temple and, after tearing through his brain, had exited below the left ear, where it left a hole into which a small fist could have been inserted. The bullet was gone, lost somewhere in the wall. A .38 automatic—the same gun, it was subsequently established, purchased by Krivitsky—lay nearby, thickly encrusted with blood. Yet no one in the hotel had reported hearing a shot, although death had taken place, according to the police surgeon, at about 4 A.M., at which hour there were few outside noises to muffle the sound. Moreover, no silencer had been found.

To Detective Sergeant D. L. Guest, it appeared to be a typical case of suicide. He attributed little significance to the fact that no one reported hearing a shot. At that hour the rumble of a passing truck, the siren of a police car or ambulance, or the noise of a train entering or leaving the nearby station—any of these sounds could have smothered the report of the gun. The dead man, who had neatly hung up his jacket and placed his shoes beside the bed, resembled many other suicides Guest had seen.

It came as no surprise to the police that a formal affidavit in Krivitsky's pocket identified him as Samuel Ginsberg, born in Russia in 1899. Many people who killed themselves in hotel rooms registered under false names. True, some of them destroyed all their personal papers; but others went no further than the false registration, intent only on hiding their identities up to the moment of suicide.

According to the police, the door had been locked. But it was not an automatic lock, and the maid did not remember whether the door had actually been locked. In any case, the lock was flimsy and could easily have been picked.

The only window in the room was open a few inches from the bottom. There was no ledge or fire escape. Nor was there any sign of a struggle. The room had not been ransacked, and Krivitsky's wallet remained in his pocket.

Based on these indicators, the police viewed it as a routine case of suicide, and no additional attempts at investigation were made. Detective Sergeant Guest completed the possession and identity checks, sent for the morgue wagon, and allowed the hotel staff to clean up the room.

The three letters left behind by the dead man were taken as further, though superfluous, evidence of suicide.

The letter in English, written in a handwriting that matched the signature on the hotel register, was addressed to Louis Waldman, New York City. When Waldman received the news, he concluded at once that Krivitsky had been murdered. On more than one occasion Krivitsky had told him, "If ever I am found dead and it looks like an accident or suicide, don't believe it. They are after me. They have tried before."[31] He flew to Washington and demanded an FBI investigation. This demand was promptly rejected. Then he asked to see the homicide division's file on the case. This request, too, was turned down.

Aside from Krivitsky's friends, other prominent people expressed the belief that he had been murdered. Alexander Kerensky, prime minister of the provisional government established after the revolution, said in New York, "I am sure it was murder. . . . If it was not a murder, then it was a suicide provoked by a direct menace. I understand that they had been menacing his son, whom he loved dearly."

Mrs. Leon Trotsky, widow of the revolutionary leader murdered by a KGB assassin the previous summer, spoke out without hesitation: "Krivitsky's death was not a suicide. That suicide theory is just one of the OGPU's many schemes to attempt to cover up its murders."[32]

The letters found in Krivitsky's room were written in his handwriting on stationery bearing the printed address of Charlottesville, Virginia. Marguerite Dobert identified the stationery as the same letter paper she had given him on the farm.

The letter to Louis Waldman read:

Dear Mr. Waldman:
  My wife and my boy will need your help. Please do for them what you can.
                                                    Walter Krivitsky
  P.S. I went to Virginia because I knew there I can get a gun. If my friends should have any trouble, please help them, they did not know why I bought the gun.

Krivitsky addressed the note in Russian to his wife and son:

Dear Tonya and Alek:
  It is very difficult, although I want very much to live, but to live is no longer allowed me. I love you, my only one. It is difficult for me to write, but think about me and then you will understand that I must go. Don't tell Alek yet where his father has gone. I believe that in time you will tell him because it is best for him. Forgive, it is very hard to write. Take care of him and be a good mother to him and be always

quiet and never get angry at him. He is very good and always very pale. Good people will help you, but not enemies. I think my sins are great. I see you, Tonya and Alek. I embrace you.

Vela

P.S. On the farm of the Doberts I wrote this yesterday, but I did not have any strength in New York. I did not have any business in Washington. I went to see the Doberts because that is the only place I could get the firearm.

The letter in German was written to Suzanne La Follette, a New York editor with whom Krivitsky had remained friendly:

Dear Suzanne:

I trust that you are well, and I am dying with the hope that you will help Tonya and my poor boy. You were a friend.

Yours,
Walter

P.S. I also think about your brother and Dorothy.[33]

Krivitsky's death was front-page news in New York and Washington, and the Hearst press continued to cover the story prominently for weeks afterward.

Almost immediately charges of bungling and ineptitude on the part of the Washington police surfaced. Most of these charges were based on the routine handling of the case before the dead man's prominence became known. No effort had been made to determine the trajectory of the bullet or to check the room for fingerprints. By the time the police reopened the investigation, the gun had been wiped clean to get rid of the blood.

The police questioned some of the hotel employees—the manager, the maid, the housekeeper, and the bellboy—but apparently did not locate any of the hotel guests. They established that a shell found on the floor had been fired from Krivitsky's .38 automatic, but they never recovered the fatal bullet.

It was certain only that Krivitsky's brains had been blown out, that one shot had been fired, and that the death wound was inflicted by a bullet of the same type he had purchased in Charlottesville. It could not be determined whether the .38 had been the weapon used to kill him and whose finger had pulled the trigger.

Nevertheless, the police were satisfied with the original finding of suicide. They thought that all the circumstances, including the notes in Krivitsky's own handwriting, spoke for themselves and left no doubt, despite widespread criticism of their handling of the case.

Notwithstanding the furor surrounding this affair, it should be acknowledged at the outset that the Washington police were probably right. Only those who closed their eyes to the circumstances and insisted on a more sinister explanation could continue to deny the probability of suicide in his case.

Krivitsky's death must be viewed against the background of his life at the time. He had managed to quarrel with or alienate most of his benefactors and allies, and felt embattled and alone in an environment that he saw as implacably hostile. Not only a sizable segment of the American public but also the government itself seemed deaf to his warnings about Stalinism, including the conspiratorial aspects about which he was so well informed.

Still clinging to a faint hope, Krivitsky had tried to convince the Doberts, as well as himself, that he could be a full partner on the farm and adjust to this unfamiliar environment. Yet even while continuing to talk enthusiastically about the idea, he must have read the doubt written on the Doberts' faces and recognized the same doubt in his own heart. By the time Marguerite Dobert drove him back to Washington, he had probably mentally abandoned the project.

And all he had in prospect, on that coming Monday, was another futile appearance before a committee where he would be pressed for additional information. Yes, he could put off his interrogators with trivial or insignificant facts, but he feared that in time it would become more and more difficult to limit his disclosures, to keep from betraying colleagues and agents to whom he was still bound by long-standing ties of friendship and loyalty. Ever since his defection he had held back this kind of information, which was often the most important, revealing only information that discredited Stalin. The agents he betrayed in England were people in whom he had no personal interest.

Once when he was walking on the Long Island seashore with David Shub, the father of Boris, who collaborated with him on his book, he kept talking about the dangers he faced.

Wishing to ease Krivitsky's mind, Shub said: "But why should you still be afraid? Why should Stalin be after you now? After all, you've already told everything and nothing further can make a difference."

"Oh, no," said Krivitsky. "I haven't told the most important."[34]

Tormented by doubt and fear, suicide probably appeared to be the only answer for Krivitsky. At one blow he would free himself from his private hell and simultaneously protect his wife and child, who would no longer be menaced by the KGB and could rely on help from his friends.

Marguerite Dobert's testimony affords a strong indication that Krivitsky was already seriously contemplating suicide after talking so long and enthusiastically about buying a share in the farm, since it was then that he apparently wrote the notes found afterward. But neither the writing of the notes nor the purchase of the gun represented an irrevocable decision. If he had changed his mind, he could have destroyed the notes and kept the gun for self-protection, as he had proposed to do several times. But both actions show the direction in which he was leaning.

If Krivitsky had seen someone he feared at Union Station and decided to hide out in the hotel, he must have had ample time and opportunity to get in touch with the police or telephone a friend. Yet he did no such thing. It seems highly unlikely, however, that a man who feared an impending attempt on his life would have failed to seek help from somebody.

The unavoidable assumption is that Krivitsky rented the room with the idea of committing suicide there. He had the three notes in his pocket and the gun and ammunition purchased only the day before in his canvas bag. Even then he may not have reached a final decision. From the time he checked into the hotel until the lethal shot was fired ten hours later he could have been wrestling with this decision—if not, it is difficult to know why he waited so long. The rental of the room provided him with the time and solitude he needed to reach a final decision.

Police ineptitude made it impossible to establish with certainty what happened in the final minutes or seconds of this tragedy. Nevertheless, there can be no doubt that, if Krivitsky had decided to take his own life, he had the means at hand to do so. Not that the KGB would not have killed him if it could. Krivitsky simply beat them to it.

Regardless of the facts, the Krivitsky case afforded Communists and anti-Communists alike the opportunity to air publicly all the rage and suspicion they wished to direct at their enemies. The left-wing press found itself split between those who viewed Hitler as the devil incarnate and those who saw Stalin in that role. By taking sides in the Krivitsky case—for or against suicide, for or against a KGB assassination—they sought to justify their own political positions.

The anti-Communist press created a furor for a few days, editorializing on the subject of other KGB assassinations with Krivitsky's case as a peg. Publications with strongly leftist editorial policies derided the idea that Krivitsky could have been a victim of KGB assassination.

Nevertheless, the Krivitsky case was soon overshadowed by much greater events. The clamor subsided and Krivitsky was forgotten by almost everybody except his wife and son. Tonya Krivitsky adopted a new name and, in subsequent years, endured great hardships while she cared for her son. Alexander also adopted another name and eventually became an engineer.

In any suicide the guilt can rarely be assigned exclusively to one party. And in seeking to apportion the guilt for Krivitsky's suicide, the same can be said. Certainly the U.S. government and the authorities with whom he had to deal, despite their willingness to grant him asylum, regarded him with varying degrees of indifference, discomfiture, and, at times, outright hostility. Many segments of the American public accorded him a hysterical and hateful reception. All in all, however, the primary guilt for this death lay with the system he had served so long and faithfully—a system already responsible for millions of deaths that now wanted his as well.

Krivitsky's widow was not far from the truth when she told reporters, "I believe the letter [to her] was written under coercion. The OGPU had threatened that they would kidnap or harm me and our child unless he did what they directed—kill himself. He made this bargain because of his great love for us. But he was murdered in this fashion just as surely as though they had pulled the trigger of the gun."[35]

6

A Man Who Could
Do Everything

THE SOVIET SPY who will be remembered even in his own country as Colonel Rudolf Ivanovich Abel adopted that name on a dusty, still, hot Tuesday, June 25, 1957, in the town of McAllen, Texas. It was a critical moment in his life.

He had found himself in the Alien Detention Facility, situated in country as flat as the top of a billiard table only a few miles from the Mexican border. Most of the other prisoners were Mexican farm workers who had illegally crossed the border in search of work. Like the Mexicans, he had been charged with illegal entry. But there was one significant difference: he had not crossed the border from Mexico.

He knew, of course, that the charge of illegal entry merely amounted to a pretext for holding him while they decided what to do with him. His captors had no idea that he would be spending his fifty-fourth birthday in prison; nor did they know his true name, date and place of birth, or anything else about his real origin, other than the fact that he came from the Soviet Union.

But the American authorities had no doubt that he was the highest-ranking Soviet spy ever caught in the United States. They had been told that he held the rank of colonel, and from this some

131

people erroneously inferred that he belonged to Military Intelligence and was a military man. Neither was true.

After refusing to answer questions, the captured Soviet spy had changed his tactics. He concocted a story and decided to make a statement. "My real name," he told the authorities in McAllen, "is Rudolf Ivanovich Abel. I am a Soviet citizen. I found by accident a large sum of American dollars in a ruined blockhouse in Russia. That gave me the idea of leaving the country. I succeeded in crossing the border and made my way to Denmark, where I bought a forged American passport. With this passport, I entered the United States from Canada in 1948."[1]

He was lying—but not about everything. The real Rudolf Ivanovich Abel had been a close friend in the KGB, a former Latvian sailor and Red Guard.[2] Their friendship belonged to the past. The real Abel was interred in the German Cemetery in Moscow.

If the bogus Abel's life as a Soviet spy was unusual, his origins could be considered equally remarkable.

It was possible to say that everything had begun in England. On the other hand, one could have gone even further back in search of the beginning. But in reality, there is no beginning or end to anything. In looking back, all he could do was try to find out when or where the chain of events became inevitable.

The man who called himself Abel was born William August Fisher[3] in Newcastle upon Tyne on July 11, 1903, the son of Russian immigrants, although both of his father's parents had emigrated to Russia from Germany. His father, Genrikh (Henry) Matveyevich Fischer (Fisher) had belonged to the tiny and ultimately select group of professional revolutionaries known after the establishment of the Soviet regime as Old Bolsheviks. His mother, Lyubov Vasilyevna Karneyeva, was a midwife by profession.

In 1900, while Lenin was leaving Siberian exile to go abroad, Henry Fisher immigrated to England. The move reflected a general conviction among Socialists that, in view of police repression in Russia, more could be accomplished if they strengthened their base abroad.

Moreover there already existed a colony of some thirty thousand Russian emigrés in London.

After settling in Newcastle, close to the Scottish border, Henry Fisher became one of the conspirators who helped Lenin smuggle the revolutionary newspaper *Iskra* [*The Spark*] into Russia. He later became one of the leaders in smuggling arms not only from Newcastle but also from Blyth and Sunderland aboard Russian ships that called at those ports.

Young Willy Fisher, the Abel-to-be, attended school, played football, and outwardly engaged in all the pastimes of a boy of his age. Yet it was impossible for any member of the family to remain unaware of the elder Fisher's single-minded absorption in underground party work or to live apart from it. Except for contacts with party comrades, the Fishers existed in an insulated world of their own, and Willy soon found that there was a barrier between himself and other young people.

When did William Fisher take the first step that led to his becoming Colonel Rudolf Ivanovich Abel? Could it have been as a boy, when he was first drawn into his father's clandestine work and felt most strongly his dedication, resourcefulness, energy, and complete devotion to the party?

There is no definitive answer to this question. Even William Fisher, reflecting on his life in his last years, probably could not have answered with any degree of certainty. Had he not gone to work for the INO (the OGPU's Foreign Department, predecessor of the KGB's First Main Administration) when he did, he told a friend at the end of his life, "I would be an artist today . . . a member of the Academy."[4]

Willy Fisher was about to enter his teens when World War I began. It was not a pleasant time for the Fishers, who were regarded as Germans, and Willy must have been very uncomfortable among his schoolmates, listening to the atrocity stories that filled the press and circulated by word of mouth after the brutal German invasion of Belgium. Ironically, his father, who considered himself a Russian and missed no opportunity to serve the revolutionary cause in Russia, suffered much of the opprobrium directed at enemy aliens.

During his school years, Willy cared less for study than for helping his father in clandestine political activities or propaganda work.

The only subject in which he excelled was mathematics, which fascinated him from the beginning. But he could scarcely wait to get outside the school walls and join his father in distributing antiwar leaflets at the gates of factories or on the docks. The message never varied: Workers everywhere should refuse to fight because the war was being waged by imperialist powers over colonies, for the conquest of foreign territory that brought only profits to capitalists and further impoverished the workers—those among them who were fortunate enough to survive the war. If forced to carry arms, the workers should turn them against their oppressors.

A new phase in the family's activities began in November 1917, when the Bolsheviks seized power. Then the Allies' stern disapproval of the Soviet regime and their scarcely concealed support of Russian anti-Bolshevik groups, as well as threats of military intervention, spurred Henry Fisher and his friends into action. They formed a "Hands Off Russia" movement, and soon Willy was helping to distribute leaflets and participating in street-corner meetings that attracted attentive listeners as well as boisterous hecklers.

As he approached maturity during his last years in England, Willy was a shy, modest youth who had little to do with people his own age. The opposite sex was a mystery to him. He shared his father's ideals, as they were later echoed by John Reed, the American reporter whose ashes were interred in the Kremlin wall. "It is still fashionable . . . to speak of the Bolshevik insurrection as an 'adventure.' Adventure it was, and one of the most marvelous mankind ever embarked upon, sweeping into history at the head of the toiling masses, and staking everything on their vast and simple desires."[5]

The adventure of which Reed spoke had an irresistible attraction for the Fishers. Henry Fisher conducted a long correspondence with friends in Moscow who encouraged him to return to Russia. In 1921 the family departed from England and, on their arrival in revolutionary Russia, went to live in the Kremlin itself, in close proximity to the rulers of the new Soviet state.

Living in the Kremlin while they waited for permanent quarters, the Fishers had little awareness of conditions in the country as a whole, ravaged, as it was, by revolution and civil war. Even in Moscow, they knew next to nothing about the lives of average Muscovites. They ate most of their meals in a common dining room, where they occasionally caught glimpses of Lenin, Trotsky, and Bukharin. Their other needs were satisfied without any effort on their part, and the people with whom they came in contact were equally or more privileged.

Henry Fisher was hoping for an important post in the government—not entirely unrealistically, for Lenin was known for his haphazard recruitment of individuals for top jobs—but weeks passed without any decision being reached. None of the jobs offered to him seemed suitable, and while continuing to wait, he busied himself with the project of his memoirs, which he had resolved to write.

Meanwhile Willy went to a special school for English-speaking students that had a full curriculum based on the Soviet system but where there was daily instruction in the Russian language. Although he had grown up hearing Russian spoken at home in England, he had never received any formal Russian-language instruction. His native language was English. He could not easily accustom himself to a situation in which he would be expected to speak Russian in all his activities, eager as he was to become a full-fledged citizen of his new homeland. His problem with the Russian language would remain with him all his life. While he eventually learned to speak and write Russian fluently, he never acquired native facility and always had a slight accent.

In his first years in the USSR, it was essential for him to study Russian in order to enter one of Moscow's higher educational institutions. His companions during this period were English and American young people who, like himself, belonged to Communist families that had emigrated to Russia after the revolution.

Nevertheless, Fisher's associations were not limited to young people in this category. Inevitably, he made the acquaintance of his father's comrades from long ago, the Old Bolsheviks.

"All of my memories of childhood," he said later in a magazine interview, "are connected with Old Bolsheviks, revolutionaries. . . . I particularly liked the aura of mystery and adventure surrounding them. They were idealistic, unselfish, and honorable."[6]

Soon after beginning his studies in the special school, Fisher left his family's temporary home in the Kremlin and moved into a student house, where he shared a room with three other students. Some of his new friends were tremendously attracted to the new technical wonder of radio, and soon he was infected by their enthusiasm. In 1966 he wrote:

> In our free time many of us diverted ourselves as radio amateurs. That was the time of detector receivers, spark transmitters—we only heard of radiotelephony as something that was in its infancy. It would be hard for today's youth to conceive of the inventiveness of amateurs of that time. We obtained the wire for coils by removing it from old apartment doorbells that did not work. We found the crystals used for detectors in rocks or in geological collections. The condensers for tuning were of all sizes and shapes. I remember how I managed in 1923 to obtain an R-5 lamp that took an incredible amount of energy to heat up. I remember how we had to improvise to make the wet cells feed this lamp, which shone while in use no worse than any good burner.[7]

Although Fisher possessed some talent for drawing and was already beginning to experiment with color, he was aware that the times called for a different kind of education. His enthusiasm for radio aroused a desire to study radio technology, and as soon as he had progressed far enough in his knowledge of Russian he secured admission to an institute where he enrolled in this discipline. In all his decisions at that time he was motivated by a determination to mold himself in such a way that he could serve the Soviet state and, ultimately, the cause of international communism.

In 1922 he applied for membership in the Komsomol, the Communist Party's youth organization. He was required to appear before some representatives of the local Komsomol organization to answer questions designed to elicit his knowledge of the Komsomol and dedication to its principles. When these representatives voted unanimously to accept him, the application was forwarded to the Komsomol committee of the area of Moscow in which he lived.

Summoned to appear there, Fisher was informed that his membership had been approved. After urging him to appreciate this honor and to justify the confidence thus placed in him by his future efforts, the secretary presented to him the dark gray membership booklet.

In reply, young Willy Fisher solemnly said, "I'll do my utmost to increase my knowledge of the works of Marx, Engels, and Lenin and to spread this knowledge among Soviet young people. I'll also do everything in my power to carry out the decisions of the Party and its Central Committee."

When the secretary nodded encouragingly, Willy added with the same solemnity, "I will always be ready to give all my strength and, if need be, my life in defense of the Socialist motherland."

It was a vow he would often have reason to recall.

When William Fisher decided to become a radio engineer, he had no thought of going into Intelligence work. This was not surprising, since the idea had not yet occurred to anyone that radio communications could be important in espionage.

"In my work as an Intelligence officer," he said many years later, "a knowledge of photography and radio technology, the ability to draw, and so forth have served me well."[8] On the same occasion he noted that he had also used such covers as draftsman, radio engineer, translator, photographer, and artist.

After passing his final examination and being qualified as a radio engineer, Fisher was required to work in the same field in order to recompense the government for its investment in his education. He found a job in a plant that produced radio components, while continuing his studies at night, concentrating on science, physics, and higher mathematics.

When, after a series of strokes, Lenin died on January 21, 1924, William Fisher, who had heard so much about the founder of the Soviet state from his father, felt as if he had lost his own father. For weeks afterward, he went around in a daze, scarcely able to reconcile himself to the fact that the Soviet state would have to go on without Lenin.

Later that year he was called up for military service. He served in a detached radiotelegraph battalion of the Soviet Army. During his military service, like many other men, he established lifelong friendships.

He was demobilized in the winter of 1926 and immediately faced a decision on his future. "I had two offers—a scientific research institute and the OGPU's Foreign Department," he wrote. "I was attracted by radio technology as well as by the romance of espionage. Comrades argued that my knowledge of foreign languages must be used in the service of the motherland. Finally the decision was made, and I became a Chekist on May 2, 1927."[9]

Was it really that simple? Hardly. No less an authority than V.

Drozdov, a major general of the KGB, spoke about Fisher's excellent command of French, English, and German and noted:

> These and other capabilities of Abel as well as his active participation in the Komsomol were probably the reason why the Komsomol recommended him in 1927 for work in the organs of state security. It must be said that Abel himself reacted to this without any enthusiasm, as he was interested above all in radio technology and dreamed of a scientific career. But, like a disciplined Komsomol member, he did not refuse the new appointment.[10]

It is a safe assumption that the OGPU had kept an eye on William Fisher for some time. His native command of English, long residence in England, and possession of a valid British passport recommended him for espionage work in English-speaking countries. His knowledge of French and German was adequate if not exceptional. Apart from all that, his background indicated that he was politically reliable.

Still, he had hesitated about entering such a career without, perhaps, having a clear idea of the root causes of that vacillation. He had been in Soviet Russia long enough to know that the "organs of state security" evoked fear and revulsion in the population. He certainly did not wish to become involved in the OGPU's bloody actions on behalf of internal security, even if they were directed against "enemies" of the Soviet state. On the other hand, he had no doubt that there were powerful enemies abroad who threatened Soviet Russia's existence and was prepared to work against them.

While he was still hesitating, Henry Fisher intervened forcefully and told his son to forget his own wishes and accept the OGPU's offer. Willy could not explain to his father why he hesitated. A feeling that came from deep in his nature told him he wanted to do something else with his life. Yet he could not bring himself to reject his father's advice.

Subjected to pressure on all sides—from the "talent scouts" of the OGPU, most of his friends, and now his father—he yielded at last, failing to realize until much later what this decision would cost.

In the years to come, he confined himself to a remark he often repeated to intimates. "You don't leave the 'organs.' "[11] The most that could be hoped for was that one day the "organs of state security" would leave you.

William Fisher became a Chekist only nine months after the death of Felix Dzerzhinsky, the father of the Cheka, and many of Dzerzhinsky's old colleagues were his teachers. It was a time of transition for the Cheka, or OGPU, as it had been renamed, not only because of Dzerzhinsky's death, but also because Stalin had virtually eliminated his other rivals since then and was, in 1927, consolidating his grip on State Security.

Dzerzhinsky's nominal successor was V. R. Menzhinsky, but the real power in the Cheka was exercised by Stalin's own man, Yagoda, nominally Menzhinsky's deputy. Presumably at Stalin's behest, Yagoda was gradually getting rid of or shunting aside the old guard that had surrounded Dzerzhinsky and placing new men loyal to him in most of the key positions.

The Cheka possessed certain significant advantages in its foreign operations. First of all, it benefited from the Russian conspiratorial tradition and suspicion of foreigners, from whom it sought to hide even the most inconsequential facts. Aside from the ingrained secretiveness of Russians, particularly those officials who came into contact with foreigners, the protracted duel between Czarist secret police (Okhrana) and the anti-Czarist underground in the nineteenth century employed clandestine tactics on both sides. Thus the Cheka that came into being after the Bolshevik coup d'état could draw on experienced conspirators from the old secret police as well as the Communist and Social Revolutionary underground for its own personnel. In fact, the Cheka was virtually without peer among secret Intelligence services, with the possible exception of Britain's M-I6, which could also draw on a long tradition of espionage. Finally, in any struggle involving Russian emigration, the Cheka possessed an obvious advantage over its opponents. It could easily place its own agents among the emigrés or exploit their longing for their homeland and relatives in order to recruit them. To those living in difficult circumstances abroad, it could also hold out the hope of future material inducements at home.

When William Fisher joined the Cheka, it was still directing most of its efforts at the emigration. Its aims were twofold: to deny the emigration to foreign enemies as a potential menace to the Soviet state and to induce large numbers of emigrés to return to Russia as a means of bringing about the emigration's moral disintegration while weakening its influence as a potential counterforce.

In addition to violence, the KGB was also willing to use the "soft" approach in order to achieve its second aim. Organizing a campaign for "return to the homeland," it sent emissaries abroad to argue that the regime wished to bring about a reconciliation with the emigrés and enlist their help in the reconstruction. "The history of Russia," they asserted, "is being made *there*, and not here." The emissaries directed their efforts at selected targets among the leaders of the emigration, such as the novelist Aleksei Tolstoy (distantly related to the great Tolstoy), who soon announced that he was returning.

Soviet State Security was good at assessing the strengths and weaknesses of its own personnel. William Fisher could not by any stretch of the imagination be seen as a gifted practitioner of strong-arm methods. Before long he was to be given a special assignment involving the KGB's second aim and employing the "soft" approach.

Like most major secret Intelligence services, the KGB, as the Cheka came to be known, subjected new recruits like William Fisher to intensive training before assigning them to active work. Willy went through a course in which he was taught the fundamentals of espionage tradecraft: recruitment, assessment, and handling of agents; conspiratorial meetings, including recognition and danger signals; detecting and throwing off hostile surveillance; selection and use of dead drops with appropriate signals; use of cutouts (go-betweens for agent and spy); surveillance of targets; audio surveillance; radio communications; secret writing; photography; and opening locks and sealed envelopes. For more specialized trainees, excluding Willy, there were the techniques of armed combat—the use of firearms, knives, and other weapons, jujitsu, and the use of poisons.

His instructors were pleased with him. They were all hard-bitten veterans, some of whom had served prison sentences, and were not easily satisfied. But they found him an apt pupil, highly intelligent, serious, and attentive. Most of all, they valued his cleverness with his hands. In anything that required manual dexterity, he was head and shoulders above the other students. He only needed to be shown something once; thereafter it was as if he had been doing it all his life.

Among Willy's fellow students at the KGB training school was a rather forthright, simple fellow named Rudolf Ivanovich Abel.[12]

When Fisher finished training, he was temporarily employed in the KGB's headquarters in the Lubyanka while he awaited a more permanent assignment. He worked in the Illegals Administration, under which, as it developed, he would actually spend most of his career.

As the name suggested, the Illegals Administration had the task of placing "illegal" residents in foreign countries. From the "illegal's" point of view, it meant that he had to survive in isolation, dependent to a large extent on his own wits, self-reliance, and self-control.

At that time William Fisher did not dream that this was the fate that lay in store for him. There were few KGB officers, however, who possessed native fluency in a foreign language and had lived as a citizen of a foreign country. These qualities set him apart from his new colleagues and marked him as a natural candidate for an "illegal."

Yet the chiefs of the KGB's foreign espionage operations were reluctant to acknowledge that they depended so heavily, in terms of language, on officers under deep cover like William Fisher, who had been born and spent his early life in England.

Sometime during his initial service at the OGPU headquarters in Moscow, William Fisher met a music student named Elena Stepanovna Lebedeva. She was three years younger, blonde, and petite, and was studying the harp at the conservatory. They went to concerts and visited art galleries together, not only sharing these cultural interests but finding a mutual sympathy that gradually drew them closer.

Soon she introduced him to her mother and older sister. Once he decided that he wanted to marry her, he probably informed his superiors in the KGB, who proceeded to check the record of Elena Stepanovna and her family in the files of the secret police. Presumably no problem arose.

After the wedding, they did not live together very long. Willy received a foreign assignment as an "illegal" and had to leave his new wife at home—the first of many separations that they were forced to endure.

"If we told some stranger," Elena Stepanovna wrote Willy when he was working under deep cover as an "illegal" resident in the United States, "that a wife and a husband could live apart for so many years and still love each other and wait for their reunion, he would not believe us. It is natural only for novels."[13]

The microfilm of her letter reached William Fisher through a dead drop filled by a Soviet courier.

William Fisher was something of an anomaly as an "illegal" on his first mission abroad for Soviet Intelligence. After all, he returned to England under his true name with his own British passport. The British government could only consider his presence in the country entirely legal. Nevertheless, from the Soviet government's point of view, Fisher was a Soviet citizen, an officer of State Security engaged in a mission on behalf of his "real" country, the USSR.

When Willy went abroad on this first mission, he met his boss, Alexander Orlov, in France and traveled with him to England. Later, accompanying Orlov to conspiratorial meetings in pubs, Willy reluctantly came to the conclusion that his new boss behaved stupidly as a clandestine operator.[14]

Always reticent about his affairs, and particularly security-conscious about operations in which he had been involved, Fisher said very little about his activities in England. He hinted, however, about his dealings with the noted Russian physicist Peter Kapitsa.

Kapitsa arrived in England in 1921, the same year Fisher went to Russia. Although he was not a political emigré—he never asked for asylum—he worked in Cambridge for the next fourteen years. In 1935 he attended a scientific conference in Moscow and was denied an exit visa by the Soviet government. There was an uproar among Western scientists, to which the Soviet Embassy in London responded: "As a result of the extraordinary development of the national economy of the USSR the number of scientific workers does not suffice."[15] Kapitsa had no choice but to remain in the Soviet Union. From then on he worked in Moscow's Institute of

Physics. Kapitsa ultimately helped to lay the theoretical ground-work for the USSR's development of the atom bomb, although he did not work on the bomb itself.

What was the nature of Fisher's connection with Kapitsa in England? It is known that Moscow had been trying for some time through various emissaries to persuade Kapitsa to return to the Soviet Union. In view of the high regard in which he was held and the excellent facilities he commanded in Cambridge, as well as the insecurity in Russia faced by all Soviet citizens, scientists not excluded, Kapitsa had good reason to hesitate.

Under the circumstances, it would have been logical to place Willy Fisher in contact with Kapitsa. Fisher was young, but not so young that Kapitsa would have been unwilling to listen to him. Fisher was an engineer by profession, knowledgeable about physics and, therefore, able to discuss the subject intelligently, even though Kapitsa would hardly have regarded him as a colleague. As a British subject who had just returned to England after working in Russia, he could provide Kapitsa with interesting information about conditions there, information that would seem less colored by political prejudice or other subjective considerations coming from an Englishman rather than a fellow Russian.

Fisher did not claim that he persuaded Kapitsa to return to Russia, but his comments could have convinced Kapitsa that conditions in Russia had improved and that he would have nothing to fear if he traveled to the USSR. Kapitsa's fateful trip did not occur until several years later anyway, and other Soviet emissaries might have also influenced his decision.

By that time Fisher was working for Soviet intelligence elsewhere.

Like his father and his father's oldest friends, William Fisher sought no benefit for himself and was indifferent to his surroundings or material acquisitions. Those few comforts that he did enjoy cost little or nothing, such as his family circle, the company of his friends, visiting art galleries or painting his own pictures, listening to his wife's music or himself playing the classical guitar, or walks in the country with his dog.

Privilege made him uncomfortable. He still believed in the ideals of the old revolutionaries, who had led humble and austere lives as a matter of principle. For a long time he hardly bothered about his dress and changed only when his lengthy sojourns in foreign countries made it important to pay close attention to such matters.

In his private life all was well. He and Elena Stepanovna (or Elya, as she was called by her husband) were happy to be reunited, after his return from England in 1931, and a year later she gave birth to their first and only child, a girl whom they named Evelina. The KGB helped the Fishers to get an apartment of their own in Moscow, two rooms in a four-room apartment. Two other families occupied the remaining rooms, but the Fishers felt fortunate, since they were much better housed than most inhabitants of that city.

Elya knew by now what kind of work Willy did. Still, she hoped that he would be allowed to work at the Center in Moscow for a few years, remaining at home with his family. He had been back only a short time, however, when he received orders to report for an intensive course in agent radio communications. Except for some study at the OGPU training school, he had done nothing with radio since his military service. He wondered what his superiors had in mind for him.

Only a few days after he completed the course, once more receiving high marks, he heard that he was being sent to Copenhagen. He would again be an "illegal," this time bearing a false Swiss passport.

He had to wait until he arrived in Copenhagen to learn more about his specific assignment. Thus he found out that State Security had removed from Nazi Germany its remaining intelligence networks—those which had not been destroyed by the Gestapo— except for a few considered capable of surviving on their own. Stalin feared that a wholesale exposure of Soviet espionage would allow Hitler to increase tension or even give him an excuse for an armed attack on the USSR, possibly in alliance with Poland. The installations were moved to Germany's periphery, in Switzerland, Denmark, Belgium, and Holland, as well as the Saarland, which was still under League of Nations administration.[16] Nevertheless, a number of the most covert operations were being run out of Copenhagen, and Willy inferred from this information that he, too, would be involved in German operations.

When he reported for duty in Copenhagen, the resident, his chief, quickly disabused him of the idea.

"In case of war, most of the small countries in this part of Europe are going to be overrun by the Germans," the resident said. "That includes not only Denmark but also Norway and perhaps Sweden. We are now engaged in organizing stay-behind operations for the eventuality of war. I intend to assign you to the preparatory work. Your area will be Scandinavia—that is, Denmark, Norway, and Sweden, without Finland, which is being taken care of by our comrades in Leningrad. You are to help in organizing the stay-behind networks, but your principal job will be to train Danes, Norwegians, and Swedes as radio operators. These networks will be activated, of course, when or if a German occupation takes place. Until then the operators will transmit only on certain occasions for testing purposes. Any questions?"

"Yes," Willy Fisher said. "You know that I don't speak any of the Scandinavian languages?"

The resident dismissed this statement with a wave of his hand. "That won't be necessary. We have principal agents who speak Russian. Anyway, you know English, and many of our agents speak that language."

For the next few years Fisher was based in Copenhagen but, under the cover of a salesman, traveled constantly throughout Scandinavia. His work was all very easy, too easy. But the KGB never relaxed its security measures. The safe houses in which he met agents and gave them their training on the "key"—in transmitting messages by radio—had been carefully chosen and were situated in locations that made surveillance extremely difficult, if not impossible. Fisher personally preferred a safe house on a dead-end street, fronting on a rail line, canal, or river, approachable on foot by various routes, via paths, driveways, alleys, even over back fences. Such precautions seemed wasted in retrospect, as there was not a single emergency involving police surveillance or a raid in that whole period.

He was satisfied with his work and thought that his superiors must be pleased too. The Germans would certainly be in for some surprises when they came up north. Then one day the world in which he lived so complacently collapsed without warning. He received peremptory orders to return immediately to Moscow. No opportunity to hand over his duties to anyone else. No period of grace. Just get on the first ship and return.

The year was 1937, and Soviet Russia had found itself in the throes of the Great Purge.

The terror of the years 1936 to 1938 in Russia was all the more horrifying because it was senseless, indiscriminate, and so widespread that it struck high and low alike. Only Stalin was safe, but even that may have been an illusion: indeed, Stalin never went anywhere without elaborate security precautions and was afraid to show himself in public. The measure of his own insecurity was the extent to which the terror cut down many of his closest collaborators.

William Fisher did not know what fate awaited him at home, but he was well aware that his status as the son of an Old Bolshevik no longer protected him. As late as 1935 the designation "Old Bolshevik" was a mark of high distinction, while membership in the Society of Old Bolsheviks conferred certain honors and privileges. But in May of that year the Society was suddenly abolished and its building seized without any public explanation.

Vaguely sensing bad things to come, William Fisher arrived in Moscow. The first blow was not long delayed. One day he came home and told Elya that he had been dismissed by the "organs." No reason had been given, and he knew better than to ask for an explanation.

Indignantly, Elya urged her husband to fight back, and she herself protested to all their friends. She proposed to go to the most influential people they knew and ask for their intercession. Everyone warned her that this was the wrong time to protest, that no one could be expected to intercede with the "organs," who were a law unto themselves. Friends also impressed upon her the danger to her husband and herself, and she soon fell silent. For his part, William Fisher had no intention of rocking the boat. He obtained a job in a factory without much trouble and went back to his old occupation as an engineer.

Nevertheless, he was under no illusion that he had reached a safe shelter. There were some who whispered that dismissal from the "organs" usually only preceded arrest. On the other hand, he knew that many State Security men were taken directly from their desks to the Lubyanka prison, without the preliminary step of dismissal.

During that terrible year of 1938 Willy and Elya lay awake night after night, listening for the automobiles that entered the center courtyard and came to take the latest victims away. Behind the darkened windows, others besides the Fishers were lying awake, listening for the muted cries and scuffling of feet as the arrested persons were led off. Some, half-dressed, listened inside their doors, trying to determine whether the elevator was stopping at their floor. A few had small bags already packed so that they would be prepared when the knock came.

Willy could only guess at what might bring about his own arrest. Most of the Old Bolsheviks had retired into seclusion, but their very silence was an indictment of Stalin, and, by association, Willy might easily be lumped together with his father's contemporaries.

And he had worked for Alexander Orlov, who had defected by then. Fortunately, he had not accompanied his former chief to Spain. Still, no one could tell whether their old association, recorded in State Security files, would not be used against him.

Meanwhile Rudolf Ivanovich Abel, Willy's friend, continued to go to work. The strong, blond man, outwardly affable and carefree, inwardly trembled in fear of an arrest that could occur at any hour. One man in his office had been summoned by his boss. He never returned. His uniform cap continued to hang on the coat rack, but no one dared remove it.

Much later, recalling those times, Willy Fisher said: "I was lucky. I escaped with a light scare."[17]

At that point it began to look as if Willy had really "escaped." And after the replacement of Yezhov by Beria as head of the KGB toward the end of 1938, the Great Purge slowly ground to a halt. Willy's career as a Chekist had also ended. Or so it seemed.

The dark clouds on the international horizon did not overly concern Willy. Now that he had nothing more to do with the Foreign Administration, he did not follow international developments. Like his fellow citizens, he could leave such problems to Stalin and the hierarchy running the country. Consequently, the events of June 22, 1941, shocked him as profoundly as they did millions of others.

It was a Sunday. He, Elya, and little Evelina rose early to take a morning stroll. In the central section of Moscow, they noticed that

loudspeakers had been set up at strategic locations. While ponder-
ing the significance of this, they met one of Willy's colleagues from
the factory who told them that Molotov was to make an important
speech at noon. The colleague joked that perhaps Molotov would
announce a forthcoming visit by Hitler to Moscow.

Joining a crowd gathered beneath one of the loudspeakers, the
Fishers instantly recognized the husky voice of Molotov, who had
just begun to speak:

"This morning at 4 A.M., without presenting any demands to the
Soviet Union and without a declaration of war, German forces
attacked our country, crossing our border at many points and
bombing Zhitomir, Kiev, Sevastopol, Kaunas, and various other
cities of ours. . . . This outrageous, perfidious invasion of our country is without parallel in the history of civilized states. The invasion
of our country occurred despite the existence of a nonaggression
treaty between the USSR and Germany and notwithstanding the
fact that the Soviet government had conscientiously fulfilled the
provisions of this treaty."

Anticipating military service, Willy had almost forgotten about
his past connection with State Security. But one day, without warning, he was ordered to report to State Security headquarters. On
entering the office to which he had been directed, he found, to his
astonishment, that the man who awaited him was a former boss,
Yakov Serebryansky. Fisher was both astonished and delighted to
see him. Of all his bosses in State Security, Serebryansky was the
one man he looked up to with both respect and deep affection.
Serebryansky had proved himself on many occasions to be a true
friend, benefactor, and protector. The reason for his astonishment
was simple. Before he lost touch with his old associates in the
NKVD, he had heard that Serebryansky had been arrested and
condemned to death.

As Serebryansky himself subsequently told him, the report was
true. But while Serebryansky was still awaiting execution, the
NKVD suddenly arranged for his release and called him back to
work—without, however, annulling his death sentence.

Fisher was assigned to the NKVD's Fourth Administration,
which had been created to conduct partisan warfare against the
Germans. During the war years, Fisher and Abel worked closely

together, training radio operators who were infiltrated overland or flown behind the German front lines in Belorussia and the Ukraine, where they joined partisan groups and set up communications with the Fourth Administration headquarters. Fisher and Abel obtained their recruits from the Fourth Administration's radio operators' school in Moscow.

One of the radio operators whom Fisher trained for partisan operations was Konon Molody, who later became famous as a spy under the name of Gordon Lonsdale. Molody was only about twenty when he first met Willy Fisher, who by then was nearly forty and must have seemed to be an old man to Molody. His health had caused him to age, and he was beginning to suffer from the physical problems that would haunt him for the rest of his life. His stomach ulcer was aggravated by wartime tension and poor diet, and he was afflicted by sinus trouble.

Fisher and Abel, virtually inseparable during the war years, also trained agents for stay-behind operations in Moscow and other Soviet cities that were expected to fall to the Germans. In the course of time, constant recruitment and training eventually provided a pool of clandestine radio operators, and they turned their attention in another direction. Fisher, in particular, became fully occupied with a type of operation that assumed increasing importance as the war continued.

When the KGB recalled him to duty, shortly after the German invasion, Willy Fisher was distressed to learn that the radio network he had constructed for stay-behind operations in Scandinavia was dissolved before the war. Such a net could have been invaluable, yet it had been abruptly abandoned without ever being used.[18] His superiors either professed ignorance or bluntly refused to discuss the matter. Fisher and a few close friends like Abel could only surmise that the decision was a by-product of the shake-up in the leadership. Perhaps those who succeeded to power distrusted operations begun by others who ended in disgrace.

Willy, a typical field man, had never held his bosses in the Moscow Center in high regard. In earlier years, however, they had at least been people with long firsthand experience in conspiratorial work and retained many of the revolutionary ideals that made them servants of a cause. The new bosses were a different breed. These self-centered careerists possessed no revolutionary tradition and had no other aim than to advance themselves and obtain privileged positions.

Willy Fisher was fond of saying: "Bosses are bosses, but it is impossible to do without them!"

In 1957, while a prisoner in New York's federal house of detention, Fisher asked Alex Krimsky, the warden, whether he could obtain more books to read. Fisher's attorney related:

> I told Abel, in front of the warden, that I thought he would be interested in the book *Labyrinth* on German wartime counterespionage, by [Walter] Schellenberg of Hitler's staff.
>
> "Schellenberg claims," I said, "that at one time during the war the Germans had captured over fifty radio transmitters belonging to Russian agents, and turned them around to feed misleading military information back to Russia."
>
> Krimsky laughed loudly but Abel quickly countered, "Did he tell how many of theirs we grabbed and did the same thing with?" Abel was said to have worked inside Germany during World War II.[19]

In reality, Fisher never worked inside Germany during the war, despite a fanciful story about "Alec" told in Konon Molody's book, which is generally filled with misinformation and lies.[20] Nevertheless, Fisher was undoubtedly well-qualified to discuss the subject of turning around agents—"doubling" them—and using their radio transmissions for counterespionage purposes. It was precisely in this area that he and the real Abel worked during the last years of the war.

In a secret war of the ether, the NKVD and the Gestapo used captured enemy agents in an attempt to deceive the enemy by feeding false information and eliciting useful information in return. The counterespionage elements of both services continued such transmissions as long as there was any possibility of outwitting the other side. If it became clear that the deception had failed, the transmissions were tapered off and eventually stopped.

Fisher and Abel, familiar with the "fists" or distinctive touch on the keys of the radio operators they had trained (which are as individual as handwriting), provided expert advice when it was suspected that a Soviet agent had been captured in German-held territory. In such cases, the agent might be forced to continue the transmissions himself or, if uncooperative, be replaced by a Gestapo specialist. Even when the Soviet agent agreed to cooperate, there were various ways in which he could send danger signals that would be recognized at the receiving site without necessarily being detected by his captors.

German agents with radio sets, of course, were captured on Soviet territory. Here again Fisher and Abel took part in the complicated game of playing back those agents against the Gestapo.

Which side won this war of the ether? Only the parties involved could provide a definitive answer. It is clear that both sides had triumphs and failures.

KGB Major General Drozdov wrote in his article about William Fisher:

> Hitler's diversionary-spy service, as is known, consisted of a multitude of conspiratorial staffs and centers. The "Staff Valkyrie" directed spying and diversionary work along the whole eastern front. "Zeppelin"—a special service of the SD created by Himmler—concerned itself with underground work deep in the Soviet rear. The commands "Orion," "Saturn," "Aries," and others carried out espionage against the Soviet Army in certain sectors of the front and inside our country.
>
> Chekists operating in the opponent's rear penetrated into these enemy nests and, apart from military intelligence information, identified spies and saboteurs whom the Hitlerites were training and dispatching into our rear.[21]

Like many Soviet citizens, William Fisher firmly believed that after the war fundamental changes would take place in the direction of liberalizing the Soviet system in all spheres, making life easier and happier for everyone. The stress placed by Stalin on "Mother Russia" and the regime's appeals to Russian patriotism, as well as its rehabilitation of the Orthodox Church after the German invasion, seemed to indicate that the leaders realized communism was unpopular with the people. The valor with which Russians and other nationalities had fought against the Germans in defense of their traditional motherlands, not of the "Soviet Union," led many people to expect that the more extreme and detested Communist measures would be relaxed.

All such hopes were destined to be disappointed. As soon as the war ended, Stalin and his Politburo colleagues lost no time in tightening up all aspects of Soviet life that had been somewhat relaxed during the war. It was made abundantly clear to the population that rigid Soviet communism would not be abandoned, and arrests in cities and towns emphasized the point. Hundreds of thousands of returning Soviet POWs, not to speak of displaced persons, old emigrés, and so-called *Ostarbeiter* in occupied Europe, were treated as traitors and sent off to concentration camps. The *Ostarbeiter* were labor deported from occupied eastern territories to work in Germany. Some found their way to other countries.

For the purpose of reimposing strict Soviet control, the Kremlin bosses thought it useful, if not indispensable, to find a replacement for Nazi Germany as the Soviet Union's number one enemy. They did not have to look far. They fastened on the USSR's principal rival in the postwar world, the United States of America.

During the war, rivalry between the two powers had been muted by the exigenices of the common struggle against Hitler. Roosevelt and his closest counselors had made a deliberate effort to overcome Soviet distrust, supposedly caused by the Western powers' intervention in Russia in 1918–19, hostility toward communism, and subsequent quarantine of the Soviet regime. Thus, Roosevelt and other American leaders believed that by subordinating political questions to the winning of the war, and by later making one-sided concessions on disputed issues, they would avoid rekindling Soviet suspicion and distrust of Allied motives.

On the Soviet side, every effort was made to exploit American feelings of guilt concerning the West's past policies toward the Soviet Union and concomitant American willingness to make concessions as a token of good faith. It never seems to have occurred to Western—particularly American—policymakers that Soviet suspicion and distrust are based on something far more deep-rooted than the real or imagined misdeeds of Western nations, and that goodwill alone will not overcome them.

The Soviet Union had never ceased to conduct espionage against the United States during the wartime alliance, and after the war, the basis for stepped-up espionage operations already existed. During the war Americans hardly concerned themselves about Soviet espionage—unthinkable in an ally—and did not begin to adopt countermeasures until after the severe deterioration in U.S.–Soviet relations.

With the United States as the major target of Soviet espionage, it was only natural that native English speakers among Soviet intelligence officers assumed much greater importance, taking into account the ever present possibility of another war and the need for deep-cover agents.

William Fisher was one of the outstanding candidates in this group. Concealing his disappointment with the renewed climate of repression in the Soviet Union, he accepted the argument that the hostility of the United States was to blame. He had long experience in the field and had proved himself to be dedicated, disciplined, resourceful, and tenacious. Aside from his native command of English, he also possessed other talents that marked him for an important espionage mission in the United States.

William Fisher's 1948 mission should be viewed against the background of an international situation that made another world war conceivable, to statesmen if not to the people they governed. In retrospect, it seems probable that Moscow was already making plans for the invasion of South Korea by Soviet-trained and equipped forces from North Korea. War with the United States could be contemplated more comfortably by the Kremlin now that the USSR was prepared to detonate an atom bomb, making a threat of retaliation credible against nuclear attack by the United States.

In any intelligence organization there is a strong tendency to prepare for the contingencies being mulled over by the people at the top. A war with the United States would result in the complete withdrawal of State Security's "legal" residencies, and all espionage would subsequently devolve upon the "illegal" residencies—apart from the relatively limited assistance of "friendly" diplomats whose countries still maintained missions in Washington. So the KGB's Illegals Administration, where Fisher worked, began to assume a larger role in future espionage operations against the United States.

Now William Fisher's special credentials became obvious. A

trained engineer, he had studied nuclear physics and had a grasp of that subject that was remarkable for a layman. The ongoing atomic espionage that Soviet intelligence had begun in the United States during World War II would become one of the duties of the new "illegal" resident by taking over the surviving networks. An even more important function was to prepare for the kind of stay-behind operation with which Fisher had acquired wide experience. No one was better qualified to plan for clandestine radio communications enabling Soviet agents in the United States to keep in touch with Moscow.

Therefore, it was hardly surprising that Fisher was selected for the job. And he had no choice but to accept, though both he and Elya knew that the assignment would involve a long separation. Worst of all, Willy was even more disturbed by the prospect of being separated from his sixteen-year-old daughter, Evelina; he had not been parted from her and his wife except for the period when they were evacuated from Moscow to Kuibyshev in 1941. At this latest separation, he was promised home leave after five years in the United States, but seven years were to pass before he could return to Moscow.

The significance attached to Fisher's mission was reflected in an invitation by Politburo member Vyacheslav Molotov for a long, serious conversation before his departure. Molotov at that time headed the Committee of Information, which briefly consolidated all Soviet secret foreign intelligence activities under one roof.[22] Molotov also gave a dinner for Fisher, his wife, and daughter—a quite unprecedented event in the case of a spy.

On a gray afternoon in November 1948, a black limousine drew up at the main entrance of the Leningrad Station in Moscow. A tall, thin man with a birdlike face, his dress distinguished by a sort of faded gentility, got out as if he found the effort laborious. The chauffeur, carrying a suitcase, accompanied him to the train.[23]

One of those watching Fisher's departure at a distance was the State Security chief, Viktor Semyonovich Abakumov, who was subordinate only to Beria in the entire Soviet security and secret police apparatus.

7

The Man Who Rose from the Dead

PRESUMABLY THERE WERE people who knew Andrew Kayotis in Detroit. He had lived in that city for many years, working, perhaps, in the automobile industry. If so, he might have helped to build some of the trucks sent under lend-lease to Russia during the war. As a naturalized U.S. citizen, he decided to return to his native Latvia after the war, hoping no doubt to find some of his relatives, for he was unmarried and had no family of his own. When he returned to Latvia, reoccupied after the war by Soviet troops, he suddenly fell ill, was taken to a hospital, and died.[1]

A very ordinary story so far. But it soon became more interesting: Andrew Kayotis rose from the dead. Resurrected, he set out on his return journey to America. On November 14, 1948, he arrived in Quebec aboard the *Scythia*, which had sailed from Hamburg.[2] Within a few days, with his American passport, he crossed the border into the United States. Although the exact point of entry remains unknown, it can be safely assumed that he did not cross over from Windsor, Ontario, to Detroit. The resurrected Kayotis had every reason to avoid anyone who could have conceivably known him.

Andrew Kayotis was the identity assumed by William Fisher for his travel to America.[3]

It is possible that he continued to call himself Kayotis for some time after arriving on American soil. He traveled around the country for more than a year before coming to New York City, where he found a furnished apartment in a four-story walk-up at 216 West 99th Street. He rented it in the name of Emil R. Goldfus.[4]

For the next seven years, continuing to live in New York City, Fisher usually identified himself as Goldfus or, less often, as Martin Collins. He possessed birth certificates in both names,[5] but the one for Martin Collins, allegedly born on July 2, 1897, was a forgery— probably made in Moscow.

The real Emil Robert Goldfus was born on August 2, 1902, in New York City and died there two months and seven days later.

The normal Soviet Intelligence technique, which Fisher must have used himself, was to go through the files of old newspapers (at the New York Public Library, for example) and study the obituary notices. Generally, it was preferable to select someone who had died at an early age (so that the birth certificate could be obtained locally) and whose year of birth more or less matched that of the person who wished to use the birth certificate. By identifying himself as Goldfus, Fisher was able to obtain his birth certificate from the Department of Health after paying a small fee. With the birth certificate, Fisher could procure an American passport without difficulty.

In any case, under one false identity or another, Willy Fisher traveled around the United States for all of 1949. Precisely where he went and what he did cannot be determined with certainty. To his later acquaintances in New York City, he mentioned that he had worked in a lumberjack camp in the Pacific Northwest.[6] On other occasions he gave accurate details of San Francisco and Los Angeles that showed he had really spent time there.

Found at the time of Fisher's arrest in the Brooklyn studio he rented were twenty or more road maps of the United States. Certain areas, circled in pencil, turned out to be national defense installations,[7] and it seems likely that he visited these areas and observed the defense installations from the outside.

Nevertheless, it is possible that Fisher's travel had another purpose besides familiarizing himself with the country and its defense installations. Considering his training and experience, as well as the background of his assignment, there is a strong presumption that he spent that year on a special project: laying the groundwork for a clandestine "stay-behind" radio net to be activated in case of war.

It would have been logical for Fisher to buy radio transmitter-receivers in American cities and bury them in "safe," strategic locations—national and state parks, game preserves, and forests. Then it would have been necessary to give Moscow their exact locations so that, if war broke out, Soviet agents could be directed to dig them up in order to communicate with the Center. If so, Fisher could have been interested in defense areas not only as targets of espionage but also as convenient areas near which to site clandestine radios.

Konon Molody (alias Lonsdale) wrote:

> Of course, it was also necessary for me to be able to speak with my headquarters. I therefore had to find a place in which my shortwave transmitter, which had an output of 150 watts, could be safely installed. I had not far to look. I was still in touch with the Krogers,* who had by now moved . . . to a bungalow at 45 Cranley Drive, Ruislip. Nearby was the Ruislip U.S. air base—a web of radio communications. I could think of no better place. Detection would be almost impossible.[8]

The radio transmitters cached by Fisher would not have had the range to reach Moscow. If they had been activated in 1949 or soon thereafter, the most likely receiving station would have been the Soviet Embassy in Mexico City, which, like most Soviet embassies, possessed the antennae and communications equipment required for such purposes. It is even conceivable that Fisher went to Mexico City during his year of travel in order to coordinate plans with KGB representatives at the embassy.

If the above assumptions have any basis in fact, those radio transmitter-receivers are still buried throughout the United States, and their exact locations can still be found in the files of the KGB's Illegals Administration.

Morris and Lona Cohen frequently entertained friends, and there appeared to be nothing remarkable about their dinner party

---

* Mr. and Mrs. Morris Cohen, Soviet agents who earlier worked for Fisher in the United States.

in February 1950 for a wealthy English businessman named Milton. In their apartment at 178 East 71st Street, the Cohens introduced Milton to a number of friends, who were impressed by his Old World manners and the authority with which he could discuss art and music. He was obviously not a conventional businessman interested only in profits and losses, they thought.

The surface, however, was deceptive; "Milton" was in reality William Fisher, Soviet "illegal" resident in New York.[9]

Morris and Lona Cohen were trusted agents whom Fisher seems to have inherited from the Julius and Ethel Rosenberg spy ring, with which they maintained contact. Soviet intelligence preferred to recruit both husband and wife as agents; this was by far the most secure arrangement, since one partner could not always account for his or her activities to an innocent partner without arousing suspicion. Morris Cohen had become a Soviet agent even before he married Lona.

Cohen came to the United States as a child with his parents, immigrants from Russia, who opened a vegetable store in the Bronx. After graduating from James Monroe High School, Cohen obtained a football scholarship at Mississippi State University. A knee injury, however, ended his football career, and he stayed on as an assistant trainer with the team, graduating with a Bachelor of Science degree in 1935. A year later he attended the University of Illinois, but did not complete the work for a master's degree.

At that time he started studying Marxism and was already gravitating into the Communist orbit, motivated, in all likelihood, by the Great Depression, which seemed to point to the bankruptcy of capitalism, and by the threat to world peace represented by fascism.

In 1937 he applied for a passport and signed an affidavit that he would not travel to Spain, where civil war was raging. Nevertheless, he went to Madrid and joined the Abraham Lincoln Brigade, which was composed of American Communists and fellow travelers, to fight on the Loyalist side.

When he returned to the United States a year later, with a passport under the name of Israel Altman, designed to conceal the fact that he had gone to Spain, his commitment to communism could not be doubted. He found a job almost immediately with Amtorg— ostensibly a Soviet trading company operating in the United States, which was in fact an NKVD cover organization.

After working as a guard at the Soviet pavilion during the 1939 New York World's Fair, Cohen became a substitute teacher in the city public school system, assigned to one of the slum districts, where he took a special interest in collecting sports equipment and organizing games for the children.

In 1940 he met Lona Teresa Petka in Communist circles. Born in Adams, Massachusetts, she was the fifth of nine children of Polish immigrants. Lacking education, she worked as a domestic servant, and by the time she met Cohen, she had advanced herself to a position as governess with a family named Winston, who lived at 1125 Park Avenue in New York City.[10] They were married in 1941.

Six months after the attack on Pearl Harbor, Morris was inducted into the army. He served as a cook in the Quartermaster Corps with units in Alaska and Canada before being sent to England in 1944. Lona, a Communist Party member, worked in a munitions plant on Long Island and, with her natural aggressiveness, soon became a shop steward.

After the war the Cohens moved into the sphere of espionage as a team. Outwardly, Morris Cohen seemed to revert to a normal peacetime life as a public school teacher, while Lona became a housewife. Since neither of them had access to classified information through their own occupations, it can be assumed that they functioned in their espionage work in the capacity of cutouts or couriers. When William Fisher took over their direction, he probably gave them their first instruction in clandestine radio and photography. There could have been no better teacher than Fisher, allowing for the lack of first-class facilities.

One of the Cohens' friends whom Fisher thought of cultivating for possible recruitment as an agent was a young man named Alan Winston, who had apparently been one of Lona's charges when she worked as a governess. Somewhat alienated from his own family, he probably maintained contact with Lona as a link with his childhood, particularly since she could give him sympathy that he missed from his own family.

James B. Donovan, attorney of the so-called Abel, wrote:

Alan Winston, said Abel, was a young pseudointellectual who was supposed to be studying for a graduate degree at a New York university.

He described him further as the son of a wealthy textile manufacturer who had rebelled against his parents and their "bourgeois" way of life, which he considered to be decadent. . . . Abel said that Winston and he had met in Central Park one day when they both happened to be sketching. They shared common interests in art, music, good food and became fast friends. They traveled together to concerts, movies, museums and restaurants. With a girl friend of Winston's, they often had dinner at his young friend's midtown apartment, with Abel choosing the wines and doing gourmet cooking. The Colonel said he had tried to talk this young critic of capitalism into cooperating "to allow all nations to share all knowledge," but Winston never gave a firm answer. His initial reaction, said Abel, was negative.[11]

Despite Fisher's pretense that their initial meeting was casual or accidental, it seems clear that if they met in Central Park, they were in fact introduced to each other by one of the Cohens. Fisher must have given up on Winston as a potential agent, but still trusted him enough to place fifteen thousand dollars in a safe deposit box at Manufacturers Trust in his name; his friendship with Winston was one of three close friendships with men enjoyed by Fisher during his years in America.

The Cohens' work with Fisher turned out to be of short duration; in the summer of 1950 Morris and Lona had disappeared. Their flight resulted from the arrest of the physicist Klaus Fuchs in England that February. Fuchs spied for Soviet Intelligence during the war and was in contact with a courier named Harry Gold while working on the atomic bomb at the Manhattan Project and in Los Alamos. After his arrest, Fuchs confessed and identified the courier to whom he passed secret information. Fuchs was unaware, of course, that his State Security case officer, Anatoly A. Yakovlev, who had official cover in the Soviet Consulate in New York, had blundered on one occasion by sending Gold to pick up material from a member of another spy ring (David Greenglass, Julius Rosenberg's brother-in-law). Gold's arrest led to the exposure of the Rosenberg spy ring, placing the Cohens in jeopardy.

It cannot be confirmed that Willy Fisher had taken over responsibility for the Rosenberg spy ring, although the evidence points in that direction; Fisher may have even met Julius Rosenberg. In such a case he would have used a false name, and even if Rosenberg decided to talk, he could not have given a good description of Fisher, who melted into almost any crowd. Certainly Fisher did not feel endangered by the arrest of the Rosenbergs. Nevertheless, the Cohens, who probably acted as couriers with the Rosenberg ring, were bound to be exposed.

One can assume, therefore, that Fisher gave orders to Julius Rosenberg and his associates to flee the country. Morton Sobell reached Mexico before he was arrested, but the FBI arrested Greenglass about the middle of June 1950 and the Rosenbergs on July 16, before they could complete their plans to escape. Only the Cohens, who closed their bank account and cashed their savings bonds almost on the same day Greenglass was arrested, got away, but they left their apartment as it was, Lona even abandoning her jewelry, cosmetics, and toilet articles, and most of her clothes.

William Fisher went on as before. There is no record of what he thought on April 5, 1951, when Morton Sobell received a thirty-year sentence, or on June 19, 1953, when the Rosenbergs were executed. In June 1955, while Sobell was serving his sentence, Fisher and his assistant, Hayhanen, went to Bear Mountain Park and buried five thousand dollars, which was to be given to Sobell's wife. Hayhanen later claimed that he had delivered the money, but actually appropriated it for his own use.[12] Ironically, Fisher was to become a fellow prisoner of Morton Sobell in the federal penitentiary in Atlanta.

In 1951 William Fisher moved to a comfortable apartment on Riverside Drive at 74th Street. He signed the lease as E. R. Goldfus, gave his occupation as photographer, and paid the rent punctually.[13] Here he set up his radio, running an aerial out the window, and prepared to listen to encrypted shortwave broadcasts from Moscow according to the transmission schedule set up for him. He also had a tape recorder for recording the transmissions, thus making it easier to transcribe these messages. All the messages were enciphered with one-time pads, which made them unbreakable. (The one-time pad is composed of randomly chosen groups of numbers that the spy adds to his numerically encrypted message, using each group only once and destroying the page after all the groups have been used. Since opposing cryptanalysts cannot recover these groups of additives, it is impossible to break the message.)

Thus Moscow could communicate with him in a timely manner, and it was necessary only to deliver money, materials, or microfilms to him through dead drops. But Fisher had no means of communicating safely with Moscow other than through drops or accommodation addresses. Such methods were slow, cumbersome, and unreliable at best, and in the long run he needed to establish a transmitting site that would enable him to send his own radio messages to Moscow.

Fisher was meeting agents, too. Who they were and what kind of intelligence they provided are known only to the KGB, since Fisher revealed nothing after his arrest and, except for what he reported to the KGB later, maintained silence about these activities to the end of his life.

During this period, he knew that the Center in Moscow was preparing to send out an officer as his assistant. The Center's preparations had already begun in 1948, only a short time after he departed from Moscow. For some reason, the Center had chosen a man of Finnish background, Reino Hayhanen, for training as his assistant. Perhaps this choice stemmed from the fact that the Center possessed documentation with which a Finn could lay claim to American citizenship.

Hayhanen was born in Soviet Russia in 1920 in a village inhabited mainly by Finns only twenty-five miles from Leningrad, close to the Finnish border. He served as an interpreter with the Red Army during the 1939–40 winter war with Finland. After Finland was forced to cede some of its territory to the Soviet Union under the terms of the peace treaty, Hayhanen remained in the Karelo-Finnish Republic, as this area was called, continuing to serve as interpreter, even though he had become an officer of State Security.

In 1948 Hayhanen was summoned to Moscow, where he learned that he was being sent to Estonia for espionage training. There, in addition to the usual conspiratorial tradecraft, Hayhanen received instruction in photography, the operation and repair of automobiles, and English. At the end of the year's course, Hayhanen was promoted to the rank of major of State Security and told that he was being given an assignment in the United States.[14] Since Hayhanen had native fluency in Finnish and now possessed some knowledge of English, he fulfilled one of the criteria for a foreign assignment in the underground mentioned by Alexander Orlov: "He had to acquire a working knowledge of the language of the country of his proposed assignment and to master the language of the country of which he would represent himself to be citizen."[15]

Returning to Moscow, Hayhanen received further instructions. He was to have the cover name of Eugene Nicoli Maki; the KGB had a birth certificate showing that he was born in Enaville, Idaho, on May 30, 1919. The real Eugene Maki, as a boy of eight, had moved to Finland with his father, a native Finn, his mother, and a brother in 1927.[16]

Hayhanen's KGB bosses did not tell him what happened to the Maki family, but he obviously had no reason to fear that any of them would ever appear and embarrass him. In applying for a passport at the American Embassy in Helsinki, Hayhanen was instructed to say that his father had died in 1933, while he and his brother accompanied their mother to Estonia and lived with her in that country until her death in 1941.[17] Since Soviet forces occupied Estonia and the KGB carried out mass deportations from all the Baltic countries in the summer of 1941, this suggests that the Maki family fell into the hands of State Security at that time and may have been deported to Siberia. In any event, Hayhanen's year in Estonia was presumably intended in part to familiarize him with that country in order to support his claim of residence there.

Hayhanen's first task was to build his cover story in Finland under the Maki name. Since he had to account for his alleged residence in Finland since 1943, he traveled to the vicinity of the Russo-Finnish border where a KGB officer, working undercover with the TASS news agency in Helsinki, smuggled him across the border in the trunk of a car. Hayhanen then spent three months working and living with a blacksmith in Lapland and found two witnesses who accepted money from him and were prepared to swear that he had resided in Finland since 1943.

Hayhanen then moved to southern Finland and spent two and a half years in two cities there, working in a factory that built safes and doing auto body repairs. On July 3, 1951, he applied for a U.S. passport at the American Embassy, claiming citizenship on the basis of Eugene Maki's birth certificate. Although Hayhanen already had a wife and son in the Soviet Union, he continued to build his new cover by marrying a twenty-seven-year-old Finnish woman.

After receiving a passport about a year later, Hayhanen returned to Moscow, again smuggled across the border in the trunk of a car. At a safe house in Moscow, where for security reasons he had no contacts outside the Illegals Administration, he received further instruction in codes and ciphers as well as in the microdot and soft-film techniques.

The microdot technique is valuable for reducing the size of photographs of, for example, stolen documents. Using a strong light projector and a lens with a very short focal length, as well as high-resolution film, the clandestine photographer can reduce a 35 millimeter negative to the size of a typewriter period, recording one thousand lines per millimeter while preserving the distinctness of black and white lines. The resulting microdot is pasted onto any handy object where a black speck would not appear out of place— a book, letter, label, printed directions—and mailed to an accommodation address.

The soft-film technique enables the clandestine operator to bend or fold specially treated film for concealment in hollowed-out coins, bolts, or pencils.

In Moscow Hayhanen received final instructions from Vitali G. Pavlov, deputy chief of the PGU's American Department, concerning his mission in the United States. Pavlov, who had been the KGB "legal" resident in Ottawa at the time of Igor Gouzenko's sensational defection, seemingly escaped unscathed from his Canadian experience. Now he informed Hayhanen about the work in New York. Hayhanen was to be assistant to the "illegal" resident, a man with the pseudonym "Mark," and would himself have the pseudonym "Vic."

Pavlov said, "In espionage work we are always at war, but if real war comes, spies must remain at their posts. Even if you no longer hear from us, continue to carry out your espionage work in the country where you are assigned. After the war, everyone will be asked what he did to help win the war."[18]

Hayhanen also met Mikhail N. Svirin, first secretary of the Soviet United Nations delegation in New York, who was to be his initial contact on arriving in the United States.

This highly unusual and hazardous arrangement violated fundamental KGB doctrine requiring strict separation of "legal" and "illegal" residencies. This approach was partly aimed at protecting the Soviet government from embarrassment caused by the involvement of its official representatives abroad in certain espionage operations. But such an approach was designed, above all, to ensure that the exposure of one type of network would not result in the destruction of the other.

This flouting of elementary doctrine by the KGB in New York could be interpreted as an expression of contempt for the capabilities of the FBI. On the other hand, it might have amounted to a calculated risk, based on the acknowledgment that Hayhanen, as a novice, was more prone to blunder at the very start of a mission; in that case, he might have exposed Fisher and destroyed the "illegal" *rezidentura* in its first stages. Apart from that, Hayhanen was more in need at such a time of money, swift communications, and similar services that could be better supplied to him through the "legal" *rezidentura*. Such might have been the reasoning in Moscow, but this approach traded short-term advantages for serious long-term risks. Indeed, the worst did come to pass, implicating the Soviet official representation as well as the "illegal" apparatus, but it did not happen because Hayhanen was arrested.

Departing from Moscow, Hayhanen retraced his illegal route into Finland. He left his new wife, Hannah, behind and traveled to England, where he boarded the *Queen Mary*, arriving in New York as Eugene Maki on October 20, 1952.[19]

In accordance with his instructions, he made it his first order of business to find a place to live. After spending the first month in a hotel, he found a furnished room on 43rd Street in Brooklyn.[20] Then it was time for Hayhanen to report his arrival by going to the Tavern-on-the-Green in Central Park and placing a white thumbtack on a sign by the nearby bridle path. From then on he had to look for marks in signal areas—a certain streetlight in Brooklyn or a railroad station in Newark—and go to a particular dead-drop where there was a message for him.

Oddly enough, the first message to Hayhanen (apparently drafted by William Fisher and delivered by him) went astray. The message, written in Hayhanen's transposition cipher, was based on a key consisting of the Russian word *snegopad* (snowfall); 3-9-45 (the day, month, and year of the USSR's "victory" over Japan); the first twenty letters taken from the stanzas of certain Russian folk songs; and the number 13.[21] Unfortunately, the hollow nickel containing the microfilm of this message—one of a type produced by Fisher's own handiwork—became the property of a newsboy in the summer of 1953. The newsboy accidentally dropped the coin, the nickel split open, and the microfilm was turned over to the FBI. The message, however, remained unread until Hayhanen himself deciphered it after his defection:

> We congratulate you on a safe arrival. We confirm receipt of your letter to the address "V" repeat "V" and the reading of letter No. 1.
> For organization of cover, we gave instructions to transmit to you three thousand in local [currency]. Consult with us prior to investing it in any kind of business, advising the character of this business.
> According to your request, we will transmit the formula for the preparation of soft film and news separately, together with [your] mother's letter.
> It is too early to send you the Gammas.*
> Encipher short letters, but the longer ones make with insertions. All the data about yourself, place of work, address, etc., must not be transmitted in one cipher message. Transmit insertions separately.
> The packages were delivered to your wife personally. Everything is all right with the family. We wish you success. Greetings from the comrades. Number 1, 3rd of December.[22]

Hayhanen's Finnish wife, Hannah, arrived in New York in February 1953.[23] Their first home was at 176 South 4th Street in Brooklyn, a ramshackle building where apartments were rented to transients,[24] in an area of decaying houses, neon-lit service stations, and dingy grocery and candy stores. None of this could have struck Hannah as the America where an immigrant's dreams came true. Nevertheless, they continued to live there throughout the spring, as if reluctant to part from familiar surroundings, however humble.

Hayhanen's instructions required him to appear on the twenty-first of each month near the Lincoln Road exit of the BMT Prospect Park subway station. He was to wear a blue tie with red stripes and smoke a pipe (although in reality he was a nonsmoker).

In April, Svirin met him at this spot and gave him a package of microfilmed letters from his family in Russia and a message convey-

---

* Literally "musical scales." Since Soviet intelligence refers to a radio operator as a "musician" and to a radio transmitter as "music," this probably means radio frequencies and broadcast schedules. See Gouzenko, *The Iron Curtain*, p. 65.

ing May Day greetings, informing him that his family was well, and wishing him success in his work.[25]

Around this time Hayhanen received his first task. Possibly this was meant to be no more than a test, to see how well he coped with the job; Fisher may have observed the whole affair at a safe distance. Hayhanen was asked to contact a Finnish seaman with the pseudonym "Asko," whose ship had just docked in Hoboken. Asko was acting as a courier between Moscow and New York. They arranged a meeting at the Seventh Avenue station of the BMT Brighton Line subway, where Hayhanen received and paid for several messages.[26] Other clandestine arrangements were used on Asko's other trips: Asko left a thumbtack in the men's room of a Brooklyn bar to tell Hayhanen that he had filled a drop in the telephone booth of a Manhattan bar.

Hayhanen and his wife moved that summer to an apartment in a narrow three-story building at 932 Madison Street in Brooklyn.[27] But Hayhanen must have been a disappointment to his KGB superiors because he made no effort to get a job or to establish a business as a cover for his clandestine work, preferring instead to pass most of his time in Brooklyn bars frequented by Finns.

He apparently had his last meeting with Svirin in the fall of 1953, but the meeting went off routinely, with Svirin showing no interest in Hayhanen's activities. In any case, Svirin was beginning to attract the attention of the U.S. authorities and may have felt insecure, for he left the United States somewhat hurriedly in April 1954 before the expiration of his normal tour of duty.

Meanwhile, in December 1953, Fisher had quit the West Side of Manhattan and moved to a dingy one-room studio in Brooklyn, in a cavernous eyesore of Civil War architecture that had once been used for manufacturing pottery. It was located at 252 Fulton Street in the shadow of the Brooklyn Bridge. He also rented a storage room on the same floor for twenty dollars a month.

Within a few days he had strung an antenna for his radio on the rooftop outside his window in plain sight of the U.S. courthouse. Inside the studio he had set up a darkroom where he developed and printed snapshots for his new friends, who were led to believe that he was a photofinisher by trade now devoting himself to the study of painting on the basis of his savings.[28]

On one wall of the studio he had a tall chest and bookshelves filled with paperbacks, many of them mysteries. The walls would later be covered with Fisher's own paintings, and scattered about the studio, apart from paints, brushes, and easels, were piles of drawing pads and sketchbooks, cans of nails, bolts, etching needles, cutting implements, parts of camera lenses, bits and pieces of optical devices, a magnifying lens, a coffee pot, and an electric burner. Fisher was addicted to a throat lozenge that came in a tin box that he filled with the ordinary objects processed by him for professional purposes—hollowed-out pencils, nails, and bolts, coins and earrings with secret compartments, tie-clips with cleverly concealed holes.[29]

The new location was ideal. The artists, writers, and poets who inhabited this whole area, on the "wrong" side of Brooklyn Heights, wanted only to be left alone and, for their part, strictly minded their own business. Nothing could have been better from the standpoint of a spy.

At first Fisher rented a room in a boarding house on nearby Hicks Streets,[30] but this was used only for sleeping; later he commuted to the studio from various Manhattan hotels. One of his closest friends was Burt Silverman, a young artist in the building, with whom he often exchanged visits and engaged in long discussions about art. In all his discussions he avoided arguments and refused to talk about politics—"Leave politics to the politicians," he said. He was prepared to argue only when the subject of abstract art came up, for he despised it.[31] Silverman and Fisher sometimes went on expeditions to take photographs that they used for their paintings. At parties Fisher made a favorable impression on women with his slightly British accent and European manners, habitually compressing his admiration of attractive women into one word, "*Fantastisch!*"

Fortunately for Fisher, his neighbors were not particularly curious. One artist used to meet Fisher coming up the stairs late at night when he received transmissions from Moscow on his short-wave radio. The painter asked him, "Why are you painting so late?" Probably concealing his annoyance, Fisher replied, "I'm so busy during the day."[32] On another occasion, Fisher was listening to a Radio Moscow broadcast when Silverman suddenly dropped in. Fisher abruptly turned off the set and followed Silverman into his studio across the hall. The phone rang, and Silverman said, "I'm here with Emil, and we're listening to Moscow on his shortwave set." Abel turned pale and said slowly, "Don't ever say anything like that again."[33] Silverman thought nothing of this incident at the time.

William Fisher's first operational meeting with Hayhanen took place in July or August 1954 in the men's smoking room of RKO Keith's Theater in Flushing. Once again Hayhanen was wearing his blue tie with red stripes and smoking a pipe.

"Never mind the passwords," Fisher said. "I know you are the right man. Let's go outside."[34] At a nearby coffee shop, Fisher was able to size up his assistant for the first time. He looked intently at Hayhanen's florid and perspiring face with its alcohol-clouded, unsteady blue-gray eyes.

"He treated me like a chauffeur," Hayhanen complained later.[35]

Reino Hayhanen had been unhappy even before he left for America. Assigned to the United States, he dreamed of an easy and comfortable post under official cover in an embassy, seeing himself as a prestigious Soviet representative. This dream world came crashing down when he was informed that he would be sent as an "illegal," rather than assigned to a "legal" *rezidentura* with its status and perks.[36]

And since his arrival in America, his situation had only worsened: as far as he was concerned, the United States was a hardship post. He was in constant need of money, while his superiors expected him to find a job or start a business. He preferred to spend his time in places where he could speak Finnish or Polish, and he detested English. Besides, he could never understand American slang. Half the time he did not know what people were talking about.

True, he had managed to buy a car with part of the three thousand dollars that his superiors had advanced to him to start a business, but even that had not lived up to his dream; he kept getting speeding and parking tickets and had to pay fines.

Nevertheless, the real trouble had started with "Mark," his pedantic boss. Unlike Svirin, Mark insisted on strict observance of all the operational rules and was quick to reproach "Vic" for his transgressions. Mark also insisted on frequent meetings, which deteriorated into lessons; their relationship had soon resolved itself into that of a severe schoolmaster and an errant schoolboy.

From the outset, Fisher made clear his disapproval. Hayhanen ought to spend more time with Americans speaking their language. How could Hayhanen have spent over twenty months in the United States and still not opened a business? And, learning how Hayhanen was spending his time, he scolded his assistant for excessive drinking.

Later, when they got down to business, Fisher found other things to criticize. He considered Hayhanen's microdots unsatisfactory and told him to use spectroscopic film, which could be purchased at any Kodak store.[37] Hayhanen should do more practicing,[38] Fisher said. When Hayhanen continued to obtain poor results, Fisher showed him how to use the spectroscopic film in order to get greater contrast.

But the gulf between them was too great to be bridged. One day, while on an automobile trip, some Morse code came over the radio, and Fisher asked Hayhanen to take it down. Hesitantly, Hayhanen confessed that he did not know Morse code. Fisher could not hide his disgust. "In illegal espionage work, everyone has to know Morse code," he said sternly. "What did they teach you in Moscow?"[39]

During the winter of 1954–55, Hayhanen struggled, within his limitations, to satisfy his exacting boss, but the harder he tried, the worse things seemed to become.

In November 1954 Fisher received a message from the Center about an American sergeant who had been compromised and recruited as a spy while in charge of the motor pool of the American Embassy in Moscow. Fisher's orders were to establish contact with the sergeant in an effort to obtain intelligence through him at his new duty station. Ascertaining that the sergeant had a sister in Colorado, Fisher sent Hayhanen to find out the sergeant's current address. Hayhanen traveled to Colorado and called up the sister, who, although alarmed by his thick foreign accent and incoherent speech, gave him the address. Perhaps recognizing Hayhanen's clumsy handling of the job, Fisher took the matter into his own hands, although for one reason or another he did not proceed further with it.

Fisher sent Hayhanen on two other brief trips. On the first,

Hayhanen was supposed to contact a Swedish ship's engineer named Olaf Carlson in Boston. On the second trip, he went to Arleigh, New Jersey, where he had the task of recruiting someone as an agent. In both cases, he failed to find the man he had been told to contact.[40]

But Fisher was unwilling to give up on Hayhanen yet, perhaps thinking that his own standing in Moscow would suffer if he did not straighten out his subordinate. At the same time, the more pressure he placed on Hayhanen, the more his assistant turned to drink as a solace.

Mercilessly, Fisher kept prodding Hayhanen to establish a business cover for his espionage work, and finally his persistence seemed to be getting results. In March 1955 Hayhanen and his wife signed a three-year lease on an empty store with a four-room apartment in the rear in Newark, at 806 Bergen Street. The store was on a bus line but far removed from the center of town.[41]

Hayhanen told Fisher that he intended to sell photographic equipment and supplies, such as film. Pleased by this belated evidence of initiative, Fisher promised to give Hayhanen all the help he could.

On a May evening in 1955, proposing to give Hayhanen some photographic equipment for the new shop, Fisher took his assistant to his Brooklyn studio, and they went up to his storeroom on the fifth floor. Fisher had previously hinted to Hayhanen that he had a small place somewhere in Brooklyn. After that evening, Hayhanen had a fairly precise idea of the studio's location. It was a mistake for which Fisher would pay dearly.

Donovan, "Abel's" lawyer, referred later to "the unthinkable espionage error of allowing subagent Hayhanen to learn the whereabouts of his superior's studio."[42] But ex-NKVD chief Orlov, speaking of an "illegal" resident, pointed out quite correctly, "His past in Russia and his new identity [name, passport, business cover, and address] are known only to one or two of his closest assistants who are themselves staff officers of the NKVD."[43] Hayhanen was not a "subagent," as Donovan called him, but an officer of State Security. While Fisher had kept Hayhanen in the dark about all such personal information up to that time, he would not have violated principles if he had chosen to reveal it to his assistant.

Nevertheless, Donovan was right in characterizing this act as an "error of judgment," in view of Hayhanen's incompetence and lack of serious motivation.

Although Hayhanen and his wife lived for a time in the rear of the Bergen Street store, he made no effort to open a business there, concealing the store's interior by whiting out the windows with an opaque cleaning wax. And he went on with his purposeless, dissolute life as before.

There would undoubtedly have been more unpleasant scenes between Fisher and Hayhanen, if Fisher had not received permission to come home on leave. He also had an agreeable surprise: as a sign of Moscow's approval of his work, he was promoted to the rank of full colonel of the KGB.[44] Before he left, however, he must have already planned to take advantage of his sojourn in the Soviet Union to clarify the situation concerning Hayhanen and arrange to get his inept assistant off his hands.

Despite his reservations, he made a trip with Hayhanen to Bear Mountain Park and separately buried the money intended for Mrs. Sobell in two packages. His last instructions to Hayhanen were to contact Mrs. Sobell, using a letter written by the KGB officer who had recruited her husband as a means of identification, and deliver the five thousand dollars to her. Taking advantage of Fisher's absence on leave, Hayhanen later dug up the money and appropriated it for his own use, although he claimed that he had delivered the money to Mrs. Sobell and "told her to spend it carefully."[45] It seems likely that he used some or all of the money for the purchase of a cottage on the outskirts of Peekskill, New York.

Fisher had missed Moscow in many ways. Despite the friendships he had formed with his neighbors, he led a solitary life. Once in a while he dropped into a local bar, the Music Box, where a barmaid recalled, "He sat alone, would drink brandy, and look lonely."[46]

Fisher was not the kind of man who ran after women; if anything, he was somewhat puritanical.[47] Moreover, he avoided sexual entanglements, knowing that they could cloud his judgment and lead to his exposure as a spy and imprisonment. Although he did have involvements with women, he tried to control the circumstances in order to keep the relationship on a casual basis.

On one occasion, he joined three other artists at the Ovington Studios in sketching a live model. A black woman of generous proportions, she posed nude and her lushness would have delighted Rubens. To Fisher, who may have been partly influenced by the official Communist sympathy for American blacks, she seemed exceptionally appealing as well as exotic, although the others did not find her attractive. The fatherly-looking Fisher astonished the young artist next to him by leaning across and saying, "Boy, I'd like to lay her."[48]

Fisher evidently succeeded in establishing a personal relationship with the model, a nightclub entertainer named Gladys. She gladly let him photograph her for nightclub display purposes, and he also lent her money (he said later) to help her out in hard times.[49] But Gladys pursued her career—as no doubt Fisher intended that she should—and sent him only an occasional postcard. The FBI found one of these postcards with a "friendly message" in Fisher's studio after his arrest.[50]

On the eve of his departure for Moscow, Willy Fisher told his neighbors that he was running short of money and planned to go to California to market a device he had invented. Soon afterward he left a note under Burt Silverman's door saying that he would be back in a few months.[51]

On June 10, 1955, William Fisher flew to Paris,[52] spending a couple of days in that city as he began his first vacation in seven years. He went to see a movie, *Monsieur Hulot's Holiday*, and enthused afterward about Tati's performance to friends in the Soviet Union.[53] From Paris he traveled by train to Vienna, where he probably picked up a passport under another name at the Soviet High Commission or embassy. During the first part of his trip he must have traveled with an American passport, either as Goldfus or Collins, for he had much to say to his friends at home about the attitude of the French toward Americans. The comments were based, no doubt, on firsthand experience.

To his more intimate friends who had belonged to the KGB at one time or another, Fisher spoke frankly about his confusion as a result of the changes in the organization. Beria was gone, and Abakumov, who had watched Fisher's departure for America, had been arrested and executed. Molotov was already headed toward political extinction. He remained a Politburo member, but the

Committee of Information, which he had headed, had been abolished years ago.

He remained tight-lipped about these events, but criticized the changes that had taken place in the First Main Administration, the part of the KGB for which he worked. He considered this apparatus vastly overstaffed; it took two hundred people today, he said, to do the work that had been done by five people in the old days. The inclusion of a single paragraph in an enciphered message required the signature of a department chief.[54]

Fisher saw a good deal of his closest friends, but he was constantly in the company of his wife and daughter, who seemed unwilling to let him out of their sight. He was astonished most of all by his daughter, whom he had left as a teenage girl, still hardly more than a child in his eyes, and now rediscovered as an attractive, poised young woman of twenty-three. Wishing to share her father's interests as much as possible, she had opted for a technical education. She had also adopted from her father, a great admirer of Dashiell Hammett,[55] the habit of reading mystery stories.

Elena Stepanovna felt that Willy had already done enough for the cause of communism, and she urged him to try to convince his bosses that he should not return to the United States. Nevertheless, she sensed that he would not put the case strongly enough.

It was true that there were good reasons why he should not return to the United States. The belief that war was imminent had originally led to his American assignment. Now, however, the post-Stalin leadership had decided that the USSR could undermine the West with far less risk by a policy of "peaceful coexistence."

Fisher had accomplished much of his original mission by shaking up and reorganizing the American spy networks for the contingency of war, and there was little more that he could be expected to do in this regard. Moreover, he had passed his fifty-second birthday, an age at which most underground operators have their careers behind them.

Finally, there was Hayhanen. The Center agreed that Hayhanen should be relieved, but it was also apparent that the job called for delicate handling. Hayhanen was an obvious danger to Fisher, and that provided another strong reason for keeping Fisher at home.[56]

On the other hand, having established himself as Hayhanen's

boss, Fisher appeared to be the right one to deal with Hayhanen. In addition, Fisher had left his studio with all of his spy paraphernalia intact in expectation of his return. While his apparent disappearance would not expose any operations, it might cause some inquiries by the police and possibly bring in the FBI. If the FBI discovered evidence of Soviet espionage, that fact could be damaging in itself.

So there were reasons that justified sending Fisher back to America, and the arguments pro and con made his superiors in the KGB hesitate.

Had Fisher known what Hayhanen was doing during this time, he would have experienced many sleepless nights.

Hayhanen had exploited Fisher's absence in other ways besides digging up and misappropriating the five thousand dollars set aside for Mrs. Sobell. Relieved of the scrutiny of his demanding boss, he no longer checked his assigned signal areas regularly. He did not have to take trips to outlying areas on operational missions or to submit to espionage lessons from his boss.[57]

The store he had rented remained closed, its windows whited out, thereby arousing the curiosity of the whole neighborhood. And he behaved strangely for a spy, who normally seeks to avoid attention. He and his wife engaged in drinking bouts that created a legend among the neighbors, disposing of whiskey bottles in such quantities that the garbage collectors threatened to refuse to take their trash.

Hayhanen had also become the talk of the neighborhood after he threw a loaf of bread on the floor of the local bakery and ordered his wife to pick it up, roaring with laughter as she got down on her hands and knees to do so. On another occasion, the landlord summoned an ambulance and called the police[58] after finding their apartment spattered with blood and Hayhanen himself badly cut or stabbed after a drunken quarrel with his wife.

None of this became known in Moscow, but the KGB chiefs finally decided to send Fisher back to the United States nearly six months after his return home. He left around the first of December 1955 and seems to have spent two or three months traveling back to the United States.

At first everything seemed to be in order. Fisher's friends and acquaintances at the Ovington Studios readily accepted his explanation of his long absence and were obviously glad to see him.

As usual, the trouble stemmed from Hayhanen. Fisher sent a message to him about his safe arrival, asking Hayhanen to meet him "in the same place as before." He was referring to their first meeting at the RKO Keith Theater in Flushing, but Hayhanen, who seemed to guess wrong consistently, took it to mean the Symphony Theater at 95th Street and Broadway, where they had last met.[59]

When they finally met in July 1956, more than a year had gone by, but Hayhanen found his boss as angry as he usually was at their meetings. Nevertheless, Fisher made an effort to control his anger, engaging in polite small talk. Both men were conscious of the tension between them, and the explosion could not be long averted.

"How is your store coming along?" Fisher asked.

"Newark is too wet, it's impossible to open here," answered Hayhanen, seeking to justify himself.[60]

Then Fisher began to scold Hayhanen, telling him that this was just one more example of his poor work. Finally Fisher changed his tone and spoke more gently, saying that in view of the fact that Hayhanen had not opened the store, there was no reason why he should not go on a vacation. Fisher said he realized that Hayhanen had been under a strain, and thus it was a good time to make a trip to the USSR.

Fisher promptly sent off a message to Moscow, and several months later Hayhanen received a communication from the Center approving his leave and informing him that he had been promoted to the rank of lieutenant colonel.[61]

Whatever his shortcomings, Hayhanen was too smart to believe that his trip to the USSR would be a "vacation." Nor was he fooled by the ostensible promotion, as he had heard of colleagues who were promoted on the eve of a trip home and subsequently disappeared. While carefully hiding his true feelings from Fisher, he was determined to see how the wind was blowing before he made such a trip.

After returning to New York, Fisher lived at the Embassy Hotel at Broadway and 70th Street. In September 1956 he moved to the Benjamin Franklin on West 77th Street.[62] To his friends in Brooklyn, he seemed unchanged. Aside from his painting, he devoted himself with great zeal to the guitar, which he had learned to play many years earlier in Moscow. Now he owned a Goya, a guitar made in Sweden, and purchased all of Andrés Segovia's records and sheet music. With a tape recorder, he recorded his own playing and practiced over and over again. He had no patience for anything but classical guitar music, calling folk music "banal" and the lyrics "too sentimental."[63]

All this time Fisher continued to urge Hayhanen to prepare for his trip. But he no longer offered any espionage instruction or had Hayhanen accompany him on operational jaunts outside New York City. He excluded Hayhanen from all aspects of his work and kept the knowledge of his operations to himself. To all intents and purposes, Hayhanen had been suspended and was only awaiting final disposition of his case.

Fisher informed Hayhanen that Moscow had decided he should travel by ship to Le Havre and then to Paris by train. From Paris he was to go by train to Frankfurt and fly from there to West Berlin. He would then cross over to East Berlin and check in at the KGB headquarters in Karlshorst, where arrangements would be made for his flight to Moscow.

Hayhanen was told to apply for a U.S. passport under the name of Lauri Arnold Ermas, which he would use during the first part of his trip.[64] Presumably he would turn in this passport in East Berlin and receive another one for travel to the USSR.

Hayhanen did his utmost to delay matters, but as 1957 began, Fisher told him emphatically that it was time for him to go. Fisher ordered him to make a reservation on the first available ship bound for Europe. He was to let Fisher know about his exact travel arrangements at their next meeting or, if that did not come off for some reason, through a message in a dead drop in a concrete staircase in Brooklyn's Prospect Park.[65]

By this time, Hayhanen had little doubt about what to expect if he returned to the Soviet Union. Obediently, however, he checked with the steamship lines and found out that the *Queen Elizabeth* was scheduled to sail at the end of January. Instead of going to the meeting, where he might have been asked inconvenient questions, he left a message for Fisher in the dead drop: *I bought a ticket for next ship—Queen Elisab. for next Thursday 1:31. Today I could not come because 3 men are tailing me.*[66]

Despite this message, Hayhanen did not depart. Summoned to an urgent meeting in Prospect Park near the dead drop, he explained to Fisher that the FBI had had him under surveillance and taken him off the ship before it sailed. But having no evidence against him, they finally released him.[67]

The whole story was a figment of Hayhanen's imagination. He had limited powers of invention and could think of nothing better as an excuse for further delaying his departure. But Fisher, skeptical perhaps, half believed the story. He later told Donovan, his lawyer, that he now thought Hayhanen had been secretly apprehended in December by the FBI and that he had met Fisher thereafter on orders from federal agents.[68]

At their mid-February meeting, Fisher insisted that Hayhanen leave as soon as possible. He went over the travel route again and instructed Hayhanen as to the Paris leg of the trip, going into pedantic detail on how to use the telephone in Paris.

Seeing no alternative, Hayhanen capitulated. He booked passage on the *Liberté* and departed on April 24. Fisher must have breathed a sigh of relief as the ship steamed out of New York harbor. On his arrival in Paris, Hayhanen telephoned the Soviet Consulate and, in accordance with Fisher's instructions, asked, "Can I send through your office two parcels to the USSR without Mori Company?"

After receiving the proper reply, Hayhanen went to the appointed meeting place wearing his usual blue tie with red stripes and smoking a pipe. There he exchanged passwords with the KGB officer who had come to see him, and they walked together to a bar a few blocks away. Over coffee and cognac, the KGB officer gave Hayhanen two hundred dollars or its equivalent in French francs and American dollars.

The following night Hayhanen went to a prearranged visual meeting, which required him to remain hatless and carry a newspaper. This was the signal that he would depart the next day for Frankfurt.[69]

Instead of leaving on the train the next day, Hayhanen went to the American Embassy, just off the Place de la Concorde. He introduced himself as a KGB lieutenant colonel and said that he had vital information he wished to turn over to the appropriate officials. To support his claim, he displayed a Finnish five-mark coin that had been converted into a microfilm container, opening the secret compartment by inserting a needle into a tiny hole.

At this point, a Soviet Russia case officer from the CIA's Paris station interviewed Hayhanen and was quickly convinced that the would-be defector was exactly what he claimed to be. Hayhanen made it clear that he had no desire to continue doing espionage work, which he thoroughly disliked, and resented the fact that the KGB had not given him a good job in a Soviet embassy or some other "legal" residency.[70]

The case officer and his superiors recognized that, based on his own statements, Hayhanen properly belonged within the jurisdiction of the FBI, which is responsible for U.S. internal security. The CIA Paris station communicated with its headquarters in Washington, and on May 4, or soon thereafter, arrangements were made to turn Hayhanen over to the FBI. Hayhanen himself, who was primarily interested in political asylum under adequate protection, agreed voluntarily to return to the United States and to cooperate fully.

Fisher still knew nothing about these events. He had succeeded in getting Hayhanen off his hands, but now some definite actions had to follow. He was like the head of an insolvent business who had to start handing out pink slips to his employees and dissolving whatever commitments he could before the bankruptcy proceedings started. Nevertheless, he had to await a final decision by Moscow before he could take any action.

By an odd coincidence, Fisher returned to New York City from a brief trip to Daytona Beach, Florida, and registered at the Hotel Latham on 28th Street just off Fifth Avenue on May 11, the same day the FBI flew Hayhanen back to New York. Fisher signed the register as Martin Collins and moved into Room 839.[71]

Hayhanen was not sure of the exact location of "Mark's" studio in Brooklyn, but he knew its approximate location, and FBI men fanned out through the neighborhood until they found the right building and identified the fifth-floor studio by Hayhanen's description of Fisher. Then the FBI staked out the building, and on May 21 their vigilance was rewarded when they saw Fisher in the studio. FBI agents succeeded in following him after he left the Ovington studio around midnight. They followed him directly to the Hotel Latham.[72]

Two days earlier, even before the FBI zeroed in on him, Fisher had visited Dr. Samuel Groopman, who had an office in the hotel, for a vaccination. Dr. Groopman, by way of casual conversation, inquired where he was going. "To the north countries to paint," Fisher replied.[73]

Aware that a vaccination was required in order to enter Mexico, Fisher had probably planned to leave by that route. A couple of slips discovered in his possession at the time of his arrest[74] contained instructions for a clandestine meeting in Mexico City to be set up through a signal area on a telephone pole.[75] In this way, Fisher could obtain logistical support for his homeward journey to the USSR.

William Fisher had kept up his friendship with Burt Silverman while moving from one Manhattan hotel to the other. After his return from Florida, he told Silverman, "I may be going away very suddenly."

Silverman sensed that all was not well with his friend. "Why haven't you written?"

"Why bother you with my problems?" Fisher answered.[76]

It cannot be determined just when Fisher learned about Hayhanen's failure to arrive in Berlin. Hayhanen would have been expected to report in East Berlin no later than May 6. Possibly a few more days elapsed before the KGB headquarters in Karlshorst decided on the basis of its inquiries that he was not the victim of an accident or foul play, nor lying sick in a hospital somewhere, nor that he had been arrested by the Allied authorities. Thus, the Center in Moscow would have known on or about May 11—the day Hayhanen was flown to New York and Fisher returned from Florida—that Hayhanen was definitely missing. Moscow must have notified Fisher of this in their next scheduled shortwave transmission, and it can be safely presumed that when Fisher visited Dr. Groopman ten days later, he already knew of Hayhanen's disappearance.

Nevertheless, one element of uncertainty for both the Moscow Center and Fisher had been injected into the situation by Hayhanen, although it is not clear whether this was intentional or fortuitous. If he had intended to defect to the Americans, it would have been logical for him to remain in the United States and simply contact the authorities there. By going to Paris and making contact with the KGB officer from the "legal" *rezidentura*, he misled the Center to some extent about his intentions. Moreover, something could have happened to him even before he left Paris.

Fisher had to await developments, and in any case, he still had unfinished business in New York. In his capacity of paymaster, he had been instructed to pass money to various Soviet agents (reportedly to Kim Philby among others). After his arrest, FBI agents found in his hotel room a briefcase containing five thousand dollars attached to photographs of the Cohens, his former agents. There can be little doubt that the money was to be delivered to them.[77]

But Morris and Lona Cohen had escaped to England, where they were working as principal agents for Konon Molody. In all likelihood, the photographs were intended to enable a courier to recognize the Cohens and deliver the money to them.

If the dismantling of his studio constituted another piece of unfinished business, Fisher certainly had not begun the job by the unbearably hot night of June 20. Hoping to get some relief, he lay naked on his bed. Sleep would not come, and he tossed back and forth, finally kicking the sticky sheet into a tangled mass at the foot of the bed.

Toward morning the temperature dropped slightly. Just before sunrise—and more out of exhaustion than relief—he finally dropped off to sleep. At 7:30 A.M. a knock on the door jolted him out of this uneasy sleep. At first he did not respond. When the knock was repeated, he staggered to the door. "Who's there?" he asked. The reply was inaudible, and after his initial hesitation he opened the door a few inches. Three men burst into the room, shoving him out of the way.

"We're agents of the FBI," one of them said.

"Colonel, we have received information about your involvement in espionage. We'd like you to cooperate. If you don't cooperate, you'll be under arrest before you leave this room."[78]

William Fisher was a brave man, but in those first moments he began to shake. Despite his nervousness, despite the way he kept swallowing as if he would devour his Adam's apple, he retained enough of his self-possession to notice the title "Colonel" by which the FBI agents continued to address him. That could mean only one thing: his worthless assistant must have defected and told the FBI everything he knew. Apart from his rank, Hayhanen knew Fisher only as "Mark."

The agents told him to sit down on the bed. They asked him again and again whether he was willing to cooperate. While he sought to cover his nakedness with a sheet, he rejected flatly all such demands. "There's nothing for me to cooperate about," he said.

"We'll see," the oldest agent said.

As the questioning continued, his captors allowed him to put on his undershorts and to put in his false teeth, enabling him to speak more clearly. If he cooperated, the agents informed him, the man in charge would call their superior at the New York office and report the extent to which he was being helpful.

But when he shook his head once more, an agent opened the door and summoned three other men, who promptly identified themselves as officials of the Immigration and Naturalization Service. While Fisher finished dressing under their vigilant eyes, an FBI agent nudged one of his companions, pointing to a Hallicrafters shortwave radio on a bedside table and to an aerial strung up the wall, across the ceiling, into the bathroom, and out the window.

"What's the radio for?" one of the agents asked.

"I like to listen to the good music station," Fisher said with a faint smile.

Although Fisher had received a transmission from Moscow on that radio only the night before, he did not worry. It was his practice to tape record each transmission, transcribe it on paper, decipher the message, and then burn everything and flush the ashes down the toilet. Now, however, he began to have an uncomfortable nagging feeling. Something was wrong. Suddenly he remembered that he had torn off the piece of tape and dropped it on the table among some pencils and brushes. He could see it lying there, ignored by the agents who had started to search through his possessions.

Something had to be done without delay. While he was thinking, he indicated the cans of paint lined up on the windowsill. "Can I throw those out?" he said. "I won't take them with me." When one of the FBI men nodded, he seized the cans and threw them into a wastepaper basket. Then, as he related much later, he grabbed the piece of tape, wiped off his artist's palette with it, and flushed it down the toilet under the eyes of the FBI agents.[79]

The government men searched through the clothes he had laid over a chair the night before, as well as the suits that hung in the closet, piling the garments on top of the bed after completing their examination. An Immigration Service officer opened Fisher's suitcases and set about carelessly throwing his clothes into it.

"May I do my own packing?" Fisher asked, unable to conceal his displeasure. The INS man watched as Fisher folded the clothes and neatly packed them. At one moment, when the officer's gaze seemed to wander, Fisher surreptitiously removed some slips of paper from the suitcase, trying to hide them in his right sleeve. But this maneuver did not work, and the INS man took possession of the strips, which contained instructions for a clandestine meeting in Mexico City. Another INS man pulled a receipted bill out of a sheaf of papers. "Who is Goldfus?" he asked.

"That's me."

Inside a zippered briefcase the searchers found a brown wrapper with $6,500 in fifty- and twenty-dollar bills. They also discovered a bankbook issued by the East River Savings Bank showing a balance of $1,386.22, as well as a key to a safe-deposit box, which later turned out to hold $15,000 in cash. Other papers included birth certificates in the names of Emil Goldfus and Martin Collins and a smallpox certificate recently issued to the latter.

While the search continued, Fisher went on with his own cleaning up, collecting various articles, books, pencils, pieces of wire, Kleenex tissue, contraceptives, paint brushes, and scraps of paper, all of which he threw into the wastepaper basket. Another object added to this collection was a block of wood wrapped in sandpaper that contained, in a concealed hollow section, the Moscow Center's transmission schedule. Later he learned that the FBI agents had gone through the overflowing basket with great care after his departure and found not only the block but also a hollowed-out pencil containing soft microfilms.

That afternoon, after being questioned all day, he was driven to Newark Airport, where he boarded a private DC-3 with two Immigration Service officers.

Aboard the plane, the INS officers removed Fisher's handcuffs.

They were the only passengers on the DC-3, and he asked where they were going. The officers said that they did not know.

As soon as they had taken off, Fisher made a note of the time, the direction of the flight in relation to the sun, the plane's air speed, and made mental calculations.

He lay down during the flight, closing his eyes but not sleeping. When the plane began to circle for a refueling stop in Mobile, he sat up suddenly and looked around for a few minutes. Then he astonished the officers by asking, "What are we doing in Alabama?"[80]

As the DC-3 continued to its final landing at Brownsville, Texas, the officers again placed handcuffs on his wrists. They then drove in a waiting car to their destination, the so-called Alien Detention Facility, in nearby McAllen. On Sunday and Monday following his arrival he was interrogated all day by two of the FBI agents who had taken part in his arrest in New York. As he had done previously, he refused to answer any questions.

On Tuesday, he changed his tactics. He stated that his real name was Rudolf Ivanovich Abel and that he was a Russian citizen.

What accounted for this sudden about-face? The FBI had Hayhanen's testimony that Fisher was a KGB colonel and that the two had engaged in espionage. This testimony already implicated the Soviet Union in their illegal activities, but Fisher's admission that he was a Russian citizen seemed, on the face of it, rather dubious for a Soviet "illegal" resident, who, after all, was expected to deny any connection with the Soviet Union.

Nevertheless, what alternative did he really have? He could continue to insist that he was Emil Goldfus, but the FBI would soon prove that the real Emil Robert Goldfus had died. The Martin Collins of the forged passport had never existed.[81] The FBI probably would have little difficulty in locating people in the Detroit area who had known the real Andrew Kayotis. Finally, he could remain mute and let the U.S. authorities prosecute the alien "known as 'Mark' and also known as Martin Collins and Emil R. Goldfus, et al."[82]

Fisher must have reasoned that by assuming the identity of his old friend Rudolf Ivanovich Abel he would accomplish two things. First of all, there was no way that the U.S. authorities could refute his claim to be Abel, and, second, he would give a clear signal to Moscow that he was not cooperating with the FBI.

The admission that he was a Soviet citizen could do little additional harm in view of Hayhanen's testimony—and it might even do some good. What if the authorities were embarrassed by the arrest of a Soviet spy who had successfully carried out his espionage work in the United States for nearly nine years before being caught? In that case, they might prefer to make as little fuss about the affair as possible. He was encouraged in this belief by the fact that they had flown him two thousand miles, all the way from New York to the Mexican border. Perhaps they would choose to treat him like the Mexicans they were holding at the detention center and simply push him across the border.

One day he learned that a formal hearing in his case was to be held in the detention camp. Told that he had the right to be represented by a lawyer, he skimmed through a local directory and selected an attorney named Morris Atlas, who practiced in Mc-Allen.

At the hearing, accompanied by Atlas, he stated again that his name was Rudolf Ivanovich Abel, that he had entered the United States illegally, and that he had used the names Martin Collins and Emil R. Goldfus at various times and places. He also repeated that he was a Soviet citizen.

Under questioning, he admitted that he had never registered as an alien and therefore had violated provisions of the Immigration and Nationality Act. He went on to give other details—all of them false—of his origin and background: he was a teacher by occupation, had attended elementary school from 1910 to 1916 and high school from 1916 to 1920 in Moscow, and his father, whose name was Ivan Abel, had been born in Moscow. The only true information consisted of his mother's name and birthplace, as well as the fact that he had left Moscow in May 1948.

"To which country do you wish to be deported?"

"The USSR," he replied.[83]

For several weeks after this hearing, Fisher remained in the detention camp, while FBI agents went on questioning him. If he chose to cooperate, they told him repeatedly, he would immediately receive special treatment—an air-conditioned hotel room, as well as good food and liquor. He could also count on a $10,000-a-year job with another government agency.

It did not take much imagination on his part to figure out that the "other government agency" was the CIA. But from the beginning Fisher had rejected any thought of cooperating and did not intend to change his mind, whatever happened. "That is out of the question," he told Donovan, who defended him at his trial, when the subject was again raised after his conviction. "Never will I do it. In that first half hour, when I sat on the bed that morning in the Hotel Latham, I decided then. I am firm in my decision."[84]

In his cell, Fisher waited. Now that the FBI agents had failed to recruit him, he was convinced that, sooner or later, they would push him across the border into Mexico. To pass the time, he played solitaire, solved crossword puzzles, or wrote out logarithm tables as a mental exercise. He was not the first prisoner who recalled all that he knew about mathematics in order to retain a grip on reality.

Instead of being quietly pushed across the border into Mexico, William Fisher found himself catapulted almost overnight into the limelight. His face appeared on the front pages of newspapers all over the world; television screens showed his tall, monkish figure being hustled by burly U.S. marshals into the federal courthouse in Brooklyn for arraignment.

On August 7 he was served by two agents of the FBI with a criminal warrant for his arrest. Then he was taken to an extradition proceeding before U.S. Commissioner J. C. Hall in Edinburg, Texas, where he waived extradition to New York.

The following day he was flown back to Newark, landing after dark, but by then his case had become a sensation, and the press was out in full force at the heavily guarded airport.[85] Escorted to a waiting automobile through the photographers and television cameramen who crowded around, Fisher observed, "I'm getting a lot of publicity." He cooperated willingly with the photographers, even consenting to vary his pose for them by smoking a cigarette.

The *New York Times*, reporting this arrival, commented: "The charges against Abel, if proved, may put him in the class of Richard Sorge as a fabulous espionage operator for Moscow."[86] It was a comparison that would later be made by KGB Chairman Vladimir Semichastny,[87] but at this point Moscow was not acknowledging Fisher. For the rest of his life, however, Fisher's name would be coupled with the designation "master spy" in world news media.

Soon after Fisher's arraignment, Judge Matthew B. Abruzzo appointed a lawyer to defend him. It was a fortunate choice. James B. Donovan, gray-haired and stocky, whose calm demeanor exuded competence, had served in the OSS with distinction during World War II. An outstanding attorney, he took on the unpopular task of defending Fisher as a "public duty." The mutual sympathy and respect that developed between them endured to the end.

Donovan struck the right note in his first press conference. "A careful distinction should be drawn between the position of the defendant and people such as Alger Hiss and the Rosenbergs," he said. "If the allegations are true, it means that instead of dealing with Americans who have betrayed their country, we are dealing with a Russian citizen, in a quasi-military capacity, who has served his country on an extraordinarily dangerous mission."[88]

Fisher's trial, which opened on October 14, lasted only eleven days. The verdict was inevitable, in light of Hayhanen's testimony and the impressive array of spy paraphernalia. Nevertheless, Donovan provided Fisher with a praiseworthy defense, asserting that his constitutional rights had been violated, especially with regard to the Fourth Amendment, which is aimed at protecting people against unreasonable search and seizure.

Aside from Hayhanen's appearance early in the trial, the most dramatic moment was furnished by the reading of six microfilmed letters to Fisher from his wife and daughter concealed in a hollowed-out pencil. Fisher showed visible emotion for perhaps the only time during the trial, his face reddening and his sharp, deeply set eyes filling with tears. "Sometimes I approach your instrument [Fisher's guitar] and look at it and want to hear you play and I become sad," she wrote.[89] Her health was bad, and, perhaps as a result of his absence, she suffered from hypertension. Fisher appeared to be still more moved by his daughter's letters, which undoubtedly added to his feeling of guilt with regard to his family. Only a few months after he ended his leave in the Soviet Union, Evelina wrote him that she was getting married to a young man who was a radio engineer (like her father). "I do wish you were here with us. Everything would be much easier for me then. I am missing you very much. I thought at first that my husband could substitute for you more or less in some respects, but I now see that I was mistaken."[90]

On November 15 Judge Mortimer W. Byers sentenced an impassive Fisher to thirty years in prison. But Donovan could take some satisfaction from the fact that Fisher was not sentenced to death. Donovan had argued against an extreme penalty, pointing out that an American intelligence officer of comparable rank could be captured in the USSR in the future, and in such a case the American government could arrange an exchange of prisoners through diplomatic channels.

"It is absurd to believe that the execution of this man would deter the Russian military," he said. "The effect of imposing the death penalty upon a foreign national for a peacetime conspiracy to commit espionage should be weighed by the government with respect to the activities of our citizens abroad."[91]

While his case was being appealed, Fisher began serving his sentence. He was sent to the federal penitentiary in Atlanta toward the end of May 1958.

Fisher made a good adjustment to prison life, and, like the gentleman he was, did not complain about his lot or his jailers,[92] or about his fellow prisoners, who addressed him as "Colonel." He had subscriptions to the *New York Times* and to *Scientific American*, and Donovan's staff regularly sent him books he requested.

The authorities found Fisher a cooperative prisoner who caused no trouble and was well liked by the other inmates. In view of his talent for art, he was assigned to the commercial art department. He became interested in the silk-screen process and, finding that no one else knew much about it, characteristically taught himself and devised his own methods for silk-screen work. For the next four years he took the lead in designing and producing Christmas cards for the inmates' families.[93]

The only real difficulty that Fisher caused his attorney and the authorities involved the privilege of correspondence with his family, which he was denied in effect because of a ban on foreign correspondence. Even before he began his sentence, Fisher pressed Donovan to have this ban rescinded, terming it "barbaric."[94]

After negotiating with both the American government and

Soviet authorities, Donovan obtained this privilege for Fisher. Soviet officials, in particular, had played an elaborate game, finally "locating" Fisher's family, who were said to live in Leipzig. Fisher was allowed to send mail to his family after the letters were inspected by the American authorities. About a year later the privilege was revoked after the FBI became convinced that his letters had transmitted secret information to the KGB. Although he ridiculed the idea that any information in his letters could be very secret, Fisher never explicitly denied that there were secret messages in the letters.

It is now known that Fisher did send concealed messages to the KGB through his family correspondence. In return, the letters originating from his wife and daughter contained words and phrases in code provided to them by the PGU.[95]

The situation changed, however, after Francis Gary Powers and his *Utility 2* plane was downed in the Soviet Union. Powers' father wrote directly to "Abel," suggesting an exchange of the two men, but Fisher responded that he could do nothing himself because he was unable to correspond with his family.[96] Even before Powers went on trial in the USSR, the *New York Daily News* editorialized about the possibility of "An Abel for a Powers" swap.[97] Powers had been captured on May 1, 1960, and on June 24 the Department of Justice reinstated Fisher's privilege of corresponding with his family.[98]

Yet more than a year was to pass before these first tentative moves achieved any concrete results. During this time Reino Hayhanen died in an automobile accident on the Pennsylvania Turnpike. At the beginning of 1962, on the basis of suggestions made in Washington, Donovan offered to travel to Germany in order to meet with "Frau Abel" at the Soviet Embassy in East Berlin.

After receiving an affirmative reply, Donovan traveled to East Berlin. At the Soviet Consulate he met "Frau Abel" and "Abel's" alleged daughter, both of whom were probably Soviet or East German Intelligence agents impersonating Fisher's wife and daughter. He was also introduced to "Cousin Dreeves," another supposed relative. After these introductions, he was received with the others by Ivan Aleksandrovich Shishkin, second secretary of the Soviet Embassy, who was ostensibly in charge of the meeting.

Nevertheless, Shishkin was nothing but a figurehead. The real negotiator on the Soviet side—although he was never identified as such—was "Cousin Dreeves," who "never spoke, only grinned," said Donovan. "He was a lean, hard-looking man about fifty-five; he kept closing and opening powerful hands and I mentally classified him as an Otto the Strangler type. He probably was from the East German police."[99]

But "Cousin Dreeves" was actually KGB Major General V. Drozdov, the number two man in the First Main Administration, responsible for all KGB espionage and counterespionage abroad. An expert on Germany who spoke German fluently, Drozdov made all the decisions in the negotiations with Donovan behind the scenes.[100]

When the Fisher-Powers exchange was finally approved on both sides, after a private luncheon limited to Donovan and Drozdov, Fisher was flown to West Berlin. At the exchange on the Glienicker Bridge, on February 10, 1962, Donovan bade farewell to Fisher, who had aged noticeably and become more gaunt while in prison.

As a mark of his gratitude, Fisher later sent Donovan via a Soviet courier two rare sixteenth-century editions of *Commentaries on the Justinian Code* in Latin.[101]

Carrying his own bag, Fisher shuffled across the Glienicker Bridge into East Germany, to which he would later return.

8

Stealing the Atom Bomb

IN TERMS OF his position, Igor Gouzenko was, at best, a small cog in the wheel of Soviet espionage, essential but easily replaceable nonetheless. He had been recruited to be a cipher clerk—a communicator or "commo man," in American parlance—the invisible man of the Intelligence business. For him there is none of the glamor of a codebreaker or a spy who, by virtue of one broken enemy message or a successful foray into a foreign embassy, can become a legend among his colleagues. Like all commo men, Gouzenko spent long hours alone in a room to which only a very few had access. Neither seen nor heard, he was a cipher of Intelligence in the arithmetical sense of the word.

Gouzenko worked for the "neighbors"—the GRU.[1] He had served at the GRU Center in Moscow, and his assignment to the GRU "legal" *rezidentura* at the Soviet Embassy in Ottawa was his first tour abroad. As a cipher clerk, Gouzenko was responsible for encrypting outgoing messages and decrypting incoming ones. Locked up in his room, he maintained the files of secret dispatches, particularly incoming ones from Moscow, which could be kept up to a year, and provided a repository for the military attaché's notebook, as well as the papers and notes of his assistants, all GRU case officers.

It is hard to believe that "this curiously unadventurous, quiet and peaceful man"[2] could have become the catalyst for one of the most sensational exposures of Soviet espionage, including Soviet Intelligence's acquisition of the secrets of the atom bomb.

Gouzenko's defection also resulted in the exposure of the KGB "legal" resident in Canada, Vitali G. Pavlov, who operated under diplomatic cover as Second Secretary of the Soviet Embassy. As the SK—Sovetskaya Koloniya, or Soviet Colony—officer in the KGB "legal" *rezidentura*, Pavlov was responsible for watching all Soviet employees in Canada; his bungling of efforts to deal with Gouzenko led to his recall and demotion. After his return to the USSR he was deputy chief of the American Department of the First Main Administration,[3] failing to distinguish himself in that position. Later he was reportedly head of the PGU's special school for training Intelligence officers.[4] Training, in most Intelligence services, is usually one of the last stops for officers who have fallen into disfavor.

Gouzenko's sins were sufficient to ensure that orders would have been sent from Moscow to "dispose" of him or "render him harmless"—both euphemisms for murder—and if his former comrades found out where he was hiding, a specialist in "wet affairs" would have been sent out to do the job.[5]

Igor Gouzenko belonged to the first generation that was born and came to maturity under the Soviet system. Of peasant stock, he was undoubtedly representative of that generation. Almost everything he knew about conditions in Russia before the revolution, apart from official propaganda and what was taught in school, had been told to him by his grandmother, a peasant woman, and his mother. What they said often conflicted with the official version of events.

Gouzenko was born in the village of Rogachev, not far from Moscow, in 1919.[6] His father died of typhus during the civil war between the Reds and the Whites, and his mother taught in local schools. Conditions of near famine in their village led his mother to send Igor to his grandmother, who lived in another village and still had some land of her own, including fruit trees.

Igor spent the next seven years there happily, far removed from the turmoil of postrevolutionary Russia that most noticeably affected the cities and towns.

Recognizing that it was time for him to go elsewhere for an education, Igor's mother took him to the village of Verkhne-Spasskoye, in the rich central black earth district, where she had received a new teaching assignment. Verkhne-Spasskoye had a population of several thousand and was a regional center, boasting three kolkhozes (collective farms).[7]

Despite the richness of the land, appearances were deceptive; the peasants were starving here, too, as in other parts of Russia. Mrs. Gouzenko protested to the kolkhoz chairman and became involved in a fight with him and his wife. Knowing that this incident boded ill for her, she wrote immediately to Moscow and requested a transfer to Moscow.

The transfer was unfortunate in one way, since Igor, as well as his brother and sister, had to live with relatives for a year until their mother could establish another home. Eventually she found quarters for herself, Igor, and his sister Ira in a so-called "model" house for teachers, a kind of two-story barracks in an industrial suburb of Moscow, in which the three members of the family shared a room with two elderly women. Still, being in Moscow was a help to Igor and his sister, in view of the educational opportunities furnished in the Soviet capital.

Igor, who was not athletically inclined, was a good student. Despite his mother's private feelings about the Soviet regime, he had taken part in Communist youth organizations, belonging to the Young Pioneers and then the Komsomol. This party affiliation, together with good scholarship, had gone far toward securing a place for him in more advanced Soviet schools. But sometimes there were unpleasant episodes at home, when his mother criticized the Soviet regime, and he felt it necessary as a Komsomol member to rebuke her for her statements. He continued to believe implicitly what he was taught in school and in the Komsomol, even if he found it necessary at times to suppress other thoughts. In this respect, he was like the Germans of his own age who belonged to the Hitler Jugend and had fallen prey to Nazi propaganda to the point where they were at odds with their own parents.

One day Igor Gouzenko would remember how he had spoken to his own mother as an irate Komsomol member.

At the age of eighteen Gouzenko began to attend art classes, paying for his lessons by teaching illiterate workers to read and write at a school connected with a foundry on the outskirts of Moscow.

He realized, however, that art did not have much to offer as a career in the Soviet Union. A great deal depended on the official party line toward art, which could shift at any moment. When someone suggested that he apply to the Moscow Architectural Institute, it struck him that this made good sense. He would still be able to use his drawing talents for work that the government considered essential in the building of socialism.

After studying art for a year, he submitted an application to the Architectural Institute. With his good academic record and a recommendation from the Komsomol chairman, he received an acceptance contingent on his passing the entrance examinations.

In the fall of 1938, he officially began his studies. Without family connections or influence, he could hope for a successful career only by being a serious student. He avoided extracurricular activities and spent long hours in the Lenin Library studying not only art and architecture but also mathematics and construction.

One day in the library he encountered a classmate named Anna. He had seen her every day at the institute but had never been able to overcome an inherent shyness and speak to her. Even now, face to face with her at the library, he could not find the words to speak to her. Anna smiled at him. "Are you here for the same purpose as I?" she asked.

"If it is to study the history of Russian architecture," he answered, "the answer is 'yes.'" When she nodded, he added: "Then perhaps we could join forces? Two heads, you know."[8]

Their friendship would endure much longer than the three years that Gouzenko spent at the Architectural Institute.

On June 22, 1941, Gouzenko was drawing placards for a workers' club, when his uncle burst into the room. "Igor, you can forget all that now. Germany has declared war on us!"[9]

Gouzenko continued his studies for the next two months, paying little attention even when a few German bombs fell on his dormitory. One day he was summoned to State Security's "Special Section" at the Institute.

Gouzenko knocked on the door, and an old man opened the small window, looking questioningly at him. "My name is Igor Gouzenko." Without a word, the old man went to a row of steel file cabinets, removed a file, and studied it for a couple of minutes. Then he jotted something down on a pad and returned to the window.

"How are you getting on with your studies?" the old man asked.

"Well, I've been among the top five students all year," Gouzenko said.

"Good," the old man said pleasantly, handing Gouzenko a slip of paper. "This will admit you to the *Voenkomat* [the military registration and enlistment office]. Report there at once."[10]

Incredulously, Gouzenko learned that he had been assigned to the Kuibyshev Military Engineering Academy of Moscow. He only had ten days to prepare for the entrance examinations, which covered higher mathematics, structural materials, resistance of materials, construction, and other elements of building.

Two days after he passed the examination, Gouzenko was interrogated by the academy commission about his motivation and political reliability. He must have made a good impression, because he was notified on the spot of his acceptance and told to report the next day for his uniform.

By the end of August 1941, he had received an appointment for training as a cipher clerk at the GRU. With no conscious effort on his part, he had embarked on a career full of unsuspected hazards, with consequences for his whole life.

In April 1942 Gouzenko completed his training at the Higher Red Army School at Filya, outside Moscow, and was assigned as a cipher clerk with the rank of lieutenant to the GRU Center. As he was well aware, he enjoyed a privileged position, earning the rather high salary of 1,400 rubles a month compared to the 600 rubles paid to a well-qualified engineer in a plant. Besides, he had access to the *Voentorg* or PX, where he could buy canned meat and other imported foodstuffs, and bring them home to his mother and sister or to Anna.

Nonetheless, his job had its drawbacks. He frequently had to work through the night, and the consequences of a mistake could be very serious—especially for the unlucky person who made it. One young lieutenant who handled the distribution of cables threw an envelope he thought to be empty into the ordinary trash. An employee at the incinerator noticed that the envelope contained a coded message—a cable from Foreign Minister Molotov to Soviet Ambassador Maisky in London. For his oversight, the lieutenant was court-martialed and shot.[11]

As a cipher clerk, Gouzenko was subjected to periodic surveillance by State Security, and above all he could have no personal association of any kind with foreigners. He was required to report any new friendships with Soviet citizens, but associations with women were even more strictly supervised. Under penalty of dismissal, he had to tell his superiors in advance of a date with a woman.[12]

When he and Anna decided to get married, he informed the GRU about these plans; permission had to be granted before the marriage could take place. This meant that State Security would investigate Anna and her entire family in order to determine whether she was acceptable for someone in his position. Even in wartime, these requirements were stringently enforced.

On November 20, 1942, Igor and Anna were married in a civil ceremony at the Registry Office, during his half-hour lunch break. He rushed back to his office, arriving three minutes late, and was reprimanded for his tardiness. Any church ceremony would have given him a black mark as a Komsomol member and probably eliminated any chance to become a Communist Party member, which was now essential to his career.

In connection with the formal dissolution of the Comintern, the GRU was reorganized in March 1943, taking over most of the Comintern's Intelligence assets, including its extensive files and dossiers. As one aspect of the reorganization, the GRU was divided into two parts: one covering Tactical Intelligence, which pertained to Intelligence work at the front and directly behind the lines, and Strategic Intelligence, which dealt with the GRU's foreign espionage as a whole.

Strategic Intelligence became the largest part of the GRU as it absorbed the Comintern's assets. A communications branch was set up within Strategic Intelligence to handle radio traffic with GRU residencies and agents abroad; and those with "commo" background and a knowledge of foreign languages, like Gouzenko, were assigned to the new communications branch.

"It amazed me to note the psychological range employed in dealing with agents throughout the world," Gouzenko wrote. "Exhaustive files, compiled over a period of years at considerable cost, held case histories on each agent, his motives, his habits, his weaknesses, his reason for being an agent. This knowledge was used to best advantage when psychology was needed."[13]

Gouzenko became very familiar with these agents in the traffic he handled, although his responsibility stopped with deciphering their incoming messages and to enciphering outgoing ones. Case officers in the area divisions wrote the replies. The agents had all sorts of problems—they needed money or supplies, they were sick, they had fallings-out with their wives, they were in danger of exposure or arrest. The case officers encouraged them psychologically, arranged for transfers of money, provided for deliveries of equipment, set up dead drops and meeting places, directed them to safe houses, and established escape routes on an emergency basis.

In some instances, the case officers went still further. One radio message to China read: PUT AWAY KIM ENTRUST IGNAT WITH THE WORK. Gouzenko was a silent witness to numerous messages of this type, many of which were sent to China, calling for the "disposal" of some agent who had become too great a risk.[14]

In the spring of 1943, Gouzenko learned that he was being sent to Canada. In preparation for his departure, he had to memorize a "legend," or cover story, in order to answer questions about himself when he arrived in Canada. As in the case of other intelligence personnel assigned abroad, he discovered that his biographical information had been changed: his birthplace, for example, was listed as Gorky.

"What am I supposed to answer if some Canadian authority wonders how I happened to be assigned abroad from the Economics Technical Institute at Gorky instead of from Moscow?" he asked.

The man who drew up Gouzenko's "legend" shrugged off this objection. "Just tell them you were sent abroad as a protegé. Just let it go at that, and if they ask more questions, simply act as if you don't understand."[15]

Moreover, Gouzenko, who was identified as a civilian employee of the Soviet military attaché's office in Ottawa, received a civilian passport even though he was a military officer on active duty. Unlike some intelligence officers, however, he retained his real name on the passport. Since he had never served abroad, there was no need to cover his tracks.

Despite regrets about their impending separation, Igor's mother was also happy about his assignment and wistfully asked whether there was any possibility of accompanying him and Anna to Canada. Gouzenko walked back through the blackout to the GRU Center to see Major Dashevsky, who had briefed him on his new assignment.

"I'm sorry, Gouzenko," said Major Dashevsky, "you will not be able to bring your mother—wives, yes, but parents, no. It is a rule and most strongly enforced."

"But why?" Gouzenko persisted.

"I do not question the rules," Major Dashevsky said coldly. "I only obey them. You will be well advised to do likewise."[16]

Gouzenko knew better than to press the matter further. His mother never raised the question again, obviously recognizing that her request had been unrealistic.

Gouzenko later found out that the parents of Soviet officials were never allowed to go abroad. They were held as hostages for the "good behavior" of the officials—in other words, as a precaution against defection.

From that moment on Gouzenko never looked back.

Colonel Nikolai Zabotin, the new Soviet military attaché in Canada, was, in the words of Igor Gouzenko, "the most intriguing man I have ever met."[17] Gouzenko was introduced to Zabotin at a military airport outside Moscow on the morning of their departure for Canada. Since Gouzenko was ostensibly a civilian, he was wearing a "sickly, sand-colored" suit made in Lithuania and obtained from a special store at the GRU Center that issued foreign clothes to employees and their wives going overseas.[18]

Gouzenko automatically started to salute Colonel Zabotin but stopped abruptly, realizing that he was now supposed to be a civilian. Zabotin at first frowned but then broke out in a booming laugh.

"You'd better get away from that habit, Gouzenko," he said, with a firm handshake. "And, above all, don't look so damned respectful. Haven't you noticed that real, bona fide civilians never act awed by a mere colonel? It takes a general, at least, to impress the ingrates."[19]

Colonel Zabotin was a tall, handsome man whose military bearing would have betrayed him if he had been wearing civilian clothes. A soldier in every sense, he was bound to impress Canadians and other foreigners already favorably disposed toward any representatives of the heroic Red Army. Diplomatic relations with Canada had just been established in 1942, and Zabotin was about to set up the first GRU "legal" residency inside the newly opened Soviet Embassy. Stalin and his Politburo associates had no intention of missing the opportunity to expand espionage work against one of the Allies, which they regarded as enemies in any case, despite the expediency of World War II cooperation.

The flight of Gouzenko and Zabotin lasted four days, with stops at two Soviet air bases and a landing at Fairbanks, Alaska. After a transcontinental train journey from Edmonton they arrived in the Canadian capital. Other members of Zabotin's staff began to arrive, and Zabotin purchased a house on Range Street as the GRU base. His staff was divided roughly into two parts: the diplomatic group and the technical employees. Zabotin, his assistant Motinov, Rogov, and later Domashev belonged to the diplomatic group. Gouzenko was one of the technical employees, which also included photographic experts and radiomen. By the end of the war the GRU's staff would comprise seventeen Soviet officials; they would be overseeing twenty Canadian agents.[20]

Within a short time, Gouzenko was admitted to the secret cipher branch of the embassy, located in a sealed-off area on the second floor. Before walking upstairs, Gouzenko had to press a concealed button under a banister. The entrance to the secret cipher branch was hidden behind a velvet curtain. Drawing back the curtain, Gouzenko stood in front of an aperture in a steel door. Once he had been recognized by the duty officer, he passed through this door and found a second door, made of even heavier steel, which the guard opened for him. Then he entered a carpeted corridor, off which there were some smaller rooms similarly protected by steel doors. The windows of these rooms, painted white to remain opaque, had steel bars and could be closed off entirely at night with steel shutters. Two incinerator rooms were located at the end of the corridor. The room on the left had a small incinerator regularly used by the employees of the cipher branch. Only Ouspensky, the branch chief, could enter the room on the right, which held a much larger and more powerful incinerator built according to specifications provided by Pavlov, the KGB "legal" resident.

Supposedly this incinerator had been specially designed for emergency burning of code and cipher books, agent dossiers, cables, and other documents, but Pavlov boasted, "It is big enough and powerful enough to consume the body of a man." This remark made Gouzenko wonder whether the giant incinerator was ever used for such a purpose.[21]

As cipher branch chief, Ouspensky was in charge of the Soviet Foreign Office's communications. Vladimir Petrov has described the procedure elsewhere: "All the cables that came to our embassy from Moscow appeared to originate in the Soviet Ministry of Foreign Affairs," he wrote. "But our chief cipher clerk could tell from one indicating group of figures the cables which he had to pass on to the MVD* office, though he could not decipher them, as he did not have access to our cipher books."[22] In Ottawa Ouspensky performed a similar function in regard to the GRU and the KGB, each of which had its own cipher.

Nominally working for Ouspensky in the cipher branch were Gouzenko, Zabotin's cipher clerk, and Farafontov, Pavlov's cipher clerk. Each jealously guarded the separate communications for which he was responsible, storing the clear-text messages and other material in safes inaccessible to the rival service.

Their precautions reflected the bitter rivalry between the two

---

* Ministry of Internal Affairs, which at that time corresponded to the KGB.

Soviet Intelligence services, each service seeking to keep its operations secret from the other. It was also reflected, in Ottawa, as in other places, in the bitter hatred between the respective GRU and KGB chiefs. Zabotin and Pavlov were constantly sending complaints about the other man back to their headquarters in enciphered messages. In the final analysis, however, Pavlov, who was the KGB's SK officer (and therefore charged with watching all Soviet personnel), seemed likely to gain the upper hand, barring some major blunder on his part.

Nevertheless, especially after his wife's arrival in October, Gouzenko began to enjoy his new life. They moved into an apartment at 511 Somerset Street, and after the birth of their son, Andrei, it seemed as if nothing could go wrong with their world.

Colonel Zabotin's spy network was built on two agents, both of whom were born in prerevolutionary Russia. They began to work for Soviet Intelligence in the 1920's, accepted money for their services, were devoted Stalinists, and were leaders of the Canadian Communist Party. While they contributed information to Zabotin, their principal value to the GRU was as spotters and recruiters of intelligence talent, particularly in Communist study circles or discussion groups—whose members themselves were being "studied."

Sam Carr, whose real name was Schmil Kogan, settled in Canada after the Russian Revolution and during the 1930's engaged in Communist organizational activities, stressing the party's revolutionary aims and recruiting Canadians for the International Brigades that fought under Soviet direction in the Spanish Civil War. As national organizing secretary of the Communist Party, he later proved to be very useful to the GRU.

Carr, who had been assigned the pseudonym "Frank," was "run" by Lieutenant Colonel Rogov, his case officer. Carr provided the GRU with leads on government workers and apparently kept close tabs on members of the armed forces who had Soviet or Communist sympathies.

For instance, Rogov gave Carr the following task on June 15, 1945: "Is there any possibility for you of developing our work in the Ministry of National Defense, in the Ministry of Air, in the

Ministry of the Navy, or else on their military staffs. At the present time these fields are of great interest to us and we want you to put forth maximum efforts in this matter."[23]

In a cable to the GRU Director dated August 2, 1945, Zabotin reported: "Sam promised to give us several officers from the central administration of the active forces. At present it is pretty hard to do it, in view of the fact that a filling of positions in the staff with officers who have returned from overseas is taking place."[24]

Carr was helpful to the GRU in other ways. One of Zabotin's important tasks was to obtain false Canadian passports for GRU agents in the United States and other countries. A problem arose in 1945 for an important Soviet agent in California, who had come to the United States seven years earlier, traveling with a Canadian passport in the name of Ignacy Witczak. The real Ignacy Witczak had served in Spain in the International Brigades, and, as often happened in those days, his passport was collected and turned over to the GRU. The real Witczak, however, had returned to Canada in 1939 and was admitted without a passport. When the false Witczak needed to have his passport renewed, Sam Carr took on the job for Zabotin against his own better judgment. He himself was paid $850 and obtained the renewal by bribing an official in the Canadian Passport Office.

Zabotin's other "rock," Fred Rose (real name Rosenberg), had worked for Soviet State Security when he was only seventeen and became a Canadian citizen in 1926. Within three years he became national secretary of the Young Communist League in Canada and served in Moscow on the International Executive Committee of the Young Communist League in 1930.

Returning to Canada, Rose was appointed to the Central Executive Committee, the Communist Party's leading body. With time out for a couple of terms in prison, where he was sent as a result of his subversive activities, he continued to be active in the party. During the 1930's he participated as a candidate in two campaigns for elective office, losing each time.

In 1937 he was appointed by the Central Executive Committee to the Central Control Commission, which, in all Communist parties, exercises quasi-police functions within the party ranks and engages in Intelligence work. Reportedly he worked secretly for the KGB through its resident in the United States, a man who used the pseudonym of "Ovakimian."[25]

Rose's first contacts with the GRU developed in May and June 1942 when a Soviet trade mission came to Canada, immediately prior to official recognition of the USSR. Rose met a member of the trade mission, ostensibly a clerk, who was in reality Major Sokolov of the GRU. According to a GRU report, Rose himself approached Sokolov and suggested working for the GRU. Again in September Rose made a proposal to Sokolov for organizing intelligence work on behalf of the GRU.[26] In view of Rose's past connections with the KGB, Sokolov had to ask Moscow to approve his employment. By the time permission was finally granted, Zabotin had taken over direction of the GRU apparatus in Canada.

Despite his Communist affiliation, Rose was elected a member of the Canadian Parliament in 1943 and reelected in 1945. By then he was in a position to obtain copies of governmental documents and report on secret sessions of the House of Commons for the GRU.[27]

Zabotin's most important spy was obtained without the help of either Sam Carr or Fred Rose. In the spring of 1945 Zabotin was instructed to contact Dr. Allan Nunn May, who was working on atomic research in Montreal. May was described as a "very valuable source," and Zabotin was told that the operation should be carried out with the greatest possible care.

"He is a corporant* and his cover name is Alek," the cable said. "I consider it best to establish contact through Sam Carr. Advise me immediately when you have established contact."[28]

Although Zabotin had not heard of him, May was a noted British experimental physicist and civil servant. He had visited the Soviet Union in 1936 and was known by his friends to have leftist sympathies, but he did not take part in political activities or publish his views outside the scientific field. In view of the fact that he was already cooperating with the GRU in England, he may have been advised to say nothing about his membership in the Communist Party.

When Dr. John Douglas Cockcroft, a Cambridge professor and

---

* Soviet Intelligence jargon for a member of the Communist Party.

internationally renowned scientist, was appointed a director of the Atomic Energy Project in July 1944 and headed a team of English and Canadian scientists collaborating on atomic research, May was selected as a group leader at the Montreal Laboratory. In this capacity, he received clearance for the most sensitive information in the project.[29]

Colonel Zabotin resented the GRU director's instruction to establish contact with May through Sam Carr. He thought that the decision as to how to establish contact should have been left up to him. Such an instruction was more appropriate for a junior case officer than the GRU chief in Canada. He replied with a cable in which he asked, "Can we trust Sam more than one of our own people?"[30]

Zabotin's unstated point was that Sam Carr had been associated with Earl Browder, former head of the American Communist Party, who had been deposed by Moscow for alleged ideological deviations and made into a nonperson. At one time Carr's work in Canada had been financed with money provided by Browder on behalf of the American Communist Party.[31]

The GRU director saw the point and immediately gave Zabotin permission to appoint his own man to make contact with May, and Zabotin thereupon gave the job to Lieutenant Angelov, one of his assistants.

Angelov traveled to Montreal and looked up May's address in the local telephone book. Without bothering to call for an appointment, Angelov went to the house and, after observing it for a few minutes, went to the front door and rang the bell.

A scholarly, meek-looking man with a bald head and a long mustache opened the door. "Yes?"

"Dr. Allan Nunn May?"

The man nodded. "Won't you come in?"

As soon as he stepped through the door, Angelov said in a low voice, "Greetings from Michael."

May blanched, looked around quickly, and ushered Angelov into the living room, firmly closing the door behind them. "I'm sorry," he said, "my old connection has been cut off. Besides, I believe I'm being watched by the local security people."

Angelov laughed. "Nonsense," he said. "Don't tell me any stories. You're no more being watched than I am."

"But I tell you—"

"Just pay attention to me, Alek. Moscow has an assignment for you. If you don't want to do it—if you refuse—that'll be your headache, not mine."

"My God, you don't know what you're asking," May said. He seemed to crumple. Then, in a lower voice, he asked: "What is it you want?"

"It's very simple. No trouble for you at all. Moscow just wants a report on the kind of research you're engaged in—both in Canada and the United States."

"All right, I'll try," May said, wiping his forehead with a handkerchief he produced from somewhere. "When do you have to have it?"

"As soon as possible."

May nodded. "Next week, then. You can come here to pick it up. But you can't come here after that. If we must meet—"

"We'll meet somewhere else," Angelov said. He took a couple of bottles of whiskey out of his briefcase and put them on a table. Then he took two hundred dollars from his wallet and handed the money to May, who took it without another word.

"Until next week," said Angelov, picking up his briefcase and heading for the door.

Dr. May nodded again. "Yes, yes—goodbye."[32]

The following week May turned over to Angelov a very long and comprehensive report. The first part dealt with the technical processes being followed in the atom bomb's production; the second part concerned the organization of the atom bomb project in the United States—the structure of the Manhattan Project and the principal officials and scientists involved in it. The report included a list of scientists closely connected with the project, secret plant sites, and the nature of the work in such places as Oak Ridge, Tennessee; the University of Chicago; Los Alamos, New Mexico; and Hanford, Washington.[33] For the GRU this simplified the selection of agents and targets in future operations.

But May's contributions did not stop there. First, he provided a couple of other lengthy and detailed follow-up reports requested by Moscow. Then, in July 1945, he turned over laboratory samples of U-235 and U-225, which were considered so important that Motinov, Zabotin's deputy, flew them to Moscow.

In late July, Angelov, who had continued to meet the scientist, reported that May was being sent back to England soon to go on with his work there. On receipt of this news, the GRU director ordered that arrangements be worked out for a conspiratorial meeting between a GRU representative and May as soon as he arrived in London.

But May was still in Montreal when the bombing of Hiroshima took place. Based on information furnished to Angelov, Zabotin could provide Moscow with facts about the atom bomb that were still top secret:

To the Director.
Facts given by Alek:
(1) The test of the atomic bomb was conducted at New Mexico (with "49," "94–239"). The bomb dropped on Japan was made of uranium 235. It is known that the output of uranium 235 amounts to 400 grams daily at the magnetic separation plant at Clinton. The output of "49" is probably two times greater (some graphite units are planned for 250 mega watts, i.e., 250 grams each day). The scientific research work in this field is scheduled to be published, but without the technical details. The Americans have a published book on this subject.
(2) Alek handed over to us a platinum with 162 micrograms of uranium 233 in the form of oxide in a thin lamina. We have had no news about the mail.[34]

Lieutenant Colonel Rogov, Sam Carr's case officer, cultivated Captain David Gordon Lunan, a native of Scotland, as an agent after he was spotted by Fred Rose. Lunan had worked his way up to the rank of captain in the Canadian Army and served on the War Information Board before becoming editor of *The Military Gazette.* He had attracted Rose's attention because of his enthusiastic participation in the activities of the Quebec Committee for Allied Victory, in which Communists exerted great influence.

Rogov, who used the alias "Jan," recruited Lunan as the principal agent for a spy nucleus that included three other agents, all involved in confidential government work. Following classical conspiratorial principles, "Jan" maintained contact solely with Lunan, who had been assigned the cryptonym "Back" by Moscow. The others, each of whose cryptonym began with the letter B, were Durnford Smith ("Badeau"), Edward Mazerall ("Bagley"), and Isidor Halperin ("Bacon"). They had contact only with Lunan and not with each other.

Lunan collected reports from the three other agents on a wide range of top secret subjects, including data on uranium-235, V-bombs, explosives, and political matters in general. Lunan's main task, therefore, was to gather data and other information from his three subordinates. If one of the agents was arrested, he could tell the authorities nothing about "Jan" or even about his fellow spies, except for "Back." "Back," on the other hand, acted as a cutout between "Jan" and the other three, as well as between each of the three spies and the others.[35] Without "Back" an investigation could make scant progress.

Durnford Smith, the most productive of the three spies, worked as a research engineer for the National Research Council. Married and the father of two children, he did not seem to be deterred by family considerations and was, if anything, an "eager beaver." He furnished information on radio techniques, optics, and the proceedings of the secret Council on Research Problems.[36] Zabotin noted in a dispatch to the GRU Director, "We have received from Badeau seventeen top secret and secret documents on the question of magnicoustics, radio-locators for field artillery."[37]

Later Rogov wrote in his notebook: "Badeau asks for permission to work on uranium. There is a possibility either by being invited or by applying himself, but he warned that they are very careful in the selection of workers and that they are under strict observation."[38]

Like Durnford Smith, Edward (or Ned) Mazerall came from a cultured background and had a university education. He was an electrical engineer by profession and worked for Westinghouse and the Canadian Broadcasting Company before obtaining a job with the National Research Council as an engineer engaged in the highly secret development of radar equipment. Mazerall, however, was not enthusiastic about his spy work, and his wife was opposed to his "political" activities.[39] As a result, although he was employed in the most secret department, which dealt with radar, technical aspects of radio, and air navigation, he contributed very little to the GRU.[40]

Isidor Halperin, Lunan's third agent, was a mathematics professor. As an expert on artillery, he had extensive knowledge of new weapons, explosives, and other military inventions. "He is definitely keen," Lunan wrote, "and will be helpful." He produced a long and authoritative report on the work of the Canadian Army Research and Development Establishment, covering various plants and laboratories and other installations.[41]

Zabotin had two other agents called "Gray" and "Ernest" who provided detailed information on Canadian war plants, giving their location, production capacity, and general description. "Gray" was Harold Samuel Gerson, and "Ernest" was "Gray's" brother-in-law, James Benning. Both worked in the Canadian Department of Munitions.

Gerson proved to be the more valuable. He began working for the GRU in September 1942 under Fred Rose and evidently wished to continue his spying even after the war. He submitted a proposal in which he asked the GRU to supply financial backing for a "geological engineering consulting office" that he planned to establish after the war.[42]

Gerson was brought into the GRU spy network through Raymond Boyer, an independently wealthy man who had been associated with the Communist Party since the mid-1930's. Boyer was a chemist and started working for the GRU before the "legal" apparatus was established in the Soviet Embassy. Fred Rose was also his superior.

A perennial student of the kind sometimes found in rich families, Boyer had spent seven years at Loyola College, nine years at McGill University, and a year at the Royal Military College. He did postgraduate work at Harvard, the Sorbonne in Paris, and the University of Vienna.[43] He seemed certain to become an expert on something, and in his case it was high explosives (VV).

Zabotin described Boyer as a "Noted chemist, about 40 years of age. Works in McGill University, Montreal. Is the best of the specialists on VV on the American continent. Given full information on explosives and chemical plants. Very rich. He is afraid to work. (Gave the formula of RDX, up to the present there is no evaluation from the boss)."[44]

RDX (Research Department Explosive) was a new high explosive whose formula was still classified secret after the war. Boyer was working on RDX research at McGill and turned over all the information that came into his possession for transmission to the Soviet Union.[45]

One afternoon in September 1944, Igor Gouzenko was called into Colonel Zabotin's office, where he found the colonel staring at a letter that had just arrived in the diplomatic mail, its torn envelope still lying on top of the desk.

Zabotin looked at him silently for a moment. Then he said, "For reasons unstated, the immediate recall of you and your family has been ordered by the director."[46]

Numbly, Gouzenko went back to his desk and sat down. After an interval he was able to resume his work, but he later remembered nothing of what he did the rest of the afternoon.

He had completed only fifteen months of what was normally a two-year tour of duty. Recalling the words that Zabotin had used, he could not escape the impression that there was an underlying tone of suspicion. What had he done to arouse such suspicion in Moscow? Had word somehow gotten back about his enthusiasm for life in Canada and his decreasing enthusiasm for everything Soviet, even though he had been very careful, even in speaking to close associates and friends?

What about Anna? Had she been spied upon and some of her anti-Soviet remarks recorded? But she was just as careful as he not to make such remarks to anybody who could report them.

Another possibility was that Pavlov had installed a listening device in their apartment and recorded their private conversations. This, however, seemed no more than a remote possibility, since he had done nothing to warrant an investigation of this kind.

Finally Gouzenko finished his work, put away his code books and locked up the safe, donned his hat and coat, signed out at the door, and walked out into a steady fall downpour. Still half dazed, he walked past his house as far as the next corner, where he stood in the drenching rain until he finally got up his courage to return home.

He walked upstairs and rang the bell. Anna opened the door. "Oh, Igor, I was getting worried—you are so late. Why . . ." She gave him a strange look. "You are drenched! What is the matter?"

He closed the door. "It's bad news, Anna." Her face changed as concern turned into fear. "We have been recalled. The order was sent to Zabotin this afternoon." Her legs sagged under her, and he picked her up and carried her to the sofa.

Later, as he was drying the dishes after supper, Anna cried out, "Igor, are you in personal trouble? I've only been thinking of what the recall will mean to Andrei and us. But you . . . you . . . did you do something so bad they are liable to send you . . ."

"I know of nothing Moscow could wish to punish me for," Igor said quickly. "But who knows what one may have unconsciously done? Today I was too amazed to speak. Tomorrow I'll try to talk with Zabotin on the subject."

The next day Gouzenko told Zabotin that he had been leading the class in English at the embassy school and could be useful as an interpreter or reports officer if it was considered advisable to replace him as cipher clerk.

Zabotin nodded. "Yes, that's right," he said, "but Moscow decides such things. I'll ask the director to reconsider your recall until further additions to the staff make your departure more practical."

Within three days a reply was received from the GRU Center agreeing that Gouzenko could continue as cipher clerk "for the time being." As soon as his daily work was finished, he rushed home to tell Anna the good news.

Her reaction surprised him. "Let's face facts," she said quietly. "It's only a reprieve. We will still have to face the crisis one day. What then?"

Gouzenko answered her automatically, as if the thought had long lain dormant in his mind. "We won't go back, Anna! Andrei deserves his opportunities in this country. You are entitled to live like these Canadian wives. We will pack up and disappear somewhere in Canada or even in the United States. We will change our names. I will take other work. I will . . ."

Anna fell into his arms, crying. At first she could not speak. Then she said, "I'm glad, so glad, Igor."

Once the decision had been made, Gouzenko recognized the necessity to caution his wife on one point. "We must not convey any impression other than resignation to future recall," he told her. "If we convey even a hint of subdued excitement those who know us might begin to wonder. And if Pavlov begins to wonder our plans will blow sky high."[47]

As fall turned into winter, and then into spring, Gouzenko began to look with new eyes at the work of the GRU's "legal" *rezidentura*. "Around me in the military attaché's office and over at the Soviet Embassy, there was open, if guarded, conversation on the possibility of a third world war," he wrote later. "It was generally agreed that the Soviet Union is preparing for another war. Those of our number who were tied up with the Communist Party were all for the war, claiming only a general upheaval would lead to the establishment of world communism."[48]

In 1945 Gouzenko could only think that it was necessary to frustrate the Soviet Union's efforts to extend its system to the new world in which he hoped to find a home with his family. His contribution should be to warn Canada and other Allied nations of the dangers they faced. Suppose that he took with him documents that *proved* what the Soviet representatives were up to?

He brought up this idea in a discussion with his wife. At first Anna seemed disturbed, recognizing that it amounted to a form of treason far more serious than defection. Perhaps she wondered how this would affect their relatives in the Soviet Union, who were directly exposed to retaliation. But at last she told him that she was in agreement, for this would demonstrate their sincerity and earn them the privilege of living in another country.

In June 1945 Lieutenant Kulakov arrived in Ottawa to replace Gouzenko as cipher clerk, and Gouzenko started to select the documents he planned to take with him when he left. Having selected a document, he would turn over the edge and replace it in the file. In this way, he would not run the risk of arousing suspicion if Zabotin discovered that a document was missing. Moreover, this simplified and speeded up the process of removing the documents at the last moment, when he was sure to have a minimum of time at his disposal.

Gouzenko also started to break in Kulakov as his replacement, but he did not hurry, hoping to win as much time as possible. Then, one day in August, Zabotin called Gouzenko into his office. "Moscow is again inquiring when you are returning," he said. "I'll be sorry to lose you, Igor, but this is it."

Gouzenko carefully concealed his disappointment. "Very well,

Comrade Colonel. It will be good to see our relatives and old friends again."

Zabotin frowned for a few seconds, but then laughed in his agreeable way. "You're an odd one, Igor. You never seem to get upset about anything. I intend commending your loyalty and efficiency to the director. I feel certain you will go far in the service."

Gouzenko thanked his boss and asked how much time he had to prepare himself and his family for the trip.

"There is a ship with space available early in October," said Zabotin. "That gives you about two months."[49]

With the time fast approaching, Gouzenko suddenly had second thoughts about stealing the documents. If he was caught, what would happen to Anna and his two-year-old son? Would it not be simpler to take his wife and son and disappear?

A new complication had been added when they learned that Anna was pregnant again. She was already in her fifth month, and with less than two months to go, the crisis would come to a head when the strain might prove to be too severe for her and the unborn baby.

On the day Zabotin informed him of Moscow's inquiry about his departure, Gouzenko returned home and discussed his doubts with Anna.

"I will not hear of you changing your mind," Anna said firmly. "This is your chance to do something big for this country and yourself and, most of all, for Andrei and the new baby. Canada is to be our home. Let us not take everything and give nothing."

The final crisis was precipitated when Colonel Zabotin told Gouzenko to turn over his cipher work to Kulakov in the near future. Thereafter Gouzenko would stand by in case he was needed to assist Kulakov. Zabotin hoped that such a transfer of responsibilities would make Kulakov a fully qualified cipher clerk by the time Gouzenko departed.

On September 5, 1945, Gouzenko returned home early. He took off his coat while little Andrei was making a racket in the high chair.

Anna looked at his face. "Is it tonight?"

Gouzenko nodded. "It has to be tonight."

Zabotin's deadline for this transfer of responsibilities was not the only reason for Gouzenko's selection of Wednesday night as the time for action. A Saturday night would have been ideal in one sense, because the documents' absence could not have been discovered before Monday morning. But he and Anna had decided some time ago that he should turn over the documents and tell his story to a newspaper, and a weekday appeared preferable. In this case Wednesday night was best because Kulakov was on night duty at the military attaché's office and would sleep until noon the next day. Since Kulakov would be acting as cipher clerk, he was likely to be the one to discover the theft.

Gouzenko left home and set out on the long walk to Range Street, where the house occupied by the military attaché was located. The documents he planned to remove were in the embassy, but he needed first to go to the military attaché's office, ostensibly to finish some work, although his real purpose was to confirm that Kulakov had the night duty as scheduled. Had Zabotin set a trap for him with his sudden deadline? For all he knew, the State Security people could be trailing him even now.

Gouzenko found to his satisfaction that Kulakov was already sitting at the watch officer's desk. Just as he entered, Captain Galkin, another intelligence officer, came out and greeted him. "How about coming to a movie with me?"

Gouzenko pretended to be interested. "Which one are you going to?"

Galkin named a neighborhood theater. It occurred to Gouzenko that this would give him a good excuse to leave the military attaché's office without the pretext of doing some work.

"That's a good idea," said Gouzenko. "It's too hot to work anyway."

The two men waited outside on the sidewalk until they were joined by several others who also intended to see the movie. When the group reached the theater, Gouzenko stopped short and said, "Damn it, I've seen that show! You fellows go ahead because it's a good picture. I'll take a streetcar and go to another show downtown."

As soon as he was out of their sight he turned in the direction of the Soviet Embassy on Charlotte Street. He nodded to the guard as he signed the book. As a cipher clerk, he had access to the embassy at any time.

As he moved toward the staircase, he suddenly saw, to his horror, Vitali Pavlov, the KGB "legal" resident, sitting in the reception room. Acting as if he had not seen Pavlov, who took no notice of him, he continued on his way.

He steeled himself for anything—for a shout behind him or footsteps pounding on the stairs—and forced himself to go on. Then he pressed the concealed button under the banister and climbed the stairs to the second floor. He drew back the velvet curtain and stood before the opening in the steel door until the man on duty unbarred the door.

Stepping inside, Gouzenko recognized Ryazanov, the commercial attaché's cipher clerk, with whom he was friendly. They talked about the hot weather, and Ryazanov asked if he was working late again.

"No," Gouzenko said, "there are just a couple of cables to do and then I'll catch an 8:30 show."

He entered his little office and carefully closed the door. Opening a drawer in his desk, he took out Colonel Zabotin's cipher pouch, which contained the current messages. He had left it there that afternoon, knowing that it contained a number of messages that he intended to take with him. Then he extracted from the file the documents with the turned down edges.

He had a considerable bundle of papers of all sizes (the police later determined that there were 109 documents at all), which he distributed as evenly as possible inside his shirt. Partly because of his excitement, the shirt was already soggy with perspiration.

At last, seated at his desk, he hurriedly enciphered two outgoing cables that he had deliberately left behind that afternoon in order to have an excuse for returning in the evening.

As soon as he had finished, he checked his shirt, making certain it was not bulging. Then he closed the safe and left the room, turning over to Ryazanov the two enciphered cables and Zabotin's cipher pouch. Still worried about his bulging shirt, he hoped that Ryazanov would attribute its untidy look to the weather. Ryazanov, however, displayed no special interest in his appearance.

Casually, Gouzenko went into the men's room and washed his hands. "It's too hot to stay around here," he called out. "Why don't you skip out with me to the show?"

"Fat chance of getting away with anything around here,"

growled Ryazanov. "Besides, Pavlov is downstairs. Thanks just the same. I'd better stick around."[50]

Mention of Pavlov made Gouzenko feel weak in his knees, but there was no turning back now. He adjusted his shirt again and bade Ryazanov good night at the door.

He walked down the steps gingerly, afraid that some sudden movement might dislodge one of the documents. As he approached the reception room on the ground floor, he broke out in a sweat but yet did not dare take out a handkerchief to mop his brow. The reception room was empty; Pavlov was gone. Gouzenko took this as a good omen. He signed out, leaving the embassy for the last time, and hastened his steps toward the streetcar stop.

He was trembling violently when he reached the downtown office of the *Ottawa Journal*. On the sixth floor he walked down the corridor until he found the door marked "Editor." He was on the point of knocking when doubt suddenly seized him again. Perhaps every newspaper had a Soviet agent working there.

He ran back along the corridor just in time to reach the elevator as someone got out. Then the elevator stopped at another floor. A girl got in, took one glance at him, and smiled. "What are you doing here? Is there news breaking at the embassy?"

Her face looked familiar, but Gouzenko could not place it. When they arrived at the ground floor, he mumbled an apology and rushed away. Panic-stricken, he walked for blocks, wondering who she was, before boarding the streetcar and riding home.

Anna did her best to calm him. The girl was probably someone he had met at an embassy reception. There was nothing to worry about. Waving the documents in the air to dry them, Anna advised him to try once more to see the editor. She wrapped the documents in some paper, and he set out again.

Finding the editor's office locked, Gouzenko wandered along the corridor until he finally reached the City Room, where he asked to talk to the man in charge.

Gouzenko took out the stolen documents and spread them on his desk. He explained that they contained proof that Soviet agents were spying on Canada in an attempt to obtain data on the atom bomb. The man glanced at one of the documents but put it down immediately, since he obviously could not read Russian.

"I'm sorry," he said. "This is out of our field. I would suggest you go to the Royal Canadian Mounted Police or come back in the morning to see the editor."

Gouzenko tried to explain that the KGB would be hunting him by the next morning and might even kill him. But he could tell that the man doubted his sanity.

"Sorry," the man said, "I'm busy." He got up and walked away, leaving Gouzenko sitting alone at the desk.

Gathering up his documents, Gouzenko decided that he had no choice but to contact a high official. At the Justice Building on Wellington Street, Gouzenko told a policeman that he had an urgent matter requiring the personal attention of the minister of justice.

"It's almost midnight," the policeman said firmly. "You can see nobody until morning. Sorry."

"But it is desperately necessary that I reach the minister right away—by telephone at least."

The policeman shook his head. "It can't be done."

Feeling discouraged and beaten, Gouzenko returned home. Anna sought to console him. "Don't worry about it," she said. "You have the whole morning to reach the minister. Have a good sleep and you will feel better."

They were still talking, when the pink light of dawn filtered through their windows.

Gouzenko had suggested that they go with their son to the minister of justice's office, and they planned to arrive when the office opened. At the Justice Building, Gouzenko told the man at the reception desk that they had urgent business with the minister.

At first it seemed as if they would be stopped right there, but finally they were conducted to the minister's office, where Gouzenko again tried to explain the nature of their business. The secretary informed Gouzenko that the minister was in his other office in the Parliament Buildings and that he would take them there.

At the other office Gouzenko was once more confronted with a secretary. Gouzenko insisted that he had to see the minister himself. There was another long telephone call, and then the other secretary was told to escort them back to the Justice Building and wait for the minister there. Two hours passed and the minister of justice did not appear. The secretary received a telephone call. After hanging up, he turned to them: "I am very sorry. The minister is unable to see you."[51]

In their disappointment, the Gouzenkos went to the office of the *Ottawa Journal*, where they asked to see the editor. The editor was unavailable, but a young reporter, who listened sympathetically, told them at last that nobody was interested in their story there. "Nobody wants to say anything but nice things about Stalin these days," she said.

They did not know that during the two hours they spent in the minister of justice's office the Canadian government was trying to decide what to do with them. The Gouzenkos were an embarrassment, and the authorities had some difficulty in determining how to dispose of them. For Prime Minister Mackenzie King, in particular, the case was a hot potato. On the one hand, there were doubts concerning the genuineness of the documents and Gouzenko's reliability. Perhaps the whole affair was an anti-Soviet scheme designed to provoke a scandal and compromise the Canadian government. On the other hand, the documents seemed to show that atomic and other state secrets had been passed to the Russians, and the nation's security demanded at least a perusal of them.

Prime Minister King refused to have anything to do with Gouzenko and recommended that he return to his embassy. Subsequently, he told the House of Commons: "I thought he should be told to go back to the embassy with the papers he had in his possession. . . . What I felt most important was to see that nothing should be done which would cause the Russsian Embassy to believe that Canada had the least suspicion of anything which was taking place there."[52]

The Gouzenkos were also rebuffed by a second government office, where they had turned for naturalization papers, as well as by other newspapers. They returned to their apartment. They had nearly abandoned hope but now sought help from their Canadian neighbors in the same apartment house. A woman who lived across the hall offered to take them in for the night, since they were afraid to remain in their own apartment.

During the course of the day Zabotin's office had become aware that Gouzenko was not only missing but that several recent messages had also vanished. At this point Zabotin turned over the case to Pavlov, the KGB resident, whose dual capacity included the responsibility of investigating such cases at the embassy.

Sometime around midnight Pavlov showed up at the Gouzenko apartment, accompanied by Farafontov, his cipher clerk, and the GRU intelligence officers Rogov and Angelov. While Gouzenko watched surreptitiously through a keyhole from the apartment across the hall, Pavlov hammered insistently on the Gouzenkos' door.

Hearing the noise, the Gouzenkos' next-door neighbor, who was aware of the situation, opened his door and asked what Pavlov and the others wanted. When someone mentioned Gouzenko's name, he said, "The Gouzenkos are away."

Pavlov and his companions went downstairs but returned a few minutes later. This time Pavlov had a jimmy and pried at the door, which suddenly sprung open with a rasping sound. The group of four entered the apartment and quietly closed the door.

The woman with whom the Gouzenkos were staying telephoned the police. Two policemen arrived and surprised the four Soviet officials in the act of rifling desk and bureau drawers. Asked why they had broken into the apartment, Pavlov said angrily, "How dare you talk to me like that? We had a key for this apartment but lost it. Anyway, this lock is Soviet property and we can do what we like with it. I order you to leave this apartment!"[53]

Later Pavlov claimed that the policemen had insulted them and violated their diplomatic immunity. Finally the police allowed Pavlov and his companions to leave while continuing the investigation.

Pavlov's feat of "breaking and entering" saved Gouzenko by finally convincing the Canadian authorities that he should be taken seriously. The next morning Gouzenko was invited by a police inspector to accompany him to the Justice Building, where he had a very different reception. High-level Royal Canadian Mounted Police and civilian investigators treated him courteously and attentively, and he answered their questions for nearly five hours.

From that time on Gouzenko and his family received the protection of the Canadian government and went into hiding. Meanwhile, the principal Intelligence figures at the Soviet

Embassy—Colonel Zabotin and Pavlov—tried to assess the damage. They hoped that Gouzenko would keep silent about the most crucial aspects of their espionage work, fearing for his own life and the lives of his family. As one observer later noted: "In the earlier history of Soviet espionage there had been more than one case of a defecting member of Intelligence who remained silent for the rest of his days."[54] Orlov and Krivitsky were prime examples; although they revealed some of what they knew, both remained silent about the most important information they possessed.

Soon after Gouzenko's defection, the Soviet Embassy opened a counterattack. Ambassador Zarubin demanded that the Canadian authorities turn over Gouzenko, who, Zarubin claimed, had embezzled funds from the embassy. Zarubin also charged that the police had displayed extreme rudeness toward Soviet diplomats, and he insisted on the punishment of the guilty parties.

When the Department of External Affairs ignored this communication, Ambassador Zarubin repeated his demand a week later:

> Confirming its communication in the Note No. 35 of Sept. 7th of the fact that Gouzenko had robbed public funds, the Embassy, upon instructions from the Government of the USSR repeats its request to the Government of Canada to apprehend Gouzenko and his wife, and, without trial, to hand them over to the Embassy for deportation to the Soviet Union.
>
> The Soviet government expresses the hope that the Government of Canada will fulfill its request.[55]

Recognizing the international ramifications of the case, Mackenzie King decided to confer with President Truman and Prime Minister Attlee, explaining the trips on other grounds so that the press would not give even greater prominence to the story. In his naiveness, King even proposed to discuss the subject with Stalin. A few months later he told the Canadian House of Commons: "From what I have heard and know about Premier Stalin, I am confident that the Russian leader would not countenance or condone such action in one of his country's embassies."[56] Fortunately, he was dissuaded from making the trip.

In December the time arrived for Anna to have her baby. Since Gouzenko feared that Pavlov would have his agents watching all the hospitals within a radius of many miles, arrangements were made for an RCMP constable to pose as her husband and accompany her to a hospital, where they pretended to be Polish immigrants who spoke only a little English, hoping to avoid the necessity of answering unwelcome questions.

Thus, at the birth of their second child, a girl, Gouzenko himself was replaced by a proxy husband.

Igor Gouzenko worked for almost nine months with the Canadian Royal Commission established to investigate his revelations. Eventually he testified under heavy guard at some twenty trials between May 1946 and 1948.

In December 1945, Colonel Zabotin left Canada without notifying the Department of External Affairs, as required by diplomatic protocol. Despite his supposed diplomatic immunity, there were reasons to believe that charges could be brought against him. He fled to New York and boarded the *Aleksandr Suvorov*, a Soviet ship, which left port without proper clearance. Zabotin, who was made a scapegoat in the Gouzenko case by his own government, found himself under virtual arrest and, after returning to the Soviet Union, was sentenced to ten years in a labor camp.[57]

Ambassador Zarubin left Canada in a completely overt manner a few weeks after Zabotin's departure. The report of the Canadian Royal Commission took pains to exonerate him of any complicity in the espionage revealed by Gouzenko, and Zarubin was later accepted as an ambassador in both Great Britain and the United States. Since Zabotin had been warned against revealing any secret information to the ambassador, and Pavlov probably received a similar warning from the KGB, there was in fact no reason to blame Zarubin for the espionage operations in Canada.

Allan Nunn May was tried in England and was sentenced to ten years of penal servitude. Of the twenty people tried in Canada, six were acquitted, including some who appeared guilty. The other fourteen received prison terms of various lengths. Fred Rose and Sam Carr, Zabotin's "rocks," were each sentenced to six years.

Gouzenko and his family were granted Canadian citizenship and assumed new identities. A permanent bodyguard was maintained nearby under a camouflage that deceived outsiders very successfully. The Gouzenkos' neighbors, their children's schoolteachers, the local authorities, and shopkeepers in the area knew them only by their assumed identities.

Igor Gouzenko apparently had no financial worries. An Ottawa businessman promised him an annuity for life. He also received about $150,000 from his book, *The Iron Curtain,* and a Hollywood film starring Dana Andrews and Gene Tierney based on his experiences. His novel, *The Fall of a Titan,* was published in 1954. A financial and artistic success, it was inspired by the case of the Russian novelist Maxim Gorky, who was practically a prisoner in his last years at a villa in Soviet Russia. Gorky had become disillusioned with the Soviet regime and lost favor with Stalin in his old age; Gouzenko indicated in his novel (as many people believed) that Gorky was murdered at the instigation of Soviet State Security.

Soviet Intelligence has had more than its share of defectors. Whether the traitor-spy is motivated by ideological considerations, money, ambition, or revenge, he is likely to be exposed by a defector with similar motivations. The Igor Gouzenko case, which has been replicated many times, shows that the traitor-spy's fate lies in the hands of strangers, people he does not know and whose existence he does not even suspect.

As Gouzenko himself said in 1957, "There are Communist-sickened Russian officials and agents who yearn for an opportunity to break for freedom and to carry with them vital documents, evidence of Kremlin-directed espionage against the West, as I did in 1945."

This was an opinion that he evidently continued to hold up to the time of his death by heart attack in June 1982. Only eight months earlier he had asked *The Times* of London to publicize his plan for offering citizenship and financial assistance to all defectors who brought with them information about Soviet espionage against the West.[59]

9

Victims of Circumstance

IF A PSYCHOLOGIST were to divide all of humanity into two types, "assertive" and "responsive," the victims of circumstance would tend to be responsive in nature. They do not dominate events; events dominate them.

Vladimir ("Volodya") Petrov, a KGB Intelligence officer formed in a hard school, was such a man. As a victim of circumstance, he became a defector, although he could have just as easily wound up in a concentration camp.

Petrov was christened Afanasi Mikhailovich Shorokhov,[1] but even as a boy he was called Vladimir or Volodya instead of Afanasi. Inspired by the revolutionary fervor of the 1920s, young Shorokhov decided to exchange his family name for the revolutionary name Proletarsky ("man of the people").

Later, while serving in the KGB, he was sent abroad under the cover of a clerk in the Soviet Embassy in Stockholm. Before his departure, the authorities, without asking him, issued a passport giving his name as Vladimir Petrov, since Proletarsky was considered too militant to be used on a "diplomatic" assignment.

Having become Petrov in Sweden, he was again Petrov when the KGB sent him to Australia, where he was assigned to the Soviet Embassy in Canberra. At home, however, he continued to be known as Volodya Proletarsky, and as time passed his feeling of embarrassment grew. Whenever a telephone call came for him in the office and someone yelled "Proletarsky!" he suspected that his colleagues were laughing at him behind his back.[2]

Nevertheless, there was no way he could cease to be a "man of the people," except by representing the KGB abroad—or by becoming a defector.

Vladimir Petrov was born in the village of Larikha in central Siberia on February 15, 1907. His ancestors were peasants, and Petrov had been brought up as a peasant. He was the first of his family to learn to read and write.[3] Russian peasants are often described as *khitriy* (cunning), and this was one of the qualities that Petrov had and never lost, long after he had ceased to be a peasant. A man who knew him many years later in Australia gave his impressions of Petrov:

> The first was one of impassiveness. No sign of expression or emotion passed across Petrov's large face. When he laughed, he sounded hearty but the laughter never showed in his eyes. He looked at the world suspiciously and talked little. . . . I immediately saw that, behind the thick frame of expressionless mobility, Petrov had a cunning and alert mind.[4]

The Russian Revolution enabled Petrov, like countless others, to escape from the peasantry and leave the land tilled by their forebears for generations. Nevertheless, Petrov did not find it easy to free himself from the inexorable grip of the land. His mother felt that he had set his sights too high.

"Son, it is as I said," she told him. "You should realize that you have not sufficient education for such high ideas. You should stay here in the village and work."[5]

But the regime needed young party activists who came from the "people," and Petrov's persistence and hard work finally paid off. Admitted as a Communist Party member on July 15, 1927, after only a year of probation, Petrov first was assigned to run a village cultural center, and then attended a trade-union course in a party school, which led to a new assignment as a youth organizer at a Urals steel plant.

Called up for military service in the autumn of 1930, Petrov expressed a preference for the Red Navy and was accordingly sent to Naval Headquarters in Leningrad to begin three and a half years of naval service. Once again his party membership worked to his advantage, for Petrov became one of only nine recruits selected for cipher training, which lasted two years.

Petrov's naval assignment was a turning point in his life. Up to that time he had lived only in villages and provincial towns; thereafter, except for tours of duty abroad, he remained close to the centers of power in Moscow and Leningrad. Moreover, his naval service as a cipher specialist opened the way for a lifelong career in Soviet Intelligence. For all that, the Red Navy left its mark on Petrov. The same acquaintance in Australia noted: "He walked with somewhat of a rolling gait, and a tattooed anchor at the base of his left thumb confirmed the impression that he had once been a sailor."[6]

Petrov served on a destroyer attached to the Baltic Fleet as a senior cipher rating, acting as custodian of the naval code books and handling incoming and outgoing messages. He liked the navy and enjoyed the comradeship of other sailors. Consequently, his decision to leave the navy was a hard one to make.

On one of his shore leaves, he met a girl named Lydia, whom he married after a brief courtship. Having acquired the added responsibility of a wife, he decided at the end of his enlistment that he should not continue going to sea, even though he had been offered the chance to become a political commissar in the navy. In any case, he had another possibility. Friends of his, who had gone through naval cipher school with him, were now working for Soviet State Security, and they urged him to apply. Aware that KGB personnel, even more than naval personnel, received preferential treatment in all the necessities of life, which the general population was denied, he did not hesitate. "My reasons were simple," he wrote twenty years later. "I was married, I wanted a job, and I wanted enough to eat."[7]

He applied without delay, complying with the seemingly endless paperwork and waiting for the security investigation to be completed. In May 1933, he was notified of his acceptance by the KGB.

Petrov reported for work in Moscow. Starting on the lowest

rung of the ladder, he was officially classified as a junior case officer, a position that carried with it the rank of KGB junior lieutenant.[8] His real post, however, was in the Special Cipher Section of the KGB's Foreign Administration, where he worked as a cipher clerk.

The Special Cipher Section handled all the cable traffic with the State Security's "legal" residencies abroad, which moved through commercial radio and telegraph channels, or, more rarely, by direct radio communications between embassies abroad and Moscow. A completely separate (and strictly isolated) cipher section processed the messages to and from "illegal" residencies, which depended on secret radio reception and transmission.[9]

There were usually seven cipher clerks on duty in the Special Cipher Section, on the fourth floor of the old Lubyanka building. Petrov found the work a hard grind, for the volume of traffic was very great, and the cipher clerks frequently did not finish all the cables before midnight.

In addition, Petrov was forced by the party to attend evening classes three nights a week in order to make up for his lack of formal education. After four years of unremitting effort, he finally passed all his subjects and received a diploma entitling him to enter any institution of higher education.

But this heavy work schedule and constant study led to a serious deterioration of his marriage. He and Lydia were incompatible in most respects anyway, for his quiet and serious nature conflicted with Lydia's shallow interests and constant need for excitement and variety. They were separated in 1938, and Lydia later married a Red Army officer.

Bored with desk work, Petrov sought to find a more congenial occupation during the period before his foreign assignment. At one point he tried to rejoin the navy, at another he wanted to attend the Stalin Tank Academy and become an army officer. On each occasion, Ilyin, the chief of the cipher section, refused to release him, claiming that the section was shorthanded.

The situation changed abruptly in September 1937. Petrov already knew that State Security border guards and internal security troops had been secretly dispatched to the southwestern Chinese province of Sinkiang, where a Soviet puppet government was on the point of being overthrown. Sinkiang, now a center of nuclear weapons research, borders on the Soviet Union and has long been of interest to Moscow.

One day Ilyin sent for him. "The chief of communications with our troops in Sinkiang has asked for a capable man to take charge of cipher duties at the headquarters there. I've decided that you're the man for the job. Hand over your present duties and be prepared to move at once."[10]

After a five-day train trip into Central Asia, Petrov finally reached Frunze, the jumping-off point for Sinkiang. From Frunze he traveled with an army convoy over a spectacularly dangerous road through the Tienshan Mountains, before arriving at the Soviet headquarters in Yarkand.

It was the sight of Yarkand, with its abject poverty and diseased population, that impressed upon Petrov the Soviet Union's civilizing mission in Asia. Here he took up his duties at headquarters, supervising a staff of eight cipher clerks.

By this time, the anti-Soviet revolt was beginning to die out. The final task of the Soviet forces at Yarkand was to carry out a thorough purge of the Sinkiang population to eliminate all pro-British, pro-American, and anti-Soviet elements. People rounded up on the basis of even the slightest rumors or whispers were briefly interrogated by a KGB colonel and automatically convicted of spying for the Americans or the British. The chief of staff signed the order for execution, and the condemned prisoners were driven in truckloads to a place outside the town where graves had already been dug.[11]

Petrov remained in Sinkiang until January 1938, when the pro-Soviet Urumchi government had been restored and Soviet forces were being withdrawn. Just before his departure, he dealt with cipher traffic concerning Agent 063, whom he remembered well from his work in Moscow as one of the most valuable Soviet agents, supplying high-level information.

The message received from Moscow on the eve of his departure contained a laconic order: "Render harmless Agent 063, found to be a British spy."

When Petrov delivered the message to the Soviet chief of staff, Voitenkov, he learned the identity of Agent 063. He was the

Chinese governor of Yarkand, a huge fat man who constantly came and went at the Soviet headquarters.

Voitenkov immediately devised a scheme for the governor's elimination. He sent an interpreter to him with an invitation to call at Soviet headquarters that evening to bid farewell to the commanding general, who was about to leave for the Soviet Union. Voitenkov correctly calculated that such an invitation would not be declined.

When the governor appeared, he was seized at once. Petrov later processed the report of his fifteen-minute interrogation, during which the governor, even though caught completely by surprise, still continued to maintain that he was not a British spy.

Meanwhile, three of Petrov's radio operators were digging a grave in the dirt corridor of the building. The governor was led out, bound and gagged, and laid in the corridor beside the grave. At a signal a truck outside in the courtyard revved up its motor, and one of the assistant interrogators fired three shots into the back of his head. Then the governor's huge body was rolled into the open grave, gasoline was ignited over it, and the remains were covered with dirt. The earth was then stamped down flat, and straw mats were replaced over it.

Petrov's last duty was to report to Moscow that the order concerning Agent 063 had been carried out.[12] He left by plane the next morning. Petrov could not suppress the thought that Agent 063's crime was not that he had been a British spy but that he knew too much.

On his return to Moscow, Petrov was transferred to a section of State Security responsible for the KGB's communications within the USSR. Later he temporarily became head of the section. The *yezhovshchina*—the purge conducted throughout the country under Yezhov's direction—was just then at its height. In this new position many of the messages from Soviet State Security headquarters in Moscow to its regional offices passed through Petrov's hands, providing an inside picture of the great purge.

One of Petrov's friends, a State Security official in a country town near Novosibirsk, told of a message from the Moscow headquarters setting a quota of five hundred people to be executed in that town. The official went through his files but could only find people listed for trivial offenses, yet he could not report to Moscow his inability to comply with this order. He went through the files a second time and made up his list of five hundred victims by selecting priests and their relatives, former members of Admiral Kolchak's White Army (who had already been amnestied), and anyone who had ever spoken critically of the Soviet regime. He then brought charges against them and had them executed, reporting fulfillment to Moscow. Petrov's friend was a decent man whose conscience troubled him for many years, but, as Petrov said, he not only wanted to stay alive, but had a mother, a father, a wife, and two children.[13]

Petrov himself narrowly escaped being purged a couple of times. In Sinkiang he had formed a close relationship with Voitenkov, at first State Security Chief of Communications and later chief of staff there. After his return to Moscow, Petrov sometimes acted as Voitenkov's secretary. Invited by Voitenkov to work for him permanently, Petrov requested a transfer from cipher work, but the chief of his section once again refused to release him, motivated by self-interest rather than any concern for Petrov. Nevertheless, as it turned out, the section chief did him a favor.

In April 1938 Voitenkov was arrested at the Kazan Railroad Station in Moscow. Not long afterward, Frinovsky, Yezhov's deputy, who had directed the Sinkiang operation from Moscow, was also arrested. Both men disappeared and presumably were shot.

On another occasion, suspicion fell on Petrov when the State Security office in Ishim sent Moscow a report about a revolt in which Petrov's brother supposedly participated. Questioned about the matter by his section chief, Petrov stated that his brother had been serving in the Red Army at the time. Besides, their name, Shorokhov, was quite common in that area. Eventually both Petrov and his brother were cleared of any suspicion. Nevertheless, he continued to feel insecure for a long time thereafter.

Evdokia ("Doosia") K. had begun work for Soviet State Security in 1933, the same year Petrov joined the organization. While he was concerned with the KGB's own communications, she worked in the branch in charge of cryptanalysis, concentrating on codes and ciphers used by foreign governments in communicating with their embassies in Moscow. They had become acquainted at the office and sometimes met on KGB outings. In June 1940 they were married.

They were just getting settled into their apartment a year later when the Germans invaded Russia. For a time Petrov was chief of the cipher section of Gulag, with twelve clerks subordinate to him.[14] Faced with a seemingly unstoppable German advance, the Soviet regime ordered the evacuation of government offices from Moscow on October 16, 1941, and State Security offices were evacuated along with the others. Doosia went to Kuibyshev, but Petrov remained behind with a special cipher group attached to the headquarters of Beria, Commissar of State Security.[15] It was expected that all the lines of communication would be transferred to Kuibyshev soon, after the anticipated German capture of Moscow.

Contrary to these expectations, the Germans were driven back, and most of those who had been evacuated returned. With Petrov's help, Doosia was among the first to return and went to work in his section.

Early in 1942 Fedor Filipovich Degtyarov, Petrov's chief, summoned Petrov and asked him if he would like a foreign assignment. Degtyarov had recommended Petrov for a job that had just opened up in Sweden. Petrov said that he was definitely interested but would have to discuss the matter with his wife. He also pretended to have certain doubts, since some people had returned from such assignments with a black mark on their record. Degtyarov, however, expressed confidence in Petrov, saying that his soundness would keep him out of any trouble.

In reality, both Petrov and Doosia were overjoyed at the news, already looking forward to their escape from the dangers and privations of wartime Russia to the peace and abundance of neutral Sweden. But they knew that it would have been the height of foolishness to express their joy openly. As dedicated employees of State Security and good Communists, they were not supposed to enjoy life abroad or, still worse, to prefer it to the life of the USSR.

In July 1942 they were ready to go to Sweden. They had bade

farewell to their relatives and friends and turned over their apartment to colleagues who would occupy it in their absence. But it was no simple matter to reach Sweden from Russia when nearly all of the western USSR was in German hands. They made the tedious overland journey to Arkhangelsk, where they were supposed to sail for London. Their ten-week wait was in vain. Because of the heavy damage sustained by the convoys from German air and sea attacks, no captain was willing to take their party, which included women and children, as passengers.

Disconsolate, they returned to Moscow, where they no longer had a home and were even denied access to the State Security restaurant because they were now under the cover of the Ministry of Foreign Affairs. They were able to stay with friends but suffered from hunger during the six weeks they waited for visas enabling them to travel to Teheran.

At last they were on their way again, and this time flew to Kuibyshev, then on to Teheran, stopping over there until they could proceed to Cairo. At Suez they boarded a British ship sailing to England around the Cape of Good Hope. It was already November, and only a few days after they left Aden, while in the Indian Ocean, their ship was torpedoed by a German submarine. Before the ship went down, the passengers managed to get into lifeboats. A British destroyer soon picked them up and took them to Durban in South Africa. Eventually they reached Cape Town, from which they sailed to England. They spent a couple of weeks in London before continuing to Aberdeen and boarding a plane to Sweden. They arrived at their destination roughly eight months after their first departure from Moscow.

Vladimir Petrov officially held the position of clerk in the Soviet Embassy, although as an officer of the KGB "legal" residency he had in reality two intelligence jobs, as a cipher clerk and as the SK officer assigned to check on all Soviet citizens in Sweden, up to and including Ambassador Alexandra Kollontai. In fact, prior to his departure, Petrov had been specifically ordered to check up on the venerable lady, a comrade of Lenin and other Old Bolsheviks, who had headed the Soviet Embassy in Stockholm for thirteen years.

Doosia Petrov remained a staff employee of State Security, but her official status in Sweden was that of a dependent, as Petrov's wife. Soon after her arrival, she began to work full time in the *rezidentura*, typing dispatches addressed to Moscow and agents' reports and stencils for the duplicating machine, photographing documents procured by agents, and doing occasional translations of material from English into Russian.

When the KGB resident, a man named Yartsev, was recalled to Moscow, his energetic and forceful wife carried on in his place until his successor arrived. The new resident, who became the Petrovs' chief after both Yartsevs had left, was named Razin. Extremely intelligent and personable, he proved to be a far more professional intelligence officer than his predecessors.[16]

Doosia turned out to be a great asset to her husband both socially and professionally. Impressed by her ease in capitalist Sweden (she was even taken for Swedish at times), Razin freed her from office work and made her a case officer.

One day Razin showed Doosia a cable from Moscow. "Doosia, I have some important news for you," he said. "I proposed to Moscow that you should take over the running of Maria and Moscow has approved. Are you happy to accept the assignment?"

Doosia's blue eyes lit up. "Yes, of course. I am happy to serve in any way I can."[17]

Doosia already knew a good deal about Maria, having typed up reports on her. Razin had met Maria at the theater and became interested in her when he found out that she worked for the Swedish Foreign Ministry. Maria knew some Russian and was amenable to a suggestion that she exchange Swedish for Russian lessons with a girl at the Soviet Embassy.

This was the task that Doosia now took on. Maria was, of course, unaware of the KGB residency's real interest in her. Doosia had to cultivate her, learning as much about her as she could, sounding out her ideas, and cautiously indoctrinating her with favorable ideas about the Soviet Union and Soviet policy—until the time came to recruit her as an agent.

Their relationship developed into real friendship. After their weekly meeting, Doosia submitted a detailed report to Razin, who reviewed it and sent it on to Moscow. At first, Doosia was intent on picking up every piece of biographical information on Maria— her full name, the names of her parents, her relatives, their occupations, significant facts about her education, interests, hobbies, events in her life, and illnesses. She wrote up a character appraisal of Maria, focusing on her strengths and weaknesses, and—with Moscow's approval and KGB funds—gave her a wristwatch for her birthday.

Doosia gradually learned details of Maria's work in the Foreign Ministry, the hours she spent there, the occasions on which she found herself alone, the people she worked with, her friends in the Foreign Ministry, and so on. Nevertheless, Doosia did not feel that the time was ripe yet to recruit her, but Moscow was critical about the delay, suggesting that she needed to be more aggressive in her ideological softening-up of Maria.

Urged on by Moscow, Doosia tried to take advantage of the fact that Maria was Jewish by talking enthusiastically about all the advantages enjoyed by Jews and other nationalities in the USSR. She talked about the enormous economic progress made by the Soviet state, the absence of unemployment, the free medical care, and the low-cost housing, and pointed out that the Soviet Union was leading the only effective resistance against Hitler. Maria seemed impressed, nodded sometimes, but seldom commented.

Then Maria confided to Doosia, at the outset of one of their meetings, that she was about to be sent to Eastern Europe. Doosia congratulated her, knowing that Maria had always dreamed of traveling and seeing foreign places.

Doosia went back to the embassy and discussed this latest development with Razin. They agreed that an attempt should be made to recruit Maria before she departed for her new post. They sent off a cable to Moscow with this proposal, and Moscow sent back its approval, but suggested that Vladimir Petrov, who had met Maria, should undertake the recruitment. In reply, Razin and Doosia pointed out that Petrov hardly knew Maria, while Doosia and Maria had become close friends. Moscow finally agreed to let Doosia make the attempt, stipulating at the same time that this should be done at Maria's home rather than the Petrovs' apartment. Moscow obviously feared that the Swedish counterintelligence service might have rigged up listening devices in the Petrovs' home.

Doosia's decisive meeting with Maria took place on a mild and pleasant August evening. She went to Maria's home, and they sat and talked about various subjects. Doosia finally brought the conversation around to Maria's preparations for her assignment in Eastern Europe. Maria spoke readily about how busy she was, what was happening in her office, and how much night duty she still had to do before her leavetaking.

Doosia saw the opening and decided that there was no time left for hesitation. "Maria, when you are working on night duty," she said, "are you ever visited by anyone or are you alone?"

"Oh, it's usually very quiet," answered Maria, "but you never know. My boss sometimes works till the early hours of the morning. He may call for something I'm typing, or want me to take dictation. Why?"

"Maria, you've known a number of us from the Soviet Embassy —Razin, Lena, and myself—and you and I have had some very frank talks about things, haven't we? I mean especially about the warlike plans of the capitalist countries against the peace-loving Soviet Union. Now that the war is over, there ought to be peace, but it isn't enough just to wish for peace. Everyone who really wants peace must be active in fighting for it."

Doosia continued: "War is a terrible thing. Even here in neutral Sweden you have felt the effects of war, though the effects here are negligible compared with the sufferings of the Russian people. Why have you escaped? Because your government deceived the people. They allowed German troops to pass through Sweden. They collaborated with Hitler. Otherwise the Nazis would have overrun Sweden. Maria, you are Jewish. Think what dreadful cruelties you would have suffered under the Nazis!"

When Maria turned pale, Doosia saw that her last remark had struck home. She quickly seized her chance. "There is only one way to fight for peace—by helping the Soviet Union, which stands for peace, against its warlike enemies. There are many ways to help the Soviet Union. It may be by campaigning for peace or it may be with information. The more information the Soviet Union has about the plans of its enemies, the more hope there is that its fight for peace will succeed."

"Doosia, what do you mean?" Maria's dark eyes searched Doosia's face incredulously. "What sort of information?"

There was no turning back now. Doosia knew that only firmness and determination could help her now. "I mean this, Maria. The

Soviet Union needs to know what secret treaties there are between capitalist countries which threaten it. It also needs to know in advance the secret discussions on treaties which are being negotiated between itself and foreign countries. At this moment, as you know, your department is negotiating a treaty between the Soviet Union and Sweden. Maria, can you get me copies of these drafts and discussions and of other material which will help the Soviet Union? From what you have told me, you are alone most of the time when you are on night duty. It should be quite easy. This would help the Soviet Union very much. Of course, it would be an absolutely secret matter between you, me, and my boss. No one else would know."

"No, I don't think I could help you, really," said Maria, who kept staring at Doosia. "As you know, I'm going abroad very soon. Time is short."

"You might be able to help us in your new post. But, in any case, couldn't you let me have the drafts of this treaty before you go?"

Maria shook her head.

Doosia remained persistent. "Why not, Maria? Are you afraid? I can assure you that no one else need ever know. And if the worst did happen, you could count on help from us."

"No, no! I couldn't get anything you would want; and I'd be too frightened anyway. I can't do it."

"Well, don't decide in haste. Think it over, Maria, and let me know later."

But Maria now shook her head with equal determination. "This is my final decision," she said in a formal manner that left no doubt about her position.[18]

Doosia parted with Maria. Before Maria went abroad, Doosia sent her a bunch of roses accompanied by a card wishing her good luck, but Maria, who had always responded to such gestures with a note of thanks in the past, did not reply. Doosia never heard from her again.

Doosia reported the failure of this attempted recruitment to Moscow, which did not comment—not surprisingly, as such recruitments are attempted by the KGB every day in all parts of the world.

The other operation assigned to Doosia was of quite a different sort. In this case there was no question of recruiting an agent. The agent Klara was a thoroughly indoctrinated Communist who had been a Soviet spy for many years. Doosia's job was to run this agent, which involved nothing more than going to meetings with her, giving her instructions, paying her money, and receiving her reports. The only real problem was how to conduct their contacts in a professional manner, using the best techniques to effect clandestine meetings and the transfer of reports and documents without being caught by the Swedish counterintelligence service.

Unlike the operation involving Maria, the operation with Klara went smoothly from beginning to end during Doosia's tenure as case officer.

Nevertheless, Doosia frequently went to Klara's apartment for meetings. Her only precaution was to have Klara call her at home from a pay telephone before a scheduled meeting; Doosia would say "hello" two or three times and if nobody spoke she knew that Klara was giving her a signal that it was safe to come. If Klara did not call at the appointed time, Doosia would know that the meeting was off and visit her at a previously arranged alternate time.

While Doosia was busy with her espionage activities, Vladimir Petrov found that he had all the work he could handle. As the KGB's SK officer, he met each month with an agent called Misha, a Soviet naval officer who was in close contact with the crews of Soviet trawlers interned in Sweden. An internee himself, Misha reported on their attitudes and activities, particularly those that raised any question as to their loyalty. Petrov's secret meetings with Misha frequently took place when Petrov pretended to be out fishing with his tackle on some deserted shore.

When the war ended, Petrov turned his attention to the repatriation of interned Soviet citizens. Most of them had enjoyed a much higher standard of living in Sweden, and some had no desire to return home.

The Soviet Ambassador, Chernyshev, who had replaced Madame Kollontai, visited the internment camps and assured Soviet internees that they had no reason to fear that their sojourn in Sweden would be held against them. According to him, everyone would be well treated and receive a good job in the USSR.

The majority of the internees chose to return to the USSR, believing that they had done nothing wrong, that they had behaved well in internment, and that as loyal Soviet citizens they would be received at home with open arms.

After his own return to the USSR, however, Petrov checked on the fates of the internees and discovered that few of them had ever seen their families again. Most of the internees were sentenced to terms ranging from ten to fifteen years in corrective labor camps as punishment for their stay abroad and as a precaution against their spreading stories about the good life in Sweden.

During the four years the Petrovs spent in Sweden from 1943 to 1947, Petrov had an excellent opportunity as the KGB cipher clerk to survey the widespread Soviet espionage network. "Neutral Sweden during our time was a rich and productive field for Soviet espionage," Petrov noted later.[19]

These espionage activities were aided in no small measure by the background against which they took place. Madame Kollontai had succeeded in creating a sympathetic public attitude toward the Soviet Union in Sweden. The Soviet Union's alliance with the West against Nazi Germany won additional popular support. Finally, the Swedes had no desire to offend a powerful neighbor like the Soviet Union. It followed that neither the Swedish government nor its security service was strongly disposed to counteract Soviet espionage.

One of the best agents of Soviet Intelligence was being cultivated by the GRU while Petrov was still in Sweden and accepted recruitment after Petrov's departure. He was Ernst Hilding Andersson, a Swedish Navy petty officer, who betrayed to the USSR many of Sweden's most important naval secrets.

Before his arrest in September, 1950, Andersson provided regular reports on the Stockholm naval base and the Swedish Baltic Fleet. He also furnished Soviet Intelligence with maps and detailed descriptions of the big Karlskrona naval base in southern Sweden.

An important agent recruited by the KGB was Fritiof Enbom, a railroadman, who provided information on the transit of German troops across Sweden, which the Swedish government permitted under strong German pressure. Enbom's information made it possible to estimate the size of the German troop movements quite accurately. Then, in 1943, Enbom was introduced to a KGB officer named Vassiliev, to whom Enbom reported thereafter. Later, in

1946, the KGB turned over Enbom to the GRU, to which he supplied military information until his arrest in February 1952.

All in all, both from a professional and a personal point of view, the Petrovs' four-year tour of duty in Sweden was a success. Unfortunately, this experience did not prepare them adequately for what they later encountered in Australia.

Returning from Sweden, the Petrovs found the Soviet Union more run-down and drab than they remembered it. The best part of their arrival in Moscow was the welcome they received from Doosia's family—her father, mother, brother, and ten-year-old sister—who met them at the railroad station. The only surviving member of Vladimir's family, his mother, still lived far away in his native village in Siberia.

Both Petrov and Doosia were assigned to work in the Committee of Information (KI) on their arrival. The KI represented an attempt to consolidate all foreign intelligence into one organization, but it was destined to fail for a number of reasons, including the resentment of the GRU people over the fact that KGB men headed all important divisions.[20] The KI was housed in a couple of ornate buildings that had once been the headquarters of the Comintern. The Petrovs, like other KI employees, had a serious commuting problem, since it took three hours to make the round trip by bus.

The office in which Petrov worked placed SK officers and co-opted agents in all Soviet delegations, cultural groups, and sport teams traveling outside the USSR. Petrov served in the Maritime Section, which kept tabs on Soviet seamen visiting foreign ports. The Maritime Section had a primary interest, of course, in ensuring that foreign intelligence services, emigré organizations, and the like did not recruit seamen as agents or utilize them as sources of information. Petrov's special sphere of work embraced Soviet seamen on ships plying the lower Danube. Their calls in countries, even "People's Democracies," such as Rumania, Hungary, and Yugoslavia, required the same sort of vigilance by the Maritime Section as their trips to other foreign ports.

At first Doosia was also assigned to SK work, watching over Spitsbergen, where Norway and the USSR met. The coal mines there employed Soviet citizens of the lowest sort, and, much to her relief, she was later transferred to the Swedish desk.

In the middle of 1948 when, at Marshal Bulganin's instigation, the GRU withdrew its people from the KI, State Security also recalled its SK and EM (emigré) sections, which returned to their old quarters at 2 Dzerzhinski Square.[21] This transfer simplified Petrov's commuting problem, but Doosia continued to work at the KI until they departed for Australia (the KI was finally abolished at the end of 1951[22]).

When they were assigned to Australia, the Petrovs welcomed the relief from the constant professional stress and material shortages of their life in the Soviet Union. The abundance in Australia lived up to their expectations, but they found Moscow waiting for them at the Soviet Embassy in Canberra.

In Canberra they moved into a house with a garden at 7 Lockyer Street within walking distance of the embassy, acquiring a dog named Jack and a cat named Pussilla. They soon settled down in their new home, hopeful that this tour would be as successful as the one they had in Sweden. During their period of service at their new post, Vladimir Petrov was promoted from lieutenant colonel to full colonel, while Doosia was a captain of State Security.[23]

Seeking to deceive the Australian authorities about Petrov's real position, Moscow gave Petrov the official cover of a clerk at the Soviet Embassy, but soon after his arrival in Australia he was promoted to Third Secretary and Consul. Doosia had two cover jobs, as the ambassador's secretary and embassy accountant.

In the "legal" residency, Petrov was originally charged with SK and EM duties. As the SK officer, he had to watch the Soviet official colony as well as some two hundred others holding Soviet passports. The Moscow Center, however, emphasized the importance of his EM duties, since after World War II Australia offered a haven to many thousands of emigrés who refused to return to countries under Soviet domination. From Moscow's standpoint, it was essential to prevent these emigrés from being used in anti-Soviet activities.

Since he was not only a Soviet consul but also represented VOKS, the All-Union Organization for Cultural Relations, Petrov became a familiar figure in places frequented by Russians in Australia. Meanwhile, Doosia served as the KGB cipher clerk, occupying an office in the Secret Section upstairs, where a man named Prudnikov functioned as head cipher clerk under Foreign Ministry auspices, in addition to her office on the ground floor where she served as the ambassador's secretary.

Vladimir Petrov also had access to the Secret Section. He spent many hours in the darkroom, photographing the residency's dispatches to the Moscow Center and developing and printing dispatches received from Moscow. As usual, the dispatches moved in both directions on undeveloped film that was automatically exposed when the container was opened by any unauthorized person.

The *rezidentura's* work was complicated by the fact that the resident, Sadovnikov, as well as his successor, Pakhomov, worked under Tass cover in Sydney, two hundred miles away. A year after Petrov's arrival, the problem was resolved with the sudden recall of Pakhomov, who believed that he was being shadowed by the Australian security service, and Petrov became acting resident.[24]

The residency, however, was badly understaffed. Petrov himself had to do a good deal of traveling in connection with his cover work, but Doosia seldom had a chance to leave Canberra. Over three years, she was able to make only two brief visits to Sydney.

Under the circumstances, Petrov was more amused than irritated when he received a dispatch from the Moscow Center with the following advice:

> The secret hiding places for documents selected by you have a number of defects. They are all located in one and the same area, which facilitates their detection by the counterintelligence, even if you move from one secret hiding place to another.
>
> The description of the secret hiding places for documents was not accompanied by sketches which would give a clear idea of the advantages and defects of the selected places, and of their exact location.
>
> In our opinion, a crack between the boards supporting the railroad bridge embankment cannot be used as a secret hiding place for documents, because the railway bridge is probably regularly inspected by the appropriate persons, and in exceptional circumstances might be guarded.[25]

Petrov commented: "In vetoing my suggestions, some MVD bureaucrat in Moscow, who had never been within 10,000 miles of the peaceful countryside around Canberra, took the opportunity to write fifteen pompous passages of general principles about secret hiding places. He even warned me to beware lest the material be destroyed by rodents. No doubt he ate a good lunch at the MVD restaurant and thought that he had written a masterly directive which would remain as a model treatise on the subject."[26]

In contrast to Western intelligence services, the KGB exercises very strict control over operations in the field and allows residents and case officers little room for personal initiative and judgment. The Moscow Center decides everything about dead drops, including their selection for given operations, utilizing only the suggestions of field case officers.

Soon after he took over as acting resident, Petrov was instructed to prepare the groundwork for the establishment of an "illegal" apparatus in Australia—one which would of course operate independently of all Soviet installations. In the dispatch the Center told Petrov:

> The aggravation of the international situation and the pressing necessity for the timely exposure and prevention of cunning designs of the enemy demand a fundamental reorganization of the whole of our intelligence work and the creation in Australia of an illegal apparatus which could uninterruptedly and effectively operate under any conditions.[27]

The conditions the Center had in mind were, of course, those of wartime or, at the very least, a complete rupture of diplomatic relations. In writing Petrov, the Center urged the *rezidentura* to take up the matter with its agents in such a way that "no panic is caused among them, and so that they would not interpret our preparations as a sign of inevitable war."[28]

Petrov worked with Antonov and another assistant on developing opportunities for establishing "illegals" in Australia. One promising candidate, however, was turned up by the Center. A man using the name Pechek (whose real name was Vincenc Divisek), a Czech by nationality, had been conscripted into the German Army, deserted to the Russians, and agreed to work as a Soviet agent. He was parachuted into Czechoslovakia during the war and proved to be an excellent agent, cooperating closely with the Czech underground. After the war, he was running a hotel in Czechoslovakia when the Communists took over. Pechek decided to emigrate to Australia with his wife. When this came to the attention of the KGB, Pechek was told that he would be allowed to leave only if he became a Soviet agent. Pechek agreed. To all appearances, he was well suited to become an "illegal," because of his Czech, rather than Russian, nationality, his clandestine experi-. ence, and his settling in Australia as an emigré. Arrangements were made before Pechek's departure for making contact secretly after his arrival. Unfortunately for the KGB, Pechek got in touch with the Australian security service when he arrived and reported the whole story. Pechek was told to go to his clandestine rendezvous, and only some mix-up between the Center and the field prevented one of the KGB men from walking into a trap.

Petrov then saw an opportunity to establish an "illegal" in Australia in a somewhat more subtle manner. An old Siberian woman, who had left Russia with her husband before World War I and emigrated to Australia, contacted the Soviet Embassy in Canberra long before Petrov arrived. Her husband had died and she was seriously ill. She wanted to bequeath her house and possessions to a son who still lived in the Soviet Union. An officer of the embassy drew up a will and sent it to Moscow. Later, the old woman contacted the embassy again and Petrov went to see her. Her health had deteriorated and she was now paralyzed. Petrov assured her that her will was intact, and in view of her desperate financial situation he helped to arrange a small mortgage on her house, which was located in a poor area of Sydney. Questioning the old woman, Petrov found out that while she would almost certainly recognize her son, although she had not seen him in many years, she would not know her grandchildren, having never seen any photographs of them. Petrov recommended to the Center that an "illegal" could be substituted for a grandson, after the KGB arranged for the cooperation of the old woman's son, who was living at Okhmolinsk in Siberia. He never learned, however, whether an "illegal" was sent to Australia to pass himself off as the grandson.

The climate for recruiting "illegals" in Australia changed for the worse when the Soviet Union ceased to be an ally of the West. The KGB was no longer able to recruit agents with the same ease, and some of its existing agents broke their connections with Soviet Intelligence. Another factor that negatively affected the KGB's work was the reorganization of the Australian security service, which became very active and increasingly effective in its counterespionage work. It was the Australian security service that came to Petrov's rescue when he reached a dangerous crisis in his life.

The arrest of Lavrenti Beria and five of his closest associates in Soviet State Security was announced on July 10, 1953, and led to the arrest and execution of a number of KGB officials, as well as the defection of KGB officers stationed abroad. Not all of those who suffered as a result of Beria's fall were closely connected with the once powerful boss of State Security. Vladimir Petrov held a relatively modest position in the KGB and had only met Beria on two occasions many years earlier.[29] Beria's fall, however, furnished a ready pretext to people inside and outside the KGB to settle personal grudges.

Before departing for Australia, Petrov had examined the SK files on the embassy staff in Canberra. He discovered Ambassador Lifanov had been denounced in his student days as a Trotskyist by two of his fellow students. Petrov attached no particular significance to this denunciation, which was very common at the time. When he reported for duty in Canberra, Petrov informed Lifanov, as he had been instructed by Moscow, that he was responsible for SK work in the embassy.

"He made no comment on my disclosure," Petrov wrote, "and promised his assistance with this important task; but I doubt whether it increased my popularity with him to know that I was the MVD secret overseer."[30]

Knowing that the Petrovs belonged to the KGB and had their own independent channel to Moscow, Lifanov was not likely to care much for them in any case. In addition, Doosia had been imposed on him as his secretary and would be in a position to keep him under close observation. Later, when Petrov became the "legal" resident, Lifanov had all the more reason to want to get rid of them. Doosia noted: "It was, in fact, quite common for Soviet ambassadors abroad to attempt to discredit the MVD residents, and to bring about a quick shuffle of replacements, lest the resident should acquire too much influence and become a threat to the ambassador himself."[31]

Doosia unwittingly complicated the situation. Mrs. Lifanov regarded Doosia, blonde, trim, and stylish, with suspicion, since the ambassador's previous secretary, a single girl, had enjoyed a cozy relationship with him. The ambassador had similar ideas about Doosia and became resentful when she insisted on maintaining correct, but rather distant, relations with him.

Doosia was the cause of further difficulty with the ambassador, since she took her duties as embassy accountant seriously and adhered strictly to the written instructions she had received from Moscow in the knowledge that her predecessor had been reprimanded for "irregularities." Lifanov had no use for a secretary or an accountant who would not permit him to override the regulations and expend money as he pleased, and it soon became clear that he regarded both of the Petrovs as enemies.

Through no fault of her own, Doosia made other enemies among the wives of embassy personnel. Her first view of them made her heart sink. "They were," she said, "a dreadfully unprepossessing lot, dumpy, drab and stolid."[32]

Vladimir Petrov, whose position enabled him to escape from the artificial constraints and petty intrigues of the embassy, spent a lot of his time in the pro-Soviet circles of Sydney, where he became acquainted with Dr. Michael Bialoguski, who eventually became his friend and confidant. Bialoguski, originally from Poland, had established a medical practice in Sydney, treating many emigrés. Although he spoke Russian, he was, in reality, anti-Soviet because of what he had seen under the Soviet occupation, his own arrest by the NKVD, and his observations of living conditions in the USSR. He volunteered to the Australian security service to penetrate pro-Soviet circles and to report on the activities of Soviet front groups. Thus Petrov and Bialoguski met, and, as often happens in such circumstances, each thought that he was cultivating the other. Bialoguski started reporting to the Australian security service about Petrov, while Petrov reported his meeting with Bialoguski to the Moscow Center and proposed to develop him. Bialoguski, without being aware of the fact, was assigned the cryptonym "Grigori" by the Center.

As their acquaintance progressed, Petrov began to express his frustration and anger about conditions in the embassy to Bialoguski. Bialoguski, of course, reported Petrov's outbursts to the Australian security service. For his part, Petrov did not vent his feelings without calculation—he assumed that Bialoguski might be a Soviet informant, in which case his complaints would get back to the ambassador, or that Bialoguski was working for the Australians, who could prove helpful if things ever came to a showdown.

Stalin's death in March 1953 cast a pall over the embassy in Canberra because of the uncertainty about the situation in Moscow. Nobody at the embassy knew about the maneuvering in Moscow that involved Beria, Malenkov, Molotov, Khrushchev, and other leaders, but Soviet officials knowledgeable about the inner workings of the system could easily imagine what was happening at home.

In May 1953 Petrov was ordered to return to Moscow to report on his KGB work. Before his departure, however, he experienced trouble with his eyes and asked Bialoguski to recommend an eye specialist. The specialist, Dr. Beckett, recommended hospital treatment, and Petrov put off his trip to Moscow and spent the next ten days in the hospital. After his release, he made a new reservation for a flight to Moscow, departing on June 21. Just before this date, Petrov received a cable from Moscow ordering him to stay in Australia until further notice.[33] Less than a week later, Lavrenti Beria, the seemingly all-powerful chief of Soviet State Security, was arrested at a CPSU Presidium meeting.

The announcement of Beria's arrest, which came in July, was an excellent excuse for opening the attack on the Petrovs at the embassy in Canberra. A party meeting was held at the embassy to hear the charges against the traitor Beria, which had been drawn up in Moscow in the form of a detailed indictment. The charges were read to the assembled CPSU members by Party Secretary Nikolai Kovaliev, who was the commercial attaché in Canberra and had been secretly co-opted as an agent by the KGB.[34] (As the Petrovs later discovered, this fact may have made him antagonistic rather than friendly toward them.) The party members listened to the catalog of charges against Beria with expressionless faces; there was no discussion, and everyone promptly went home.

Some time later, Prudnikov, the chief cipher clerk, showed the Petrovs two cables that had been sent from the embassy to Moscow. One cable was from Ambassador Lifanov to the Ministry of Foreign Affairs; the other was from Party Secretary Kovaliev to the Central Committee. The collusion of Lifanov and Kovaliev was obvious not only from the timing of the cables but their content. In almost identical language, the cables accused Doosia of "splitting the collective," i.e., causing dissension in the embassy, and charged that the Petrovs were plotting to form a Beria faction there.[35] Prudnikov's motivation for showing them the cables was obvious. He saw a fight shaping up between Foreign Ministry and party representatives on one side and KGB representatives on the other, and he wanted to play it safe until he was certain which side would win.

Vladimir and Doosia Petrov were greatly alarmed when they read these cables, recognizing the seriousness of the charges at once. They sent a cable to Moscow through their own channel to the KGB, telling their side of the story, but they received no response from Moscow. Preoccupied with its own internal troubles and demoralized by the purge of Beria and his top subordinates, the KGB either could not or would not intercede on behalf of the Petrovs.

At about the same time, Petrov heard from Bialoguski that Dr. Beckett wanted to examine his eyes again. On July 23 Petrov went with Bialoguski to Dr. Beckett's office. Petrov was not aware that the whole business had been instigated by the Australian security service, which, on the basis of Bialoguski's information, had decided that Petrov might be ripe for defection after Beria's fall from power. Consequently, Dr. Beckett, who had won Petrov's confidence while treating his eye illness, was chosen to sound out Petrov about his intentions.

Alone with Petrov, Dr. Beckett proceeded to question him. Petrov shrewdly guessed what was behind these questions, but liked Beckett's direct, honest manner. When Petrov remarked that it was not easy to find a job in Australia, Beckett told him that it was a matter of having the right people to help him. On that note Dr. Beckett terminated the conversation, but he gave Petrov food for thought in the weeks and months ahead.

The Petrovs still hoped that their situation at the embassy would improve, but instead it got worse. Although Lifanov was recalled, before he left he openly brought his charges against them at another party meeting.

"Comrade Petrova," said Lifanov to the assembled party members, "has been a harmful influence here ever since her arrival. She has caused division and dissension in our embassy, and she has used her husband as a mouthpiece for her schemes. This pair has presumed too far; they have tried to set themselves above the party secretary here, and above myself, as ambassador."

Lifanov studied the faces in front of him before continuing. "I charge them with plotting to form a Beria faction in our embassy!"[36]

It would have taken a very stupid Soviet citizen indeed to "plot to form a Beria faction" *after* Beria's arrest, but that consideration did not deter Lifanov or his confederates in the embassy from leveling these accusations against the Petrovs. Everyone knew that in terms of "Soviet reality," a lack of logic did not make such accusations any less frightening. Lifanov's purpose was to have them recorded in the minutes of the meeting with the endorsement of the sheeplike party members, who dutifully supported him. Lifanov departed in September 1953, after this final salvo at the Petrovs. While waiting for his successor, the Petrovs still hoped that there would be a change for the better, but their hopes faded rather quickly.

The new ambassador, Nikolai Ivanovich Generalov, arrived in October, and both he and his wife showed hostility toward the Petrovs from the outset. One of Generalov's first moves was to dismiss Doosia from her job as the ambassador's secretary. This action was a clear indication that he had been briefed about the Petrovs before he departed from Moscow. Mrs. Generalov set about encouraging the other wives to snub Doosia or to boycott her entirely.

The campaign against them affected the nerves of both Petrovs, but Vladimir felt the pressure even more than his wife. "After the Beria accusation, he was hardly recognizable as the same man," she said later. "Instead of his normal placid self, he became nervous and haggard and distraught. He knew too much, had seen too many tragedies which had their origin in the sort of lies and calumnies that were now being directed at us."[37]

Vladimir Petrov was already beginning to think seriously about defection, but the problem was simpler in one way for him than for Doosia. After his mother died, he had no living relatives in the

Soviet Union, while Doosia's parents, brother, and sister were still alive. It was not surprising that when he tried to broach the subject of defection very cautiously, she refused to discuss it.

Petrov next enlisted Bialoguski's help in raising the matter with Doosia. Bialoguski visited the Petrovs at home in Canberra, and expressed indignation about the unfair treatment they were receiving from their colleagues at the embassy. Then he asked why they did not stay in Australia. Doosia became furious and railed at Bialoguski, saying that neither she nor her husband would think of deserting Russia. Her violent reaction convinced Petrov that he would have to defect without her, if it came to that.[38]

Petrov reached the turning point after a bad automobile accident in late December 1953. He escaped serious injury but suffered severe shock and painful cuts and bruises. His Australian acquaintances showed genuine sympathy and concern, while his colleagues in the embassy treated him with indifference. Early in the new year, Petrov told Bialoguski that he wished to see Dr. Beckett again. He had two meetings with Beckett, and finally informed him of his desire to stay in Australia. Dr. Beckett promised to arrange a meeting with G. R. Richards, who represented the Australian security service.

Petrov's initial meeting with Richards took place on Saturday, February 27, 1954, at Dr. Bialoguski's apartment. At this meeting Petrov repeated that he wished to stay in Australia. He said that he still hoped to persuade his wife to stay too, but that, in any event, he had made up his mind to defect and wanted to have the protection of the Australian authorities. Richards assured Petrov that he had the authority to offer Petrov political asylum. For the time being, however, Petrov refused to sign a formal request, although he said that he would fully cooperate with the Australian government by revealing all he knew about Soviet activities in Australia.

After his first meeting with Richards, Petrov began his preparations for defection by removing documents from the secret files. He found a safe method of accomplishing this without revealing what he was doing to Doosia or risking premature discovery by anyone else. Under the existing rules laid down by the Center, the *rezidentura* was permitted to retain one year's file of Moscow-originated dispatches in addition to the current year. Since it was now 1954, the file for 1953 could be retained for reference purposes, but it was in constant use and Petrov could not spirit it away. The file of Moscow dispatches for 1952, however, was due for destruction. He checked through the 1952 file with Doosia and prepared a destruction certificate, which he and she signed. Then he switched the 1952 file with some papers he had prepared in advance to look like the 1952 file, took them over to the incinerator, and threw them in. "There go the 1952 letters; they're overdue for destruction," he said.[39] Doosia paid no attention, and the destruction certificate was duly forwarded to the Moscow Center. For temporary safekeeping, Petrov sealed the 1952 file in an envelope and concealed it in another safe in the secret section used by Doosia for the cash box and accounting books. He was sure that she would not notice the inconspicuous envelope, and she did not.

Three weeks later, on March 19, Petrov met Richards again at Bialoguski's apartment. On this occasion, Richards informed Petrov that his chief realized Petrov's need for financial assistance and, therefore, had approved the payment of five thousand pounds to him when he finally requested political asylum.

Petrov described the plan he had worked out for his actual defection, which would simply entail his going to Sydney on business as usual and not returning. He tried to persuade Richards to speak to his wife and to talk her into coming with him, but Richards shook his head. The Australian government was willing to help anyone who wanted to have political asylum, he said, but would not attempt to persuade a representative of another government to defect. Obviously, Richards doubted that Doosia would stay. Moreover, he saw no reason why he would be successful in such an effort when her own husband had failed.

Much as he wanted Doosia to accompany him, Petrov would not change his mind. Whatever happened, he intended to go ahead, and all he could do under the circumstances was to keep Doosia in the dark so that she could truthfully say she had known nothing about her husband's plans. To that extent he might be able to protect her.

———◆———

As the defection moved toward a climax, Petrov had several meetings in Canberra with Richards. At their first meeting in that city, Petrov reported that all his preparations for defection had apparently remained undetected. His departure would also be assisted by his scheduled meeting with a group of new arrivals from Moscow in Sydney on April 3. Filled with optimism, he expressed confidence that he could learn the latest news from Moscow before he defected.

At a party meeting at the embassy the next evening, which Petrov had to attend, Ambassador Generalov chose to renew the attacks against Doosia, accusing her of divisiveness, insubordination, and rudeness. Despite the fact that the Petrovs were scheduled to return to Moscow in late April, Generalov endeavored to do them as much damage as possible. He further reprimanded Doosia by forcing the meeting to eliminate her name from a motion commending the work of all the party women in the embassy.

Vladimir Petrov had another shock in store for him. The next morning when he reported for work, the chief cipher clerk called Petrov into his private office. Self-importantly, he informed Petrov that he and the ambassador had checked all the safes in the embassy and found a number of papers in Petrov's safe that should not have been there.

This news upset Petrov. "What documents, Comrade?"

"Oh, drafts of cables and other secret material left in the safe in your consular office."[40]

Petrov felt greatly relieved, though he realized that the matter was serious enough. He had feared for a moment that they had somehow discovered the envelope in the secret section upstairs. The night before, in his tired and disturbed state, he had left some classified documents in his safe on the ground floor instead of taking them upstairs to the safe in the secret section, as the regulations required.

Petrov went immediately to see Generalov, who showed him the documents but would not allow him to have them. "I shall have to send Moscow an adverse report on this laxness," Generalov said severely.[41]

Petrov realized that the raid on the embassy safes had been aimed mainly at him. Any hesitation he might have had about defection disappeared entirely. "This new charge, coming on top of the others," Petrov wrote, "would be a deadly weapon in the hands of my enemies; I could get ten years in a labor camp for that offense alone."[42]

Petrov lost no time in removing the hidden documents from the embassy. During the morning, he took out the buff-colored envelope, opened his jacket, and slipped the envelope into his shirt. Rebuttoning his shirt and jacket, he strolled out of the embassy and went home. He concealed the envelope under the mattress of his bed and returned to the embassy.

On Friday, April 2, Petrov removed the envelope from under his mattress and packed it inside a copy of *Pravda* in his traveling bag. He ran out to the waiting car without bothering to say good-bye to Doosia or his dog, Jack. He merely called back over his shoulder, "Back on Saturday or Sunday at the latest."

Petrov and Richards traveled from Canberra to Sydney on the same plane, but pretended not to know one another. In Sydney Petrov was busy most of the morning making reservations for travel to Canberra for the Soviet group arriving by ship the next day. That afternoon he met Richards at the latter's apartment and signed a formal request for political asylum. As planned, he stayed overnight with Bialoguski and was up early the next morning to go to the pier where he welcomed the new arrivals.

Among the group was Kovalenok, his replacement as resident, and they had a brief private conversation. Kovalenok gave Petrov a message from Topeshko, a senior KGB officer, who was an old friend of Petrov's.

"I bring you greetings from Topeshko," said Kovalenok. "He asked me to tell you that you have no need to worry about how you will get on back in Moscow."[43]

Petrov thanked Kovalenok for the message, but was not in the least deceived.

Petrov accompanied the group of Soviet representatives to the airport and saw them off for Canberra. He walked out of the terminal to a car where Richards was waiting. On the way to the safe house where he was to stay, he stopped off at a hotel to give some money for travel expenses and a ticket to another Soviet representative bound for New Zealand. Later he mailed the receipts, some remaining cash, and his own used air ticket to the ambassador's new secretary for accounting purposes, thereby tying up all the loose ends. His job was done.

At the safe house, Richards gave Petrov the promised five thousand pounds, and Petrov turned over to him the buff-colored envelope he had carried around with him in his bag since leaving Canberra.

Doosia did not begin to worry until Monday. During the afternoon Ambassador Generalov called her to his office and asked when Petrov would be back. She pointed out that Kovalenok had talked in Sydney with her husband, who said that he might not be back until Monday.

On Tuesday, however, the situation had changed dramatically. Generalov again spoke to her and said he was seriously worried about her husband. He intended to ask the Australian government to investigate Petrov's whereabouts and would also have to report Petrov's absence to Moscow. Moreover, he directed her to move into the embassy at once for her own protection.

The uncertainty and suspicion were cleared up by an Australian radio announcement on Tuesday, April 13, that Petrov had been granted political asylum. On April 19, in accordance with orders from Moscow, Doosia left the embassy under guard to drive to Sydney, where she was due to leave by plane for Moscow. A large crowd had gathered outside the embassy, a long two-story brick building behind a tall cypress hedge. It was obvious that many representatives of the media were lying in wait for her there too.

This was the first indication she had received that anyone outside the embassy felt concern over her fate. She was not aware that the public at large had been informed about her situation and was considerably agitated by the idea that she might be taken back to Moscow by force. Just before her departure, she asked Kovalenok, who was the most recent arrival from Moscow, what he thought would happen to her.

Kovalenok was at least honest. "Oh, various things could happen—perhaps a labor camp—possibly even the death sentence, since by the look of things your husband deserted of his own free will."[44]

Nevertheless, Doosia was still uncertain whether her husband had chosen to defect. She feared that he might have been kidnapped by the Australian security service and compelled to write the letter to her in which he said he had voluntarily asked for asylum in Australia. For that reason, it seeemed to her that Ambassador Generalov was possibly truthful when he said that he wanted to protect her against kidnapping.

When she and her guards arrived at the airport in Sydney, she was horrified to see an even larger and noisier crowd. She suddenly began to worry about her safety, thinking that the crowd was hostile because of the spying. Crying uncontrollably, she allowed herself to be dragged by the guards through the crowd, losing a shoe in the process. The closer they came to the plane, the more violent the crowd became. Only the intervention of the police enabled them to climb the gangway to the plane.

After the takeoff, a stewardess seized an opportunity to speak with her privately and asked if there was anything she wanted. She said that she wanted to see her husband. But she gave up hope when she learned that the plane's first and last stop in Australia would be at Darwin.

A little later Doosia went to the rest room. The stewardess was there, and she said to Doosia: "I do realize how awful it must be for you not being able to get in touch with your husband. Do you want to stay in Australia, too?"

"I want to see my husband," Doosia replied.

"You look very frightened. What are you afraid of? Is it the people who are escorting you?"

"Yes, the couriers; they have guns."

"Don't be afraid. Stay here a moment while I see the captain."[45]

The stewardess came back with another member of the crew, who asked Doosia if she wished to remain in Australia. Doosia replied again that she wished to see her husband, but was afraid of the couriers with their guns. The crewman assured her that everything would be all right. Then he went away.

Doosia did not suspect that the plane's captain was in radio contact with the Australian authorities throughout the night, informing them of her statements.

Early the next morning, the plane landed at Darwin. Doosia's chief escort reminded her and the other guards that they were to remain on the plane during the stop at Darwin. But the situation developed differently. A steward told them politely that they would have to leave the plane, as the regulations did not permit passengers to remain on board during refueling. When the four Soviet passengers descended from the plane, Doosia failed to notice that her guards had been separated from her and speedily disarmed. In the air terminal, Doosia finally received the opportunity to speak to her husband on the telephone.

Although her escorts were once more at her elbow, Doosia could clearly hear everything Vladimir Petrov had to say. But she pretended that she did not recognize his voice. She kept saying, "No, no—that's not my husband," yet all the time she was listening intently as Petrov told her that he had made the decision to defect of his own free will. "I beg you, face facts before it is too late," he said in conclusion. "I ask you to stay not just because you are my wife, but as one human being to another. You still have life ahead of you if you do. If you go back now, you will never see your family anyway because of what I've done. Doosenka, believe me, you will never cross the threshold of your home."[46]

Doosia answered, "No, you are not my husband, good-bye," and hung up.

Despite her words, Petrov had convinced her of what she already feared—that even if she returned to Moscow, she would never see her family again. Doosia then gave an unobtrusive signal to the Australian official who had spoken to her when she left the plane. The official immediately came over to her. She now informed him that she, too, wished to remain in Australia. Her escorts were helpless once the Australian officials had decided to intervene.

Vladimir and Doosia Petrov testified at length before the Australian Royal Commission on Espionage, which examined their evidence for many months. As the report of the Royal Commission stated: "Petrov was in the witness-box on thirty-seven days for approximately seventy-four hours in all, and Mrs. Petrov on twenty-one days for approximately thirty hours in all. . . . We feel that in the final result we should find, and we do find, that the Petrovs are witnesses of truth."[47]

It is an ironic reflection of the realities of life in the KGB that two such people as Vladimir and Doosia Petrov, who were typical products of the Soviet system, should have ever defected. Both were completely loyal to the KGB as well as their country and had provided dedicated service for twenty years. If Beria had not fallen, the Petrovs, who simply belonged to Beria's organization, would have retired from the KGB and joined many of their former colleagues as pensioners in Moscow. They were simply victims of circumstance.

10

A Little Bit of Capitalism

THERE HAVE BEEN Soviet spies—good Communists—who, by a-
dopting a business cover to mask their covert activities, have turned
out to be such successful capitalists that they have had difficulty
remembering their political creed, which stresses the evils of capitalism. Such a man was Max Klausen, a spy ring's radio operator,
who became something of a business tycoon in Japan while engaging in German-Japanese trade.[1]

Another convincing (if not convinced) capitalist was Konon
Molody, the KGB's "illegal" resident in England in the late 1950's
and early 1960's. Molody possessed a capitalist's talent for spotting
a potential market. He wanted to start a small business that would
not take too much time away from his Intelligence work, and he
noticed that jukeboxes were almost unknown in England.

"During my stay in the United States I had become accustomed
to this essential ingredient of American culture," he wrote, "and
had even transacted a little business in jukeboxes." He added
wryly: "At the risk of doing permanent damage to my English
hosts, I decided that the spread of these instruments in England
would be desirable, at least for myself."[2]

Molody bought interests in vending machine businesses and

became a company director. He also invested in the stock market. These business activities provided him with a certain aura of respectability while he went about his espionage work.

"All this enabled me to get about London, to explore its remoter districts, and to gain a better insight into British life," he wrote later. "It did nothing to convert me to a belief in the virtues of capitalism."[3]

Probably not. But of all KGB Intelligence officers, Molody was one of the few who had been exposed to the free enterprise system in formative years and could really understand how it functioned.

Konon Trofimovich Molody was born in the Soviet Union in January or February of 1922. He apparently lost his father at an early age and was brought up by his mother, with whom he shared difficult times. In a letter to his wife, he once wrote that "it all started as far back as 1932 when Mother decided to dispatch me to the nether regions.* At that time she could not imagine, of course, the consequences of this step. I do not blame her."[4] The year 1932 was one of famine in the USSR, and the "nether regions" to which his mother dispatched him were the United States. The "consequences" to which he referred were his recruitment in his youth into Soviet Intelligence.

Probably to spare her son the hardships of life in Russia at that time, Molody's mother sent the ten-year-old Konon to live with her sister in California. Molody pretended to be his aunt's son, and the aunt registered him under her name in a private school in Berkeley, where he learned to speak English fluently.[5] In 1938, as war approached in Europe, he was called home, possibly because his mother feared that the separation would become permanent, or possibly because Soviet State Security, which was keeping an eye on him, wanted him to come back.

Nobody knows about young Molody's life during his years in America, but evidently he was unhappy. He came away with anti-American feelings that lasted throughout his life. "For personal reasons, I was glad to leave the U.S.A.," he wrote. "I could never come to terms with the American Way of Life. The contrast be-

* "Tartarus" in the original.

tween the American myth and the American reality was too glaring."[6]

On his return to the USSR, Soviet State Security took Molody under its wing because of his stay in the United States and his ability to speak fluent American English. While the German invasion of Soviet Russia in 1941 postponed State Security's long-range plans for Molody, they did not intend to lose its hold on him. At the age of nineteen, he was assigned to the KGB's Fourth Administration, which conducted partisan warfare behind the German lines.

Molody's memoirs, *Spy*, written under the name of Gordon Lonsdale, was designed to preserve his Lonsdale legend and, therefore, blended fantasy and fact (with the former predominating). Molody did not acquire his Lonsdale identity until 1954, but, in the best tradition of Intelligence cover stories, he tried to make certain facts of his own biography a part of the Lonsdale legend.

The real Gordon Lonsdale was born in the mining town of Cobalt in Canada's northern Ontario on August 27, 1924. Lonsdale's father, a miner, came from English stock. His mother was Finnish. The marriage soon broke up, and she took her child to another town, where she met a Finn named Hjalmar Philaja and moved in with him. When the Great Depression began, Philaja persuaded the young woman to accompany him back to Finland with her child. Since she could not obtain a passport for Gordon until his birth was registered, she registered the birth in the Province of Ontario on September 2, 1931, a full seven years after Molody's birth.[7]

If Molody's memoirs can be believed, the three did not reach Finland. In Sweden, while they were awaiting onward passage to Finland, Philaja heard about a mechanic's job in Lvov, Poland, and they went instead to Lvov.[8] But Soviet forces occupied the eastern part of Poland, including Lvov, in 1939 as a result of the Molotov-Ribbentrop pact, and Philaja, Lonsdale, and his mother fell into the grasp of Soviet State Security. Nothing is known of their fate, but Gordon Lonsdale's papers ended up in the possession of the KGB.

In his own account, Molody has Lonsdale moving overland

from Warsaw (where he had supposedly been living) to join partisans near Orsha after the German invasion in 1941. Orsha was a major rail link between Moscow and the Belorussian capital of Minsk, as well as a key point linking Leningrad and the Ukraine. The city had been turned into a large supply base by the Germans. The Fourth Administration flew Molody to a remote airstrip in the Orsha region, where he joined his assigned partisan detachment.

Toward the end of the winter Molody suffered a concussion in an attempt to blow up a locomotive. The injury was serious enough to require his evacuation, and he convalesced in a Moscow hospital.[9] After his recovery, his superiors in the Fourth Administration decided to train him as a penetration agent and drop him in German-occupied territory. He first attended the State Security school for radio operators, which was actually run by the Fourth Administration. It was here that Molody first met William Fisher, alias Colonel Rudolf Abel, who supervised his later training.

Molody stayed at an apartment in a large block of flats near Zubovsky Boulevard. "My landlady was a member of the intelligence service, and I posed as her nephew on leave," recalled Molody. "She had no children of her own and took a great liking to me. Eventually she started calling me 'son' and I called her 'mother.' "[10] Indeed, the lady could have been his own mother, who was still living, and if so it suggests that she was already working for State Security in 1932, when she sent her son to California. In that case, she probably did realize the consequences of her action, even if Molody later was unwilling to admit this to himself.

After completing the school course, Molody received his training in the apartment. Fisher, an old hand as a clandestine radio instructor, visited him daily and took a fatherly interest in him. Fisher showed him how to assemble the radio receiver, then took it apart and had him reassemble it. Undoubtedly they availed themselves of the opportunity to speak English with one another and exchange impressions about the United States and England.

During Fisher's absence, Molody practiced on the key and established radio contact at specified times with other students scattered about the city.[11] Molody was also visited regularly by other instructors who taught him basic concepts of intelligence and conspiratorial techniques. When he was not busy with instruction, he worked in a military garage, putting in up to twelve hours a day, with the idea of passing himself off as an experienced driver or auto mechanic, if the need arose.[12]

After several months of training that lasted until the end of 1942, Molody was ready for his mission. In January 1943 he jumped from a plane and landed in the vicinity of Minsk. He buried his parachute in a forest and set out for the city on foot. His transmitter and other equipment were to be supplied after he had established himself. With his false papers, he had no trouble obtaining a job in Minsk at an office recruiting local labor for work in Germany—the so-called *Ostarbeiter* who would take the place in factories and on farms of Germans called up for military service.

Precisely what Molody did thereafter is not clear. According to his own story, he was rounded up with other Russians while visiting a village outside Minsk. His eventual release came about with the aid of a State Security officer who had penetrated the local branch of the Abwehr (German Military Intelligence) and was engaged in recruiting Russians as German agents. He saw to it that Molody was recruited as an agent for the Germans and had him turned loose after he was rejected on physical grounds. Molody identifies this State Security officer as "Alec," the pseudonym he uses for William Fisher,[13] even though Fisher never served under the German occupation during the war. There is no reason, however, to doubt Molody's story that the Abwehr had been penetrated by a State Security officer, and it may be true that Molody acted as radio operator for a network that included such a penetration, which enabled the KGB to learn in advance about German agents dispatched into Soviet rear areas.

Molody claims that in the summer of 1943, after the Soviet forces inflicted a crushing defeat on the Reichswehr at Kursk, the advance of the Red Army seemed likely to reach his spy ring's area of operations around Minsk. Therefore, they received orders to move westward before they were bypassed by the Red Army. Molody thereupon became an *Ostarbeiter*, and went to Berlin, where he was employed in the Daimler-Benz factory on the strength of his experience as an automobile mechanic.

He managed to conceal the separate parts of his transmitter in his personal possessions and was able to set it up whenever he found a safe place from which to transmit, assisted by Soviet agents among German Communists who had survived during the Nazi regime or other *Ostarbeiter*, escaped POWs, and the like.

Molody remained in Berlin until the end of the war, transmitting intelligence received from other members of the ring. When the war was over, a new phase in his life began.

Recognizing his potential as a spy, Soviet State Security sent him to a university to complete his education. During the next few years, he studied international law at a university he did not name. He was a few months short of graduation when State Security sent him on his next assignment. The available evidence indicates that Molody was sent to Prague shortly before the Communists seized power in Czechoslovakia. What he did there, however, remains unknown.

Molody either married before or during his assignment in Prague. One source suggests that his wife, Galina ("Galyusha"), was Czech,[14] although it seems more likely that she was Russian. Galina was a teacher who also served as chairman of the Communist Party Cultural Commission for her community, but she had difficulty reconciling herself to the long separations from her husband that reflected the exigencies of his Intelligence work. While serving as an "illegal" resident in England, Molody, who traveled regularly, in accordance with his business cover, to countries in western Europe, made secret trips at rare intervals to Moscow and European Communist capitals for brief reunions with his wife, and sometimes his children. At the end of 1960 Galyusha reported that Liza, their twelve-year-old daughter, and Dima (the familiar form of Dmitri) were doing badly in school, with the latter also being marked down for deportment and diligence. Their son, Trofim, who was approaching kindergarten age, worried Galyusha because of his sensitivity and delicate health. At some point the precocious Trofim told his mother, "When is Daddy coming, and why has he gone away, and what a stupid job Daddy has got."[15]

Konon Molody received his most important assignment in 1954, when he was sent to England as "illegal" resident. His assignment, of course, was only part of a larger undertaking, although as director of the spy ring, he had the leading role. Whether the project originated in the Illegals Administration or came from the top level of the PGU cannot be determined, but it certainly involved a vast amount of preparation and a not inconsiderable allocation of resources. Molody must have spent at least the first half of 1954 getting ready for his assignment.

Morris and Lona Cohen, who came to Moscow after their flight from New York in the summer of 1950, as the FBI closed in on the Rosenberg spy ring, had spent a couple of years in training before they were assigned to the same project. Morris Cohen learned all about radio transmitter-receivers and how to send and receive Morse code, became acquainted with call signs and signal plans, and found out how to deal with antennas and power supply. Together he and Lona were instructed in all the elements of photography used in espionage and became experts at making microdots. They mastered the encipherment and decipherment of messages, as well as the use of one-time pads, which were destroyed immediately after their use (so that only the Center in Moscow could decipher a message).

Gradually, the participants' roles became sharply delineated. As director of the spy network, Molody would occupy himself primarily with operations, while the Cohens, under his supervision, took care of the network's communications, including radio and postal communications (with the requisite photographic processing), the servicing of dead drops, and the handling of funds and the accountings prepared for the Center.

In this connection, it is interesting to note that Molody and the Cohens' funds came from money paid in New York into Swiss bank accounts.[16] Since William Fisher was acting as paymaster for the KGB in New York (until his arrest in June 1957), there appears to be good reason to believe that he had some responsibility for the Molody spy ring in England.

Final preparations for England entailed passports and cover stories for Molody and the Cohens. It was highly desirable that the documentation be issued at some distance from England, making any check that much harder. It was decided in Moscow that Molody should adopt the identity of Gordon Lonsdale, in order to secure a passport in Canada. For this purpose, the KGB furnished Molody with all the particulars of Lonsdale's birth and life story available in its files. The Cohens were instructed to assume the names Peter John Kroger and Helen Kroger, a New Zealand couple who had died many years earlier.[17] (It is not known how this couple came under the KGB's range of observation.) The Cohens, therefore, had to first travel to New Zealand, although the Center considered it safe for them to submit their passport applications at a consulate in Europe, since the applications had to be supported with false birth certificates and a marriage license, and the forgeries might have been exposed if the applications were made in New Zealand itself.

For various reasons, it was logical for the three spies to go to their destinations by way of the Far East. They traveled together to Japan, where they parted company. Molody embarked on a Soviet grain ship bound for Vancouver while the Cohens set out for Australia and New Zealand.

Going ashore illegally in Vancouver at the end of November, Molody rented a room in a boardinghouse on Pendrell Street. He told his landlord that he was a salesman and represented a large company in eastern Canada, but there is no evidence that he actually worked at any time during his three-month stay in Canada.

"I chose Vancouver as my home town," he wrote. "I had never been there, but it was as far from England as one could get, and it seemed as if there would be less chance of meeting people from Vancouver when I reached my destination."[18] Moreover, he probably found it easier to go ashore in Vancouver, and he would cross most of Canada on his way to Europe, thereby acquainting himself with a great deal of the country.

From the beginning, Molody did not lose sight of his main objective in Canada. He reported his arrival promptly to an accommodation address, and then proceeded to collect documentation supporting his cover story as Gordon Lonsdale—a driver's license, a Young Men's Christian Association membership card, and various professional cards that apparently attested to his occupation of salesman.[19]

At the end of 1954, he moved to Toronto, where he lost no time in requesting a copy of Gordon Lonsdale's birth certificate at City Hall. With the birth certificate, a forged affidavit, and his own photograph, he made a formal application for a Canadian passport. The passport was duly issued in the name of Gordon Lonsdale in January 1955.

Molody was elated because he had achieved his objective of obtaining a passport some four months ahead of the schedule he had mapped out for himself. Feeling no need for haste, Molody did some sightseeing for about a month. On February 22, 1955, he crossed the border into the United States at Niagara Falls, and, like most tourists, he paused to look at the spectacular view. He then proceeded to New York City, where he set up conspiratorial meetings with William Fisher. They met on a bench near a "well-known landmark" in Central Park and discussed his mission in England. The discussion continued over the course of the next few days. "Alec gave me the names and particulars of various people whom I would have to meet in Western Europe, and elaborate arrangements had to be made to ensure safe contact," said Molody.[20]

Molody had given a great deal of thought to his cover in England, and according to him, Fisher had agreed that study would be the best pretext for Molody's stay in that country. He decided on the London University School of Oriental Languages and African Studies located in Russell Square. "I had long wanted to study the Chinese language and Chinese history for its own sake," he wrote, perhaps thinking that one day the KGB might wish to send him to China. "But, in addition, Alec had information that the school was heavily subsidized by the War Office, because British Intelligence officers, both military and political, were sent there for courses in Chinese and other Asian and African languages."[21] In answer to his query, the university administration informed him that the school year would commence on the first Wednesday in October, and that he should report a few days earlier to register.

This reply took care of his cover, and as soon as his business in New York had been completed he sailed for England aboard the *America* at the end of February.[22]

Meanwhile, the Cohens reached Vienna in December 1954, and Morris Cohen wrote a letter to the Consulate General of New Zealand in Paris. He explained that he and his wife had British passports, but wished to have documents from their own country. They submitted applications for passports supported by forged birth certificates, showing they were born in the Gisborne district of New Zealand, and a marriage license attesting to the fact that they had married in New York in 1943.[23] They received the New Zealand passports without any complications and, late in February, just at the time Molody was sailing from New York, entered Great Britain.

The "illegal" *rezidentura* headed by Konon Molody was about to go into business.

Molody landed at Southampton on March 3. He must have taken some secret pleasure in a dispute with a customs official at the port, who ruled that, as a student, Molody was not a tourist but a resident and, therefore, had to pay duty on his camera. Rather than pay the duty, Molody arranged to leave the camera in customs until he left the country through Southampton.[24] His refusal to pay any duty also helped to reinforce his image as a student with limited means. In reality, he was not suffering from any lack of money on arrival at Southampton, for he had about twenty thousand Canadian dollars in cash.[25]

For the first two months in London, he stayed at the Overseas Club on St. James's Street, where foreign visitors could rent rooms for less than two dollars a night. In May he managed to rent a furnished flat in the White House, Regents Park, where he asked for an apartment on an upper floor, stating that he liked lots of fresh air. The real reason, however, was that he wanted to be as high as possible in order to get better reception when he installed his shortwave radio.[26]

Meanwhile, the Cohens were also getting established in London. After living in a hotel for a few weeks, they rented a small terraced house in Catford, in southeast London, for five guineas a week. Unable to provide any personal references, the Cohens, who claimed to have come from Switzerland, gave a Swiss bank as a business reference and arranged for the rent to be paid through the same bank.[27]

Soon after they moved into the house, Morris Cohen began commuting every day into central London, where he made himself known to antiquarian dealers and started attending book auctions.

He informed his new contacts that he was interested in Americana and Victoriana on behalf of overseas clients.[28]

Molody had not yet contacted the Cohens since he was waiting for further instructions. As he related later, he paid a daily visit to a telephone booth on the Thames Embankment behind the Savoy Hotel. He pretended that he was making a telephone call, but each time he felt under the wooden shelf that held the directories for a map pin, which was a signal to him. One day he found the map pin in place and knew that a message had been hidden in a certain dead drop, whose existence was known to him before he came to England.

The dead drop was an inconspicuous hole in a stairway used by thousands of people every day. Making sure that he was not observed, he extracted a package about the size of a ring box and slipped it into the pocket of his raincoat. Then he walked along, looking in store windows, until he was sure that he had not been observed. He took a bus back to the Overseas Club and, once in his room, undid the package, which contained tissue paper tightly folded into the shape of a cube. On the tissue paper there was a message that he quickly deciphered. He was to go to Paris for a meeting in which the Cohens would also participate.[29]

Also attending the meeting in Paris was a man from the Center whom Molody called "Jean." Whatever else they discussed, it is clear that Jean gave Molody and the Cohens last-minute instructions on how they were to proceed, after they had outlined their own situations in London. Molody also made arrangements with the Cohens for future operational meetings. Their cover story was that Molody had met the Cohens by chance at a Paris café, and that they had maintained a social relationship ever since.

A few months after the meeting in Paris, Morris Cohen opened his own business by renting a back room over a tobacco shop in the Strand, opposite St. Clement Danes Church. He became actively involved in buying and selling old books. In the weekly trade journal *Critique*, he ran an advertisement: *Americana—from the North Pole to the South Pole—want lists and reports always welcome.*[30]

Soon after Molody moved into the White House, he checked with the School of Oriental Languages and African Studies and confirmed that he could start studying Chinese there in October. Since he had enough time before the course began, he decided to take a guided tour of Europe. He noted with interest how easily the group on the tour bus crossed borders, with the guide handling all the formalities.

At the school he found himself studying in the company of many British intelligence officers and was also able to mix socially with them and their wives. He told them that he had decided to study Chinese in the hope that he could represent his firm, a large Canadian engineering company, in Communist China.[31]

Molody's main concern at this time, however, was to set up the Cohens in a house that would provide a more secure location for their transmitter and photographic facilities. Early in 1956 they finally came across an ideal spot near the U.S. air base in Ruislip, whose busy radio communications would help to hide the "illegal" *rezidentura*'s transmissions to Moscow.

The house in question was a Tudor style bungalow at 45 Cranley Drive, a dead-end street lined with two-family homes, each fronted by a miniature lawn. The last house on the left, a one-family bungalow, stood out because of its individuality—whitewashed, what appeared to be half-timbering, bow windows, and an attached garage on the right side. In front there was a low brick wall reinforced by a taller hedge that enclosed a neatly clipped lawn with a magnolia and flowering cherry.[32]

From the standpoint of spies like Molody and the Cohens, the house's location possessed certain advantages in addition to its proximity to the American air force base, which added up to a knotty surveillance problem for M-I5. Since the house was situated on a dead-end street, cars could not cruise by very easily. The bow windows, which had an unobstructed view of the street, made it impossible to conduct surveillance from parked vehicles. There was a recessed entry to the front door, preventing direct observation of that door by watchers in adjoining houses. A playground in back would make watchers on that side too conspicuous. The only place from which the house could be watched without alarming the inhabitants was the house directly across the street.

The "Krogers" were able to buy the house with operational funds from a former sergeant of the Metropolitan Police for 4,200 pounds (about $12,000). They spent another 800 pounds (roughly $2,000) on improvements, such as built-in bookshelves, an extension ladder to the attic, locks and bolts of a special type on all the doors and windows, and installation of a burglar alarm, letting the neighbors know that in view of "Peter Kroger's" valuable books, they were worried about possible robbery.[33] "Helen Kroger" also told the neighbors that her hobby was photography, thus providing an explanation for the fact that the windows of the bathroom were sometimes blocked by boards in order to turn it into a darkroom.

There were other special things in the bungalow that were less conspicuous. One such item in the living room was a Ronson lighter with a secret compartment in which negatives of a signal plan had been hidden. Among the furnishings was a radio-phonograph console that Molody and Morris Cohen used for short-wave reception from Moscow, with headphones plugged into the back. In Cohen's book-filled study, there was an innocent-looking camera, a typewriter, and a tape recorder that they connected to the radio in the living room in order to record Moscow's transmissions.

They had placed numerous secret containers in the bedroom, bathroom, and kitchen; some of these containers also provided hiding places for money, which they kept on hand in fairly large amounts for emergency use. The Cohens hid two forged Canadian passports, complete with their own pictures, in the lining of a leather writing case in a drawer of the bedroom dressing table. They intended to use the passports for their escape, in case it was inadvisable to use their "genuine" New Zealand passports.

With Molody's help, Morris Cohen constructed a trapdoor in a corner of the kitchen floor. The trapdoor gave access to the concrete slab on which the house had been built, leaving a cavity three or four feet deep under the floorboards of the house. At the far end of this cavity, they broke through the concrete to make a hole two feet in depth, which they could cover with a concrete lid. This was where they concealed the transmitter, wrapped in two heavy plastic bags. The transmitter was of the most modern design, completely transistorized, and had been built in Moscow with parts from a number of European countries. They also hid in the same hole an automatic device for sending out Morse on a tape at high speed; a Minox camera and holder for photographing documents;

a couple of lenses; and spare transmitter parts. Since this equipment was needed only rarely, they cemented the lid over the hole and sprinkled dust on top, seeking to give the impression that the concrete slab had never been touched. They concealed the trap door in the kitchen by covering it with a piece of linoleum and moving the refrigerator on top of it.

It took time to get all these things set up to their satisfaction, but the spy ring with Molody as *"Kapellmeister"* (orchestra leader)[34] and Morris Cohen as "pianist," was ready to take action early in 1956, a year marked by unusually important events.

In the spring of that year, Khrushchev and Bulganin made a state visit to Great Britain, traveling on a Soviet cruiser. While the cruiser was in Portsmouth, Commander Crabbe of the British Navy, an expert frogman, mysteriously disappeared. He had apparently been carrying out a secret underwater exploration of the bottom and sides of the Soviet cruiser. Doubtless Molody and his friends sent reports to Moscow about this incident, making use of various Admiralty sources controlled by the spy ring.

In October 1956, at the Eighteenth Party Congress in Moscow, Khrushchev delivered his secret speech denouncing Stalin. The contents of the speech soon leaked out, and shortly afterward, as one of its repercussions, the Hungarian Revolution erupted. The KGB, of course, considered it of vital importance to find out what the Western powers, including Great Britain, intended to do in this situation. Directives must have been sent to Molody and other key KGB residents abroad to exploit all available sources for information, but it is not known how Molody responded.

While Moscow was still hesitating about military intervention in Hungary, a new crisis developed. Great Britain and France, joined by Israel, attempted to seize the Suez Canal in answer to Nasser's threats to close the canal. Did Molody's "illegal" residency have any advance knowledge of this military action? Whatever the case, the move by Great Britain and France against Egypt diverted world attention from Hungary and encouraged Soviet military intervention.

As the end of his eighteen months of study at the School of Oriental Languages approached, Molody realized that he would have to find some other cover for his espionage work. He decided that, like Morris Cohen, he should start a small business. One of the first things that came to mind was the jukebox business, which could be profitable to a small entrepreneur, while the size of his income would be difficult to check, since it would depend, after all, on the patronage of his jukeboxes.

Molody made his first contact in this field after reading an advertisement in a London evening newspaper. Molody got in touch with the vending-machine firm, but their deal was not the type he had in mind. However, the firm's representative referred him to another company that handled jukeboxes. He paid a deposit on five Minstrel brand jukeboxes and set up his own route by placing them in taverns and cafés.[35] "Looking after my round of machines," he wrote in his book, "gave me an excuse to buy a car, which was also of great help in my intelligence activities."[36]

To his acquaintances he told tall stories about his experiences with vending machines in the United States, where he supposedly had to struggle against gangsters who intimidated bar owners into using their machines and discouraged competitors by smashing their machines, or, if this did not work, beating up or killing them. "I was shot at once," said Molody, "and mark my words, it'll get as bad over here."[37]

By the time he finished his studies, he was ready to branch out into vending machines. With a man he met when he bought his jukeboxes, he formed a partnership in the Automatic Merchandising Co. Ltd., investing £500 (about $1,400). Then he became a partner in two other firms, the Thanet Trading Co. Ltd., which operated chewing-gum machines, and the Peckham Automatic Co. Ltd., specializing in gumball machines. Together these firms had two hundred sites in London, giving Molody a good excuse for going into many odd places and making all sorts of contacts.[38] Soon he was describing himself as a managing director and acquired a Ford station wagon to go about his work. Best of all, however, was his idea of appointing himself export sales manager, which provided him with a pretext like that of Cohen for frequently traveling abroad.[39]

In late 1958 Morris Cohen gave up his store in London and ran the antiquarian business out of his home, explaining later that he wanted to save the rent on the store and the expense of commuting.[40] Still, the new arrangement had advantages that did not escape Cohen and his wife, who complained to her friends in the neighborhood about the nuisance of running a taxi service for her husband's business associates—"foreign booksellers"—she picked up at the London Airport.[41] In all likelihood, there were real booksellers among them, but some of their visitors must have been fellow Soviet agents.

As the years passed, Molody's business interests continued to grow. At one point he surprised and gratified his partners by coming back from Milan, where he had succeeded in selling a firm bubble-gum machines at a price of $300,000. The Automatic Merchandising Company ordered the machines from the manufacturer, but when the machines were ready for delivery, the deal fell through and, in March 1960, the company went into receivership, with liabilities of £30,000 (about $84,000).

In August 1959, however, he had purchased a directorship in the Master Switch Company Ltd., which was manufacturing an electronic device for car and truck dashboards that automatically locked the doors, trunk, and hood.[42] The device could also be adapted, as the advertising stated, for use in "banks, prisons, offices, factories, and homes." Presumably, it would have been useful in the bungalow on Cranley Drive.

This new business offered an outlet for Molody's considerable energies, and he was soon deeply involved in solving the firm's start-up problems of administration and production.

In March 1960, the month in which the Automatic Merchandising Company failed, Molody and three other directors of the Master Switch Company went to Brussels, where the firm's electronic device was being exhibited at the annual International Inventors' Exhibition. "I got a good belly laugh when our exhibit won a gold medal as the best British exhibit," wrote Molody.[43]

Thus, the KGB's relatively modest capital investment of no more than five thousand dollars in all these enterprises had contrived to turn the "Canadian" into a respected British businessman and provided him with exactly the cover he needed.

Since Konon Molody and the Cohens, after their arrest, adhered strictly to the code of Soviet spies by sealing their lips about their intelligence activities, only the Moscow Center knows what they actually did during the five years they conducted espionage in England.

Two-way communications were maintained on a regular basis in accordance with the signal plan. Their own radio messages to Moscow dealt only with the most urgent and important matters and never amounted to more than a hundred words or so at a time, for their transmissions were measured in seconds rather than minutes in order to escape detection.

The Molody spy ring microfilmed bulky reports and documents for dispatch through dead drops serviced by couriers and reduced less bulky materials to microdots for transmission in packages (usually Morris Cohen's books) or letters mailed to accommodation addresses outside the country.

The British authorities' revelations about the espionage carried out by Molody and the Cohens were limited to the Portland spy case, which formed the "conspiracy" for which they and the two others involved in the case received prison terms. The authorities excluded everything else they learned about the Molody spy ring from the trial and never made additional information known to the public.

Implicated in the Portland spy case were two British subjects employed at the Portland naval base, Henry Frederick Houghton and Ethel Elizabeth "Bunty" Gee. Because of the Royal Navy's experience in dealing with German U-boats during World War II, NATO decided that the development of antisubmarine weapons, in the face of a massive Soviet submarine threat, should be entrusted to the British. Closely related to the work conducted at Portland's Underwater Weapons Establishment was the development of Britain's first nuclear submarine, *Dreadnought*, which was modeled on the U.S. nuclear submarines *Nautilus* and *Skipjack*, but modified by the British to become an antisubmarine submarine.[44]

Houghton had served for twenty-five years in the Royal Navy, retiring as a chief petty officer in 1945 at the end of the war. He had served on armed merchantmen in convoys during the war— work that was dangerous enough but did not provide much occasion for heroics. After his retirement, Houghton became a navy civilian clerk, and in 1951 he was sent to the British Embassy in Warsaw to fill a job in the naval attaché's office.

Houghton had always had a drinking problem, but he drank so heavily in Warsaw that he was often intoxicated and had to be warned several times. He had also become deeply involved in black market activities, smuggling scarce penicillin and strepto-mycin into Poland from England and reaping huge profits. After quarreling with his wife, he became intimate with a Polish woman named Christina, who was obviously an agent of the secret police. But Polish Intelligence did not have much time to exploit Hough-ton as an agent in Warsaw, since his drunkenness and other dubi-ous activities led the British Embassy to conclude that he was a security risk. He was sent home when his tour of duty had only been half completed.[45]

Houghton's bad record in Warsaw should have disqualified him for employment in a defense establishment engaged in secret experimental projects. Nevertheless, after he returned to England in October 1952, he was assigned to the Underwater Weapons Establishment at Portland. His heavy drinking continued, and he was spending far more money than he earned.

Exactly when Houghton established contact with Polish Intelli-gence in England is not known. Houghton, whose cupidity was well-known to Polish Intelligence, probably required little urging to sell them information.

It is also uncertain whether it was Houghton's own idea or a suggestion from his case officer to develop a love affair with Bunty Gee. Houghton's job limited his access to information, but Bunty Gee, with whom he had been acquainted for some time, worked in the Portland office responsible for the handling, filing, and circu-lation of test pamphlets that dealt with research and development in antisubmarine warfare. Bunty Gee was constantly engaged in the handling of documents—some of them highly secret—taking them from the vaults and filing them on their return.

Bunty Gee could, therefore, be a valuable asset in expanding Houghton's access to Portland's secrets. And Miss Gee was a prime asset from another point of view. As a spinster, she had led a dull life, going back and forth between her office at the naval base and the cottage in Portland where she took care of an eighty-year-old mother, an invalid aunt, and a seventy-six-year-old uncle.[46]

By this time Houghton's marriage had broken up. Although no impartial observer would have found him attractive, it was different with Bunty Gee, who had never been seriously involved with a man and was immediately flattered by Houghton's attentions. To Bunty Gee, Harry Houghton was a war hero who opened up an exciting world of lovemaking.

The more serious phase of their relationship began sometime in 1957. By then Harry and Bunty were spending nights together in London and elsewhere. How she explained her overnight absences to her old and sick relatives is not known, but she must have hinted that Houghton had proposed marriage to her, and that she had postponed any idea of marriage while her relatives continued to need her at home. It was not long before Houghton enlisted Bunty's aid in smuggling out test pamphlets requested by his case officer. She usually removed the documents on a Friday night so that he would have the weekend to photograph them, before she returned them on Monday morning when she went to work.

Aside from the desire to please her lover, Bunty also began to enjoy the money that came her way. Her job paid her only £10 ($28) a week, and now she found herself in a position to save money on a scale she had never dreamed of. By the time of her arrest, she had accumulated nearly £5000 ($14,000) in bank accounts, National Savings certificates, cash, and shares. Despite his lavish expenditures on drink, entertainment, and new cars, Houghton's finances were also looking up. He had £1,500 ($4,000) in a bank account, Premium Bonds, and cash.[47] In 1959 he bought a cottage in Portland which cost him £9,000 ($25,000) with improvements, and Bunty Gee helped him redecorate it.[48]

Konon Molody apparently entered the picture in 1960. It was the KGB's practice to take over operations in which it had exceptional interest from the "Socialist Commonwealth's" intelligence services, and in this case someone in Moscow decided that the KGB should take over the Portland agents from the Polish service. The reason for doing so is less obvious. Normally military and naval intelligence are a GRU, not KGB, responsibility, although there is no clear-cut or absolute line of demarcation between the two Soviet services.

The motive for assigning the operation to Molody's "illegal" *rezidentura* is also unclear. Previously Houghton had been handled by the Polish Intelligence "legal" residency in the London embassy, and it might have seemed normal to have the KGB's "legal" residency take over the operation. On the other hand, if Molody was already handling a penetration of the Admiralty, it would be understandable why he took over the Portland operation.

In October 1962, William John Christopher Vassall, a British Admiralty clerk, thirty-six years old, was convicted of spying for the Russians and sentenced to eighteen years in prison. Vassall confessed that he had photographed secret documents for transmission to the Russians. His spy work began in July 1956 in Moscow while he was working in the naval attaché's office (as Houghton had done earlier in Warsaw). Vassall had been compromised by several Russians and a Pole when he was photographed committing homosexual acts. Vassall's spying continued after he returned to London and worked at the Admiralty.[49] If Molody was already running Vassall as an agent, this might explain why the Portland spies were turned over to him.

Evidently Bunty and Houghton were full-fledged partners in crime by the time Molody became the case officer, since they both took part in operational meetings with Molody—meetings that were observed by MI-5 agents.

According to British intelligence, Houghton's extravagant life style and apparently inexhaustible supply of money finally aroused suspicion. The subsequent investigation uncovered Houghton's intimate relationship with Bunty Gee and raised some questions about what they were up to, and the pair led the Special Branch to "Gordon Lonsdale," who in turn led the investigators to the "Krogers" in their bungalow at Ruislip.

So much for the official version, but Konon Molody clearly did not accept this version of his own exposure and arrest. "The truth is quite different," said Molody. "MI-5 was given the tip by a traitor who handed it over on a plate. Without that, they would never have got me."[50] Was that Molody's ego speaking? Naturally it would be hard for him to admit that MI-5, the despised foe, was smarter than he and that he had blundered and fallen into a trap.

Yet one can doubt that Molody was simply trying to save face. When a KGB officer is caught red-handed, it may reflect on his professionalism in a negative sense and make the KGB itself look bad, but is it better to admit that the KGB has traitors in its ranks? One is forced to conclude that on this occasion Molody was expressing a truthful opinion. He also asserted that he knew the traitor's identity and implied that the traitor was still living.

If so, the question must be asked, what traitor? Only MI-6 or MI-5 could answer this question, assuming that the traitor ever really existed. If, indeed, Molody was betrayed by a high-level Soviet Intelligence defector, then MI-5 zeroed in on Molody from the beginning. In that case, Houghton, inept conspirator that he was, did not lead MI-5 to Molody; on the contrary, Molody led MI-5 to Houghton and Bunty Gee at one end of the chain and to the Cohens at the other end. Moreover, Molody must have led MI-5 to other agents whose identities have not been divulged.

In other words; after Molody became known to MI-5 as a Soviet spy, special agents followed him to the first rendezvous with Houghton and Gee on July 9, 1960, opposite the Old Vic Theatre.[51] Thereafter, it was only necessary to identify these agents of Molody's by tailing them to their homes or offices.

Molody was kept under surveillance until August 27, when he went abroad.[52] This raises another interesting question: How could MI-5 be sure he would return? If Molody had developed the slightest suspicion he was being watched, the only logical step would have been to leave the country and never come back. Or did MI-5 see no other alternative than to run that risk, since the case against him was not complete? The risk was all the greater because Molody seems to have met the Cohens in Frankfurt on this occasion.[53]

On August 26, the day before he went abroad, Molody had deposited a brown attaché case for safekeeping at his bank, the Great Portland Street branch of the Midland Bank. Superintendent Smith of the Special Branch, who obtained a secret search order, examined the contents of the case, which included such items as a Praktina camera, a magnifying glass, and some film holders.[54] Molody retrieved the case on October 24, the day after he returned. He recognized immediately that the case had been tampered with: "I realized that the hunt for me was on."[55] If this was true, it is difficult to understand why he did not seek to escape or at least get rid of incriminating evidence during the two months he still remained at liberty.

At the July 1960 meeting with Houghton, the British security officers had succeeded in tape-recording a conversation in a lunchroom where Molody told him, "We will meet on the first Saturday of every month, especially the first Saturday of October and November, at Euston."[56] On Saturday, October 1, Molody still had not returned to England. If he and Houghton met according to the schedule set forth in their lunchroom conversation, their first meeting after his return to England must have taken place on Saturday, November 5.

At the beginning of November, Molody moved back into the White House, where he lived until his arrest.

The arrest took place at one of the usual Saturday meetings on January 7, 1961. After going through a number of standard maneuvers to throw off surveillance, Molody parked his car on a side street and strolled toward the Old Vic, where he had previously met Houghton and Gee.

Showing that they had been well-schooled in clandestine techniques, the pair made a visual contact with Molody on Waterloo Road, walking past him without any sign of recognition. They continued on their way, but Molody suddenly swung around and went after them, pretending to have just recognized them. When he caught up with them, he put his arms around their shoulders, greeting them with feigned excitement. In a moment he made a little bow to Miss Gee and smoothly took the shopping bag she was carrying. That and a separate parcel in her possession contained a number of secret test pamphlets, pictures of Admiralty fleet orders, and Houghton's photographs of the second half of a basic handbook of the Royal Navy, *Particulars of War Vessels*, amounting to hundreds of pages that included the designs and specifications of the then uncommissioned nuclear submarine *Dreadnought* and other advanced types of warships.[57]

Special Branch and MI-5 officers had been waiting for this moment and swiftly closed in, placed the three under arrest, and whisked them off to Scotland Yard.

When Detective Superintendent George Gordon Smith of the Special Branch asked Molody for his full name and address, Molody snapped back, "To any question you might ask me, my answer is no, so you need not trouble to ask."[58]

Thus, MI-5 obtained no more information from Molody than

the FBI obtained from William Fisher. Nevertheless, the evidence found in Molody's apartment in the White House and in the Cohens' house at 45 Cranley Drive furnished ample proof of the espionage activities of the three. Taken together with testimony concerning Harry Houghton and Bunty Gee, their conspiratorial meetings with Molody, and the material they passed to him at their last meeting, this evidence ensured the conviction of all those accused in the case.

At the Old Bailey trial, which took place from March 13 to March 21, 1961, the most dramatic moment came when letters from Molody's wife and children, transmitted in the form of microdots and a letter of reply from Molody himself, which had not yet been microfilmed, were read in court. It was reminiscent of a similar moment in the trial of William Fisher in Brooklyn when letters from Fisher's wife and daughter were read in court. Like Fisher, Molody could not quite hide his emotion.

Molody and the Cohens did not go into the witness box. In a somewhat unusual procedure, however, all three were allowed to make statements based on prepared notes from the dock.[59]

There was nothing unusual about these statements except for a bit of dramatics on Molody's part. While Morris and Lona Cohen persisted in their masquerade as the Krogers and claimed complete innocence, Molody stole the show as he stood up in his casual tweeds and attempted to take upon himself complete responsibility for all the spy paraphernalia found in their home, characterizing them as innocent victims.

"I realize it is too late for me to make amends now," concluded Molody, "but I feel the least I can do in the circumstances is to accept full responsibility for my action, irrespective of the consequences to me personally."[60]

It took the jury only eighty minutes to find all the defendants guilty. The judge sentenced "Lonsdale" to twenty-five years in prison, the "Krogers" twenty years each, and Harry Houghton and Bunty Gee fifteen years each. The five defendants appealed their sentences, but all appeals were denied on May 9, 1961. By this time they were already serving their sentences. Molody, Morris Cohen, and Harry Houghton were sent at the outset to Wormwood Scrubs, where Molody and Cohen worked in the tailor shop and Houghton worked in the canvas shop manufacturing mail-bags. Lona Cohen and Bunty Gee were sent to the Holloway Prison for Women.[61]

Shortly after denial of the appeals, Morris Cohen was transferred to Winson Green Prison, Birmingham, and Harry Houghton to Winchester Prison.

Konon Molody had a longer stay at Wormwood Scrubs, but in the autumn of 1961 he was moved to Strangeways Prison, Manchester, where he remained for six months. In the spring of 1962 he was transferred to Winson Green and spent the next two years there. While still at Strangeways, he was encouraged in February 1962 by the news that William Fisher had been exchanged for U-2 pilot Francis Gary Powers. This news convinced him that a similar exchange would be arranged for him as soon as a suitable British subject was found.

Prisoners were allowed to receive their local newspaper, and Molody demanded *Pravda* on the ground that the Soviet party newspaper in Moscow was *his* local newspaper[62] (evidently untroubled by the inconsistency, since he claimed to be a Polish citizen and should therefore have read *Tribuna Ludu*). So, he read *Pravda* regularly, and his hopes soon soared higher when he read several articles about the arrest and trial of Greville Wynne, sentenced to a prison term in May 1963 for his espionage work in connection with Oleg Penkovsky, who had spied for M-16 and the CIA.

"The idea of a possible exchange began to take shape in my mind," wrote Molody.[63]

Such arrangements take time, however, but he had already received a hint that a possible exchange was in the wind. On January 15, 1963, some "important gentlemen from Whitehall" came to Birmingham and asked to see him, even before Wynne and Penkovsky's trial in Moscow.[64]

A few months later he received a letter from his wife that gave him further encouragement. Maintaining the fiction that they were Polish citizens, Galyusha wrote that she had approached the Soviet Embassy in Warsaw and suggested an exchange of Wynne for her husband.[65] According to Molody, receiving an affirmative reply from the Soviet government soon afterward, she wrote a letter in which she asked Mrs. Wynne to approach the British government with a similar suggestion.

Galyusha thought that the exchange could be arranged within a few weeks, but she was overly optimistic, because the matter dragged on for many months. The final stage was reached in March 1964, when Mrs. Wynne received permission from the Soviet government to visit her husband, who was brought to Moscow from Vladimir Prison for the purpose.

On April 9 Molody received a clear indication that his release was imminent when he was summoned by the prison's senior medical officer for a complete physical examination.[66] On April 21 he was told to pack his belongings for departure. After some brief formalities, he left the prison, escorted by two police officers, and traveled by car to Northold airfield, where he boarded a Royal Air Force transport. Three hours after the takeoff from Northold, the plane landed at the RAF base Gatow in the British sector of West Berlin. He spent the night in the military prison, supplied with books and a transistor radio.

Very early the next morning he was driven through the misty, wind-swept streets of West Berlin. Newsmen who knew about the impending exchange had spent the night at the Glienicker Bridge, where Fisher had been exchanged for Powers more than two years earlier. But this exchange was to take place at a different location. The car took him to the highway leading to Hamburg, where all traffic had been temporarily halted.

He and his escorts passed the West Berlin checkpoint without stopping and drove into the no-man's-land formed by that checkpoint and the border station of the East German authorities. The exchange had been arranged for 5:30 A.M., before many Berliners were awake and on their way to work.

As the car that carried Molody approached, the barrier of the East German border post was raised and another car raced straight toward them, suddenly veering at the last moment into a U-turn and stopping on the left side of the highway, facing the East German barrier.

It had been agreed that the center of the highway would be treated as the border to effect the exchange, and a short white line had been painted down the middle for this purpose. One man from each side went over to the other party in order to make sure of the identity of the prisoner who was being exchanged. Molody recognized the man who came over to him as an old friend and colleague. A British MI-6 man confirmed the identity of Greville Wynne, who was still sitting in the car.

When Wynne got out of the car, Molody recognized him from newspaper photographs. Molody turned to his escorts and said, with his typical black humor, "I sure hope that my favorite Englishman won't kick the bucket just now."[67]

Finally the Soviet representative in charge of the operation on the other side pronounced the word "Exchange" in English and Russian. Molody and Wynne promptly crossed the center line to the other side, got into the waiting cars, and drove off in opposite directions.

There is a certain irony in this exchange that probably did not escape Konon Molody. He had been exchanged for Greville Wynne, the MI-6 man imprisoned for his dealings with Oleg Penkovsky, who may have been responsible for Molody's arrest.

11

The Man Who Knew Too Much

IN THE HISTORY of Soviet State Security there have been many men who knew too much and were executed in order to silence them.

KGB Major Peter Deriabin said, "I went down a road which took me deep inside the Soviet leadership. I saw the diseased body as it really is, as very few Russians are ever permitted to see it. After this I could not remain. In a very real sense I think of myself as a counterpart of that fictional character of Chesterton's, *The Man Who Knew Too Much.*"[1]

Deriabin's knowledge was not the kind for which other men had received "nine grams of lead"[2]—a bullet in the back of the head. But his knowledge of the rottenness of the Soviet state and its leadership, even when supported by irrefutable examples, sounded convincing only to those in the West who were already convinced; the Communists and most liberals did not believe a single thing he said.

The purge of Old Bolsheviks and the Red Army in the 1930's had contributed to the defection of Soviet Intelligence officers, many of them old-line Communists, who became disillusioned with the Soviet system. On the other hand, Stalin's death and Beria's elimination created an atmosphere of uncertainty and insecurity among Soviet Intelligence officers in the early 1950's.

281

It undoubtedly appeared to Deriabin, Petrov, and other Soviet Intelligence defectors of the 1950's that there were hard times ahead for the KGB. The post-Beria leadership had succeeded in bringing the State Security apparatus under its control, but was bound to regard that apparatus with suspicion, if not outright hostility for some time to come.

To an ambitious young KGB officer like Deriabin, then only thirty-three years old, future prospects must have loooked bleak indeed. Thus, he had strong professional reasons—in addition to personal ones—to seize the opportunity provided by his close proximity to the West to clear out and seek his fortune elsewhere.

Peter Sergeyevich Deriabin was born in the village of Lokot in southwestern Siberia on February 13, 1921.[3] The area in which he grew up belonged to the Altai Krai, one of the best farming regions in the country and comparable to the black soil region of the Ukraine. His father owned a small farm at the time of his birth.

Thus, Deriabin came from peasant stock, and in this way, he resembled other KGB officers, such as William Fisher, whose grandparents were peasants, Igor Gouzenko, and Vladimir Petrov, who also grew up in Siberia. Of course, there is nothing strange about the fact that many people of peasant origin went to work for Soviet State Security. The new Soviet regime was to be based on workers and peasants, but by strictly applying class origins to the personnel requirements of State Security, it proved impossible to recruit many people with a working-class background, since there were relatively few workers in terms of the overall population at that time.

Young Deriabin's career was aided by the fact that his family remained neutral during the first chaotic years that followed the revolution. After the Bolshevik victory, the Deriabins quickly adapted themselves to the new situation. Peter's brother, Vladimir, joined the Komsomol and acquired a reputation as an activist. His father, who had disposed of most of his land earlier, became the chairman of a *kolkhoz* and was regarded as a supporter of the Bolsheviks.[4] With such a background, Peter Deriabin had no difficulty in advancing himself rapidly under the Bolsheviks.

The prime elements in this rapid advancement, however, were

his own intelligence, energy, and party dedication. After his graduation from high school with top honors in 1937, he took some
teaching courses and became a history teacher at a school about a
hundred miles away. As secretary of the Komsomol organization
there, Deriabin wielded considerable influence in the school despite his youth. Before long he was instructing third-year students
in Communist Party history and the USSR Constitution (the so-
called Stalin Constitution of 1936).

As war approached, Deriabin was conscripted in October 1939
and, in view of his party activities, assigned as a political commissar with a military unit. He first attended a regimental noncom-
missioned officers school, where he became a deputy political
commissar. When he was assigned to a regiment, he served as
secretary of the Komsomol bureau. His division was stationed
along the borders of Manchuria and Mongolia, facing Japanese
forces.

Although he was less than twenty years old, Deriabin learned to
throw his weight around in the army. It was a reflection of his
youthful cockiness that others began to call him the "Komsomol
god."[5] If a superior officer tried to make him perform his military
duties, Deriabin immediately complained to the political commissar above him that the officer was interfering with his political
work. In the Soviet context, this was a serious charge, and few
military officers wished to have it raised against them. Deriabin
himself was only reflecting a political indoctrination that stressed
the primacy of the Communist Party (and its representatives) in
all spheres, including the military. This arrogance could only increase, for in August 1941, on the threshold of World War II, he
won full membership in the Communist Party, which made him
part of an elite that constituted about five percent of the USSR's
population.

When the German invasion came, Deriabin found himself serving as a political commissar at the front. Commissar or not, he and
his battalion were continually under fire, first near Moscow, then
at Stalingrad, and later, after the German surrender at Stalingrad,
close to Odessa. By the spring of 1944, he had been wounded
four times and was glad when he received an assignment to the
Higher Army Counterintelligence School in Moscow.

Run in reality by Soviet State Security, this counterintelligence school was designed to train SMERSH officers, who had the task of watching out for disaffected or politically unreliable elements in the armed forces. During Deriabin's period of training, with the war drawing to a close, emphasis was placed on the control of the population in areas occupied by the USSR. The problem of imposing Soviet control extended to many millions of Soviet citizens in territories formerly occupied by the Germans, as well as millions of foreigners in those areas of Eastern Europe overrun by the Soviet Army during the German retreat. But even in those parts of the USSR that had never fallen under enemy occupation, Soviet control had loosened as a result of the war. Deriabin and his fellow students were given to understand that Moscow planned to give first priority to the tightening of this control.

The instructors at the school sought to strengthen in the students a feeling of uniqueness as Chekists, who, it seemed, differed from ordinary party functionaries and government officials in that they were Communists first, last, and always. As Chekists, the students were not to let themselves be misled by the Soviet Union's wartime alliance with the United States and England: "Today's allies are tomorrow's enemies." In general, Chekists had to remember that all non-Communist parties, organizations, leaders, and activities belonged potentially to the "class enemy"; they were, whether they knew it or not, "objectively counterrevolutionary" and should be dealt with accordingly.[6]

The course concentrated on counterintelligence subjects—such as the use and handling of informers, investigation, and surveillance—all aimed at the detection of anti-Soviet elements in the population. During the course the students did field work, carrying out surveillance under real conditions (in later courses they shadowed diplomats and other foreigners in the Moscow area). Considerable attention was also paid to the preparation of reports and the question of notifying (or not notifying) local party organizations about arrests.[7]

When Deriabin, with his spotless party record, was graduated from the school in the top ten of the class in April 1945, he received a post at naval counterintelligence headquarters in Moscow.

In the fall of 1945 he was promoted to captain. His pay was increased to two thousand rubles a month—far above the income of average people of the same age and educational background, who earned perhaps six hundred rubles monthly. In addition, he received a number of fringe benefits: better clothes, food, housing, and medical care. As a Communist he belonged to the elite, but as an officer of State Security he belonged to the cream of that elite.

Yet Deriabin was not happy. His mother and father were dead and his brother had been killed during the war. There remained only a sister, Valya, for whom he had a special fondness. Unfortunately, the twelve-year-old Valya lived far away in his native part of Siberia. Hoping to make a home for Valya, who was living with an uncle, he requested a transfer to Biysk. His request was turned down.

In his depressed state, Deriabin pulled some strings and managed to secure a discharge from military service. He traveled on a slow train over the Trans-Siberian Railway to Novosibirsk, where he changed to a branch line. Five days later he reached Biysk and was reunited with Valya.

His homecoming, however, was not as he had pictured it. He found conditions so catastrophic there that his spirits sank to a new low. Most of his surviving male relatives had been seriously wounded or crippled. Other relatives could scarcely earn enough to keep alive. After buying some clothes for his sister, he had hardly any money left from his savings.

Searching for a job, he discovered that even if he could find an opening as a teacher, he would have to start at the bottom, since all the better posts were already filled. In despair, he turned to the head of the State Security office in Biysk, who was a friend. With this man's help, he was reinstated as a captain in Soviet State Security and was assigned as a case officer to Barnaul, one of the few industrial cities of the Altai Krai.

Thus his feet were at last firmly set on the path that fate seemed to have marked out for him. He followed that path unswervingly until he left the Soviet Union nearly a decade later.

Deriabin married Tanya Zakharova in May 1946, a month before he was reinstated as a captain of State Security. They moved to Barnaul where, much to Tanya's displeasure, they found that they were to live in a safe house. Inside the Soviet Union, the KGB preferred to have its safe houses occupied by State Security officers and their families. This arrangement was advantageous from the standpoint of security and also simplified the problem of finding housing for these officers. Nevertheless, Tanya flew into a rage about sharing the house with other officers and their agents for meetings at all hours. Because of her excitable nature, she had a number of painful scenes with her husband that Deriabin's new bosses chose to overlook.

Deriabin was placed in charge of a surveillance group similar to those existing in all cities of the USSR where there were State Security offices. The group watched suspects for the KGB and collected additional evidence against them. Surveillance of a particular suspect seldom lasted more than a month, but at any given time, there were several hundred under surveillance in Barnaul, a city of two hundred thousand.[8] Most of the suspects were people of other nationalities forcibly deported to the Altai Krai after the war—Lithuanians, Latvians, Estonians, Volga Germans, Poles, and so on. Deriabin took command of the surveillance group without any previous experience and based solely on his training at the Higher Counterintelligence School. The majority of his subordinates had attended special surveillance schools, where they were trained for three to six months. Despite his lack of experience, Deriabin quickly took hold and began to run the operation smoothly.

The surveillance group had at its disposal a fully stocked wardrobe that included both men's and women's clothing for every conceivable occasion and purpose. They were also provided with specialized equipment, such as built-in cameras and concealed binoculars.

Deriabin did not like his job, which involved spying on people in his native region. He was also troubled by personal problems. Although he had hoped to make a home for his sister, Valya, the situation was not working out, since his wife bitterly resented his attachment to his sister. Also, Tanya was in ill health. She needed air and sunshine, and a doctor recommended some part-time teaching in a school outside the city for sick or physically handicapped children. Tanya was pleased with this work, and for a time things improved. Nevertheless, the improvement was of short duration. Tanya became very sick with pleurisy and died suddenly.

The death of his wife saddened Deriabin, but in a certain sense he felt relieved. The marriage had not been a success for either of them, and Tanya's death forced him to come to grips with a problem he had been avoiding for some time. He had no future outside State Security, yet he was finding it increasingly hard to contemplate spending the rest of his life in the Altai Krai. When Tanya died, he submitted a request for a transfer to Moscow. It came as no surprise when his request was rejected. But his past experience had already taught him the value of personal contacts, and he decided to try a different route.

He requested a leave of a few weeks in the Caucasus, which was approved. He had no trouble obtaining accommodations in the Caucasus in January, since few people were interested in a vacation there at that time of the year. On his way to the Caucasus, Deriabin stopped off in Moscow. As soon as he arrived at the Yaroslavsky Station, he went to State Security headquarters where he looked up an old friend, Pavel Zuikov.

Zuikov had been one of Deriabin's fellow students at the Higher Army Counterintelligence School. Since his grades were not outstanding, Zuikov did not rate an assignment in Moscow—instead, he was sent to Murmansk. But being quick-witted, he convinced his Moscow boss, while he was in Murmansk on a business trip, that he needed another clever young assistant on his Moscow staff. So, Pavel Zuikov was transferred to Moscow, and after a few months of intricate maneuvering, he obtained a job as personnel assistant to Major General Svinelupov, the deputy minister of State Security under Colonel General Viktor Abakumov.

Abakumov disliked Svinelupov, but could not replace him (presumably, he would have had to have Beria's approval for that), and there was very little communication between them. Since Svinelupov, who was not a strong man, made little use of his authority, Zuikov did not hesitate to fill the gap, transferring generals, dismissing colonels, and staffing Svinelupov's office with his own trusted friends.

When Deriabin spoke to him, Zuikov unhesitatingly used his connections on Deriabin's behalf. Moscow requested Deriabin's file from Barnaul, and then ordered a transfer to State Security headquarters.

Deriabin returned to Barnaul and settled his affairs. Realizing that a widowed brother's home was no place for his sister, he arranged for Valya to live with an aunt and uncle, who could provide her with a more stable environment.

Then he set out on the five-day trip to Moscow, happy to turn his back on Barnaul, which he visited only once thereafter on an emergency leave.

For the next six years—from 1947 to 1953—Deriabin worked for State Security in Moscow. Fortunately, Deriabin could do his work in those years without coming into contact with Abakumov, who was high-handed in his management of State Security. He made himself useful at first by performing any tasks Zuikov chose to assign him. After a while he grew restive and asked Zuikov to give him something more specific to do. As a result, he spent several months on a special project that involved screening soldiers in Kremlin military units to determine their eligibility for further training in the State Security school as personnel to be assigned to the Guard Administration, which was responsible for the protection of high party and government leaders. This task involved a check of both military records and State Security files, and where ambiguities or inconsistencies existed, local KGB offices were called upon to investigate and submit their findings.

In the spring of 1947 Zuikov finally found a permanent job for Deriabin—a post on the staff of KGB Colonel Serafim Goryshev, who was scheduled in the near future to head the Personnel Department at State Security headquarters. Goryshev's assignment, however, was suddenly changed. He became an assistant to Lieutenant General Nikolai S. Vlasik, the chief of the Guard Administration, and when he moved into his new job he took Deriabin with him.

"I didn't think you'd mind," Goryshev told him. "It is a better job and more restful."

Nevertheless, Deriabin made a point of checking with Zuikov, who said, "Well, you'll have good food and good clothes . . . and Goryshev will take care of you. Otherwise I wouldn't let you go over there. The Guard Administration can be pretty sticky. It's awfully close to the top."[9]

Nikolai Vlasik owed his position as chief of the Guard Administration to the fact that he had been Stalin's bodyguard as far back as 1919, when Stalin was considered a nonentity by other Soviet leaders. Having attended a village school for only three years, Vlasik could barely sign his name. Not surprisingly, Vlasik was antiintellectual and used his powerful position to exclude from the Guard Administration anyone who had more than eight years of schooling. His view that highly educated people were dangerous reflected the viewpoint of the Soviet leadership, but it contributed to his dismissal later in 1947, when the Central Committee concluded that Vlasik's anti-intellectualism was depriving the Guard Administration of able personnel. Vlasik was able to secure reinstatement by making a direct appeal to Stalin, only to be dismissed once and for all five years later.[10] In addition to being Stalin's watchdog, Vlasik had also functioned for some time as the leader of a squad of killers expressly dedicated to the task of executing any Soviet leaders Stalin wished to eliminate with a minimum of fuss.

In view of the key role played by the Guard Administration, nothing was left to chance, and its personnel were constantly being checked and rechecked in order to detect promptly any sign that an individual might become a security risk. Thirteen sections in the Personnel Department carried out counterintelligence functions, covering all the organizational components of the Guard Administration.

Deriabin, who had eleven officers working for him, headed a section responsible for the behavior of about 2,350 Guard officers working in uniform or plainclothes in and around the Kremlin. If anything in the pattern of behavior of these Guard officers *or* their relatives raised a question, Deriabin instituted an investigation without delay, in order to find out whether this break in the pattern indicated a real or potential danger to the officials under the Guard Administration's protection.

Tired of his bachelor life, Deriabin met a young woman who worked in the Kremlin, and their relationship quickly became serious. Marina Makeyeva, a staunch party member, worked as a stenographer in the office of Politburo member Lazar Kaganovich, who remained in power until he was ousted as a member of the "antiparty" group in June 1957. Deriabin married Marina in June 1948, and six months later they were given an apartment in the ten-story State Security apartment house at 48a Chkalova

Street.[11] They could consider themselves fortunate by Soviet standards, since they had one large room and only had to share a kitchen with two other families (normally a kitchen was likely to be shared by anywhere from five to ten households). His new wife was earning a good salary and had some useful contacts high up in the Soviet regime. Deriabin himself was earning 4,200 rubles a month by this time, about twice as much as a factory manager earned, and had numerous perks in clothing and food that were beyond the reach of the bulk of the Soviet population. In his job he also rated a car and chauffeur. When his wife gave birth to a child in 1949, she went to the Kremlin hospital, where she received treatment far superior to that usually available in other Moscow hospitals. With their combined salaries, they could afford a small dacha in some pine woods at Mamontovka, twenty miles from Moscow.[12]

To all intents and purposes, their lives revolved around State Security, since it was safer and more comfortable to see only those who belonged to the same institution, which greatly reduced the chances of a security breach or an association with someone whom the regime considered politically unreliable.

Deriabin worked very hard. His working day began at 11 A.M. and ran until 5:30 P.M. Then he took a three-hour break, when he went to dinner or visited friends. At 8:30 P.M. he returned to the office, often working until 1 A.M. or later. His office was in a spacious room on the second floor of the Lubyanka. From a window he could look into the courtyard where prisoners were exercising.

Throughout his career Deriabin performed party duties along with his regular work. In 1942 he became the party secretary at his regimental headquarters. When he graduated from the Higher Counterintelligence School in 1945, he was posted to Naval Counterintelligence headquarters in Moscow and was "elected" to carry out the duties of Komsomol secretary. After joining State Security's Guard Administration, he became a lesser party secretary in the Personnel Department.

In 1949, availing himself of a change in his working hours, Deriabin decided to register for a course at the Institute of Marxism-Leninism. He had to attend classes three times a week for four hours in the evening, leaving him little time for his family or social activities. He spent two full years at the institute, finding most of the classes monotonous and uninteresting, but the completion of this study was essential if he hoped to be promoted into leadership echelons of the KGB. Moreover, it was another step in qualifying him as a member of the *nomenklatura*, the Communist Party's elite group of activists, then numbering in the neighborhood of a quarter million (and now about a half million), for whom all key jobs in the Soviet Union are reserved and who receive their assignments from the Central Committee.

Although he remained very conscious of the drawbacks, Deriabin liked his job. He had every chance of moving up in the State Security organization. He was only occasionally overcome by misgivings, but, for the most part, he was able to banish such thoughts and go on living the good life, Soviet style.

In Russian history there is a period known as the "Time of Troubles," which began when the despotic Ivan the Terrible died in 1584 and ended in 1613, when the first of the Romanovs was crowned as czar. The "Time of Troubles" was marked by political turmoil, civil strife, and famine as one pretender to the Russian throne after the other appeared, and a succession of czars met violent ends before any one of them could cement his rule.

In modern times, the period from 1949 to 1953 became known to officers of the Kremlin Guard as the "Years of Trouble."[13] The trouble began when Andrei Zhdanov, a leading Politburo member who was regarded as a possible successor to Stalin, died in August 1948. Zhdanov may have died a natural death, but it was suspected that he had been poisoned, perhaps on Stalin's orders. After Zhdanov's death, Georgi Malenkov, his principal rival, moved to eliminate all of Zhdanov's lieutenants, and in this effort he must have had (at least) Stalin's concurrence. The outcome was the so-called "Leningrad affair," for Leningrad had been Zhdanov's power base, and the top officials there were arrested and executed. Two Soviet officials closely identified with Zhdanov, however, were in Moscow—Nikolai Voznesensky, a Politburo member, and Aleksei Kuznetsov, a CPSU Central Committee secretary with an overall responsibility for the Guard Administration. Both fared no better than the men in Leningrad.

Stalin doubtless enjoyed the bloodletting among his immediate subordinates, and may have even kept his hand in by encouraging it. Moreover, his paranoid suspiciousness continued to grow as he felt his own physical and mental powers waning. Based on the available evidence, it appears that Stalin planned to dispose of some Politburo members, like Beria and Malenkov, in a purge similar to the ones he had successfully directed in the 1930's. But Stalin died first, in circumstances that are far from clear, and his death simply gave a new impetus to the deadly maneuvering for power. Both of Stalin's intended victims—if such they were— vanished from the scene. First, Beria was executed, and then Malenkov suffered a political demise and was never heard from again.

Deriabin survived the "Years of Trouble" because he had not reached a level high enough to become a target, nor was he identified in a subordinate capacity with any of the "losers."

General Viktor Abakumov was arrested in late 1951, but Deriabin continued to enjoy favor from above. He was given a choice of two jobs—chief of the Personnel Section of the Kremlin Guard or party secretary of the whole Personnel Department of the Guard Administration.

As usual, Deriabin consulted Pavel Zuikov, who also managed to survive in his exalted position in the office of the deputy minister of State Security. Zuikov recommended caution and suggested that he delay his decision, since both jobs were potentially very dangerous, exposing him to the risk of a sentence in a labor camp.

By this time Deriabin was anxious to get out of the line of fire. He asked Zuikov what chance he would have of getting a job in the Foreign Administration. He knew that State Security's foreign espionage apparatus had remained relatively untouched by the recent upheavals. Zuikov made a few telephone calls and put Deriabin in touch with the right man.

KGB Colonel Evgeni Ignatyevich Kravtsov had spent his whole career in foreign espionage work, joining State Security in the 1930's and spending most of the intervening years abroad. There was an intelligence and sophistication about him that impressed Deriabin from the outset.

Kravtsov headed the Austro-German Branch of the Foreign Administration. He had originally come from Leningrad and was posted before the war to Latvia, where he served as "legal" resident in Riga. During the war he remained at the Moscow Center as Party secretary. In 1946 he went on a KGB mission to Switzerland under the cover of first secretary of the embassy in Berne. In 1947 he served as State Secretary representative on the Soviet repatriation commission in Turkey. After that he moved to Berlin, where he was the resident for two years, presumably having his office in the huge intelligence complex at Karlshorst in East Berlin. Returning to Moscow, he became the Austro-German Branch chief in 1951.

During his interview with Kravtsov, Deriabin found that Kravtsov was less interested in Deriabin's knowledge of German, which was only rudimentary, than in his ability to write reports. Even more meaningful were Deriabin's qualifications in counterespionage and counterintelligence and his impeccable party record. As Deriabin discovered, Kravtsov had no lack of junior officers who were first-class German linguists, all graduates of the KGB's Leningrad Foreign Languages Institute.

In May 1952, only a few days after the interview with Kravtsov, Deriabin moved to his new office in the low-ceilinged rooms occupied by the Austro-German Branch at 1a Tekstilshchikov Street. A few weeks after his transfer, Deriabin was elected the branch's new party secretary, replacing an obnoxious young officer who had been acting secretary.[14]

Not much changed for Deriabin except that he no longer had to spend long hours on night duty, he acquired a private telephone in his apartment, and the atmosphere was far more informal in his new office, for Kravtsov's eighty-one officers in the Austro-German Branch greeted their chief with a relaxed "Hello, boss!" in English.

The three thousand officers of the Foreign Administration at the Moscow Center constituted still another elite group; within State Security they stood out in terms of intelligence, education, and knowledge of the world. There were another fifteen thousand officers and agents working in the field. Officers were regularly rotated between headquarters and the field to ensure that there was no warping of viewpoints because of excessively long service in Moscow or abroad. The "illegals," who had to spend most of their service in the field, were the exceptions to this rule.

The Austro-German Branch was subdivided into three sections:

intelligence in Germany, counterintelligence in Germany, and intelligence and counterintelligence in Austria. Deriabin was rotated through these sections in order to familiarize him with their
work before settling down in the German counterintelligence section.
His duties as the branch's party secretary also helped him to acquire
a special insight into the problems of all the sections.

Deriabin served as the deputy head of a "sector," being in exclusive custody of a large group of files. At the end of each working
day, he would seal up his papers in a case that was stored in a safe
sealed with his personal stamp. If anyone in authority needed to
have access to the files, Deriabin had to be called in to open the
safe. In this way, security could be strictly maintained, and there
was always a clear delineation of responsibility for any security
violation.

One of Deriabin's first tasks involved the preparation of a report
on the activities of the Association of Free German Jurists, an anti-
Communist organization, whose work disturbed the Soviet authorities because it had an efficient intelligence network inside
East Germany. The Association of Free Jurists was planning a
world congress in Berlin in July, seeking to focus international
attention on the violations of human rights in the Soviet zone of
Germany.

After reading Deriabin's report, Kravtsov recommended that
this congress be disrupted, preferably by taking direct action
against its organizers. Lieutenant General Fedotov, deputy chief of
the Foreign Administration, approved Kravtsov's recommendation, ordering Major General Kaverznev, who commanded the
huge State Security headquarters at Karlshorst, to organize a task
force to kidnap Dr. Theo Friedenau, the president of the Free
Jurists. The order itself was signed by Lieutenant General Sergei
R. Savchenko, chief of the Foreign Administration. As in the case
of all orders calling for the use of "terror," e.g., murder or kidnapping, the order was drafted in handwritten form by Deriabin to
eliminate the need for a typist. In addition to Savchenko's signature, Kravtsov and Fedotov approved the order. These four men
were the only ones in Moscow to see the written order.

Plans for the kidnapping went ahead accordingly, but at a late
date Friedenau suddenly left for Sweden, leaving Dr. Walter
Linse, an able, reserved lawyer who was in charge of his Economic

Section, to handle the preparations for the congress. Kaverznev proposed to Moscow that Linse be kidnapped instead. Deriabin checked with his superiors and promptly replied: "Under orders of Savchenko take all measures to sabotage the congress." Kaverznev was not satisfied with this reply. He could interpret it as an order to take *all* measures, including Linse's kidnapping, but he wanted something more. He sent another cable: "Operational group for Friedenau has all information against Linse. Request permission." On July 2 Deriabin notified Berlin that permission had been granted.

On July 8, 1952, Dr. Linse was kidnapped outside his home in a quiet, attractive suburb of West Berlin by several men who, after a brief struggle, threw him into a taxicab, which roared off in the direction of East Berlin. When they had trouble getting Linse's leg inside the door, one of the gunmen coolly shot a bullet into his leg. There were vehement official protests from the Western powers and the West German authorities, but Soviet spokesmen rejected all such protests by denying any knowledge of the kidnapping.

Linse, suffering from shock and intense pain due to the wound in his leg, underwent prolonged interrogation at Karlshorst. He was in no condition to resist, and soon revealed all that he knew. Thus, the kidnapping turned out to be a great counterintelligence success. Within a few days, twenty-seven members of the Free Jurists in East Germany were under arrest, while many others were being hunted or kept under surveillance. Linse ultimately wound up in Vorkuta, a Soviet labor camp, where in 1955 some German prisoners of war encountered him.

Deriabin was congratulated by Kravtsov on the success of his first effort in the Austro-German Branch. His conscience did not bother him at the time, since he bore the Germans no love after his experiences at the front during the war.

But somewhere in the back of his mind, the idea of defection must have already lodged.

Deriabin continued to keep his thoughts on such matters to himself. But the possibility of a better life kept recurring to him—a better life somewhere, anywhere beyond the reach of the system that the State Security so sharply symbolized.[15]

Early in 1953, it looked as if Deriabin might get a TDY (temporary duty) assignment in East Berlin. Although he told himself at the time that it would be pleasant just to take a walk in West Berlin to look around, the probability is that if the opportunity had presented itself, he would not have come back at all.

But the East Berlin TDY never materialized. Deriabin did not lose hope, and, as luck would have it, he soon came up with an even better opportunity to go abroad. In the spring of 1953 Colonel Kravtsov suggested that he might like to go to Vienna. Deriabin pointed out that he would probably be disqualified for such an assignment in view of his former service in the Guard Administration. Kravtsov disagreed. The existing confusion in the new Soviet leadership, Kravtsov said, would result in this feature of his record being overlooked. Without further discussion, the two men struck a bargain.

Kravtsov was about to become the "legal" resident in Vienna and, therefore, had considerable latitude in choosing his staff. On the other hand, Deriabin was in a position to help Kravtsov when the latter's new assignment came up before the party committee. Deriabin, as the Austro-German Branch's party secretary, unreservedly supported the appointment. Kravtsov, in turn, offered Deriabin the post of SK officer in the Vienna "legal" residency.

Everything went smoothly after that. Deriabin, accompanied by his wife and four-year-old daughter, arrived at the Ostbahnhof in Vienna on September 28, 1953, a full month before Kravtsov, the new resident, arrived to take up his assignment.

On his arrival in Vienna, Deriabin occupied a palatial two-room suite with his family in the Grand Hotel, where most of his colleagues were billeted. Under his cover as assistant to General Sergei E. Maslov, the chief administrative officer of the Soviet High Commission (later the embassy), Deriabin had a private office in Room 19 of the Imperial Hotel, where the Soviet headquarters was located. Deriabin and Maslov shared the same secretary, whose office was between their offices with connecting doors.

Deriabin had come to Austria under his real name, since the

speed of his departure did not allow enough time for the usual State Security switch of names. Nevertheless, few of his agents knew him by his real name. Aside from his official cover, he had several other cover positions under false names. He used the name Korobov as chief of a section in the Soviet Commercial Administration in Austria, and on other occasions he called himself Smirnov, displaying the documents of an employee in the same administration. He also passed himself off at times as Voronov, a clerk in the Soviet High Commission office. Deriabin had five officers working for him as the Vienna residency's SK chief, but each of them had his own individual cover in other parts of the Soviet-occupation regime in Austria.

At first there were files for forty agents under Deriabin's jurisdiction, but this number was cut back by about a fourth when orders came from Moscow to break off the residency's connections with agents who had a local Communist background or were foreign Communists.[16] Of the remaining thirty, less than half were Soviet citizens in official positions. Among the others there were a few Austrians, a Greek, and some Russian emigrés.[17] On the whole, this distribution of agents was appropriate for the head of an SK section whose job called for spying on Soviet citizens either stationed in Austria or visiting that country under official auspices.

In contrast to Deriabin, Kravtsov assumed a new name, Evgeni Kovalev, with the rank of counselor, first in the Soviet High Commission and subsequently in the embassy. Kravtsov had under his command a sizable residency, which included fourteen "groups": Anglo-American, French, Austrian, West German, Yugoslav, Russian emigré, and "illegal," not to mention the SK element.

In terms of his SK duties, Deriabin had received strict instructions from the resident: "You must always keep your eye on any GRU personnel."[18] By doing so, Deriabin was constantly adding bits and pieces to individual files.

During the congress of the World Federation of Trade Unions in October and a session of the World Peace Council in November 1953, Deriabin had to mobilize all his men and obtain reinforcements from Moscow in order to conduct surveillance of the Soviet representatives. Both organizations were international Communist front groups, but this fact made no difference to State Security, which saw enemies everywhere and trusted fellow travelers no more than anyone else.

"A fine thing," Kravtsov observed on the eve of the World Peace Council session. "Over two thousand American agents swarming around the city and they give us seventy-one officers to fight them with."[19]

From time to time, Deriabin was assigned special tasks by Moscow. At one point the Center ordered him to arrange for the shadowing of a high Soviet official named Berezin, who was attending the WFTU Congress. This would not have been worthy of note had it not been for the fact that Berezin was the deputy of Nikolai M. Shvernik, then chairman of the Soviet All-Union Council of Trade Unions, who led the USSR's delegation to the Congress. Each night after the delegation had returned to its hotel, Deriabin received the written report of a three-man surveillance team from a Soviet army counterintelligence unit stationed at Baden. After reviewing the report he sent it off to Moscow. Deriabin never learned what Berezin was suspected of, but Shvernik, himself a Politburo member, did not know about Berezin's surveillance. Deriabin could not help wondering where Shvernik stood in the post-Stalin maneuvering for power inside the Soviet leadership.[20]

One thing was clear to Deriabin from his experience in the Guard Administration: no matter how high you rose in the Soviet Union, your position did not protect you. Indeed, the higher you rose, the more dangerous your situation became. Such thoughts registered in his mind without causing him to reach any firm decision about his future.

For such decisions a catalyst is necessary, and the catalyst appeared at five o'clock in the morning on February 13, 1954, when Colonel Kravtsov telephoned Deriabin at his apartment in the Grand Hotel. Excitedly, Kravtsov told him that an official of the Soviet Petroleum Administration, named Anatoli I. Skachkov, had disappeared and might have defected. Skachkov's wife was frightened, but felt that she had to report his disappearance since he had come home drunk, packed two overcoats and two suits, and left, telling her that he was "going to the Americans." Skachkov had spent the previous night carousing at the Maxim Night Club with a State Security lieutenant colonel from Moscow. Kravtsov ordered Deriabin to make an immediate investigation and take any necessary action without delay.

Deriabin dressed as rapidly as possible, called for his car, and drove over to see the security officer of the Soviet Petroleum Administration. On the way he asked himself whether there was any special significance in the fact that Skachkov had been accompanied by a State Security officer from Moscow during his binge. Could Skachkov's defection be a fake, stage managed by the Moscow Center as another attempt to penetrate American Intelligence? If so, the Moscow Center would be unlikely to tell anyone in Vienna, with the possible exception of the resident himself. Nevertheless, the resident, Kravtsov, would be obliged to go through the motions of investigating the case in order to make the defection look genuine.

Over the next twenty-four hours, Deriabin launched a full-scale investigation of Skachkov's business and personal life. With one of his subordinates, he went through Skachkov's desk at the office and searched the Skachkovs' apartment. He appropriated any papers of value in the apartment and removed them to the embassy's offices. The following night, acting on Kravtsov's fear that the Americans might raid the Skachkov apartment, he stationed an officer overnight at the apartment.

During the investigation, Deriabin could not avoid thinking more and more about his own defection. He no longer had any illusions about his work. Even if he imagined that he could hold himself aloof from the dirty aspects of his job, he knew that sooner or later he had to soil his hands, more than he had in the Linse kidnapping. And Deriabin was not much happier in his private life than in his professional one. His wife was far more committed to Communism and could not be expected to share his desire to defect. In a nutshell, he was fed up with his whole life. By the simple act of crossing a line, he could leave his life with all its cumbersome baggage behind him forever.

As the SK officer in charge, Deriabin was in an ideal position to carry out his own defection. He had the overall responsibility of watching all Soviet personnel, the officers in his group had to obey his orders, and he already knew by sight all the agents assigned to the surveillance of Soviet personnel.

Just before noon on February 15, having worked through the night, Deriabin briefly went by his apartment. His wife, disgusted with his erratic working hours, spoke sharply to him. "When do you expect to come home again?" Ordinarily he would not have replied to such a remark, which was the prelude to a domestic quarrel, but this time he said over his shoulder, as he was slamming the door behind him, "Maybe I'll never come back."

Deriabin's next step was to make another check of the Skachkov apartment, which he did with a junior officer. After he did, he said goodbye to the officer outside the door. It was about half-past three in the afternoon, but on this dark gray winter day it seemed like evening and lights were already coming on. A few snowflakes caught by the wind left no doubt that it was very cold, and the temperature was dropping.

Deriabin stopped at a stand and ate a steaming wurst, which he washed down with a bottle of beer. He hailed a taxi and drove to a well-known department store at the corner of Mariahilfer Strasse and the Stiftgasse, near the boundaries of the French and U.S. sectors. He looked down the Stiftgasse and saw no one he recognized among the passersby or those loitering in doorways. He stopped a streetcleaner with a long broom and asked him if the building across the street, the one with two sentries in front, was the American headquarters. The streetcleaner nodded yes.

Deriabin crossed the street and went up to one of the sentries, saying he wanted to see an American officer. The sentry gestured toward the entrance. Deriabin walked through the courtyard and into the lobby. He approached the Austrian receptionist behind the desk, who asked Deriabin his business. "I would like to see a Russian-speaking officer," Deriabin said in his poor German. The receptionist left for a moment and returned with an American civilian. Deriabin repeated his request. "Ah, you wish to speak with a Russian officer," the civilian said. Deriabin violently shook his head. "Someone in Intelligence," Deriabin said. "Is there anyone here from CIC or CIA?" The American civilian finally understood and said, "Wait here."

Shortly after, a young captain came into the room. He spoke good if American-accented Russian. Deriabin told the captain his official rank and position and asked for political asylum. The captain whistled. "Look here, you know what you're doing, don't you?" It was not a particularly encouraging response, but since he had passed the point of no return, Deriabin assured the captain that he did indeed know what he was doing.

The weather had turned bad. Vienna was swept by strong winds off the Hungarian plains and intermittent snowstorms, which made it extremely hazardous to take off in a small plane from the single emergency airstrip inside the American sector. Deriabin knew that the other two methods of leaving Vienna were dangerous, and he feared he might fall into Soviet hands. He could be brought out of Vienna by means of larger airfields outside Vienna, but he would have to pass through control points in the Soviet zone where he might be recognized. The other route was by the military train, which also had to pass through the Soviet zone.

While being interrogated, Deriabin kept asking when he would leave Vienna. "Don't worry," said an intelligence officer. "We'll get you out in a week or so." Deriabin jumped up and cried, "A week! A week will be too late. Get me out immediately."[21]

The Americans also realized that no time was to be lost. The next day, August 16, they smuggled Deriabin aboard the Mozart Express, as the military train was called. Soviet agents conducting surveillance outside the train in the drab, dirty gray Westbahnhof focused their attention on passengers boarding the train. They took no notice of a hot-water tank that the Austrian freight handlers loaded on the train as a shipment consigned to a quartermaster unit at Camp Truscott in Salzburg, headquarters of the American forces in Austria. Deriabin, concealed in the tank, was able to breathe through inconspicuous air holes.

Three hours later, as darkness fell, the train reached Linz, the first stop in the American zone. Deriabin's American escorts cut open the tank and released him from his temporary confinement, then drove him to a safe house in an isolated chalet outside Salzburg.[22]

At 8 A.M. on February 17, the Soviet occupation authorities imposed strict controls on all rail and highway routes leading out of Vienna. Soviet troops took up positions along these routes, and for a week every conveyance leaving the city was checked. A United Press dispatch of February 20 reported that "Soviet officials asked Austrian police to join the hunt today for two Russian factory officials who vanished after a drunken night-club spree and may try to escape to the West." The same Soviet statement named Deriabin and Skachkov and accused them of misappropriating official funds.[23]

Skachkov, who had indeed defected to the CIA, was flown out of Vienna before Deriabin walked into the American military police office at the Stiftskaserne. He was useful because of his intimate knowledge of Soviet economic policy in Austria. A year later, as it happened, Skachkov died after slipping out of the safe house where he had been interrogated and making the rounds of Frankfurt's sleazy bars. The ostensible cause of death was a heart attack, but victims of KGB assassinations have been killed with prussic acid vapor that simulated the effects of coronary disease.[24]

After being flown to the United States for further interrogation, Peter Deriabin was taken under the wing of the CIA and worked for them as a consultant. He did not surface until he published an account of his experiences in a two-part series that appeared in *Life* magazine in 1959, five years after his defection. During the intervening period he provided the CIA with a valuable fund of information. He may even have had something to do with the unsuccessful CIA operation to bring about the defection of B. Y. Nalivaiko, who was officially listed as Second Secretary of the Soviet Embassy in Vienna.

According to one source, several CIA officials privately admitted that Deriabin's defection was prompted by opportunism, not ideology, and that many other important defectors have been motivated by practical considerations.[25] There is no reason to doubt the truth of these assertions. Nevertheless, there can be no doubt that Deriabin was a "man who knew too much" about the system under which he had spent all his life up to his defection. Even if the different life he wanted for himself had its material side, it is impossible to separate this aspect from an ideology that denies to an individual freedom in all spheres, material as well as spiritual.

12

The Spies Who Came In from the Cold

WHEN THE QUESTION OF exchanging William Fisher ("Colonel Abel") for U-2 pilot Francis Gary Powers came up in January 1962, James B. Donovan, Fisher's lawyer, went to Washington and conferred with U.S. officials. Donovan brought up the question of Fisher's value to the Soviet government if he was returned to Moscow. He pointed out that Fisher might be appointed to head up the North American desk at the KGB Center. Later, Donovan described the negative reaction of one of the U.S. officials—probably a CIA representative—to this idea.

> "We don't think so," I was told. "If we took back such a man, abroad and isolated from us for so many years, there always would be a lingering question as to his individual loyalty. You can't afford to gamble on such things. Now, if we would be hesitant to have such a man head a 'top secret' operation, surely the ultra-suspicious Soviet would be even more reluctant. Abel has been here almost nine years; his own assistant defected. The very fact we agree to release him would create a doubt in the Russian mind and they would worry that he had 'made a deal.' The great probability is that he would serve only to instruct others in techniques. Even there, at his age and in poor health, his usefulness is limited, if they decided to use him at all."[1]

Those remarks were prophetic. William Fisher had also correctly foreseen that his usefulness would be limited in the future. In a discussion with Donovan, he said, "I am no longer of much use to my service. I can never again be used outside my country."[2]

Trusting a returned spy is not the kind of mistake the KGB makes. It has profited too often when others have made that mistake. For example, George Blake, who worked for MI-6, was captured in Seoul when the North Korean forces invaded South Korea in 1950. During his three-year captivity, he changed sides and became a Soviet agent. After being convicted of spying for the Soviet Union in 1961, he received a lengthy prison sentence but escaped from Wormwood Scrubs in 1966 and fled to the USSR. The KGB, however, would not reinstate a Blake of its own (as MI-6 did after 1953) and place even a *potential* traitor in its midst.

For a while the only mention of William Fisher in the Soviet press after his return to Russia appeared in a letter written by his wife and daughter to the government newspaper, *Izvestiya.*

Dear Comrade Editor:

We, Helen and Lydia Abel, Rudolf Abel's wife and daughter, ask that our letter be published in your newspaper so that the whole public of the Soviet Union may know about the humane act of the Soviet government.

Our husband and father Rudolf Abel, while in the United States of America in 1957, was arrested without grounds upon the denunciation of a swindler and provocateur, accused of antistate crimes for allegedly performing intelligence work for the Soviet Union and illegally sentenced to thirty years of hard labor.

All our numerous appeals, including appeals to the President of the United States, for the pardon of our dear father and husband who was sentenced even though he was innocent, failed to yield any positive results.

We then addressed ourselves to the Soviet government and established contact with the relatives of F. Powers, who was sentenced in the USSR; they in turn addressed themselves to the Soviet government with a request for his pardon and asked the U.S. government to help them in every possible way.

The Soviet authorities took a sympathetic view of our request. As is known, F. Powers was released. February 10, 1962, was a holiday for us as well. On this day the American government returned our father and husband to our family.

With all our hearts, we thank the Soviet government and its chief, N. S. Khrushchev, personally for their human magnanimity.

H. Abel and L. Abel[3]

The low level of credibility in *Izvestiya* obviously was not raised by this letter. Apart from the fact that the letter continued the falsification of the Fisher name as Abel (as Soviet media have done to this day), it also took more than three years for the Soviet Union to admit openly that Fisher was a career KGB officer who spied on the United States.

On his return to Moscow, Willy Fisher no longer lived in the two rooms of the apartment on the 2nd Lavrsky Pereulok occupied by the Fishers for so many years. While he was in an American prison, the First Main Administration secured another apartment for his wife and daughter on the Prospekt Mira.[4] Although it was shabby and cramped—two rooms with a total of twenty-seven square meters—the new apartment had the distinct advantage of being completely separate, unlike their old apartment, which they had to share with two other families.

During the first year or more of his return to the USSR, Fisher underwent "debriefing" in the Illegals Administration answering questions that had accumulated during his long stay in the United States. He also wrote long and detailed reports on many other subjects, such as American prisons, with an emphasis on methods of escape and circumvention of security measures.

It was a rather quiet life in the beginning. Since the Prospekt Mira apartment did not please either Fisher, his wife, or his daughter, Evelina (who had obtained a divorce), they centered their lives more and more on the dacha Fisher had inherited from his mother, in the Old Bolsheviks' settlement outside Moscow. It was little more than a cottage, without sewerage, running water, central heating, or a connection with gas mains. Because of Fisher's absence, very little in the way of repairs had been done and the dacha clearly showed the effects of this neglect.

Fisher spent all his money putting the dacha in order. Despite his colonel's rank, position, long service, and extra pay for decorations, he received only five hundred rubles monthly ($600 at the unrealistic official rate of exchange). This reflected the Soviet

Union's currency reform of 1961, when old rubles were exchanged for new at the rate of ten to one. The dacha ate up this small income and even his savings. He did his own work, but materials like nails and paint were both difficult to obtain and expensive; he had to repair the entire roof, which was leaking badly.[5]

In the course of time, he was able to get a water connection, installed a bath, and built in central heating. But he never succeeded in getting a connection to the gas main, only fifty yards away. This would have been simple if the PGU had been willing to intercede on his behalf, but he was told that its involvement would reveal his intelligence association—despite the fact that by that time the fame of "Colonel Abel" had spread so far that his neighbors knew who he was and that he had been invited by a deputation of students to speak at the local school.[6]

Soon after the exchange of British spy Greville Wynne for Konon Molody ("Gordon Lonsdale") in April 1964, the KGB leadership decided that it was time to counter publicity in the West on the Penkovsky case and Wynne's own story with a Soviet propaganda campaign. Who was better suited to such a campaign than the legendary "Abel," about whom CIA director Allen Dulles had said, "I wish we had a couple like him in Moscow."

So "Colonel Rudolf Ivanovich Abel" reemerged into the limelight. Major General V. Drozdov, deputy to the chief of the PGU, General Anatoli Ivanovich Lazarev, went on television on May 4, 1965, to discuss Soviet espionage work during World War II and singled out "Abel" as an outstanding Soviet intelligence officer. This was the beginning of Fisher's travels all over the Soviet Union and to countries of the Socialist bloc, such as Czechoslovakia, Hungary, and the German Democratic Republic. A Reuters correspondent described a trip Fisher made to East Germany as follows:

> One of his rare appearances after his return was at one of the strangest reunions held in recent times. He and other former Soviet spies gathered in a bleak East Berlin street to honor the memory of Richard Sorge, a Soviet master spy who was arrested in Tokyo in 1941 and executed three years later.
>
> Col. Abel and other surviving former Soviet spies stood to attention as the street was renamed Richard Sorge Street.[7]

Less than a year later, it was noted in the Soviet press that William Fisher had been awarded the Order of Lenin,[8] but Fisher resented the fact that he had been denied the title "Hero of the Soviet Union," an honor bestowed even on Ramon Mercader, Trotsky's murderer, after being released from a Mexican prison.

"They didn't give Willy the title of 'Hero of the Soviet Union,'" said his wife, Elena Stepanovna, "because the decree would have to be published in the newspaper. But the name Fisher could be taken for Jewish."[9]

Thus, rumors circulating in Moscow that William Fisher had received the title "Hero of the Soviet Union," as well as an open-ended bank account, were without any foundation.

Konon Molody returned to Moscow and resumed his life with his family in one of the modern apartment blocks in a new residential area of Moscow, enviable housing by Soviet standards.

At first, Molody went through the same process of debriefing that Fisher had undergone. Debriefing involved the writing of a seemingly endless succession of reports in response to questions posed by all elements of the PGU. Molody, however, was less able to respond with the necessary care to such questions because of his restless temperament and the lack of Fisher's type of pedagogical inclination. Fisher's reports were models of clear, incisive, scrupulously detailed information and analysis; Molody's careless, hurried, and skeletonized.

Nevertheless, the two men were invited together to a ceremony at the KGB Club, where they were presented with gold watches for their long and spotless service in the presence of many of their colleagues. At one point, whispering into Fisher's ear, Molody wisecracked: "It's obvious they're oversupplied with watches."[10]

The two men also resumed their close personal friendship. Molody was called "Ben" by Fisher's family, probably due to an old pseudonym Molody had used in the past. But Molody also had his own circle of friends with whom he and his wife, Galyusha, shared outings into the countryside around Moscow. Since these trips usually ended in drinking bouts in which the participants became completely drunk, William Fisher, who drank alcohol very sparingly, did not go on such excursions.

As with Fisher, the KGB used Molody and his story in a propaganda campaign. His first undertaking, the book *Spy*, was reasonably successful. It was published in England in 1965 and attracted some attention abroad.

Then, in 1969, a Russian film based on Molody's purported adventures in England played to full houses in movie theaters in Moscow and other Soviet cities. The film, *Dead Season* (*Myertvy Sezon*), featured an introduction by the renowned "Colonel Abel" and was unmistakably inspired by the career of Molody, alias Gordon Lonsdale. The hero of the film is an experienced Soviet spy named Konstantin Ladeinikov, who uses the pseudonym of Lonsfield and runs a firm that sells jukeboxes.

The movie's action takes place at a seaside resort in winter and depicts the efforts of Soviet agents to obtain information about a secret chemical-warfare center, where a former Nazi physician has developed a nerve gas capable of turning human beings into automatons. The setting is reminiscent of the Royal Navy's Underwater Weapons Establishment at Portland on England's south coast, a prominent target of Molody's espionage. Like Molody, the movie's hero is finally caught and serves several years in prison before being exchanged.

Dead Season, which was produced by Savva Kulish, represented a lavish expenditure of time and money. Some brief sequences were shot in London, but most of the shooting was done in and around Tallin, the Estonian capital, which is the most European-looking of cities under Soviet rule. Except for the hero, the cast was composed almost entirely of Latvians, Lithuanians, and Estonians, because of their greater physical resemblance to Britons, Germans, and Americans.[11]

Other than the book and the movie, Konon Molody's propaganda work was minimal. He rarely participated in the training of young KGB officers, for which he was unsuited temperamentally and intellectually, and he rarely lectured to groups of case officers belonging to intelligence services inside the USSR or in neighboring socialist countries. William Fisher, however, was enthusiastically involved in these activities, and he was greeted with similar enthusiasm from his audiences.

Molody was assigned to desk work, but he chafed under this sort of inactivity. William Fisher had realistically assessed his own future while still in jail, but Molody had long continued to cherish the hope that he could still be useful on foreign assignments, even after his return to the Soviet Union. Gradually, however, he realized that the PGU took a different view of his future and had decided that Molody could never be sent abroad again.

With that realization something died in Konon Molody. He knew that life for him was simply intolerable without the excitement and action of foreign espionage work, now closed to him forever. And so he began to drink more heavily, to brood, to burst out in angry tirades against Galyusha that made her break down and cry. Nothing seemed to relieve the interminable boredom of his life and the pain of contemplating the deadly dull future that stretched before him.

Wherever he traveled to deliver lectures, William Fisher never came back from his trips empty-handed. He returned from Odessa with several jars of scarce instant coffee; after lecturing at the KGB's special school, he came back with a box of the finest cigars, presented to him by Cuban students (he did not smoke the cigars himself but liked to display them to guests); but, best of all, he brought back from the GDR such gifts as an electric toaster, a coffee maker, a set of kitchen knives, a dozen bottles of Liebfraumilch (his favorite wine, which he used to buy for his meals in New York), and tools for the workshop he had installed in the dacha.[12]

Fisher was in fact very popular in East Germany, possibly because of his German heritage as well as the fact that, despite all the years of struggle against the Nazis, he was a Germanophile. He grumbled that everyone there was eager for instruction, insisting, in their usual thorough way, on having every detail explained and making copious notes of all that he had to say. But he was very fond of those trips.

In Hungary he also received the red-carpet treatment, lecturing not only to intelligence officers but also to selected groups of agents. Once, he related with delight later, he had a meeting with a high church dignitary at a safe house.[13]

As time went by, however, he began to speak deprecatingly about himself as an "exhibit," in a tone that left no doubt about his growing disillusion. As early as 1965, he must have begun to sense that despite his lectures all over the USSR, as well as in Eastern Europe, he had become nothing more than a kind of holy effigy.

He once encountered an old friend he had not seen for forty years outside the KGB building. The two men recognized each other instantly and exchanged greetings.

"How are you?" the friend asked.

"Not bad. And you?"

The friend shrugged, smiling faintly. "Are you retired now?"

"No," said Fisher, "I'm working."

"What do you do? Where do you work?"

Fisher gestured toward the KGB building behind them. "In there."

"How did you land there?"

"Oh, I'm just a museum exhibit," Fisher replied.[14]

Nevertheless, Fisher would have been content to spend the rest of his life as a "museum exhibit" rather than retire. Disillusioned as he was about the people who had moved into top positions in the KGB, most of whom had gotten their jobs by virtue of their political connections, he remained loyal to the institution and did not question orders from the top, no matter what his reservations.

Characteristically, what disturbed him most of all was the fact that his loyalty toward the top did not have any reciprocal effect of loyalty from the top downward. When his wife lay sick in the hospital, he asked his superiors to help him obtain some caviar for her from the KGB closed store, which sold normally unavailable gourmet items and luxury goods at nominal prices to high-ranking employees. "Write a memorandum to Andropov," said one boss, "and I'll endorse it. But don't request more than two hundred grams." Instead a friend obtained the caviar from a local delicatessen by paying a small bribe.[15]

After a while there seemed to be less and less for him to do at his work, but he still had private interests that made his life meaningful. He went on with his painting, which art critics in the United States considered too much like "Socialist realism."[16] He also kept up his music, although he was hampered in playing the guitar by a hand injury he sustained in 1966 while making repairs at the dacha.[17] But he remained fond of Bach, lute music, and Spanish gypsy melodies, which he played for his own amusement.

The ordinary routine of his life was briefly interrupted when he heard that Burt Silverman, one of the young artists he had known in Brooklyn, was in Moscow with the express purpose of seeing him. Silverman was involved in the writing of a book about "Abel," but his trip was also motivated by a desire to reestablish something of the old relationship with the man he had known as Emil Goldfus.

Seeking a meeting with Fisher through Victor Louis, a Soviet correspondent who had KGB ties, Silverman waited in Moscow, but the meeting never came about. The reason was simple: the KGB chiefs categorically forbade Fisher to see Silverman. Fisher was embittered by this order and regarded it as a symptom of the poisonous envy the KGB bosses felt toward anyone who had achieved fame, conveniently forgetting that he had done so at considerable personal risk.

Unable to see Fisher, Silverman left him a gift in the care of Victor Louis; it included some brochures of an exhibit of Silverman's own paintings and an album of drawings by their mutual friend David Levine, with an unobjectionable, deliberately impersonal dedication. Fisher received the brochures without any difficulty, but the album was never delivered to him.

Willy Fisher could only shake his head with amusement about the sequel to this incident. Some time later, bibliophile Morris Cohen was glancing through the shelves of a secondhand bookstore at No. 10 Kachalov Street and noticed the album. When he saw the inscription, he knew immediately for whom it was intended, and bought the album on the spot, later presenting it to Willy. "What class!" Willy said with exasperation. He did not suspect Louis of stealing the album; he guessed at once that one of the lower-level KGB chiefs had simply sold it for whatever it would bring and pocketed the money.[18]

Incidents of this kind soured Fisher and his family, and they found, as they went on with their lives, that their greatest peace was at the dacha, a world away from all that they had come to resent and detest.

———————•———————

After he was exchanged for Francis Gary Powers, William Fisher understandably followed with intense interest the developments in the exchanges of his friends Konon Molody and Morris and Lona Cohen. Fisher remained completely orthodox in his reactions to these developments.

On the one hand, he expressed resentment that, supposedly, his rights under the U.S. Constitution had been violated in connection with his arrest and conviction. On the other hand, he was angry because the Soviet authorities "stood on ceremony" and sentenced Greville Wynne to only eight years.

"What if there's no proof?" he said. "This Wynne should be given the works, keep him in a death cell, put the fear of God into him. Then the English will talk a different language."[19]

To his great satisfaction, Molody's exchange for Wynne was finally arranged, after which he anticipated an exchange that would free the Cohens. Although as a rule he had no sympathy with traitors (even those from the other side), he had a special affection for Morris and Lona. So he was pleased when one of his superiors in the KGB said that within three months State Security would find a suitable person to exchange.

Four months later, the KGB arrested Gerald Brooke, a young Englishman, who had undertaken a mission to the USSR to distribute leaflets on behalf of the Russian emigré organization Narodno-Trudovoi Soyuz (NTS), which had as its goal the overthrow of the Soviet regime. Brooke was sentenced to five years in a labor camp.

Fisher considered this method of finding a hostage for eventual exchange entirely normal. Moreover, he rejoiced when the Soviet authorities threatened to add twenty years to Brooke's sentence if the British refused to exchange him for the Cohens. Fisher may have even suggested this tactic.[20]

The exchange of the Cohens came about in October 1969, when Gerald Brooke and two other Britons were allowed to return to England. Morris and Lona Cohen, who still called themselves Peter and Helen Kroger, had served eight and a half years of their original twenty-year sentences. Since they claimed that they were Polish nationals and had a home in Lublin, the first stage of their journey took them to Warsaw, where they arrived on October 24.

From there the Cohens went to Moscow, receiving a warm welcome from the KGB. They were soon installed in a beautiful apartment, far superior to that of the Fishers, in a building at the corner of Malaya Bronnaya and Bolshaya Bronnaya streets. One of their neighbors was the concert violinist Svyatoslav Richter.[21]

If the Fishers envied the Cohens their housing, they managed to conceal such feelings and give them a welcome that was unquestionably sincere.

Once again the KGB had demonstrated that it would not rest until it had succeeded in freeing its own spies from capitalist prisons. But the reunited friends did not have long to enjoy one another's companionship. Death, after all, was the one factor that the KGB could not *entirely* control.

Konon Molody had a day off during the Indian summer of 1970. On October 9, a Friday, he and Galyusha drove out into the country with the usual group of friends. They found a campsite in the woods and put up a tent. Before setting out to collect mushrooms, the members of the group had a couple of rounds of vodka. Later, they returned to the campsite with a nice batch of mushrooms, made a fire, and fried the mushrooms.

They were a merry bunch, and as they ate, they drank still more vodka. After a while no one was sober, and hardly anyone noticed when stocky, vigorous Konon Molody, who had been laughing hardest of all, suddenly slumped over to one side. Someone said, "Molody, that fine fellow, he's had a bit too much again." The party continued with unabated merriment until someone else looked at Molody and decided that he seemed very odd. There was something alarming about the greenish tinge of his complexion and the rasping sound of his breath.

Galyusha, who was tipsy, looked wonderingly at her husband. "What should we do?"

"Let him sleep it off!" one of the others said.

But growing alarm finally sobered them up, and they decided to put him in a car and find a doctor. All of these preliminaries took still more time. They drove back to the city, but when they arrived at a hospital, the doctor examined him and shrugged, saying that Molody was already dead. He had sustained a fatal heart attack.

The Fishers and other friends believed that Molody had in

effect committed suicide. It appeared that he had been deliberately destroying himself with alcohol. As one observer commented: "He did it for one reason only: despair over his own uselessness, a recognition that there was no way out, that everything that had made life interesting was past. Before him there was only mere existence."[22]

In the summer of 1971 William Fisher suffered an unexpected blow. Although his superiors had found little for him to do at work, he still cherished the hope that this was simply a lull, an idle interlude shortly to be succeeded by a furious storm of activity. In any case, he had enough to keep him busy at the dacha, and he decided to request some leave. He stopped in one day at the personnel department.

"Why go on leave, Vil'yam Genrikhovich?" said one of the women in the personnel department with a smile. "We're just processing your papers for retirement. Once you're retired, you'll be able to rest to your heart's content."[23]

Thus the famous spymaster "Rudolf Ivanovich Abel" learned from a secretary about his compulsory retirement. None of his superiors in the PGU was considerate enough to arrange a personal meeting and inform him of this decision and the reasons for it.

It is reasonable to think that a man like Fisher, who had reached the age of sixty-eight and whose career in a difficult profession spanned more than forty years, not to speak of the vicissitudes of war and a long prison term, should retire and enjoy a well-earned repose. On the other hand, he deserved special consideration in view of the services he had performed and the dangers to which he had been exposed. Fisher himself considered this abrupt dismissal an affront of the worst kind.

His wife, Elena Stepanovna, and daughter, Evelina, shared his wounded feelings. They indignantly told everyone they knew that "Papa was fired." Their unhappiness, however, only made the situation worse. Willy Fisher became even more unhappy because of their reaction. But facts were facts, and soon the realism that had been so helpful to him as an Intelligence officer enabled him to face the situation as soberly as he had faced bad situations throughout his career.

He began to think of what he could do in the future. His knowledge of foreign languages would be useful if he became a translator. Through his fame as "Colonel Abel," he had made contacts with influential people at Radio Moscow and all the major newspapers—*Pravda, Izvestiya, Komsomolskaya Pravda, Trud*—and those contacts could pave the way for him. The more he thought about it, the more optimistic he became.

There was only one comparatively small cloud on the horizon. That was the matter of his health, which he had been reluctant to discuss with his family. While he did not consider it a serious problem, he knew that merely raising the subject would worry them. Nevertheless, before he could take on new work, he would have to do something about it. In recent months he had not felt at all well. He was conscious of a general malaise, but apart from that, he had acquired a persistent cough he could not shake, and he was having trouble breathing, especially at night.

He had always been a regular cigarette smoker from the time he was a small boy in England, when he used to collect his father's discarded butts and smoke them secretly. Since the trouble with his throat began, however, he had tried, with indifferent success, to cut back on his consumption of cigarettes. But moderation seemed to have little effect. He began to feel pain, and with every week the pain grew more intense.

Finally he could no longer keep his condition a secret from his wife and daughter. They urged him to have an examination. He delayed, hoping that the condition would pass, and tried to anesthetize his throat by sipping brandy. Yet he found it more and more difficult to swallow. He yielded to his wife and consulted a doctor. The diagnosis was not encouraging: he had a tumor.

In the end, knowing he would have to endure an operation, he went into the KGB's own hospital. The date was October 25, 1971. He was an ambulatory patient for a short time, still talking about his plans to work as a translator and his aim of helping Evelina to get a better job.

He did not remain ambulatory very long. Soon the doctors decided that his tumor was inoperable. His condition rapidly worsened, and one day when Elena Stepanovna came to visit him, he was no longer able to get out of bed.

Even with the pain dulled by morphine, he could not eat. He

also had difficulty speaking, but he remained conscious and did not groan. Two security officers were on duty to check on him and make certain that he revealed no secrets in his delirium.

Elena Stepanovna lost her self-control. She kept bustling about the hospital room in a sort of frenzy. Filled with grief, inclined to say the first thing that came into her head, and possibly wishing to show her political orthodoxy, she cried out: "Those Americans injected him with cancer. You'll see, wait until the autopsy and we'll prove it!"[24]

William Fisher heard all of this without any display of emotion. He was sinking rapidly. Before the end, he beckoned to his daughter, who came close and bent over him. He whispered, "Don't forget that we're Germans."

He died on November 15, 1971.

William Fisher's body lay in state for a short time in a building just behind the KGB's Lubyanka headquarters. A line of mourners, presumably composed of KGB colleagues, waited to enter the building. He was cremated several days later.

An obituary was published in the military newspaper *Krasnaya Zvezda* two days after Fisher's death:

> Colonel Rudolf Ivanovich Abel, one of the oldest Chekists, a well-known Soviet Intelligence officer, distinguished employee of the organs of State Security, and member of the CPSU since 1931, died after a serious illness in his 69th year.
>
> R. I. Abel was assigned to work in the organs of the OGPU in accordance with a Komsomol levy in 1927. From then on, for a period of nearly 45 years, he faultlessly carried out complex tasks in the maintenance of our Motherland's security in various sectors of Chekist activity. Rudolf Ivanovich proved to be a daring, experienced Intelligence officer and capable leader. He was always distinguished by love of the Motherland, a high sense of duty, party principle, impartiality, and honor.
>
> Being abroad, working there in complicated and difficult circumstances, R. I. Abel displayed exceptional patriotism, tenacity, and steadfastness. His high moral character and manly conduct are widely known, evoking a deep response and arousing sympathy throughout the world.
>
> The Communist Party and the Soviet government highly esteemed the services of R. I. Abel, conferring upon him the Order of Lenin,

three Orders of the Red Banner, two Orders of the Red Banner of Labor, the Order of the Red Star, and many medals.

Rudolf Ivanovich remained at his combat post until the very last days, he contributed all his strength and knowledge to that honorable cause to which he had dedicated all his magnificent life. He devoted considerable attention to the training of a younger generation of Chekists, transmitting to them his rich experience and inculcating the qualities inherent in the first Chekist-Leninist F. E. Dzerzhinski.

Great personal charm, modesty, simplicity, and a sympathetic nature won Rudolf Ivanovich universal esteem and well-deserved authority.

The bright memory of Rudolf Ivanovich will be preserved forever in our hearts.

A Group of Comrades[26]

A year passed. On the first anniversary of Fisher's death, Elena Stepanovna, who would survive her husband by less than three years, invited a small and very select group of his KGB bosses and old personal friends to a brief ceremony at the cemetery where his ashes had been interred and to a memorial supper at the dacha.

The group that assembled at the dacha was a peculiar one, made up as it was of a few of the most powerful men in the KGB and a number of insignificant outsiders who had simply been Willy Fisher's friends. During the supper Elena Stepanovna, glass in hand, said:

"Today Willy's closest friends have assembled at this table. We have gathered to pay our respects to his memory." After a silence, she continued: "I wish to request each of you in turn to relate how you first met Willy."[27]

It was obvious that none of the guests had anticipated this sort of challenge. But Elena Stepanovna took no notice of the awkward silence and started at one end of the table, asking one of Fisher's old friends to speak. The old man, stumbling over his words, described how he had met Willy when they did their military service in the same radio battalion.

Morris and Lona Cohen were also present, and Morris spoke next in his atrocious Russian. He related the story of Fisher's appearance at their home in New York at Christmas, bringing with him a roast goose. (An interesting story, since the only Christmas that came into consideration was either in December 1948, a month after Fisher landed from a ship in Canada, or December 1949, at the very beginning of his stay in New York.)

A deputy of General Lazarev expressed regret about only meeting Fisher for the first time just before his death.

Then General Anatoli Lazarev, head of the First Main Administration, who was, therefore, in command of all KGB foreign espionage, spoke. He made a typically Soviet speech that might have been used on almost any occasion, and succeeded in saying a great deal without really saying anything.

Another deputy, Drozdov, alluding probably to his conduct of negotiations for the Fisher-Powers exchange, noted that he had known Willy well long before he actually met him.

The others also paid tribute to the dead man and then the guests departed, some in their limousines and others on foot, bound for the closest railroad station. Thus, this occasion quietly passed without leaving a trace, except for the consolation it must have brought to Elena Stepanovna.

The ceremony at the Cemetery of the Don Monastery earlier that day was held to commemorate the unveiling of a new epitaph on the gravestone, which bore a picture of William Fisher and prominently displayed this name, with the name Rudolf Ivanovich Abel shown only in small letters beneath it. And so, one year after his death, William Fisher at last publicly recovered the name with which he had been born.[28]

Epilogue

"The More Things Change..."

BALZAC ONCE WROTE: "In revolutions as in storms at sea solid worth goes to the bottom, while the current brings light trash floating to the top."[1]

Balzac's comment is not only applicable to the Russian Revolution, but also applies in particular to Soviet State Security. The "light trash" came floating to the top at an early point. While fanatical Communists of Dzerzhinsky's stripe were at first in command, the "Red Terror" required men who did not mind getting blood on their hands, the brutes who are usually kept at the bottom of society, where, as a rule, their violence and baseness bring them into conflict with the law and they can seldom succeed in placing themselves above the law, as the Chekists did in Russia.

It is true that State Security officers have changed in the half century or more of Soviet rule. There have been generations of Chekists that, to some degree, reflect the greater generations of which they are a part. And the ways in which they have changed (or not changed) tell a great deal about the Soviet regime and State Security as an institution.

———◆———

Aside from the riffraff that inevitably found a ready reception in the ranks of State Security, the first generation of Chekists was composed largely of Communists who had worked in the prerevolutionary underground and spent many years in prison and exile. These were Communists who had remained steadfast as revolutionaries long before there was any real prospect of victory. They had learned their lessons in the hardest school of all—experience—and paid the price out of their own hides. After the revolution they simply carried on the same conspiratorial work in which they had been engaged before Lenin seized power.

But these same men, even as representatives of the new Soviet state, continued to regard themselves as revolutionaries; only the focus had changed as they fought counterrevolution inside Soviet Russia and attempted to foment revolutions abroad. This was the period when Trotsky could still speak of "permanent revolution," and many other top Soviet leaders believed that revolutions were about to break out all over Europe—and they were not entirely wrong. Nevertheless, they also had reason to be concerned about the survival of the "first socialist state." The revolutionary Chekists applied a principle that is valid in many sports as well as in war: the best defense is a good offense. They used the conspiratorial techniques they had perfected in the prerevolutionary underground, hoping to trigger the expected revolutions elsewhere and overthrow foreign governments they regarded as bitter enemies. They were experts in the forging of documents, the use of codes and ciphers, the minutiae of clandestine meetings, the illegal crossing of borders, and the smuggling of arms and propaganda; it had become second nature with them to carry on a duel with the police of many countries, to be hunted, to endure arrest, and survive imprisonment.[2]

Thus, the Soviet Intelligence system they created resembled in many respects the prerevolutionary underground. But thereafter, the first Chekists ceased to be despised members of a splinter revolutionary group and became representatives of a state that had won respect and had instilled fear in Europe as far back as the times of Peter the Great. The Chekists spoke and acted with this newly acquired authority, recruiting their agents abroad among communist Party members and leftist workers, constantly invoking the name of the "party" on behalf of Moscow.

In *Darkness At Noon*, the doomed Rubashov spoke for these Chekists in the diary he kept in prison:

> We were the first to replace the nineteenth century's liberal ethics of "fair play" by the revolutionary ethics of the twentieth century. In that also we were right: a revolution conducted according to the rules of cricket is an absurdity. Politics can be relatively fair in the breathing spaces of history; at its critical turning points there is no other rule possible than the old one, that the end justifies the means. We introduced neo-Machiavellianism into this century.[3]

Nevertheless, the first Chekists were not cynical men. Walter Krivitsky said that "the Bolshevik Revolution came to me as an absolute solution of all problems of poverty, inequality and injustice. I joined the Bolshevik Party with my whole soul. I seized the Marxist and Leninist faith as a weapon with which to assault the wrongs against which I had instinctively rebelled."[4] Like Rubashov, the old Chekists—Krivitsky among them—perished because, despite their bad deeds, they still clung to their revolutionary ideals in the face of a totalitarian regime that cared for nothing but power and more power. It could be asserted that they really helped, regardless of their intentions, to make such a regime possible. Be that as it may, Soviet State Security had gotten rid of its Rubashovs by the end of the 1930's.

From that time on, State Security was still staffed by Communists, but those Communists belonged to a different breed. They were Communists because they were careerists, and *no* career worthy of the name was conceivable in the Soviet Union without joining the Communist Party.

The men who stepped over the bodies of the first Chekists were opportunists pure and simple. The more prescient among them had foreseen that the Bolsheviks would succeed in pushing aside the stumbling Provisional Government. Others later scented a Red victory in the civil war. Still others waited until the Bolsheviks had actually won. But, early or late, they all came forward as soon as they were sure of the victors.

The opportunists obviously had an eye for the main chance and were not overly burdened with principles; the only principle most of them knew was to get in on the spoils, and since they would take on any coloration in order to advance their egocentric interests, it was not difficult for them to become convinced Communists almost overnight, shout their new beliefs from the rooftops, and sanctimoniously punish others as class enemies.

They served the first Chekists as long as they felt inferior to such men, but as soon as it became apparent that the position of their chiefs was growing shaky, they shifted their loyalties to the new, all-powerful ruler and prepared to pull these Chekists down.

The opportunists were quick to recognize that Stalin would be the victor inside the party, just as they had been quick to recognize the victory of the Bolsheviks. They also took on Stalin's coloration, becoming torturers, assassins, and just plain butchers, doing so at first to get ahead, but finally in order to save their own skins. Such a man was Alexander Orlov, although he anticipated the type of Stalinist bureaucrat that came after the opportunists and would have done well in the subsequent period, if he had not been selected as one of Yezhov's victims and fled for his life. Those who were most ruthless and unscrupulous, like Orlov, went farthest, but they, too, often died with a bullet in the back of the head during the purge years. They found themselves caught up in a game of Russian roulette where they could no longer predict the odds.

Yezhov did away with most of them before they had a chance to put their stamp on State Security, but it is doubtful that they would have ever contributed to the future development of the KGB. Their energies were used up in an effort to anticipate the "boss's" (i.e., Stalin's) wishes, and they had no ideas of their own.

The last fifteen years of Stalin's rule coincided with an era of gray, faceless bureaucrats in Soviet State Security. These were typical Stalinist bureaucrats, many of whom had been recruited from other branches of the *apparat*, including even the army, as a means of filling the KGB's ranks, which had been severely decimated in the last phase of the Great Purge. They were proletarians with limited horizons, lacking both imagination and initiative, attributes that the leaders did not prize and were more likely to view with suspicion, especially in KGB officers. Vladimir Petrov and Peter Deriabin, who came from the peasantry, were examples of this type, although Deriabin was bright enough to have fitted in well with the more highly educated KGB officers who came along later. It was an anti-intellectual era; even so, a few intellectuals managed to find their way into State Security during those years, due to the pressing need for certain rare talents. Konon Molody was also a product of this era, but he made a good case officer in the field and proved to be particularly useful as an "illegal" resident precisely because he was an "operator" who enjoyed living by his wits and functioned only marginally as a bureaucrat.

During this same era of Stalinist bureaucrats in the KGB, the USSR went through a world war, from which it emerged as one of the victors, absorbing great chunks of territory and population. In that era Soviet State Security achieved some of its greatest triumphs.

On the face of it, there would seem to be a certain contradiction between the bureaucratic character of the KGB during that era and the triumphs it achieved. One might well ask how an Intelligence organization that "went by the book" could be very successful. It is certainly true that the KGB executives of that day were cautious, plodding, and fearful of making any move without sanction from above.

Nevertheless, State Security enjoyed very significant advantages, and it could draw on a rich tradition of Russian espionage. If its executives followed the book, smarter men than they had originated those rules, and it paid to observe them. The KGB of that era also benefited from a climate of antifascism, which brought to their side many brilliant and influential people who eagerly embraced Soviet espionage as a means of fighting against Hitler and all he stood for. The KGB of that day also benefited from operations initiated by the old Chekists that only began to pay off during the wartime and postwar years, such as those involving the "moles" inside the British establishment (Philby, Maclean, and Burgess) or the spy rings inside the U.S. government, with which the name of Alger Hiss is associated. Finally, the KGB could operate with impunity in foreign countries, since the security services of those countries seemed to have completely forgotten about the KGB's existence, possibly blinkered as a result of their preoccupation with German, Italian, and Japanese espionage.

The period during which Stalinist bureaucrats dominated State Security also coincided with the tenure of Lavrenti Beria as overseer of the Soviet secret police. The coincidence was not surprising, since Beria had distinguished himself as an administrator of the Stalinist school, notwithstanding the dissolute life he led. But Beria differed from other leading Stalinist bureaucrats in that he went out of his way to look after his people.[5] With the passing of Stalin and Beria, State Security began to acquire a new image, despite the fact that lesser Stalinists remained in the ascendancy for a few years.

The anti-intellectual bias lost ground swiftly in this period. It should not be forgotten that throughout its history the KGB has always had its pick of the best men available. Communist Party and Komsomol organizations are regularly called upon to recommend the brightest and most promising party members for a career in the KGB. Those who were invited to join the KGB could not refuse without having an unfavorable notation made in their files, which would follow them everywhere. In earlier years, the KGB bosses did not put a premium on higher education, preferring people with proletarian origins and solid party orthodoxy. At the end of the Stalin era, most of the young party members selected for the KGB had completed their higher education and, therefore, unwittingly started to have an effect, at least in this respect, on the composition of State Security.

Only William Fisher succeeded in bridging all these periods. He was something of a universal man for the KGB, bringing revolutionary ideals into the organization with him, working with the opportunists and the Stalinist bureaucrats, and finding common ground with the bright young men who came along later. Yet he did not belong to any period. Perhaps that was his greatest tragedy.

Another factor became operative in the "new" KGB. Young representatives of the "New Class" who came from privileged backgrounds—sons and daughters of high party and government officials—studied foreign languages or received technical educations in the USSR's most prestigious institutes and were posted to the KGB's foreign espionage administration, where they received coveted assignments abroad. Having lived most of their lives in Moscow and Leningrad under the most affluent circumstances, these golden young men and women possessed a degree of sophistication that the earlier State Security officers from the peasantry or humble working-class backgrounds had not.

To those foreigners who remembered their cruder predecessors, the new KGB officers seemed refreshingly personable, showing a lively interest in Western clothing, music, and movies. They wanted to learn to mix cocktails and do modern dancing. In their politics, too, these same officers seemed more open to new ideas, more liberal, less defensive, and even inclined to suggest the possibility of reforms in the Soviet system.

The latest generation of KGB officers remains much the same today. They have become even more scientifically and technically specialized, since modern Intelligence services are increasingly concerned with nuclear physics, guided-missile systems, microelectronics, and computerized technology in general.

However open-minded and liberal they may seek to appear, the newer State Security officers stationed abroad have a vested interest in the Soviet system, in which they occupy a privileged status. They are well aware that their own position could only be damaged by an effort to make changes in that system. They engage in espionage work with a dedication and persistence equal to their predecessors but with greater intelligence. Moral considerations have no more importance for them than for the others, although terror will only be used as a last resort. At the same time, they are just as determined to undermine and destroy the West. Any change in what they do is more a matter of style than substance, but this very difference in style makes them far more effective. It is the same old song set to new music, but it has the virtue of lulling its victims to sleep.

Over twenty years ago, Peter Deriabin observed that the KGB's Foreign Administration included "some of the most intelligent, technically accomplished, and sophisticated members of Soviet society. Their level of education is the highest in the country, generally including years of graduate as well as normal Soviet university study."[6]

The West needs to take these changes in the KGB seriously and be on its guard, if it cares anything for its own survival in a world that is possibly more dangerous today than ever.

In more recent times, a Soviet source privately struck a clear note of warning when he said:

"The KGB is our elite. They are the sharpest, smartest cadres we can find—and don't you Americans forget that for one minute."[7]

Notes

Chapter 1   STATE SECURITY, SOVIET STYLE

1. George Orwell, *Nineteen Eighty-Four* (New York: Harcourt, Brace & World, Inc., 1949), p. 300.
2. Simon Wolin and Robert M. Slusser (ed.), *The Soviet Secret Police* (New York: Frederick A. Praeger, 1957), p. 68.
3. David J. Dallin, *The Changing World of Soviet Russia* (New Haven: Yale University Press, 1956), p. 82.
4. Aleksandr I. Solzhenitsyn, *The Gulag Archipelago* I–II (New York: Harper & Row, 1973), pp. 353–54.
5. Igor Gouzenko, *The Iron Curtain* (New York: E. P. Dutton & Co., Inc., 1948), pp. 70–72.
6. Boris Baschanow, *Ich war Stalins Sekretär* [*I Was Stalin's Secretary*] (Frankfurt/M: Ullstein, 1977), p. 173.
7. V. I. Lenin, *Sochineniya* [*Works*] (Moscow: State Publishing House of Political Literature, 1950), v. 31, p. 120.
8. Robert Conquest, *The Great Terror* (New York: The Macmillan Company, 1968), p. 437.
9. Claire Sterling, *The Terror Network* (New York: Holt, Rinehart and Winston, 1981), p. 285.
10. Albert Parry, *Terrorism: From Robespierre to Arafat* (New York: The Vanguard Press, 1976), p. 542.
11. Sterling, *The Terror Network*, p. 14.
12. *Ibid.*, p. 221.
13. John Barron, *KGB* (New York: Reader's Digest Press, 1974), pp. 56, 79, 175–76, 256.
14. Parry, *Terrorism*, p. 288.
15. Walter Laqueur, *Terrorism* (Boston: Little, Brown and Company, 1977), pp. 200–01.
16. Sterling, *The Terror Network*, p. 15.
17. *Ibid.*, p. 247.
18. *Ibid.*, p. 285.
19. *Ibid.*, pp. 49–50, 53–55, 62–64.

Chapter 2   GRAND INQUISITORS

1. Ernst Neizvestny, "Tri fragmenta" ["Three Fragments"], *Kontinent*, No. 21 (Berlin: Kontinent Verlag, 1979) p. 15.
2. Wolin and Slusser, *The Soviet Secret Police*, p. 67.
3. Georges Haupt and Jean-Jacques Marie, *Makers of the Russian Revolution* (Ithaca: Cornell University Press, 1974), p. 342.
4. Baschanow, *Ich war Stalins Sekretär*, p. 171.
5. Haupt and Marie, *Makers of the Russian Revolution*, p. 346.
6. Leo Trotzki, *Mein Leben* [*My Life*] (Berlin: S. Fischer Verlag, 1930), p. 432.
7. *Malaya Sovetskaya Entsiklopediya* [*Small Soviet Encyclopedia*], 3rd edition, 1958, pp. 1159–60.
8. Baschanow, *Ich war Stalins Sekretär*, p. 172.
9. H. Montgomery Hyde, *Stalin* (New York: Farrar, Straus and Giroux, 1971), p. 226.
10. Baschanow, *Ich war Stalins Sekretär*, pp. 78–81.
11. Wolin and Slusser, *The Soviet Secret Police*, p. 41.
12. Hyde, *Stalin*, pp. 212–13.
13. Boris Souvarine, "Boris Suvarin o Staline" ["Boris Souvarine Talks About Stalin"], *Kontinent*, No. 22 (Berlin: Kontinent Verlag, 1980), pp. 442–43.
14. Wolin and Slusser, *The Soviet Secret Police*, p. 14.
15. *Ibid.*, p. 44.
16. Baschanow, *Ich war Stalins Sekretär*, p. 174.
17. Wolin and Slusser, *The Soviet Secret Police*, p. 53.
18. Alexander Orlov, *The Secret History of Stalin's Crimes* (New York: Random House, 1953), pp. 257–58.
19. *Malaya Sovetskaya Entsiklopediya* [*Small Soviet Encyclopedia*], 2nd edition, 1935, vol. 4, p. 218.
20. Hyde, *Stalin*, p. 241.
21. Orlov, *The Secret History of Stalin's Crimes*, p. 59.
22. Nikita Khrushchev, *Khrushchev Remembers* (Boston: Little, Brown and Company, 1970), vol. I, pp. 94–96.
23. *Ibid.*, p. 94.
24. Hyde, *Stalin*, p. 377.
25. Khrushchev, *Khrushchev Remembers*, p. 312.
26. Vladimir Petrov and Evdokia Petrov, *Empire of Fear* (New York: Frederick A. Praeger, Inc., 1956), p. 83.
27. Khrushchev, *Khrushchev Remembers*, p. 104.
28. Petrov and Petrov, *Empire of Fear*, pp. 83–84.
29. Khrushchev, *Khrushchev Remembers*, p. 332.
30. Hyde, *Stalin*, p. 583.
31. Khrushchev, *Khrushchev Remembers*, p. 337.
32. Wolin and Slusser, *The Soviet Secret Police*, p. 385.

33. Khrushchev, *Khrushchev Remembers*, p. 338.
34. *International Herald Tribune*, July 18, 1953.
35. Wolin and Slusser, *The Soviet Secret Police*, p. 55.
36. *Ibid.*, p. 29.
37. Khrushchev, *Khrushchev Remembers*, p. 115 (footnote).
38. *Ibid.*, p. 115.
39. Wolin and Slusser, *The Soviet Secret Police*, p. 18.
40. *Washington Post and Times Herald*, April 3, 1956.
41. Wolin and Slusser, *The Soviet Secret Police*, p. 51.
42. *New York Times*, December 10, 1958.
43. Khrushchev, *Khrushchev Remembers*, p. 401.
44. *New York Times*, November 23, 1956, p. 1.
45. *Ibid.*, November 18, 1956, p. 1.
46. *Ibid.*, December 27, 1956, p. 3.
47. *Ibid.*, November 24, 1956, pp. 1–2.
48. Khrushchev, *Khrushchev Remembers*, p. 115.
49. *Bol'shaya Sovetskaya Entsiklopediya* [*Great Soviet Encyclopedia*, BSE], Moscow, 2nd edition, 1957, vol. 47, p. 648.
50. Radio Moscow, October 29, 1958.
51. *Kommunistichesky Kalendar'-Spravochnik* [*Communist Calendar-Guide*], *1968* (Moscow: Publishing House of Political Literature, 1967), p. 349.
52. *New York Times*, May 28, 1982.
53. *Spiegel*, June 7, 1982, p. 132.
54. *Deputaty Verkhovnovo Soveta SSSR. Desyati sozyv* [*Deputies of the Supreme Soviet of the USSR. Tenth Convocation*] (Moscow: Presidium of the Supreme Soviet of the USSR, 1979), p. 452.
55. *Spiegel*, June 7, 1982, p. 132.
56. *Radyans'ka Ukraina*, September 15, 1973, and February 14, 1976.
57. Radio Liberty Samizdat Archive, Munich, AS 4532, *Polozhenie na Ukraine* [*The Situation in the Ukraine*], p. 1.
58. Radio Liberty Research 422/81, "Ukrainian KGB Chief Warns of Ideological Sabotage," October 22, 1981.
59. *Deputaty Verkhovnovo Soveta SSSR, Desyati sozyv* (1979), p. 473.
60. *Bolshaya Sovetskaya Entsiklopediya* [*BSE*], Annual for 1981, p. 608.
61. *Ibid.*, p. 608.
62. Radio Liberty Research CRD 342/69, October 16, 1969, p. 2.
63. *BSE*, Annual for 1981, p. 608.
64. Radio Liberty Research CRD 342/69, October 16, 1969, p. 2.
65. *International Herald Tribune*, December 18–19, 1982, p. 2.
66. *Newsweek*, January 3, 1983, p. 9.
67. *BSE*, Annual for 1981, p. 608.
68. Reuters, December 17, 1982.
69. *Krasnaya Zvezda* [*Red Star*], Moscow, April 4, 1982.
70. *BSE*, Annual for 1981, p. 608.
71. Radio Liberty Research CRD 342/69, October 16, 1969, p. 3.

Chapter 3   ON THE FIRING LINE

1. Bruce Page, David Leitch, and Phillip Knightley, *Philby* (London: Andre Deutsch, 1968), p. 87.
2. Sanche de Gramont, *The Secret War* (New York: G. P. Putnam's Sons, 1962), p. 295.
3. *Ibid.*, p. 303.
4. Kermit Roosevelt, *Countercoup* (New York: McGraw-Hill Book Company, 1979), p. 139.
5. Petrov and Petrov, *Empire of Fear*, p. 293.
6. W. G. Krivitsky, *I Was Stalin's Agent* (London: Hamish Hamilton, 1939), pp. 113–14.
7. Kirill Khenkin, *Okhotnik vverkh nogami* [*Hunter Upside Down*] (Frankfurt/Main: Posev, 1979), p. 158.

Chapter 4   THE SPY WHO REPORTED TO STALIN

1. Krivitsky, *I Was Stalin's Agent*, p. 101.
2. Orlov, *The Secret History of Stalin's Crimes*, pp. 330–31.
3. Alexander Orlov, *Handbook of Intelligence and Guerrilla Warfare* (Ann Arbor: University of Michigan Press, 1963), pp. 108–109.
4. Krivitsky, *I Was Stalin's Agent*, pp. 100–01.
5. Khenkin, *Okhotnik vverkh nogami*, p. 20.
6. Krivitsky, *I Was Stalin's Agent*, p. 124.
7. Orlov, *The Secret History of Stalin's Crimes*, p. 208.
8. Krivitsky, *I Was Stalin's Agent*, pp. 124–25.
9. Harris Greene, *FSO-1* (Garden City: Doubleday & Co., 1977), p. 29.
10. Krivitsky, *I Was Stalin's Agent*, p. 127.
11. *Ibid.*, p. 128.
12. *Ibid.*, pp. 129–30.
13. *Ibid.*, p. 132.
14. Orlov, *The Secret History of Stalin's Crimes*, p. 238.
15. *Ibid.*, p. xi.
16. *Ibid.*, pp. 215–16.
17. *Ibid.*, p. 189.
18. *Ibid.*, p. xii.
19. *Ibid.*, p. 232.
20. *Ibid.*, p. xiii.
21. Khenkin, *Okhotnik vverkh nogami*, p. 22.
22. Orlov, *The Secret History of Stalin's Crimes*, p. xv.
23. Petrov and Petrov, *Empire of Fear*, pp. 57–58.
24. *New York Times*, November 24, 1962, p. 11, and November 27, 1962, p. 16.

Chapter 5   THE NEIGHBORS

1. Krivitsky, *I Was Stalin's Agent*, p. 8.
2. Paul Wohl, "Walter G. Krivitsky," *Commonweal*, February 28, 1941, p. 463.
3. Krivitsky, *I Was Stalin's Agent*, pp. 47–48.
4. Boris Souvarine, "Boris Suvarin o Staline," *Kontinent*, No. 22 (Berlin: Kontinent Verlag, 1980), pp. 437–38.
5. Krivitsky, *I Was Stalin's Agent*, p. 64.
6. Wohl, "Walter G. Krivitsky," p. 464.
7. Flora Lewis, "Who Killed Krivitsky?" *Washington Post*, February 13, 1966, p. E3.
8. Krivitsky, *I Was Stalin's Agent*, p. 275.
9. *Ibid.*, p. 34.
10. *Ibid.*, p. 35.
11. *Pravda*, November 29, 1936, p. 2.
12. Krivitsky, *I Was Stalin's Agent*, p. 98.
13. *Ibid.*, p. 100.
14. *Ibid.*, p. 239.
15. *Ibid.*, p. 269.
16. *Ibid.*, p. 272.
17. Orlov, *The Secret History of Stalin's Crimes*, p. 213.
18. Krivitsky, *I Was Stalin's Agent*, p. 275.
19. *Ibid.*, p. 278.
20. *Ibid.*, p. 277.
21. *Ibid.*, p. 279.
22. *Ibid.*, p. 287.
23. *Ibid.*, pp. 288–89.
24. *Ibid.*, p. 293.
25. Wohl, "Walter G. Krivitsky," p. 466.
26. Lewis, "Who Killed Krivitsky?" p. E4.
27. Wohl, "Walter G. Krivitsky," p. 462.
28. Isaac Don Levine, *Eyewitness to History* (New York: Hawthorn Books, 1973), p. 191.
29. Lewis, "Who Killed Krivitsky?" p. E5.
30. *Ibid.*, p. E1.
31. *Ibid.*
32. *Ibid.*
33. *New York Times*, February 11, 1941, p. 8.
34. Lewis, "Who Killed Krivitsky?" p. E4.
35. *Ibid.*, p. E5.

Chapter 6   A MAN WHO COULD DO EVERYTHING

1. James B. Donovan, *Strangers on a Bridge* (New York: Atheneum, 1964), p. 44.
2. Khenkin, *Okhotnik vverkh nogami*, p. 36.
3. Barron, *KGB*, pp. 75–76.
4. Khenkin, *Okhotnik vverkh nogami*, p. 310.
5. John Reed, *Ten Days That Shook The World* (New York: Random House, 1960), p. lii.
6. *Smena*, No. 20, Moscow, October, 1968, p. 23.
7. *Trud*, Moscow, February 17, 1966.
8. *Smena*, No. 20, Moscow, October, 1968, p. 23.
9. *Komsomol'skaya Pravda*, Moscow, November 19, 1971.
10. *Nedelya*, No. 19, Moscow, May 2–8, 1965.
11. Khenkin, *Okhotnik vverkh nogami*, p. 63.
12. *Ibid.*, p. 36.
13. Donovan, *Strangers on a Bridge*, pp. 220–21.
14. Khenkin, *Okhotnik vverkh nogami*, p. 203.
15. *New York Times*, April 25, 1935.
16. David Dallin, *Soviet Espionage* (New Haven: Yale University Press, 1955), p. 123.
17. Khenkin, *Okhotnik vverkh nogami*, p. 36.
18. *Ibid.*, p. 63.
19. Donovan, *Strangers on a Bridge*, pp. 72–73.
20. Gordon Lonsdale, *Spy: Twenty Years in the Soviet Secret Service* (London: Neville Spearman, 1965), p. 50.
21. *Nedelya*, No. 19, May 2–8, 1965.
22. Petrov and Petrov, *Empire of Fear*, pp. 210–11.
23. Khenkin, *Okhotnik vverkh nogami*, pp. 122–23.

Chapter 7   THE MAN WHO ROSE FROM THE DEAD

1. Khenkin, *Okhotnik vverkh nogami*, p. 124.
2. Louise Bernikow, *Abel* (New York: Trident Press, 1970), p. 15.
3. De Gramont, *The Secret War*, p. 200.
4. Bernikow, *Abel*, p. 16.
5. Donovan, *Strangers on a Bridge*, p. 42.
6. Bernikow, *Abel*, p. 32.
7. Donovan, *Strangers on a Bridge*, p. 85.
8. Lonsdale, *Spy*, pp. 116–17.
9. Arthur Tietjen, *Soviet Spy Ring* (New York: Coward-McCann, Inc., 1961), p. 64.
10. De Gramont, *The Secret War*, p. 322.
11. Donovan, *Strangers on a Bridge*, p. 80.

12. *Ibid.*, pp. 153–155.
13. Bernikow, *Abel*, p. 18.
14. Donovan, *Strangers on a Bridge*, pp. 129–30.
15. Orlov, *Handbook of Intelligence and Guerrilla Warfare*, p. 41.
16. Donovan, *Strangers on a Bridge*, p. 130.
17. *Ibid.*, p. 131.
18. De Gramont, *The Secret War*, p. 226.
19. Bernikow, *Abel*, pp. 51–52.
20. *Ibid.*, p. 53.
21. De Gramont, *The Secret War*, p. 229.
22. Donovan, *Strangers on a Bridge*, p. 185.
23. *Ibid.*, p. 170.
24. Bernikow, *Abel*, p. 54.
25. Donovan, *Strangers on a Bridge*, p. 142.
26. De Gramont, *The Secret War*, p. 230.
27. Bernikow, *Abel*, p. 55.
28. De Gramont, *The Secret War*, p. 238.
29. *Life*, International Edition, September 16, 1957.
30. Bernikow, *Abel*, p. 21.
31. De Gramont, *The Secret War*, p. 240.
32. *Ibid.*, p. 236.
33. *Ibid.*, p. 237.
34. Donovan, *Strangers on a Bridge*, p. 24.
35. De Gramont, *The Secret War*, p. 230.
36. *Ibid.*, p. 234.
37. *Ibid.*, pp. 232–33.
38. Donovan, *Strangers on a Bridge*, p. 164.
39. De Gramont, *The Secret War*, p. 231.
40. *Ibid.*, p. 231.
41. Bernikow, *Abel*, p. 65.
42. Donovan, *Strangers on a Bridge*, p. 146.
43. Orlov, *Handbook of Intelligence and Guerrilla Warfare*, p. 89.
44. De Gramont, *The Secret War*, p. 233.
45. Donovan, *Strangers on a Bridge*, p. 155.
46. *Life*, International Edition, September 16, 1957.
47. Khenkin, *Okhotnik vverkh nogami*, p. 38.
48. Bernikow, *Abel*, pp. 75–76.
49. Donovan, *Strangers on a Bridge*, p. 95.
50. *Ibid.*, p. 85.
51. Bernikow, *Abel*, pp. 40–41.
52. Donovan, *Strangers on a Bridge*, pp. 147–48.
53. Khenkin, *Okhotnik vverkh nogami*, pp. 144–45.
54. *Ibid.*, p. 144.
55. *Ibid.*, p. 146.
56. *Ibid.*, p. 145.
57. De Gramont, *The Secret War*, p. 233.

58. *Ibid.*, pp. 233–34.
59. Donovan, *Strangers on a Bridge*, p. 157.
60. De Gramont, *The Secret War*, p. 234.
61. *Ibid.*, p. 234.
62. Bernikow, *Abel*, p. 93.
63. *Ibid.*, p. 33.
64. De Gramont, *The Secret War*, p. 234.
65. Bernikow, *Abel*, p. 81.
66. *Life*, International Edition, September 16, 1957.
67. Bernikow, *Abel*, p. 81.
68. Donovan, *Strangers on a Bridge*, p. 39.
69. *Ibid.*, p. 158.
70. *Ibid.*, p. 159.
71. *Ibid.*, p. 40.
72. *Ibid.*, pp. 209–210.
73. *Ibid.*, p. 187.
74. *Ibid.*, p. 43.
75. Bernikow, *Abel*, p. 110.
76. *Ibid.*, pp. 239–40.
77. Donovan, *Strangers on a Bridge*, p. 362.
78. *Ibid.*, p. 41.
79. *Moskovsky Komsomolets*, February 13, 1966.
80. Donovan, *Strangers on a Bridge*, p. 44.
81. *Ibid.*, p. 42.
82. *Ibid.*, p. 116.
83. *Ibid.*, p. 45.
84. *Ibid.*, p. 342.
85. *Ibid.*, p. 46.
86. *New York Times*, August 9, 1957.
87. *New York Herald Tribune*, May 8–9, 1965.
88. *New York Times*, August 21, 1957.
89. Donovan, *Strangers on a Bridge*, p. 217.
90. *Ibid.*, p. 215.
91. *New York Times*, November 16, 1957.
92. Donovan, *Strangers on a Bridge*, p. 283.
93. *Ibid.*, p. 292.
94. *Ibid.*, p. 267.
95. Khenkin, *Okhotnik vverkh nogami*, p. 187.
96. Donovan, *Strangers on a Bridge*, pp. 347–48.
97. *Ibid.*, p. 346.
98. *Ibid.*, p. 350.
99. *Ibid.*, p. 382.
100. Khenkin, *Okhotnik vverkh nogami*, pp. 270–72.
101. Donovan, *Strangers on a Bridge*, p. 424.

Chapter 8   STEALING THE ATOM BOMB

1. Dallin, *Soviet Espionage*, pp. 288–89.
2. Gouzenko, *The Iron Curtain*, p. vi.
3. Donovan, *Strangers on a Bridge*, p. 132.
4. Khenkin, *Okhotnik vverkh nogami*, p. 221.
5. Gouzenko, *The Iron Curtain*, p. 62.
6. *Ibid.*, p. 14.
7. *Ibid.*, p. 20.
8. *Ibid.*, p. 50.
9. *Ibid.*, p. 149.
10. *Ibid.*, p. 56.
11. *Ibid.*, pp. 68–69.
12. *Ibid.*, pp. 59–60.
13. *Ibid.*, p. 67.
14. *Ibid.*, pp. 62, 67.
15. *Ibid.*, p. 174.
16. *Ibid.*, p. 179.
17. *Ibid.*, p. 181.
18. *Ibid.*, p. 189.
19. *Ibid.*, p. 181.
20. Dallin, *Soviet Espionage*, p. 277.
21. Gouzenko, *The Iron Curtain*, pp. 190–91.
22. Petrov and Petrov, *Empire of Fear*, p. 293.
23. Report of the Canadian Royal Commission (Ottawa: 1946), p. 104.
24. Gouzenko, *The Iron Curtain*, p. 254.
25. Dallin, *Soviet Espionage*, p. 405.
26. Gouzenko, *The Iron Curtain*, pp. 250–51.
27. Dallin, *Soviet Espionage*, p. 279.
28. Gouzenko, *The Iron Curtain*, p. 237.
29. *Ibid.*, p. 235.
30. *Ibid.*, p. 237.
31. *Ibid.*
32. *Ibid.*, pp. 237–38.
33. *Ibid.*, pp. 238–39.
34. *Ibid.*, p. 240.
35. Dallin, *Soviet Espionage*, p. 281.
36. *Ibid.*
37. Gouzenko, *The Iron Curtain*, p. 231.
38. *Ibid.*
39. *Ibid.*
40. Dallin, *Soviet Espionage*, pp. 281–82.
41. *Ibid.*, p. 282.
42. *Ibid.*, p. 284.
43. Gouzenko, *The Iron Curtain*, pp. 245–46.

44. *Ibid.*, p. 246.
45. *Ibid.*
46. *Ibid.*, p. 215.
47. *Ibid.*, pp. 218–19.
48. *Ibid.*, p. 233.
49. *Ibid.*, p. 257.
50. *Ibid.*, pp. 264–65.
51. *Ibid.*, p. 270.
52. Dallin, *Soviet Espionage*, pp. 290–91.
53. Gouzenko, *The Iron Curtain*, p. 276.
54. Dallin, *Soviet Espionage*, p. 292.
55. Report of the Royal Commission, pp. 645–46.
56. Dallin, *Soviet Espionage*, p. 294.
57. *Ibid.*, p. 294.
58. De Gramont, *The Secret War*, p. 363.
59. *The Times* [London], July 2, 1982.

Chapter 9   VICTIMS OF CIRCUMSTANCE

1. Petrov and Petrov, *Empire of Fear*, p. 15.
2. *Ibid.*, p. 52.
3. *Ibid.*, p. 18.
4. Michael Bialoguski, *The Case of Colonel Petrov* (New York: McGraw-Hill Book Company, Inc., 1955), p. 60.
5. Petrov and Petrov, *Empire of Fear*, p. 42.
6. Bialoguski, *The Case of Colonel Petrov*, p. 60.
7. Petrov and Petrov, *Empire of Fear*, p. 42.
8. Peter Deriabin and Frank Gibney, *The Secret World* (Garden City, New York: Doubleday & Company, Inc., 1959), p. 104.
9. Petrov and Petrov, *Empire of Fear*, pp. 56–57.
10. *Ibid.*, p. 60.
11. *Ibid.*, pp. 63–64.
12. *Ibid.*, pp. 65–66.
13. *Ibid.*, pp. 75–76.
14. *Ibid.*, p. 101.
15. *Ibid.*, p. 84.
16. *Ibid.*, p. 175.
17. *Ibid.*, p. 177.
18. *Ibid.*, pp. 181–83.
19. *Ibid.*, p. 200.
20. *Ibid.*, p. 211.
21. *Ibid.*
22. *Ibid.*
23. *Ibid.*, p. 246.
24. *Ibid.*, p. 263.

25. De Gramont, *The Secret War*, p. 154.
26. Petrov and Petrov, *Empire of Fear*, p. 266.
27. *Ibid.*, p. 265.
28. *Ibid.*
29. *Ibid.*, p. 84.
30. *Ibid.*, p. 257.
31. *Ibid.*, pp. 248–49.
32. *Ibid.*, p. 282.
33. *Ibid.*
34. De Gramont, *The Secret War*, p. 155.
35. Petrov and Petrov, *Empire of Fear*, p. 251.
36. *Ibid.*, p. 252.
37. *Ibid.*, p. 256.
38. De Gramont, *The Secret War*, pp. 352–53.
39. Petrov and Petrov, *Empire of Fear*, pp. 293–94.
40. *Ibid.*, p. 252.
41. *Ibid.*, p. 292.
42. *Ibid.*
43. *Ibid.*, p. 296.
44. *Ibid.*, p. 312.
45. *Ibid.*, p. 324.
46. *Ibid.*, p. 328.
47. Report of the Royal Commission on Espionage (Sydney: 1955), pp. 63–65.

Chapter 10   A LITTLE BIT OF CAPITALISM

1. Hans-Otto Meissner, *The Man With Three Faces* (London: Evans Brothers Ltd., 1955), pp. 132–33.
2. Lonsdale, *Spy*, p. 111.
3. *Ibid.*, p. 112.
4. Tietjen, *Soviet Spy Ring*, p. 115.
5. De Gramont, *The Secret War*, p. 307.
6. Lonsdale, *Spy*, p. 88.
7. Tietjen, *Soviet Spy Ring*, pp. 34–36.
8. Lonsdale, *Spy*, p. 11.
9. *Ibid.*, pp. 33–34.
10. *Ibid.*, p. 45.
11. Khenkin, *Okhotnik vverkh nogami*, p. 32.
12. Lonsdale, *Spy*, p. 46.
13. *Ibid.*, pp. 47–48.
14. De Gramont, *The Secret War*, p. 305.
15. *Ibid.*, p. 304.
16. Tietjen, *Soviet Spy Ring*, p. 6.
17. De Gramont, *The Secret War*, p. 324.

18. Lonsdale, *Spy*, p. 89.
19. De Gramont, *The Secret War*, p. 307.
20. Lonsdale, *Spy*, p. 90.
21. *Ibid.*, pp. 90–91.
22. Tietjen, *Soviet Spy Ring*, p. 39.
23. *Ibid.*, p. 69.
24. Lonsdale, *Spy*, p. 93.
25. Tietjen, *Soviet Spy Ring*, p. 39.
26. *Ibid.*
27. *Ibid.*, pp. 53–54.
28. *Ibid.*, p. 54.
29. Lonsdale, *Spy*, p. 94.
30. De Gramont, *The Secret War*, p. 324.
31. Tietjen, *Soviet Spy Ring*, p. 39.
32. De Gramont, *The Secret War*, pp. 319–20.
33. Tietjen, *Soviet Spy Ring*, pp. 55–56.
34. Gilles Perrault, *The Red Orchestra* (New York: Simon and Schuster, 1969), p. 15.
35. De Gramont, *The Secret War*, p. 309.
36. Lonsdale, *Spy*, p. 112.
37. De Gramont, *The Secret War*, p. 108.
38. Lonsdale, *Spy*, p. 112.
39. De Gramont, *The Secret War*, p. 309.
40. Tietjen, *Soviet Spy Ring*, p. 157.
41. *Ibid.*, pp. 57–58.
42. De Gramont, *The Secret War*, p. 311.
43. Lonsdale, *Spy*, p. 113.
44. De Gramont, *The Secret War*, p. 294.
45. Tietjen, *Soviet Spy Ring*, p. 73.
46. De Gramont, *The Secret War*, p. 297.
47. Tietjen, *Soviet Spy Ring*, p. 88.
48. De Gramont, *The Secret War*, p. 298.
49. Facts On File, November 1–November 7, 1962.
50. Lonsdale, *Spy*, p. 199.
51. Tietjen, *Soviet Spy Ring*, p. 109.
52. *Ibid.*, p. 110.
53. *Ibid.*, p. 48.
54. *Ibid.*, pp. 21–22.
55. Lonsdale, *Spy*, p. 120.
56. Tietjen, *Soviet Spy Ring*, p. 20.
57. *Ibid.*, pp. 25–26.
58. *Ibid.*, p. 26.
59. *Ibid.*, p. 153.
60. *Ibid.*, p. 156.
61. De Gramont, *The Secret War*, p. 335.
62. Lonsdale, *Spy*, p. 195.

63. *Ibid.*
64. *Ibid.*, pp. 196–97.
65. *Ibid.*, p. 197.
66. *Ibid.*, p. 198.
67. *Ibid.*, p. 212.

Chapter 11   THE MAN WHO KNEW TOO MUCH

1. Deriabin and Gibney, *The Secret World*, p. 285.
2. Solzhenitsyn, *The Gulag Archipelago*, p. 104.
3. Deriabin and Gibney, *The Secret World*, p. 17.
4. *Ibid.*, p. 31.
5. *Ibid.*, p. 43.
6. *Ibid.*, p. 63.
7. *Ibid.*, p. 62.
8. *Ibid.*, p. 85.
9. *Ibid.*, pp. 109–110.
10. *Ibid.*, pp. 126, 168.
11. *Ibid.*, p. 130.
12. *Ibid.*, pp. 130–31.
13. Peter Deriabin, *Watchdogs of Terror* (New Rochelle, N.Y.: Arlington House, 1972), p. 309.
14. Deriabin and Gibney, *The Secret World*, pp. 152–53.
15. *Ibid.*, pp. 238–39.
16. *Ibid.*, p. 255.
17. *Ibid.*, pp. 256–57.
18. *Ibid.*, p. 244.
19. *Ibid.*, p. 259.
20. *Ibid.*, pp. 261–62.
21. *Ibid.*, p. 265.
22. William Hood, *Mole* (New York: Norton, 1982), pp. 160–63.
23. Deriabin and Gibney, *The Secret World*, p. 266.
24. Hood, *Mole*, pp. 152, 169.
25. De Gramont, *The Secret War*, pp. 338–39.

Chapter 12   THE SPIES WHO CAME IN FROM THE COLD

1. Donovan, *Strangers on a Bridge*, pp. 371–72.
2. *Ibid.*, p. 82.
3. *Izvestiya*, Moscow, February 23, 1962, p. 4.
4. Khenkin, *Okhotnik vverkh nogami*, p. 83.
5. *Ibid.*, pp. 244–45.
6. *Ibid.*, pp. 249–50.
7. *International Herald Tribune*, November 17, 1971, p. 4.

8. *Trud*, Moscow, February 17, 1966.
9. Khenkin, *Okhotnik vverkh nogami*, p. 243.
10. *Ibid.*, pp. 190–91.
11. Reuters, January 4, 1969.
12. Khenkin, *Okhotnik vverkh nogami*, pp. 266–67.
13. *Ibid.*, p. 265.
14. *Ibid.*, p. 263.
15. *Ibid.*, p. 243.
16. *New York Times*, August 26, 1957.
17. *Smena*, Moscow, No. 20, October, 1968.
18. Khenkin, *Okhotnik vverkh nogami*, pp. 307–08.
19. *Ibid.*, p. 148.
20. *Ibid.*, p. 149.
21. *Ibid.*, p. 244.
22. *Ibid.*, p. 266.
23. *Ibid.*, p. 262.
24. *Ibid.*, p. 268.
25. *Washington Post*, November 19, 1971.
26. *Krasnaya Zvezda*, Moscow, November 17, 1971.
27. Khenkin, *Okhotnik vverkh nogami*, p. 271.
28. Reuters, August 23, 1972; Khenkin, *Okhotnik vverkh nogami*, pp. 268–69.

Epilogue   "THE MORE THINGS CHANGE . . ."

1. Honoré de Balzac, *Cousin Bette* (London: Penguin Books, 1974), p. 124.
2. Dallin, *Soviet Espionage*, pp. 1–2.
3. Arthur Koestler, *Darkness At Noon* (New York: Modern Library, 1941), pp. 97–98.
4. Krivitsky, *I Was Stalin's Agent*, p. 8.
5. Petrov and Petrov, *Empire of Fear*, p. 86.
6. Deriabin and Gibney, *The Secret World*, p. 181.
7. *International Herald Tribune*, December 24, 1975.

Sources

Balzac, Honoré de. *Cousin Bette*. London: Penguin Books, 1974.

Barron, John. *KGB*. New York: Reader's Digest Press, 1974.

Baschanow, Boris. *Ich war Stalins Sekretär* [*I Was Stalin's Secretary*]. Frankfurt/Main: Ullstein, 1977.

Bernikow, Louise. *Abel*. New York: Trident Press, 1970.

Bialoguski, Michael. *The Case of Colonel Petrov*. New York: McGraw-Hill Book Company, Inc., 1955.

Bol'shaya Sovetskaya Entsiklopediya [*Great Soviet Encyclopedia*], 2nd ed. Moscow, 1957.

Conquest, Robert. *The Great Terror*. New York: The Macmillan Company, 1968.

Dallin, David J. *The Changing World of Soviet Russia*. New Haven: Yale University Press, 1956.

————. *Soviet Espionage*. New Haven: Yale University Press, 1955.

De Gramont, Sanche. *The Secret War*. New York: G. P. Putnam's Sons, 1962.

Deputaty Verkhovnogo Soveta SSR. Desyati sozyv [*Deputies of the Supreme Soviet of the USSR. Tenth Convocation*]. Moscow: Presidium of the USSR, 1979.

Deriabin, Peter, and Frank Gibney. *The Secret World*. Garden City, N.Y.: Doubleday & Company, Inc., 1959.

————. *Watchdogs of Terror*. New Rochelle, N.Y.: Arlington House, 1972.

Donovan, James B. *Strangers on a Bridge*. New York: Atheneum, 1964.

Gouzenko, Igor. *The Fall of a Titan*. London: Cassell & Company, Ltd., 1954.

————. *The Iron Curtain*. New York: E. P. Dutton & Co., Inc., 1948.

Greene, Harris. *FSO-1*. Garden City, N.Y.: Doubleday & Co., Inc., 1977.

Haupt, Georges, and Jean-Jacques Marie. *Makers of the Russian Revolution*. Ithaca: Cornell University Press, 1974.

Hood, William. *Mole*. New York: Norton, 1982.

Hyde, H. Montgomery. *Stalin*. New York: Farrar, Straus and Giroux, 1971.

Khenkin, Kirill. *Okhotnik vverkh nogami* [*Hunter Upside Down*]. Frankfurt/Main: Posev, 1979.

Khrushchev, Nikita. *Khrushchev Remembers*. Boston: Little, Brown and Company, 1970.

345

Koestler, Arthur. *Darkness at Noon*. New York: Modern Library, 1941.

Kommunistichesky Kalendar'-Spravochnik [*Communist Calendar-Guide*], *1968*. Moscow: Publishing House of Political Literature, 1967.

Krivitsky, W. G. *I Was Stalin's Agent*. London: Hamish Hamilton, 1939.

Laqueur, Walter. *Terrorism*. Boston: Little, Brown and Company, 1977.

Lenin, V. I. *Sochineniya* [*Works*]. Moscow: State Publishing House of Political Literature, 1950.

Levine, Isaac Don. *Eyewitness to History*. New York: Hawthorn Books, 1973.

Lewis, Flora. "Who Killed Krivitsky?" *Washington Post*, February 13, 1966.

Lonsdale, Gordon. *Spy: Twenty Years in the Soviet Secret Service*. London: Neville Spearman, 1965.

Malaya Sovetskaya Entsiklopediya [*Small Soviet Encyclopedia*], 2nd ed. Moscow, 1935.

Meissner, Hans-Otto. *The Man with Three Faces*. London: Evans Brothers Limited, 1955.

Neizvestny, Ernst. "Tri fragmenta" ["Three Fragments"]. *Kontinent*, No. 21. Berlin: Kontinent Verlag, 1979.

Orlov, Alexander. *Handbook of Intelligence and Guerrilla Warfare*. Ann Arbor: University of Michigan Press, 1963.

————. *The Secret History of Stalin's Crimes*. New York: Random House, 1953.

Orwell, George. *Nineteen Eighty-Four*. New York: Harcourt, Brace & World, Inc., 1949.

Page, Bruce, David Leitch, and Phillip Knightley. *Philby: The Spy Who Betrayed A Generation*. London: Andre Deutsch, 1968.

Parry, Albert. *Terrorism: From Robespierre to Arafat*. New York: The Vanguard Press, 1976.

Perrault, Gilles. *The Red Orchestra*. New York: Simon and Schuster, 1969.

Petrov, Vladimir, and Evdokia Petrov. *Empire of Fear*. New York: Frederick A. Praeger, Inc., 1956.

Reed, John. *Ten Days That Shook The World*. New York: Random House, 1960.

Roosevelt, Kermit. *Countercoup*. New York: McGraw-Hill Book Company, 1979.

Solzhenitsyn, Aleksandr I. *The Gulag Archipelago I–II*. New York: Harper & Row, 1973.

Souvarine, Boris. "Boris Suvarin o Staline" ["Boris Souvarine Talks About Stalin"]. *Kontinent*, No. 22. Berlin: Kontinent Verlag, 1980.

Sterling, Claire. *The Terror Network*. New York: Holt, Rinehart and Winston, 1981.

Tietjen, Arthur. *Soviet Spy Ring*. New York: Coward-McCann, Inc., 1961.

Trotzki, Leo. *Mein Leben* [*My Life*]. Berlin: S. Fischer Verlag, 1930.

Wohl, Paul. "Walter G. Krivitsky." *Commonweal*, February 28, 1941.

Wolin, Simon, and Robert M. Slusser (ed.). *The Soviet Secret Police*. New York: Frederick A. Praeger, 1957.

Index